D0909993

Recovering the U. S. Hispanic Literary Heritage, Vol. II

Edited by Erlinda Gonzales-Berry
and Chuck Tatum

Arte Público Press
Houston
Texas
1996

The publication of this book is made possible through support from the Rockefeller Foundation. Support for the conference from which these articles were drawn was also provided by the Rockefeller Foundation. The supporters of Arte Público Press include the National Endowment for the Arts (a federal agency), the Lila Wallace-Reader's Digest Fund and the Andrew W. Mellon Foundation.

Recovering the past, creating the future

Arte Público Press
University of Houston
Houston, Texas 77204-2090

Cover design by Mark Piñón

Recovering the U. S. Hispanic literary heritage, vol. 2 / edited by Erlinda Gonzales-Berry and Chuck Tatum

  p. cm.
 ISBN 1-55885-139-9 : $34.95.
  1. American literature—Hispanic American authors—History and criticism. 2. Hispanic American literature (Spanish)—History and criticism. 3. Hispanic Americans—Intellectual life. 4. Hispanic Americans in literature. I. Gonzales-Berry, Erlinda. II. Tatum, Chuck.
PS153.H56R43 1993   92-45114
                       CIP

Contents

Foreword 11

Introduction
Erlinda Gonzales-Berry and *Chuck Tatum* 13

PART I: The Recovery Project Comes of Age

Romancing Hegemony: Constructing Racialized Citizenship in
María Amparo Ruiz de Burton's *The Squatter and the Don*
John M. González 23

Textual and Land Reclamations: The Critical Reception of
Early Chicana/o Literature
Manuel M. Martín Rodríguez 40

"Who ever heard of a blue-eyed Mexican?": Satire and
Sentimentality in María Amparo Ruiz de Burton's
Who Would Have Thought It?
Anne E. Goldman 59

PART II: Assimilation, Accommodation or Resistance?

"Fantasy Heritage" Reexamined: Race and Class in the Writings of
the Bandini Family Authors and Other Californios, 1828-1965
F. Arturo Rosales 81

Outlaws or Religious Mystics? Public Identity and Los Penitentes in
Mexican-American Autobiography
Margaret García Davidson 105

"We can starve too": Américo Paredes' *George Washington Gómez*
and the Proletarian *Corrido*
Tim Libretti 118

PART III: History in Literature/Literature in History

Having the Last Word: Recording the Cost of Conquest in
Los Comanches
Sandra Dahlberg 133

Luisa Capetillo: An Anarcho-Feminist *Pionera* in the Mainland/
Puerto Rican Narrative/Political Transition
Lisa Sánchez González 148

The Recovery of the First History of Alta California:
Antonio María Osio's *La historia de Alta California*
Rose Marie Beebe and *Robert M. Senkewicz* 168

Adina de Zavala's Alamo: History and Legendry as Critical
(Counter-Alamo) Discourse
Richard R. Flores 185

PART IV: Writing the Revolution

Práxedis G. Guerrero: Revolutionary Writer or Writer
as Revolutionary
Ward S. Albro 199

Before the Revolution: Catarino Garza as Activist/Historian
Elliott Young 213

PART V: Recovering the Creation of Community

Spanish-Language Journalism in the Southwest: History and
Discursive Practice
Gabriel Meléndez 239

Cultural Continuity in the Face of Change: Hispanic Printers
in Texas
Laura Gutiérrez-Witt 260

The Tradition of Hispanic Theater and the WPA Federal Theatre
Project in Tampa-Ybor City, Florida
Kenya C. Dworkin y Méndez 279

Contributors 295

Recovering the U. S. Hispanic Literary Heritage

Volume II

Foreword

This volume is a product of the Recovering the U. S. Hispanic Literary Heritage, a project whose purposes include locating, rescuing from perishing, evaluating, disseminating and publishing collections of primary literary sources written by Hispanics in the geographic area that is now the United States from the Colonial Period to 1960. The ten-year project focuses on the implementation of the following programs:

     I.   An on-line data base
     II.   A periodicals recovery program
     III.   A consortium of Hispanic archives
     IV.   Grants-in-aid and fellowships for scholars
     V.   A publishing program
     VI.   A curriculum development project
     VII. Conferences and dissemination of information

This is the largest project of its kind undertaken in the history of scholarly efforts to study Hispanic culture in the United States. Its importance lies in filling the large gap which exists in American literature: the Hispanic contribution. The broad scope of the project includes recovery of all conventional literary genres as well as such forms as letters, diaries, oral lore and popular culture by Cuban, Mexican, Puerto Rican, Spanish and other Hispanic residents of what has become the United States.

It is hoped that the project will have an immediate as well as long-lasting impact on education and on our knowledge about a large and important dimension of U. S. culture. It will shape for decades to come academic scholarship in the disciplines of literature and history and it will have a major influence on the curriculum and teaching of English, Spanish and bilingual education in K-12 schools as well as in institutions of higher education.

Introduction

Erlinda Gonzales-Berry and *Chuck Tatum*

This is the second volume of essays resulting from the second (University of Houston, May 17-18, 1991) and third conferences (University of Houston, December 2-3, 1994) held under the auspices of the "Recovering the U.S. Hispanic Literary Heritage Project." Nicolás Kanellos, the Project Director, convened the first conference on November 9-11, 1990 at the National Humanities Center in Research Triangle Park, North Carolina. The essays of many of twenty scholars who came together at that conference were eventually published in a volume appropriately titled *Recovering the U.S. Hispanic Literary Heritage*. As Ramón A. Gutiérrez and Genaro M. Padilla, the editors of this volume, tell us in their introduction, Professor Kanellos "had brought together twenty of this country's most noted scholars of Hispanic literature to imagine a long-term research, restoration, and publication project that would disseminate widely the literary heritage of Hispanics in the United States" (17).

Many of the essays included in this first volume form a kind of compendium of guidelines, advice, and precautions that future critics and researchers should take into consideration in recovering, documenting and shaping the immense regional and national diversity of the U.S. Hispanic literary heritage. This is not to say, however, that this collective scholarly enterprise was meant to establish a permanent and static conceptual framework; in fact, many of the scholars who participated in the first conference and subsequently published their essays in the first volume explicitly caution future generations to be open to considering new literary categories and as yet unexplored critical/theoretical approaches.

Although the first volume of essays has just barely had time to exert an influence on the recovery, restoration, and study of U.S. Hispanic literary texts from the nineteenth through the first half of the twentieth century, some of the participants at the second conference, and to a much greater extent, those who participated at the third conference, have already begun to respond

13

to and challenge the intellectual wisdom of the scholars who came together in 1990 at the National Humanities Center to ponder and deliberate on a project that could shape the scholarship on U.S. Hispanic literature for years to come.

Many of us that presented and discussed position papers for three days in the solitude of the Center glimpsed and now have come to realize—perhaps the broad scope of writings unearthed, published, and written about so far has taught us—that the U.S. Hispanic community is far too complex to conflate or to reduce to simple formulas. Each recovered text points to the complexity of our historical experience, to the vast differences within, including class differences. Much of the critical work presented at the Recovery Project's second and third conferences revolves around an analysis of how internal differences contributed to a variety of discourses, some of them openly resistant, others ambivalent about assimilation, and still others, somewhere in-between.

As the reader will learn from the essays included in "Section I. The Recovery Project Comes of Age," the joint efforts of Professor Kanellos and scholars such as Rosaura Sánchez and Beatrice Pita to publish and critically comment on recovered texts has borne fruit. María Amparo Ruiz de Burton's *The Squatter and the Don* (1992) has already produced a body of criticism. The three scholars whose essays we include in this section demonstrate, along with Sánchez and Pita, a willingness to broaden the horizon of expectations of what can and should be studied as U.S. Hispanic literature. Initially, the so-called "shapers" of the Recovery Project—including the co-editors of this volume—were eager to privilege those texts that met our present day expectations: texts that resist cultural assimilation or demonstrate working class alliances, that is, the predominant cultural nationalist ideology of the Chicano Movement. All of the three essays in this section present a balanced and critical assessment of María Amparo Ruiz de Burton.

For John M. González in his essay, "Romancing Hegemony: Constructing Racialized Citizenship in María Amparo Ruiz de Burton's *The Squatter and the Don*," the first volume in the series of reprints published by Arte Público Press and the Recovery Project "evokes questions about the institutional sites, contexts and methodologies involved in the production of knowledge about 'recovered' texts written by Latinas/os in the United States." González identifies the ideological underpinnings of recovery projects and the texts they produce: the cultural nationalist contestations of race, class and colonialism. *The Squatter and the Don*, however, is not for González just—or even primarily—a novel of communal resistance of Californios against the Anglo Occupation, but an example of a drive for acculturation and intermarriage with whites in nineteenth-century California. The novel shows how Californios traded upon their status as class elites a peace structure that allowed them to gain political concessions and material advantages from the ascendant Anglo elites.

In "Textual and Land Reclamations: The Critical Reception of Early Chicana/o Literature," Manuel M. Martín Rodríguez compares two novelists, María Amparo Ruiz de Burton and Daniel Venegas, both of whom have been hailed as precursors to the contemporary Chicano novel. Drawing an analogy between land and textual restoration, Martín Rodríguez urges us to recognize that intragroup differences, particularly class stratification, contributed to the production of texts that predate contemporary politics of positionality. Just as we cannot forget that not all Chicanos had the same relation to Aztlán—some owned portions of it while others made it productive for its owners—neither can we forget that not all Chicano novelists write Aztlán from the bottom up. This is not to say that Martín Rodríguez argues for the privileging of any one ideological position. What he does call for is that reclaimed texts from the past such as *The Squatter and the Don* and *Las aventuras de don Chipote* "be read for what they are: diverse accounts of a diverse experience."

While recognizing the sustained classism present in both *The Squatter and the Don* (1885) and in an earlier Ruiz de Burton novel, *Who Would Have Thought It?* (1872), Anne E. Goldman shows how the novelist delivers a subtle but scathing critique of New England—and by extension, Anglo-American—mores in the latter. In "'Who ever heard of a blue-eyed Mexican?': Satire and Sentimentality in María Amparo Ruiz de Burton's *Who Would Have Thought It?*," Goldman shows how the novelist's placement of Lola, a young orphaned Mexican girl in an upper class New England household not only "complicates the ethnic dichotomies written into the history of the United States but stands as a metaphor for its gendered polarities." Goldman shows how María Amparo Ruiz de Burton's feminized discourse and gendered polarities serve to undergird the novelist's satire of American nationalism on the eve of the Civil War and to celebrate the gentility of the Mexican upper class.

In "Section II: Assimilation, Accommodation or Resistance?: Broadening the Parameters of Our Definitions," we include three essays that deal with a group of writers who, like Ruiz de Burton, challenge our assumptions about the creation and debunking of racial myths and defy our once neat categories of who should be included in the cultural nationalist project of canonization. In "'Fantasy Heritage' Reexamined: Race and Class in the Writings of the Bandini Family Authors and other *Californianos*, 1828-1965," Arturo Rosales traces the origins of nineteenth- and even twentieth-century Californians of Mexican descent's adherence to the myth of their Spanish, non-Mexican (and therefore non-Indian) heritage. Rosales takes on both radical California writers of the 1940s as well Mexican American intellectuals of the 1950s and the 1960s who had explained and then proceeded to debunk the so-called "Fantasy Heritage" of pure Spanish ancestry as an adaptation to the Anglo Occupation. Rosales shows how, in the early nineteenth-century writings of the Bandini family, the "Fantasy Heritage" predates the Anglo takeover of California and has its origins in a much earlier version of Mexican Eurocentrism.

In her "Outlaws or Religious Mystics?: Public Identity and Los Penitentes in Mexican-American Autobiography," a discerning analysis of gendered nuances in the work of two New Mexican writers, Manuel Otero and Nina Otero Warren, Margaret García Davidson calls our attention to the fact that these two cousins have been ignored or dismissed because they fail to meet the prevailing ideological position of the majority of Chicano critics. García Davidson's bold statement that "in judging these early biographies in the contemporary terms of cultural conflict and social resistance, Chicano literary critics have failed to recover the works on their own terms and have, in effect, dictated Chicano theory," is an open challenge to expand the parameters of the Recovery Project.

In "'We can starve too': Américo Paredes' *George Washington Gómez* and the Proletarian *Corrido*," Tim Libretti also resurrects an earlier text, a 1930s novel that might have easily been dismissed by many contemporary Chicano literary critics as passé. Like García Davidson, he challenges our facile definitions of what constitutes cultural resistance by viewing Paredes' novel as a blueprint for Chicano Marxism. Inherent in this model is a critique of the Americanization models proffered by organizations such as the League of United Latin American Citizens (LULAC) and the American Communist Party in the 1930s. According to Libretti, the latter stressed class struggle as an avenue to liberation and Americanization. What this model failed to take into account is the importance of culture and the distinct historical nature of the exploitation and oppression that affected Mexicans in the United States in the 1930s. Libretti sees the similarity between Paredes' novel and the work of Franz Fanon and Amilcar Cabral, both of whom stressed that culture and class struggle are central to the formation of a national identity. In this sense, Paredes' novel falls very much in the tradition of the nineteenth-century *corrido* which was a genuine expression of class resistance.

"Section III deals with the topic History in Literature/Literature in History. By reading Pedro Bautista Pino's *Los Comanches* in tandem with his report to the Spanish *Cortés* (1812), Sandra Dahlberg in her essay, "Having the Last Word: Recording the Cost of Conquest in *Los Comanches*," argues that what appear to be historical inaccuracies in this eighteenth-century drama are deliberate strategies employed by the author to draw attention to New Mexican Governor Juan de Anza's blatant disregard for the Comanche people and the treaties which governed frontier life before his arrival. While the historical record bears testimony to the defeat of the Comanches and their intrepid leader Cuerno Verde, Dahlberg sustain that there are no true victors in the dramatic verses that make up this historical drama. Instead, there is an invitation to the audience to consider the price of victory: the deterioration of the Christian ideals of Spanish frontier mission and the triumph of greed and pride. Jumping ahead almost more than a century, Lisa Sánchez González analyzes in her essay, "Luisa Capetillo: An Anarcho-Feminist *Pionera* in the Mainland Puerto Rican Narrative/Political Tradition," Capetillo's fiction and experimental prose collected and published in 1916 as *Influencias de las ideas modernas*. Dispersed throughout this work are the author's insights on a wide range of social, political, and historical issues. Sánchez González adroitly teases out of Capetillo's writings her anarcho-feminist views of Puerto Rico's colonial relationship to the United States, her abiding faith in the working class—especially working class women—and her advocacy of a progressive sociosexual agenda for both women and men. Capetillo offers a good example of how literature can serve a political agenda and not lose its inherent artistic value.

Rose Marie Beebe and Robert Senkewicz turn to an historical and autobiographical text for philosophical insights and literary creative impulses. In their essay, "The Recovery of the First History of Alta California: Antonio María Osío's *La historia de Alta California*," the authors show how this historical document is an explicitly self-reflective work that contributes significantly to our understanding of Osío himself as well as to the period from 1821-1846 of California history. Osío relied on personal experiences as well as on oral accounts to reconstruct and interpret the period he covers. Beebe and Senkewicz show how the document's literary form allows Osío to maintain complete authorial control over his historical narrative to develop a consistent voice that resonates throughout. Its dialogic tone differentiates *La historia de Alta California* from other historical accounts of the period. In "Adina De Zavala's Alamo: History and Legendry as Critical (Counter-Alamo) Discourse," Richard Flores examines De Zavala's collection of legends and historical writing to reveal her critical counter-discourse of Texas history and the Alamo. Drawing on Paul Ricoeur's discussion of historical narrativity, Flores shows how De Zavala's nonchronological legendry informs her historical writing and allows us to understand the Alamo "as an event whose meaning is situated within the larger process of Texas social life." De Zavala's "poetics of restoration" thus are shown to be a response to the historical displacement and resulting degradation of *mexicanos* brought about by the cultural, economic, and social reorganization of Texas as an industrialized territory.

"Section IV: Writing the Revolution," includes two essays, one, "Praxedis G. Guerrero: Revolutionary Writer or Writer as Revolutionary," by Ward Albro, and a second, "Before the Revolution: Catarino Garza as Activist/Historian," by Elliott Young. In the first, Albro traces the short revolutionary career of Praxedis G. Guerrero, a Mexican intellectual of radical leanings, who entered the U.S. in 1904 and thereafter wrote and actively participated in anti-Porfirista armed resistance in northern Mexico. Albro shows how his writings in *Regeneración* vaulted him into a leadership position in the *Partido Revolucionario Mexicano* while Ricardo Flores Magón, one of its founders, was in custody in U.S. jails. Albro considers Guerrero to be Flores Magón's equal in terms of his incisive analysis of social conditions in Mexico and his inspired calls for the overthrow of the repressive regime of Porfirio Díaz. Young proposes to rescue from obscurity the life of journalist turned border revolutionary Catarino Garza. Like Guerrero, Garza also was active in resisting Porfirio Díaz. According to Young, Garza's 1891 armed insurgency did not emerge as a full fledged historical event until Garza had constructed himself as a "speaking subject" situated between racial harassment in the United States and political attacks from the Porfirista government. In his 1888 autobiography, Garza weaves race and gender together to construct a collective national identity which bears witness to the complex and ever-shifting ethnic relationships between and among groups along the Texas-Mexico border. Of special interest in Young's essay is the discussion of the role of gender and patriarchal values in the construction of self as a "paradigmatic border hero" whose primary mission is to defend border Mexicans against Anglo discrimination.

Section V deals with the topic of Recovering the Creation of Community. In "Spanish-Language Journalism in the Southwest: History and Discursive Practice," Gabriel Meléndez stresses the role of *periodiqueros* [newspaper journalists] in the creation of community and the promotion of cultural resistance during the late nineteenth and early twentieth centuries in New Mexico. Leading the way in the professionalization of Spanish-language journalism was Camilo Padilla, publisher for twenty-seven years of *Revista ilustrada*, a journal that rivaled Anglo-American publications which consistently ignored or patronized Nuevo Mexicano culture. Padilla's struggle to give legitimacy to the Spanish language and to promote Nuevo Mexicano literature and art were quickly forgotten after his death in 1933. Like Meléndez, Laura Gutiérrez-Witt focuses on the role that print culture played in the preservation of cultural continuity among Hispanics in the Southwest. In "Cultural Continuity in the Face of Change: Hispanic Printers in Texas," she highlights the contributions of four Hispanic printers in Texas: Ignacio E. Lozano, Rómulo Munguía, Eduardo Idar, Sr., and José García Roel. All four founded newspapers: Lozano and Idar in San Antonio, Munguía and García Roel in Laredo. Both Meléndez and Gutiérrez-Witt make valuable contributions to an area that merits much greater attention by the Recovery Project: the role of editors

and journalists as cultural workers throughout the Southwest during the nineteenth and early twentieth centuries.

Related to the preservation of Mexican-American cultural identity during a period of intense Anglicization of the Southwest is Kenya Dworkin y Méndez's historical study of the development and demise of Spanish-language theater in Tampa-Ybor City, Florida. In "The Tradition of Hispanic Theater and the WPA Federal Theatre Project in Tampa-Ybor City, Florida," Dworkin y Méndez demonstrates that Anglo-American society in the 1930s was unwilling to accept as part of the corpus of American theater this Spanish language popular tradition cultivated by Cubans. She takes her analysis a step further, demonstrating that it was not aesthetic taste alone that accounted for this exclusion. Federal legislation in 1937, which removed non-citizens from relief roles, had a devastating impact on the thriving working class community of Tampa-Ybor City. Ironically, while the mission of the FTP was to use community theater tradition as an avenue for "Americanization," concurrent federal legislation contributed to the disappearance of this particular community theater. Of special interest in her essay is her indictment of scholars of American theater history who have remained silent on the connection between exclusionary political legislation, xenophobic social attitudes and the demise of non-mainstream cultural practices.

If the first collection of essays linked to the Recovery Project "overturned the all too pervasive notion that Hispanic literature is a recent phenomenon," thereby calling for a reconsideration of the national demarcations of the American literary canon, this collection of essays in parallel fashion calls for a reconsideration of internal boundaries, thereby expanding the ethnic, gender and class parameters of the Hispanic literary heritage. The effect of this maneuver is at once centripetal and centrifugal; the inward-flowing reverberations caused by calling attention to difference with the culturally specific space of literary production turn back upon themselves and spread outward, making their presence felt in ever larger concentric circles. Thus, the internal difference of local expression makes itself felt, aggregates to and expands further the contours of the American literary canon.

PART I
The Recovery Project Comes of Age

Romancing Hegemony: Constructing Racialized Citizenship in María Amparo Ruiz de Burton's *The Squatter and the Don*[1]

John M. González

As the first volume in the series of reprints published by Arte Público Press and the Recovering the U.S. Hispanic Literary Heritage Project, María Amparo Ruiz de Burton's 1885 novel *The Squatter and the Don* immediately evokes questions about the institutional sites, contexts and methodologies involved in the production of knowledge about "recovered" texts written by Latinas/os in the United States. The issue of what sort of cultural work literary recovery projects and their recovered texts perform, or should perform, in the extension and elaboration of U.S. Latina/o culture comes into focus as a site of contestation over interpretation and pedagogy. The very name of this specific recovery project—Recovering the U.S. Hispanic Literary Heritage— itself indicates a certain interventionist trajectory that would claim the textual productions arising out of the co-existence and conflict between Spanish colonizers, enslaved African workers and Indigenous colonized within what would become the United States; that the project recovers texts of the Spanish colonial and Mexican Republican periods along with those produced after various U.S. invasions and annexations points to a contestatory sense of what "American" cultural production encompasses.[2]

As Ramón Saldívar has written about the interventions of Chicana/o narrative within dominant liberal discourses of consensus and dissent that have defined discussions of "American" literature, "Chicano narrative fills the gaps and names the silences that are the limits of the ideological consensus of American literary history" (214-15). Calling into question the theoretical assumptions of the academic analysis of "American" literature through the vectors of power that Chicana/o narrative dissects, Saldívar's "dialectics of difference" articulates and extends a "radical reconstruction of American literary history" (215). Cultural critics, including people of color, feminists, and

23

the queer community, have made remaking structures of knowledge, including canon formation, a central project in the contestation of discursive and institutional spaces. If the cultural right views these interventions as proof of a balkanized, disuniting sense of nation, then the narratives, poetry and scholarship that analyze gender, race, class, and sexuality in the making of U.S. nationalism ultimately "challenge American literature to live up to its potentialities and provide a culture commensurate with its political opportunity" (Saldívar 217). In other words, where cultural conservatives see a destructive Civil War of ethnic cultures, cultural critics see a Radical Reconstruction of what it means to be an "American."

In restoring a communal memory of lived experiences before the U.S. occupation and beyond a dominant common sense of racial hierarchy, the recovery project maps the genocide of indigenous peoples and the colonization of mestizo, black and mulatto peoples onto a U.S. nationalist historiography that would celebrate Manifest Destiny's triumphant progress of "civilization." Situated within and against an Euro-American academy that has historically served to legitimate and perpetuate discourses of cultural and racial inferiority about Latinas/os, this particular recovery project contests the academy's production of state and national knowledges and strives to create a counter discourse about "the Hispanic contribution" to U.S. culture (Kanellos 13). In questioning the mythohistorical genealogy of the U.S. nation, the recovery project makes possible a discursive space from which to critique U.S. nationalist narratives of progress and "civilization" that have structured and justified exploitation and other forms of racialized violence.

Recovery projects themselves have grown out of cultural nationalist contestations of race, class and colonialism in academic and other institutional settings since the late 1960s, and as such function to generate genealogies and practices of cultural nationalist resistance. In texts rescued from an obscurity to which they were relegated by dominant racialized disciplinary practices of historiography, sociology and literary studies, cultural nationalism's oppositional intellectuals recover articulations of communal resistance to exploitation, oppression and oblivion, articulations which can then serve to educate and organize disenfranchised people of color to act against the legal and social manifestations of white supremacy, and to imagine their community as united in and through this struggle.[3] In that national imaginings are not only horizontal but historical as well, the construction of a geneological narrative becomes a central project for nationalism.

In *Imagined Communities: Reflections on the Origins and Spread of Nationalism*, Benedict Anderson argues that the spread of vernacular literacies and the creation of a mass market for printed materials coalesced the new sense of nation.[4] The novel became the privileged location of making narra-

tive national, functioning as the clock and calendar of the homogenous, progressive, and utterly typical time of the secular and sociological existence of the nation. As a recovered text, *The Squatter and the Don*, along with other cultural productions of Mexicans and Mexican Americans in the U.S. before the Chicano Movement, comes to be read as expressive, or at least pre-figurative, of a greater communal resistance fostered by Chicano nationalism. Certainly the story of the U.S. dispossession of the land from the Californios resonates with cultural nationalist aspirations to recover the lost lands of Aztlán by various legal, extralegal, and symbolic means. Wahneema Lubiano has argued that, for black nationalism, cultural production and consumption of a black aesthetic has become the site of the imagined community itself, given the lack of actual lands for national sovereignty; in the case of Chicano nationalism, the connection between cultural production and land recovery takes on a more immediate relationship as Mexican lands were forcibly alienated not only from specific Mexican individuals and families but from the Mexican people as a *nation*.[5] Any recovery of this land can hardly be imagined by Chicano nationalism as having solely specific, self-interested motives, such as those of individual land owners; if land is recovered by a particular owner, its significance lies in its prefiguration of the recovery of all of the lost territory of the nation. Imagining the loss of Aztlán as a communal, national loss enables its recovery to be imagined as communal, and (cultural) nationalist.

The documented history of land dispossession across the U.S. Southwest after the Treaty of Guadalupe Hidalgo provides for the continuation of land recovery as a site of Chicano nationalist imaginings of resistance and autonomy.[6] In this sense the recovery of texts (p/re) figures the recovery of land; the desire for the Aztlán nation finds its romance of reunion in recovery projects. The romance between subjectivity and land (or the promise of its recovery) underscores the nationalist framework and the creation of community along those contours. Chicano nationalism thus articulates a political response to the communal experiences of migration and displacement, exploitation and oppression, deterritorialization and proletarianization; it represents a critical engagement with modernity through the specific modality of the nation-state.[7] As a specifically counter-hegemonic practice to U.S. nationalism, Chicano nationalism has tended to limit its critique and imaginings of community within the general framework of the national. That cultural nationalism would take the horizontal and temporal aspirations of the modern nation is not surprising; it is not a critique of nationalism in general but rather of a specific manifestation. Rather, it accepts the nation's temporal horizons of development, and nationhood as the only social form of organization capable of embodying modernity for sub-altern groups.

But feminist critics have contested precisely cultural nationalism's own erasures of "internal" differences in the name of the Chicano nation. Subsuming the private, ahistorical gender and sexual divisions of *la familia* under the public realm of history and politics, cultural nationalism naturalizes patriarchal constructions of the family as one of its givens, as an assumed term that merits little, if any, analysis. In this it has generally accepted the division of public and private that Carole Pateman has described as the hallmark of a "modernized" nationality (47). As Chicana feminists such as Norma Alarcón, Cherríe Moraga and Sonia Saldívar-Hull have demonstrated, the nationalist genealogy with its masculinized subject of resistance has often reinscribed patriarchal modes of domination of men over women, with the family, gender, and sexuality as vectors of power (Alarcón 188; Moraga 142; Saldívar-Hull 216). With this growing consciousness of the limits of cultural nationalist interpretive strategies, both feminist- and marxist-influenced critics have wrestled to incorporate into critical practices the insights of Chicano nationalism without its theoretical blind spots, thus introducing a profound ambivalence with respect to Chicano nationalism (an ambivalence no doubt apparent in this essay as well).

This ambivalence appears in Beatrice Pita's and Rosaura Sánchez's extensive critical introduction to the Arte Público edition of *The Squatter and the Don*. In considering this novel "a narrative space for the counter-history of the sub-altern" and consequently "a form of empowerment for the collectivity," Sánchez and Pita make the most of the enormously creative and often obscurantist tensions between Chicano nationalism and other interpretive methodologies in examining *The Squatter and the Don* as a historical romance (5). Following Fredric Jameson's appropriation of A. J. Greimas's semiotic rectangle, Sánchez and Pita analyze the novel as a split discursive construct which identifies History as California's transition from a quasi-feudal subsistence agricultural economy under Spanish and Mexican regimes to a U.S. capitalist large-scale extractive economy, and Romance as the fictional love-story between Anglo Clarence Darrell and Californiana Mercedes Alamar that posits an imaginary resolution to the historical proletarianization of the Californios. For Sánchez and Pita, the marriage between Darrell and Alamar may provide a temporary salvation for one fictional Californio family, but cannot redress the steady decline of the Californios as an elite class before the encroachments of monopoly capital represented by the railroad corporations.

But what the novel can provide is an articulation of collective protest, which, even if clearly class-based and coded for a Californio elite, nonetheless figures a later, greater oppositional collectivity "as citizens, or as descendants of Californios" (51). Or, as Sánchez and Pita write,

> The identity the novel constructs of the Californio is itself class-based (aristocracy), but collective rather than individual ("We, the conquered"), regional ("native Californians"), continental ("Spano-Americans"), linguistic/national ("native Spaniards" or "Spanish Californians" and "Mexican"), religious (Catholic), political ("the conquered natives" or "the enemy") and racial ("my race"). (39)

What these and similar statements from the Introduction make visible is the Utopian allegory functioning beyond the known narrow interests of class, such that a small number of nineteenth-century elite Californios can represent, or at least prefigure, a twentieth-century Chicano working-class; that is, articulations of collectivities of any kind, however situated in terms of the perpetuation of a dominant culture, come to figure in the transcendence of class society itself in what Jameson calls the wresting of a realm of Freedom from the realm of Necessity (*Political Unconscious* 19, 291). This is indeed the ambivalence of cultural nationalism, which, despite its shortcomings, nonetheless continues as a powerful articulation of communal memory and resistance; since the 1960s, Chicano nationalism has been both the critical awareness of Chicanos/as within structures of U.S. nationalism and the primary social practice that has given form to the Utopian visions of Chicanos/as.

But to the extent that Chicano nationalism legitimates the unequal relationships of *la familia* along vectors of power such as gender and sexuality even as it challenges U.S. nationalist narratives of civilization and progress, it remains a necessary but not sufficient condition for a critical practice. Even as *The Squatter and the Don* offers the possibility of collective imaginings, the narrative also works through Romance to consolidate terms of whiteness for the Alamar family through intermarriage. Even as a greater collectivity is prefigured, the novel's immediate cultural work is to make visible the Californios as "white" and to obscure the indigenous labor that made possible this translation. Apprehending the cultural work of Romance highlights how the gender, racial, and class dynamics of erotically familial relationships enable the making of nation itself. What is recoverable from the novel is not History *per se* but rather its representation as narrative, or the very processes by which hegemony is established, maintained, negotiated and contested. Romance is not solely the patina of History, but a mode of its narrativization, and as such but one of the many practices in the reproduction of the relations of production and of power in the name of the nation. Interpreting *The Squatter and the Don* as a historical romance in the light of the post-Reconstruction consolidation of U.S. nationalism around race, together with subsequent implications for Californios as a newly proletarianized class faction, opens new considerations about the ways class, race and gender mediate the contingent nature of nationalism and citizenship.

Certainly, Reconstruction and its aftermath have historically served as indices of competing versions of U.S. nationalism, from turn-of-the-century characterizations as a dark period of black misrule propagated by Colombia University historian William Dunning and *The Klansman* author Thomas Dixon to the characterizations of Reconstruction by W.E.B. DuBios and Eric Foner as "America's unfinished revolution," in which the extensions of citizenship and civil rights fought for by the freedmen moved the nation a gigantic step towards realizing a truly democratic society.[8] The social meaning of Reconstruction highlights, then, precisely the sense in which there are *only* reconstructions of race, gender, and class as the social processes by which racialized, gendered and classed subjects are made and legitimized, as a constantly contested subject of knowledge. Reconstruction corresponds to the continuous re-negotiations of hegemony itself, emphasizing the constructed nature of social relations and the uses of "history" as a site for intervention into nationalist discourses. I propose to examine some implications of considering Ruiz de Burton's own intervention within imagining family and U.S. citizenship in negotiating the specifically racialized constructions of class in the post-Reconstruction era, and how the novel's drive for acculturation and intermarriage with whites reflected the restructuring of citizenship along lines of race in the construction of national unity I will label the "white nation."

I

The Romantic plot of *The Squatter and the Don* focuses upon the vexed relationship between the Darrell and Alamar families in Southern California during the last years of Reconstruction. William Darrell, the squatter of the title, has encroached upon the lands of Don Mariano Alamar, the patrician Mexican *ranchero* whose livelihood has been threatened by squatter challenges to his ancestral title. In order to avoid strife, Darrell's wife Mary tells their son Clarence to purchase the land outright from Don Mariano, and in the process Clarence and Don Mariano's daughter Mercedes meet and fall in love. But when Darrell finds out about the secret land purchase, he attacks the Don, forcing the cancellation of Mercedes' and Clarence's wedding. Without Clarence's rapidly growing fortunes to sustain them, the Alamars can only watch helplessly as the traditional pastoral economy disappears by the 1870s; attempts to diversify into real estate prove disastrous when local San Diego land values collapse following the Big Four's (Mark Hopkins, Collis P. Huntington, Charles Crocker and Leland Stanford) successful attempts to prevent a second, Southern transcontinental railroad, with its western terminus at San Diego, from being built. The Alamar and Darrell families are eventually reunited through the marriage of Clarence and Mercedes, which hardly pre-

vents the loss of the *rancho*, the source of the Californios' independent wealth, but does halt the Alamar family's precipitous slide into a rapidly-forming mestizo and indigenous working class.

Despite this romantic resolution, the novel ends with a plea for a "Redeemer who will emancipate the white slaves of California," calling for a civil uprising which would re-enact the Civil War not for the emancipation of African Americans from chattel slavery but for the release of Californios and Californians alike from an economic dependency fostered by monopolistic railroad corporations (372). According to Ruiz de Burton, the machinations of autocratic corporate monopolies had replaced the democratic ideal of enlightened self-governance with the selfish, avaricious and immoral corruption of the very governmental institutions created for the good of the people as a nation. In particular, the regional railroad monopolies of the Central and Southern Pacific Railroads, headed by the Big Four, had succeeded in bribing Congress into opposing any legislation that would have helped construct Tom Scott's transcontinental Texas Pacific Railroad to San Diego. In effect, enforced underdevelopment of Southern California's economy had completed the work of dispossession of the Californios that had started with the U.S. conquest and greatly accelerated by the Federal Land Act of 1851, which placed the burden and expense of proving and perfecting title to Spanish and Mexican land grants upon the land-rich yet capital-poor Californios. Indeed, the novel's narrative revolves around the various problems the Alamar family faces in settling title to the 47,000-acre Alamar *rancho*. The failing *rancho* economy, compounded with the encroachments of professionalized leagues of squatters, unscrupulous judiciaries, high taxation and title battles, has reduced the people of California to "poverty, overwork and discouragement," or, in other words, to the slavery of low-paying wage labor without the prospect of upward mobility (319).

The stranglehold the Big Four have upon California's economy creates a crisis of embodiment in which the markings of racialized servitude have been transferred from the South's black bodies to the West's "white" ones under the post-War political formation of what Abraham Lincoln, the Redeemer of the Civil War, had called free labor.[9] The narrative's trajectory from wage-labor (proletarianization) to white slavery stands in marked contrast to David Roediger's description of the white working class's movement from the rhetoric of white slavery in the 1840s to the one of wage slavery after the Civil War (65-87). If white slavery denoted not a challenge to capitalist labor relations but to a consolidation of a racialized labor ideology of identity in making a "white" working class before Emancipation, then wage slavery during Reconstruction signified the reorganization of that identity not solely around a self-conscious awareness of class but around nationalism and race as well. Alexander Saxon points out that in California this movement was particularly pronounced; by 1867, Governor Henry Haight would link racial feeling to a consolidated sense of white U.S. nationalism.

> "We protest…against sharing with inferior races the Government of our country…and this protest of ours will be re-echoed in thunder tones by the great central states until the Southern States are emancipated from negro domination, and restored to their proper place as equals and sisters in the great Federal family." (qtd. in Saxon 296)

If *The Squatter and the Don's* invocation of white slavery highlights the historical contingency of "race" in its easy effacement of the Californios' mestizo origins, it also illustrates the narrative's claims of a juridical failure in the nature of U.S. citizenship in that the Thirteenth Amendment's injunction against involuntary servitude hardly stops the monopolies from using a corrupted government itself as the agent of what Pita and Sánchez have termed the racialized proletarianization of the Californios.

This mobility of "race" within the narrative occurs at a moment when the post-Reconstruction reconsolidation of U.S. nationalism around "whiteness" takes on a new and virulent urgency; the novel's concluding plea indexes a fundamental change in structures of class and racial hegemony during the post-Reconstruction consolidation of reaction. The use of the term "Redeemer" in this context marks the ambivalent positioning of the cultural work Ruiz de Burton's narrative performs. On one hand, Redeemer invokes typological imaginings of Christian salvation, and, more specifically in the immediate post-Civil War era, Lincoln's Emancipation Proclamation; on the other, the Redeemers also refers to the group of Whiggish Southern Democrats whom early historians of the New South (such as William Dunning, James Rhodes and Woodrow Wilson) enshrined as the liberators of a distraught (white) South from the ravages of black misrule. The uneasy ambivalence of the term in the post-Reconstruction period suggests the treacherous parameters of race and class that *The Squatter and the Don* attempts to negotiate in creating a place within the newly ascendant "white" nation for the Californios.

II

The historical romance participates within what Benedict Anderson calls "the grammar of nationalism." In essence, what novelistic union between Californios and Anglos do in economic and cultural terms is attempt to complete the transformation and integration of the Californio pastoral economy into the capitalist world system through specifically U.S. channels. In his discussion of this process in nineteenth-century Texas, David Montejano has termed this process of economic and cultural incorporation as "the assertion of national authority, the penetration of a national market, and finally, the establishment of the national culture and settlement of citizens from the national core" (75). What I would like to argue is that Ruiz de Burton contests not the process of incorporation of California's economy and culture into the national core as such, but rather the social position accorded to the Californios within that capitalist order. The Californios show themselves more than willing to participate in emergent capitalist economies. For example, Don Mariano Alamar speculates heavily in San Diego properties while his son Gabriel readily takes a job as a bank worker; Elvira and Mercedes' voyage to the East Coast merely confirms the ability and desirability of integrating the Californios with the nation's cultural and economic elite.

Intermarriage between Anglo men and Californianas in Mexican Alta California had served to incorporate foreigners into the Mexican Republic as citizens even as such unions helped facilitate the consolidation of Alta California's social and economic power as a virtually independent province beyond the control of central Mexican authorities during the 1830s and 1840s. As Antonia Castañeda has shown for the Mexican period, the increasing commercial contact between Yankee traders and the Californio elite brought about by the hide and tallow trade lead to mutually beneficial marriages: "Marriage solidified class alliances between Anglo merchants and the Californiano elite, who were jointly establishing control of California's economy" (223). Marriages between Anglo men and Californio women also introduced commodities produced around the world into everyday life of Californio homes, thus marking the convergence of this elite class into an increasingly globalized bourgeoisie. By the mid-nineteenth century in Alta California, intermarriage had become one of the most important aspects of what Montejano has termed "the structures of peace," or the process by which a culturally, politically and economically dominant class negotiates (always from a position of power) a series of alliances with other classes or class factions to gain their consent in ruling civil society.

While the Californios were no longer an ascendant ruling class by the early 1880s, the romance narrative of *The Squatter and the Don* replicates residual social practices which had earlier assured Californio ascendancy in the Mexican period as well as some measure of social and political integration into the new U.S. order. According to Leonard Pitt, the peace structure of Anglo-Californiana intermarriage "made the Yankee conquest smoother than it might otherwise have been" (125). To the extent that intermarriage helped consolidate Californio control over the region's economy before the Treaty of Guadalupe Hidalgo, it also gave the Californios room to maneuver politically in the post-1848 political landscape. It is important to keep in mind that the pauperization and proletarianization of the Californio population did not happen in 1848 with the U.S. conquest; rather it occurred over a period of three or more decades (approximately 1846-1881) during which the relative political and economic strength of the landed Californio elite ebbed away, weakening that population's ability to renegotiate its position within the constantly shifting class and racial hierarchies of Anglo California.

But for a brief time the post-conquest peace structure did allow the Californios to assert political power in their own interests. Present at the creation and ratification of California's first state constitution, Californios were powerful enough to be considered "white" for the purposes of holding elected governmental offices, having laws printed in Spanish as well as English, and exercising the franchise, whereas they also helped block citizenship status for the indigenous peoples who had created the wealth that had purchased whiteness. Californio rancheros were subsequently able to influence the passage of laws that virtually guaranteed a cheap and vulnerable labor force for exploitation at a moment when labor shortages hampered their ability to profit from the boom in cattle prices brought about by the Gold Rush. Vagrancy laws allowed for the lease of offenders (usually indigenous and mestizo men) for a specified time as labor with only room and board in a preview of the post-Reconstruction South's notorious convict lease system; the Indenture Act of 1850 allowed for the involuntary bonding of Indians to a citizen for at least a decade with no payment but food and shelter (Monroy 185).[10] According to Tomás Almaguer, "This legislation represented the still-powerful rancheros' successful use of the state apparatus to promote their economic interests despite the decline of the old rancho economy" (137). Despite this maneuvering, the demise of the Californios, envisioned by Ruiz de Burton as possibly avoidable even as late as the early 1870s, had become by the time of the novel's publication a confirmed reality with the complete collapse of the pastoral economy, loss of even token political representation in state and local government, endlessly expensive litigation over land grant titles, high taxation on squatter improvements to *rancho* lands, a major influx of Anglo immigrants, and, most importantly for Ruiz de Burton, a general lack of access to entrepreneurial capital and speculative opportunity.

Significantly, the Federal retreat from Radical Reconstruction and the refiguration of political inclusion along the lines of race made the begrudged racial and class negotiations of the 1850s a near impossibility after Reconstruction. Certainly the national reconciliation of regional divisions became a major political project in the forging of post-Civil War U.S. nationalism, as Reconstruction proved in some ways even more divisive and traumatic than the War itself. The violence of the War would haunt the literary imagination at least until the publication of Stephen Crane's *The Red Badge of Courage* in the 1890s, but Reconstruction's dramatic restructuring of the institutional and specifically governmental functions, powers, and responsibilities toward the millions of ex-slaves who, by virtue of the Thirteenth, Fourteenth, and Fifteenth Amendments, became citizens, fundamentally challenged the notion of U.S. citizenship being exclusively white. The sense of nationhood itself had to be reconstructed; thus Reconstruction was not only the assertion of Federal control over the defeated Confederacy, but also a racialized struggle over the War's institutional meaning for U.S. social and political structures. The lingering traces of Reconstruction's dramatic restructuring of U.S. nationalism during a rapidly developing regime of post-war capitalist expansion haunt *The Squatter and the Don's* project of renegotiating the class and racial standing of the Californios within the state's own legal, political and economic processes.

Something of this process of national consolidation occurs via the multiple marriages that express the grammar of nationalism in *The Squatter and the Don*. The younger generation of Mechlins, Alamars and Darrells join not only as family generally but specifically as brothers- and sisters-in-law. Technically, in terms of nation, this was what the Treaty of Guadalupe Hidalgo was supposed to do in transforming Mexican citizens into American citizens: making fraternal bonds through (inter)national law. Given the increasingly precarious political and economic position of the Californios, Ruiz de Burton attempted to reclaim a national niche for the Californios by repeating, with a difference, the relationship between race, narrative, and nationalism. Thus romance and nationalism converge on the original wedding date of Clarence and Mercedes. Ruiz de Burton picked September 16, 1874, to mark the zenith of the fortunes of both Anglo settlers and Californio dons; Clarence has struck it rich with the Arizona mining operation he has recently bought, and Mercedes' father Don Mariano has finally perfected, before the highest Federal authorities, his title to the ancestral Mexican land grant upon which his *rancho* is located. The union of the two families promises to secure the fortunes and futures of both through the affective ties of marriage; this celebration of conjugal joining for the Alamar family comes appropriately on the date marking the anniversary of Hidalgo's legendary launching of the *criollo* nationalist Mexican revolution.[11] The wedding date marks for the text a potential moment of Californio integration into the economic and cultural elite of Anglo civil society, as well as possible relief from corrupt local judiciaries, an unresponsive and irresponsible Congress, professionalized leagues of squatters and monopolist railroad corporations that stand in contrast to the enlightened, cultured Anglo upper- and upwardly mobile families such as the Mechlins and the Darrells.

The Alamar-Darrell wedding, as initially planned and eventually consummated, promises to rearticulate what Doris Sommer has termed the "erotics of politics" underwriting the nationalism of the foundational fictions of nineteenth-century Latin America (*Foundational Fictions* 6). Sommer examines how the cultural work of nationhood performed by the romances of nineteenth century Latin American novels corresponded to the narration of hegemony, making visible the cultural negotiations by which liberal *criollo* elites established a sense of national order through affective ties of mutual consensual desire between the representatives of different regional, racial, and class factions. Reviewing Latin American novels written within the first decades after political independence, Sommer describes the construction of the nation as the basically inclusive consolidation of various, now-national interests within the novelistic genre of the historical romance.[12] Noting that the authors of these novels were strikingly often (but not always) the military and political leaders of the wars of national liberation, Sommer postulates that the romantic narrative of nineteenth-century Latin American novels "provides a model for apparently non-violent national consolidation during periods of internecine conflict"("Irresistable Romance" 76). In other words, the novelistic reconciliation of historically "internal" (once considered from the viewpoint of "the national") conflicts could be managed by the liberal *criollo* elites within the framework of the erotically familial.

Consequently, these authorizing Latin American "founding fathers" worked to naturalize and legitimate the hegemony of a liberal vision of national citizenship by depicting what Benedict Anderson has described as the "deep, horizontal comradeship" of an imagined fraternal community; their narratives, situated within the empty, homogenous, measured time of the novel, strive to represent the nation's constituents as citizens and not as subjects (7). But rather than depict national unity as a patriarchal will to power (coercive father-figures were still associated with the all too recently overthrown patriarchy of the oppressive king-colonizer), the authors of these national romances figured national unity as the cooperative consent of the many sociologically-enumerated ethnic, racial, regional and economic constituents of the new nation. Within the print medium through which the *criollo* elite could imagine itself nationally, unequivocal consent is figured as the natural and, above all, mutual erotic attraction between characters who represent the various "national" factions whose interests are eventually reconciled through the marriage of their representatives. If a normative heterosexuality is assumed in these erotic attractions, Sommer points out that the hegemonic cultural work of these historical romances is the (re)production of legitimate citizens, figured as siblings who populate the land in the fraternal bond of nationhood. Many of these foundational fictions were published during Ruiz de Burton's lifetime (1832-1895) including, for example, Argentine José Marmol's 1851 novel *Amalia*, Colombian Jorge Issacs's 1867 novel *María*, Chilean Alberto Blest Gana's 1862 novel *Martín Rivas*, and Peruvian Clorinda Matto de Turner's 1889 novel *Aves sin nido*.

While Ruiz de Burton was no leader of a war of national liberation, she was, as she identified herself on the title page of the 1885 edition of the novel published by Samuel Carson and Co., "C. Loyal," or, as Sánchez and Pita have pointed out, a *Cuidadano Leal*, [Loyal Citizen] in the convention of Mexican government communiqués of the nineteenth century. Highly educated in the novelistic and political literatures of the English and Spanish languages, Ruiz de Burton was intimately familiar with the Latin American nationalist novels (Sánchez and Pita, 10). The historical romance of Latin America provided a narrative strategy for articulating Californio citizenship within the post-Reconstruction reformation of national interests around race; where Ruiz de Burton's romance of nation and the Latin American one differ is in the relative power of the author(iz)ing class factions. Californios, while wielding some power after annexation, could not authoritatively adjudicate all the competing interests of post-Reconstruction California in the same way the ascendant criollo elites of Latin America could consolidate the nation after anti-colonial struggles and civil wars. Rather, all *The Squatter and the Don* could hope to do is carve out a discursive space for articulating the Californios' stakes and interests in definitions of citizenship. Certainly, as Sommer points out, the liberal consensus model of the Latin American romance in fact enabled unequal relations of power to operate as the foundation of the nation itself; but in comparison to the narrowing of U.S. nationalist discourses that transformed regional resentment, economic dependency, and political differences stemming from the War and Reconstruction into romantic reunion of Northern and Southern whites over the racialized menace of black misrule, the liberal expansive vision of Latin American nationalist romances provided a strategy to negotiate citizenship, or, in other words, "whiteness," for an otherwise economically and politically defeated Californio class.

In saying that the Californios participated and in some ways benefited from the emerging institutionalized class and racial hierarchies of Anglo California is not to diminish the vitriolic nature of Anglo racism towards Californios, working-class Mexicans or Native Americans during the nineteenth century. Clearly, the practices of racial terror—dispossession, exploitation, lynching, and genocide—will not allow us to forget. Rather, it is to acknowledge the political and contingent uses of a hatred made to seem as a self-evident and "natural" basis to assert cultural and economic domination over a specific labor force. Certainly Ruiz de Burton acknowledges the contingent, class-based nature of racism, emphasizing how only the most unsavory, "lowest-class" of the squatters insist upon calling the Alamars "greasers." But my main point is that Californios traded upon their status as an elite class in post-1848 California to construct a peace structure that at some fundamental political level granted them rights and privileges as white citizens, and that these political concessions resulted in real material advantages from the resultant control of indigenous and mestizo labor. Thus the decline of the Californios as a landed elite by the 1880s signified not just demotion into the ranks of wage-laborers but also loss of the privileges of "whiteness" maintained under previous negotiations of hegemony. In this way the romance and intermarriage of *The Squatter and the Don* allows for retaining the real material advantages of being white even if Californios as class were proletarianized. Sánchez and Pita have demonstrated how the romance of the novel attempts to reconcile the cultural and economic interests of the declining Californio landed elite (represented by the Alamars) with the old Northeastern mercantile and financial capital (the Mechlins) and the newly ascendant Western immigrant entrepreneurial capital (Clarence Darrell) in an imaginary solution to the unresolvable historical question of the proletarianization of the Californios. In Gabriel Alamar's transformation "from 'Don' to 'hod carrier,'" Sánchez and Pita identify this historical trajectory of the Californios as a class as one of a "change in class status, from upper-class to working-class…that constitutes the central resentment at work in the novel" (34).

The index of this fall in class status in the novel's passage is how wage-labor transforms Gabriel from a European into a California Indian: "The fact that Gabriel was a *native Spaniard*, [his wife Lizzie Mechlin Alamar] saw plainly, militated against them. If he had been rich, his nationality could have been forgiven, but no one will willingly tolerate a poor *native Californian*" (351). It would seem that even his fair complexion, which made him and his brother Victoriano "look like Englishmen," according to Clarence, is insufficient to arrest his refiguration as a Californian native or a Native American (89). But through the romance between Mercedes and Clearance, Gabriel is able to convert a renewed class status into whiteness, and whiteness into "white-collar." Together with a fall in class status for the Californios came the post-Reconstruction making of the white nation in which even the white proletariat gained what Roediger, following W.E.B. DuBois, has termed the "wages of whiteness," or the innumerable, if seemingly insignificant, confirmations of their social, political and economic superiority in preferential access to skilled jobs, separate but clearly better public schools, parks, and hospitals, and the general sense of broad police powers over any person of color.

As Sánchez and Pita point out, the closure of Romance cannot resolve the contradictions of decline for the Californios; rather, what Romance reveals are the historical limits of national and nationalist imaginations, or, in other words, the dialectics of Utopia and hegemony. On one hand, the acknowledgment of the power of allegorical re-appropriations of even class-based unities makes possible other, non-hierarchical imagined communities; on the other, the exercise of (relative) class privilege requires a critical examination of the dynamics of race and class within those imaginings. By analyzing the creation of hegemony in *The Squatter and the Don* we can imagine what Jameson calls a cognitive mapping of our own positions in the era of late capital ("Cognitive Mapping" 353). Cognitive mappings trace the various expansions and contractions of the borders of citizenship to understand the needs of an imagined and made Chicano community as multiply situated vis-à-vis U.S. citizenship. It allows us to realize, on one hand, the material privileges, however seemingly small, of citizenship, and on the other, the contingent nature of liberal civil rights in our own era of conservative retrenchment.

Notes

[1]This essay is part of an ongoing project on the politics of post-Reconstruction narrative strategies titled "In the Wake of Reconstruction: Cultural Citizenship and Narrative Form 1877-1907." I would like to thank Ramón Saldívar, Lora Romero, Susan Gillman, Tiffany López, Eric Shocket, Dianne Espinoza and David Cantrell for their lucid commentaries.

[2]In their introduction to the first volume of critical essays published under the auspices of the Recovery Project, Ramón Gutiérrez and Genaro Padilla answer cultural nationalist claims of the implied Euro-assimilationist connotations of the term "hispanic" with the historicist argument that this is how the mestizo and mulatto peoples of *Hispanoamérica* identified themselves. Their own recovery of a term that in the nineteenth century invoked the Americas instead of just the United States thus figures a sense of resistance to U.S. nationalism. But also see Gutiérrez's own explorations in the same volume of the *hispanidad* movement as Spain's post-1898 attempt to retain a virtual empire.

[3]One of the earliest examples, if not the paradigm, for cultural nationalist recovery projects is Schomburg's library collection begun at the turn-of-the-century as one manifestation of black nationalism's intervention within an apartheid state and its racialized constructions of "lesser breeds without the law." Despite being best known by his anglicized first name of Arthur, Arturo Schomburg was a Puerto Rican immigrant to New York City in the late 1800s, circumstances which should complicate matters of his collection being simply, purely expressive of an African American experience of black and white. Schomburg's library not only indicates what Paul Gilroy has described as the complexities of the lived experiences of migration and translation in the making of the Black Atlantic, but also its extensions and overlaps with the diasporic experiences of the indigenous, blacks, mestizos and mulattos of the Latin Caribbean and Latin America, a connection Gilroy overlooks in his construction of the Black Atlantic.

[4]The mass technologies of radio and television have greatly supplemented (if not supplanted) the possibilities of national imaginings in the present day for both state nationalisms and cultural nationalisms. Jeffery Decker's article on hip hop nationalism outlines these new technological parameters of black cultural nationalism.

[5]For Lubiano the claim to land in the U.S. is problematic for anyone not Native American or Chicano; I would add that claim is ultimately problematic for Chicanos as well, at least to the

extent that the Spanish and Mexican land grants were part of colonization strategies of the Spanish Empire and the Mexican Republic to secure the frontiers not only against the imperial encroachments of other European nations but against the autonomous existence of the indigenous peoples as well.

[6]Richard Griswold del Castillo chronicles some of the more prominent examples of land recovery attempts by Chicanos since the 1960s. These include the Balli family's legal attempts to reclaim to Padre Island off the South Texas coast, Reies López Tijerina's 1968 Tierra Amarilla, New Mexico courthouse takeover, and the Brown Berets' occupation of Santa Catalina Island off the California coast in 1972.

[7]Even when Chicano nationalism celebrates the flux of *mestizaje*, hybridity, and creolization, it makes these qualities the mark of authenticity in judging cultural production as expressive of some imagined Chicano totality. For Chicano nationalism, *mestizaje* metaphorically resolves the differences of class, gender, sexuality, etc., in constructing community. Much of the influence of mestizaje as a concept can be traced to Chicano nationalism's appropriation of José Vasconcelos's *La Raza Cósmica*; not coincidentally, Vasconcelos, as a state intellectual consolidating a sense of post-Revolutionary national consensus, developed *mestizaje* as the expressive essence of the Mexican nation. *Mestizaje* functioned as a metaphor for national consolidation, as a permutation of what Doris Sommers terms "the erotics of politics" in the foundational fictions of Latin America.

[8]It is in this latter sense that Manning Marable named the Civil Rights Movement of the 1950s and 1960s as "the Second Reconstruction."

[9]Eric Foner's *Free Soil, Free Labor, Free Men* details the political formation of free labor as articulated by the Republican party during the 1850s, while his *Reconstruction* examines free labor's mutations after Emancipation until the great strikes of 1877.

[10]Heizer and Almquist have noted the similarity between the Indenture Act and the notorious Black Code laws enacted in Mississippi during Presidential Reconstruction (48).

[11]Not surprisingly, Mercedes's birthday is May 5th, or the Cinco de Mayo, and yet another indicator of Mexican nationalist pride.

[12]The "national" itself is constructed, as Benedict Anderson points out, from the regional divisions of the colonial administration (53-64).

Works Cited

Alarcón, Norma. "Chicana's Feminist Literature: A Re-Vision Through Malintzin/or Malintzin: Putting Flesh Back on the Object." *This Bridge Called My Back: Writings by Radical Women of Color*. Eds. Cherríe Moraga and Gloria Anzaldúa. New York: Kitchen Table, 1983.

Almaguer, Tomás. *Racial Fault Lines: The Historical Origins of White Supremacy in California*. Berkeley: U of California P, 1994.

Almquist, Alan F., and Heizer, Robert F. *The Other Californians: Prejudice and Discrimination under Spain, Mexico, and the United States to 1920*. Berkeley: U of California P, 1971.

Anderson, Benedict. *Imagined Communities: Reflections on the Origin and Spread of Nationalism*. 2nd, revised ed. New York: Verso, 1991.

Burton, María Amparo Ruiz de. *The Squatter and the Don*. Houston: Arte Público, 1992.

Castañeda, Antonia. "The Political Economy of Nineteenth Century Stereotypes of Californianas." *Between Borders: Essays on Mexicana/Chicana History*. Ed. Adelaida R. Del Castillo. Encino, CA: Floricanto, 1990.

Decker, Jeffrey. "The State of Rap: Time and Place in Hip Hop Nationalism." *Social Text* 34, 11.1: 53-84.

DuBois, W.E.B. *Black Reconstruction in America 1860-1880*. New York: Atheneum, 1992.

Foner, Eric. *Free Soil, Free Labor, Free Men: The Ideology of the Republican Party before the Civil War*. Oxford: Oxford UP, 1970.

_____. *Reconstruction: America's Unfinished Revolution 1863-1877*. New York: Harper and Row, 1988.

Gilroy, Paul. *The Black Atlantic: Modernity and Double Consciousness*. Cambridge: Harvard UP, 1993.

Griswold del Castillo, Richard. *The Treaty of Guadalupe Hidalgo: A Legacy of Conflict*. Norman: U of Oklahoma P, 1990.

Gutiérrez, Ramón. "Nationalism and Literary Production: the Hispanic and Chicano Experiences." *Recovering the U.S. Hispanic Literary Heritage*. Eds. Ramón Gutiérrez and Genaro Padilla. Houston: Arte Público, 1993.

Gutiérrez, Ramón, and Padilla, Genaro. "Introduction." *Recovering the U.S. Hispanic Literary Heritage*. Eds. Ramón Gutiérrez and Genaro Padilla. Houston: Arte Público, 1993.

Jameson, Fredric. "Cognitive Mapping." *Marxism and the Interpretation of Culture*. Eds. Cary Nelson and Lawrence Grossberg. Chicago: U of Illinois P, 1988.

_____. *The Political Unconscious: Narrative as Socially Symbolic Act*. Ithaca: Cornell UP, 1981.

Kanellos, Nicolás. "Foreword." *Recovering the U.S. Hispanic Literary Heritage*. Eds. Ramón Gutiérrez and Genaro Padilla. Houston: Arte Público, 1993.

Lubiano, Wahneema. *Stanford University Talk*. Stanford, 1 April 1994.

Marable, Manning. *Race, Reform and Rebellion: The Second Reconstruction in Black America 1945-1990*. 2nd ed. Jackson: UP of Mississippi, 1991.

Monroy, Douglas. *Thrown Among Strangers: The Making of Mexican Culture in Frontier California*. Berkeley: U of California P, 1990.

Montejano, David. *Anglos and Mexicans in the Making of Texas 1836-1986*. Austin: U of Texas P, 1987.

Moraga, Cherríe. *Loving in the War Years/lo que nunca paso por sus labios*. South End P, 1983.

Padilla, Genaro. *My History, Not Yours: The Formation of Mexican American Autobiography*. Madison: U of Wisconsin P, 1993.

Pateman, Carole. *The Disorder of Women: Democracy, Feminism and Political Theory*. Stanford: Stanford UP, 1989.

Pita, Beatrice, and Sánchez, Rosaura. "Introduction." *The Squatter and the Don*. Houston: Arte Público, 1992.

Pitt, Leonard. *The Decline of the Californios: A Social History of the Spanish-Speaking Californians, 1846-1890*. Berkeley: U of California P, 1966.

Roediger, David R. *The Wages of Whiteness: Race and the Making of the American Working Class*. New York: Verso, 1991.

Saldívar, Ramón. *Chicano Narrative: The Dialectics of Difference*. Madison: U of Wisconsin P, 1990.

Saldívar-Hull, Sonia. "Feminism on the Border: From Gender Politics to Geopolitics." *Criticism in the Borderlands: Studies in Chicano Literature, Culture, and Ideology*. Eds. Héctor Calderón and José David Saldívar. Durham: Duke UP, 1991.

Saxon, Alexander. *The Rise and Fall of the White Republic: Class Politics and Mass Culture in Nineteenth-Century America*. New York: Verso, 1990.

Sommer, Doris. *Foundational Fictions: The National Romances of Latin America*. Berkeley: U of California P, 1991.

_____. "Irresistible Romance: The Foundational Fictions of Latin America." *Nation and Narration*. Ed. Homi Bhabha. New York: Routledge, 1990.

Textual and Land Reclamations: The Critical Reception of Early Chicana/o Literature[1]

Manuel M. Martín Rodríguez

The recent debate centered around the issue of communal essence vs. individual or group difference, has added a new dimension to the field of Chicana/o studies. A previous stage in which cultural nationalism sought to unite all Chicanos/as in a large "family" (*la Raza*) is now being questioned systematically by historians, sociologists, literary critics, artists and, in particular, by feminist and homosexual members of each of those disciplines.[2] As a consequence, the powerful nationalistic symbol of Aztlán—the mythical land from which the ancestors of the Aztecs started south to found Tenochtitlán—is also being revised by scholars and writers. For instance, Daniel C. Alarcón warns us in a recent essay that "Aztlán has been used to obscure and elide important issues surrounding Chicano identity, in particular the significance of intracultural differences" (36), and he goes on to point out how—in spite of its being used by Chicana/o activists as a symbol of freedom and equality—the myth of Aztlán could be seen as a mere "construct of the Aztec elite, created to ensure its members' power over other social classes and to legitimate their privileged status" (58).[3] This is not to say that the myth's influence in all aspects of Chicana/o intellectual life has come to an end. As proved by the recent publication of a volume of essays devoted entirely to the topic,[4] as well as by the constant reference to the same in numerous articles, journals, etc., Aztlán and its connotations continue to be a necessary point of reference for questions regarding Chicana/o culture.

Thus, I begin this essay by discussing what Aztlán did and does represent for contemporary Chicanos/as, even if the literature that I will analyze predates the most recent popularization of the term. By invoking the presence of their indigenous ancestors in Aztlán (thought to be somewhere in the present day Southwest U.S.), cultural nationalists of the 1960s and 1970s aspired to claim a moral and even legal right to the lands inhabited and worked by them. After all—they reasoned—their presence in the area preceded that of Anglo-

Americans. They supported this last point by invoking the 1848 treaty of Guadalupe Hidalgo which ended the war between the United States and Mexico and reconfigured the border: by that treaty, Mexico lost almost half of its territory to the United States; the population of that territory was given the choice of moving south of the newly created border—abandoning their homes—or staying in them and becoming U.S. citizens. The latter was, in principle, the only way to retain their possessions. As history shows, most of those who stayed eventually lost their property anyway. Nationalist Chicanos/as were quick to argue these historical facts in order to legitimize their claim to the Southwest and California, either by reclaiming the lands that had been taken away from their ancestors (as did the Alianza Federal de Mercedes in New Mexico) or by invoking the right to live and work in the areas that had been Mexican territories prior to 1848 (as did many civil rights groups).

The internal colony model was, therefore, much in vogue among scholars at the time, and powerful images such as "occupied America" and "the lost land" reinforced the sentiments of dispossession and of having lost the land of their forefathers.[5] Notwithstanding the fact that the majority of the Chicana/o population at that point was of immigrant descent and lived in the cities, and that most of the land had belonged prior to the Treaty of Guadalupe Hidalgo to a small elite of proprietors, the feeling of dispossession was a general one. The knowledge that the Southwest and California had once been part of Mexico, and that the Mexican presence in the area had always been strong, contributed to the perception of an equal right to the fruits of the land among Chicanos/as, regardless of actual family history; that is to say that the question was usually framed around political and ethnic issues rather than personal or familiar ones. This stance, as we shall see, failed to take into account the class distinctions among Mexican Americans that were already present before the annexation of the territory by the U.S.A., distinctions which divided the Hispanic population (at least for our purposes here) into two groups: those who owned land and those who did not. Needless to say, such an acritical reclamation of land also overlooked the textual accounts produced by writers of Mexican descent from 1848 to the 1960s, and the way in which they dealt with issues of land and labor. Those texts had largely been lost or neglected for decades in archives and libraries and only recently are they being brought to light in modern editions.   My intention, as I engage in the essence vs. difference debate, is not to address the diversity among the Chicana/o community that affects present day Chicanos/as; this has been the subject of several other essays.[6] Rather, I intend to delve into how those differences had already manifested themselves long before the Chicano Movement and, more specifically, into how they were portrayed in literature touching precisely on the issues of land ownership and wage-earning labor. To that end, I have chosen to discuss two early novels published in California: the first (*The Squatter and The Don: A Novel Descriptive of Contemporary Occurrences in California*) was published in San Francisco (1885) by María Amparo Ruiz de Burton, under the pseudonym C. Loyal);[7] the other (*Las aventuras de don Chipote o cuando los pericos mamen* [The Adventures of Don Chipote or When Parrots Suckle Their Young]) was published in Los Angeles (1928) by Daniel Venegas.[8] Both novels have been rescued from oblivion within the last ten years and are now available to a wider readership thanks to the efforts of their respective modern editors. Since in both cases the editors have deemed it necessary to preface the novels with an introduction, I will also devote some attention to their position as critics and readers. Hopefully, my analysis of these two texts—and their exegetes—will contribute something to the current debate on the historical diversity of the Chicana/o experience since the two novels seem to have very little in common (perhaps just a strong autobiographical content, as well as the ethnic background of their authors) and a great many differences (language choice, gender and social status of their authors, genre, tone, etc.). In order to account for and compare these differences and similarities, my analysis of the novels will focus on the treatment of class, ethnicity, and gender issues, as well as on the dissimilar ways of engaging with their respective audiences.

The Squatter and the Don: A Novel Descriptive of Contemporary Occurrences in California, as its subtitle implies, promises to deliver a political and social commentary, and the many narrative asides and narratorial remarks—extending at times to occupy whole chapters—indeed fulfill this function. The main narrative plot, however, is contained within the romance genre, depicting an almost impossible love between Mercedes (the daughter of Don Mariano Alamar) and Clarence Darrell, the son of the squatter in the title. The trials confronting their love are caused, to a large extent, by the brutal socio-economic transformation of the state, which constitutes the background of the narrative; the result is a compelling story about the loss of land and the decline of one Californio family. In the end, the Alamars are virtually destroyed as the newcomers and their new legal system strain the family's financial situation by disputing their right to the land.[9] This, by the way, seems to be a reflection of Ruiz de Burton's own plight and misfortunes, as her letters to George Davidson demonstrate.[10] In addition, a third genre contributes to the structure of this novel: the promotional literature which portrayed California as the land of milk and honey in order to encourage its colonization by Anglo Americans, represented in the novel by the Mechlin family. Compare, for instance, the following passages. The first is taken from A. M. Shew's *California as a Health Resort*:

> Add to these [climatological] advantages the choicest and most tempting array of fresh fruits and vegetables for every month of the year, and you have all the requisites in a climate for invalids. Thus far only a commencement has been made in settling this great State. At no distant day, *when it shall have been cut up into small farms and occupied by thrifty eastern people*, we must expect a veritable Paradise on earth, and such a Sanitarium for invalids as the world has not known. (8, emphasis added)

The second is from Ruiz de Burton's novel:

> Mr. James Mechlin had come to San Diego, four years previously, a living skeleton, not expected to last another winter…. He [had] tried the climate of Florida. He spent several years in Italy and in the south of France, but he felt no better. At last, believing his malady incurable, he returned to his New York home to die…. With but little hope, and only to please his family, Mr. Mechlin came to San Diego, and his health improved so rapidly that he made up his mind to buy a country place and make San Diego his home. (68)[11]

What interests me most about this promotional literature and its attendant problematics is that the Alamars, rather than opposing Anglo immigration, are quick to second this type of initiative (in particular as it relates to the building of a railroad all the way to San Diego and the subsequent real estate opportunities), and they seem eager to transform their way of life from a ranch economy to the industrial capitalism brought by the new conquerors.[12] In fact, Mr. Alamar's only business initiatives throughout the novel consist of promoting the fruit industry business, first (see pages 91-96), and then, in parceling his land for sale (see page 238); interestingly, these are also the two endeavors emphasized by Shew in his cited contemporary report to the Connecticut Medical Society, dated also 1885.

Hence, the Alamars' effort to retain their land is not portrayed in Ruiz de Burton's novel as a nostalgic clinging to a fading social order nor as a confrontational attitude against the new power block. It is depicted instead as a will to participate in the development and exploitation of the new opportunities for enrichment brought about by the U.S. economy, conscious of the fact that such action will enable them to preserve their social status. The Alamars are, thus, clearly privileging their class position over their ethnic origin, and they are putting their own economic welfare before any cultural, political, or national allegiance previously pledged.[13] The fact that the narrator, who clearly aligns itself with the Alamars, refers to them as "Spano-Americans" is evidently another class-marked strategy to deal with their ethnicity, and to differentiate them from the rest of the Spanish-speaking characters in the novel—usually referred to in the text as the "(lazy) indians."[14]

Even the fact that the question of property rights is framed primarily around the squatter controversy (instead of the controversy around U.S.

expansionism and Mexico's national sovereignty) reveals that ethnicity is constantly downplayed in favor of class relations, a factor also supported by the constant declarations of loyalty to the new laws by the patriarch of the Alamar family.[15] The Alamars's aversion toward the squatters stems mainly from the fact that they belong to a "lower" social echelon than theirs, one that does not allow them to buy land. By contrast, the Don and his family have no trouble at all accepting either the Mechlins, who buy a fair amount of land, or the Darrells (who secretly pay for the land they occupy); that, of course, after they embark upon certain "purifying" rites which refine their newly acquired riches.[16] Following the death of Don Mariano and the infirmity of his male offsprings (who become ill after undertaking manual jobs in construction and agriculture, thus losing their privileged class status), the ultimate demise of the Alamar family can only be reversed—or so the novel seems to imply—by the marriage of one of Don Mariano's daughters (precisely the one named Mercedes)[17] to a wealthy representative of the new order: Clarence Darrell. This could be read as a symbolic way of portraying the blending of past history with new realities, in which the rights to the land of the "noble Californios" are merged with the economic puissance of a rising class of Anglo capitalists. (Clarence Darrell owes his fortune to stocks and mining enterprises.) In such a merger, the latter brings the money and the former the social status; that negotiation would seem to be the easiest way for the Californios to retain land and privileges in a changed social order.

As for the author and the narrator, the negotiation of class, ethnicity, and gender within the novel is similarly complex, since their identities are concealed, in the case of the former, by the pseudonym and, of the latter, by the non-gender-marked language. In both cases these are strategies meant to validate their discourse vis-à-vis a readership that is envisioned as predominantly Anglo-American.[18] For the benefit of a (presumably smaller) Californio readership, however, a symbolic web of ethnic historic reminders is carefully woven, thereby adding historical perspective which serves to legitimize the Californios' rights to the land, while partially revealing the author/narrator's ethnicity. This subtext is mainly composed of dates and names that would be easily recognizable to an audience of Mexican descent. Mercedes, for instance, is born on the 5th of May, the day on which Mexico celebrates the defeat of the French invading army (in 1861, a date that was—no doubt—still fresh in Ruiz de Burton's mind in 1884 when she wrote her novel). Similarly, her wedding with Clarence is first set for the 16th of September, the anniversary of Mexico's independence from Spain. Mercedes' own name seems to be an implicit reminder of the name given in Spanish to the land grants conferred first by the monarchs of Spain and then by the Mexican governors.[19] Though mostly suppressed by the main plot, the subtext that I have just outlined

nonetheless remains visible and creates a number of ambiguities which culmi-
nate in the final chapter of the book, entitled "Out With the Invader."[20] This
chapter opens with a devastating critique of the railroad barons, whose fortunes were amassed through public subsidies and land appropriations (and
who are accused of extortion and other crimes by the narrator); this denunciation subtly brings us back to the question of land ownership.[21] The chapter
continues with praise, in the name of the "Spanish population of the State [of
California]," for "*their* countryman Reginaldo del Valle, who was one of the
first to take a bold stand against the [railroad] monopoly" (369, my
emphasis).[22]

The issue is one of class struggle: the owners of the land trying to control
the monopolies which—in their almost legal impunity—threaten even their
superior social status, thereby relegating them to, as the last lines of the novel
put it, that of "white slaves" waiting for a Redeemer to emancipate them. The
title of the chapter, though, remains ambivalent, for the invaders are both the
railroad monopolists (in a literal reading) and the non-"Spanish" population of
the state (in a figurative reading that would take into account the subtext that I
have just described).[23] It is, thus, as if María A. Ruiz de Burton were writing
her novel with two different audiences (and two different agendas) in mind:
for the Anglo-American reader, she carefully constructs a plot that lets her
narrator *explain* the abuses against the Californios in order to induce sympathy; for a Californio readership, she *encodes* her narrative with the historical
reminders that provide the informed audience with a second level of meaning:
a level in which the landed Californios' right to the land is hinted at in a reas-
suring way by evoking the grants they received under the Spanish rule, their
lingering privileged status after the independence from Spain, and a previous
instance of foreign invasion which ended up being unsuccessful for the
invaders.[24]

As for gender, although the narrator's and the author's gender is not distinctly marked, there are several passages that might reveal their identity to a
careful reader. In two of these passages, two different characters criticize the
ways of contemporary men, one even warning them of the changes that
women's suffrage would bring about. The third passage is even more important for our discussion, since it is the voice of the narrator, and not that of a
character, that tells us: "The heads of families all came [to the meeting]—the
male heads, be it understood—as the squatters did not make any pretense to
regard female opinion with any more respect than other men" (89). As these
passages suggest, in Ruiz de Burton's *The Squatter and the Don* we have not
only a text that challenges our perception of early Californio society, but also
a challenge to the contemporary perception of the social role of women. In so
doing, Ruiz de Burton's novel alerts its readers against any identity-oriented

position that prevents subjects from negotiating their own diverse and multi-fold selves.[25] This may not be apparent in a literal reading of the novel, but it is indisputable—I believe—if we read it with attention to its suppressed and allegorized impulses.

After this necessarily brief analysis of *The Squatter and the Don*, I would like now to address the issue of its relevance to a new history of Chicana/o literature, in particular as this touches upon the issues of textual reclamation and intracultural differences. I also intend to state my position and to mark my agreement and disagreement with certain elements of Sánchez and Pita's analysis of the novel. While it is undeniable that "the exclusionary dynamics of hegemonic culture erase minority discourses, silence denunciatory voices and leave tremendous lacunae in the history of marginalized groups that recovery projects and research are today compelled to fill" (50), as Sánchez and Pita state in their concluding remarks, the rest of their conclusion is far more debatable from the perspective that I am adopting in this essay.

Hence, for instance, when Sánchez and Pita propose that Ruiz de Burton's novel is "an interpelation of today's readers, as citizens, or as descendants of Californios, to resist oppression" (51) and when they conclude that "such are the contestation and defiant discourse with which the literature of the population of Mexican origin in the United States emerges" (51) I believe that they have failed to take into account class and gender differences among that population (then and now), and that they have posited a rather static and simplified vision of Ruiz de Burton's readership (once again, then and now). This is not to imply that Chicana/o literature does not emerge with contestary discourses; neither is it meant to deny the protest aspects of *The Squatter and the Don*. But Ruiz de Burton's protest emanates from a very definitely class-oriented position that many Chicanos/as would not share today, and her social class gives shape to a perceived ethnic identity that many others could not share either. In fact, as opposed to Ruiz de Burton, much of today's Chicana/o population is of working-class origin, and so were many of her contemporary Californios whose experiences the novel refuses to engage, that "broader base of Californio workers, including those who were never landed nor aristocratic" (34) whose existence Sánchez and Pita acknowledge but do not incorporate in their analysis. *The Squatter and the Don* should be read, then, with an eye for unmasking those aspects that make it an ideological construct of the Californio elite. As such, this novel served the landed Californios in a way similar to that in which the myth of Aztlán has been said to serve the Aztec elite: that is, as an intellectual legitimization of their privileged status.

Similarly problematic is Sánchez's and Pita's interpretation of the ending of the novel, in which the narrator tells us that, unless the legislators correct the abuses perpetrated by the monopolists in Southern California, "we shall—

as Channing said 'kiss the foot that tramples us' and 'in anguish of spirit' must wait and pray for a Redeemer who will emancipate the white slaves of California" (372). According to Sánchez and Pita,

> By the novel's end, the victims are seen to be not only the Californios and their immediate antagonists, the squatters, but also the city of San Diego and, in the long run, the entire state population…who suffer the consequences of the collusion of state government, congress and monopoly capitalism. (6)

Hence, argue Sánchez and Pita, it is the all-embracing nature of Ruiz de Burton's denunciation that allows her to refer to her characters as "white slaves" waiting for their liberation by a Lincoln-Christ figure (36).   The fact that the narrator is able to speak of the Alamars as part of the "white slaves" speaks less—I believe—of a universally shared victimization than of a situation that affects wealthy (or formerly wealthy) individuals and families. As I pointed out earlier, the narrator constantly reminds us of the Alamars being "Spano-Americans" and she tirelessly insists on their white countenances when describing them. "White" is implicitly used in this sense to designate Californios of the social elite; therefore, it comes as no surprise that they will rhetorically join other "white slaves" (such as the Mechlin family, who also lost their California land to squatters and lawyers) as victims. But this process of unifying the Californio with the Anglo elite, rather than making theirs a universal situation, works to separate them from the rest of the population of Spanish-Mexican descent, those fellow construction workers of Gabriel Alamar, for instance, who neither owned land nor had someone like Clarence to help them get ahead.

María A. Ruiz de Burton wrote a protest novel not from a general Mexican American point of view but, rather, from an aristocratic Mexican American point of view—and this contrasts sharply with protest novels written later during the Chicano Movement. The cultural, economic, and social reclamation in *The Squatter and the Don* has more to do with maintaining a privileged status than with social justice in any broad sense of the term. One must not overlook this fact when reclaiming this text for the history of Chicana/o literature nor when addressing its importance to contemporary readerships.

Consequently, when Sánchez and Pita state that "if the authorship is given in code, so is the readership which undoubtedly is meant to include Californios—men like M.G. Vallejo, residents of San Diego—and, it could be argued, the descendants of Californios and Mexicans in the United States today" (50), it may be worth repeating how the subtext of this novel (presumably intended for a Californio readership) serves as a historical justification of privilege as much as it is an implicit protest against the U.S. occupation. It may also be of interest to recall what in 1972—during more militant times—

one of those in the audience now envisioned by Sánchez and Pita for *The Squatter and the Don* stated when talking about that occupation:

> few conquests can be maintained without the continuous collaboration of some native faction. California and the Southwest were no exception. In California men like Mariano Vallejo and Pablo de la Guerra…played important roles in bringing California and the Southwest under Gabacho [Anglo] control. These political opportunists had much to gain by way of land speculation, increased commerce, and the hopes of political aggrandizement. They were men of influence and power who hoped to continue in privileged positions and even increase their power through a Gabacho hegemony. (R. V. Padilla 35)[26]

It is clear to me that Ruiz de Burton's narrator and her characters are speaking precisely from the point of view that R. V. Padilla describes and not in defense of the general population of Mexican descent. Even if one concedes that Ruiz de Burton's novel has many contestatory passages (particularly bold and modern in the realm of women's rights), one would still have to be careful not to attribute to the text an ideological and social position—that of the predominantly working-class Chicano Movement—that is foreign to it. Ruiz de Burton's *The Squatter and the Don* is a most interesting early component of Chicana/o literature, and a unique text that gives us the perspective of a specific sector of the early Mexican American population; but it could hardly be described as the direct origin of more recent contestatory discourses.

In sharp contrast with the Alamars, Don Chipote, the hero of our second and much shorter novel, is a landless peasant. At the beginning of the story he is a sharecropper in Mexico, and his family is so large—we are told in the first page of the text—that he stoops from daybreak until dusk to put a little food on their table. Enticed by the tall tales of a fellow countryman, Pitacio, Don Chipote decides to try his luck in the U.S., where he is sure to improve his lot very quickly.[27] After many difficulties, he manages to cross the border and becomes, by virtue of his new situation, an unskilled worker subject to the worst abuses. He first works "en el traque," that is, for the very same railroad companies that so much worried Ruiz de Burton. Then, after suffering an accident he is sent by the railroad company to a hospital in Los Angeles, where, upon recovery, he works as a dishwasher.

Los Angeles was, at that time, experiencing a boom of Mexican American theater which captivates Don Chipote among its faithful audience.[28] So enthralled is Don Chipote that he decides to participate in one of the numerous talent shows in hopes of winning the heart of one of his fellow workers, a waitress simply referred to as "La Pelona." Much to his chagrin, his artistic debut coincides with the day of his entire family's arrival in Los Angeles, accompanied by Pitacio. They, sitting in the audience, immediately recognize don Chipote and, after a free-for-all fight, the novel ends with the deportation and return of the Chipote family to sharecropping in Mexico. The moral of this ending (stated in the last lines of the text as "los mexicanos se harán ricos en Estados Unidos: CUANDO LOS PERICOS MAMEN" (155) [Mexicans will become rich in the U.S. WHEN PARROTS SUCKLE THEIR YOUNG], is as problematic as it is effective for Venegas's purposes, as we shall immediately see.

Since it inserts itself in the satirical tradition of the myth of quick riches— a variation of which myth, as we saw, land developers were using to attract Anglo colonizers—, *Las aventuras* reveals itself to be scarcely critical of social reality in Mexico, an aspect which we must keep in mind when considering the novel's ending. Don Chipote's lot may not improve in the U.S. as much as he dreamed, but we know his economic position in Mexico cannot be any better. At a time when the Mexican novel was starting to address the question of land distribution to peasants, *Las aventuras* stands out because of its failure to deal with land issues. But this may very well be intentional, since Venegas is clearly more concerned with talking about the urban working-class in the U.S. (his potential audience) than seriously delving into the problems of land ownership and the rural population of Mexico. In fact, Mexico and life in Mexico serve only as a frame for the novel, appearing precisely for the purpose of exposing injustices in the United States. In other words, the moral of his story—go back to Mexico and forget about making it big in the U.S.— should not be taken literally, since it is clearly undermined by Venegas's solidarity with those who have been uprooted from Mexico and have become "permanent" Chicanos/as.[29]

Although Don Chipote himself is only a Chicano in the strictest sense of the term at that time—a recent immigrant from Mexico—, the novel depicts a whole community of foreign workers, some of whom are eventually forced to go back to Mexico while others decide or manage to stay in the U.S. The author, who sympathizes with the immigrant working-class community as someone who belongs to or has been part of it, is thus split between his denunciation of the myth of quick riches that brings immigrants to economic exploitation in the Southwest and California, and his more severe denunciation of the conditions to which those immigrants and other residents of Mexican descent are subjected.[30] The following long quote from the novel should suffice to document my point. The narrator, while discussing the supply store system, accuses the U.S. government of involvement in the situation; at the same time, his accusation allows him to chastise those among the immigrants who are indirectly responsible for the misfortunes of others:

> Casi no se puede creer que las autoridades de los Estados Unidos no se hayan dado cuenta de este robo de que son víctimas nuestros compatriotas, pues es imposible que tales abusos no se los sepan. En este caso lo único que se puede

pensar es: o que no hacen caso porque somos mexicanos, o que son cómplices de las sinvergüenzadas de las compañías. El que esto escribe, en la temporada que tuvo que entrarle al traque, no recuerda haber recibido un cheque conforme al tiempo trabajado; ni que le hayan mandado la provisión tal como la ordenó; pues la famosa tienda manda lo que se le pega la gana y lo cobra como quiere.... Sin embargo de estos abusos que son víctimas todos los paisanos que vienen al camello a los Estados Unidos, no hay uno que regrese a México y que llegue y cuente la verdad; pues todos llegan recantoneándoselas y contándoles las costillas a los que les preguntan cómo les fue en el país del oro. Es debido a esto que la mayoría de los que andamos por estos rumbos, nos hemos dejado venir dizque a barrer el dinero con la escoba. (71-72)

[It is hard to believe that U.S. authorities haven't acknowledged the abuses that our fellow countrymen suffer, since it is impossible that they would not know about it. In this case, one can only think the following: either they do not care because we are Mexicans, or they are accomplices in the shameful acts that companies perpetrate against us. In his years as a railroad worker, this writer does not remember receiving a single check reflecting the hours he actually worked; neither did he receive the provisions as ordered; for the infamous store sends what it fancies and charges what it wants.... In spite of the abuses endured by our fellow workers, not a single one tells the truth on returning to Mexico; instead, they all come back singing the States' praises to the skies and snickering at the thin ribs of those who ask how it went in the land of gold. That is how most of us ended up here, coming as they said to sweep money from the streets].

Although the conclusion of Venegas's novel literally aims to discourage his readers from trying their luck in the North, and it could very well be interpreted as a rhetorical expression of nationalist discourse in post-revolutionary Mexico, his true intention seems to be that of addressing the wrongs which the laws permit against the Chicana/o population in the U.S. in spite of international treaties with Mexico. In this sense, Venegas distances himself from other Mexican expatriates (such as Julio G. Arce), who were much more critical of Mexicans in the U.S.

The story of Don Chipote also allows Venegas to document the culture and speech of the working-class in Los Angeles, and to pay particular attention to the mixture of Spanish and English that results from the new social and economic conditions that Chicanos/as find in California. Venegas' use of the vernacular Spanish throughout the novel reflects not only his class allegiance, but also his desire to reach a different type of audience than the one sought by Ruiz de Burton. A clear demarcation of Venegas' intended audience as working class Chicanos/as is found on page 53 of *Las aventuras*: "Ahora, lectores, aquí tienen a don Chipote camino de California. ¿Llegará? Tú que te has reenganchado dime, ¿le faltará mucho?" [Now, dear readers, here you have don Chipote on his way to California. Will he get there? You, who re-enlisted, tell me: does he have far to go?]. In fact, Venegas is probably courting the same audience that had already made him a popular playwright: the Chicana/o working-class majority.[31]

To that end, he also resorts to using and alluding intertextually to popular genres, mainly those of the oral tradition (there is a strong parallel between the plot of his novel and "El corrido del lavaplatos" [The Dishwasher's Ballad]; there is also a fair amount of text devoted to the theatrical scene in Los Angeles, as already indicated). Nonetheless, he grounds his story in popular literary modes as well, not only through the obvious parody of Don Quijote, but also through the picaresque tradition kept alive both in folklore and in print. The many repetitions in the text even suggest that *Las aventuras* was conceived (if not published) as a serial novel to be printed in newspapers, the most accessible form of literature for Chicana/o workers. In contrast, the intertextual references in *The Squatter and the Don* belong to the world of Anglo-American so-called high culture (Emerson, Carlyle, Spencer, etc.), as would be expected from an author intent on delineating an international elitist position.[32]

The two novels are also dissimilar in their treatment of gender issues. While Ruiz de Burton feels the need to conceal her gender identity, as we saw, Venegas is quick to stress his, resorting to language as well as to authorial comments which leave no doubt about the author's and narrator's attitude. Language is pervasively sexist throughout *Las aventuras*, and this is an aspect that feminist criticism will, no doubt, have to address in discussing the novel. It is obvious that there was hardly a need for Venegas to conceal his gender identity in order to publish, since class and ethnicity—not gender—were the main disadvantages confronting the publication of his novel. By contrast, had Ruiz de Burton been of working-class origin, her novel—if written at all— would probably have remained buried somewhere around her home.

Therefore, with respect to views on class, gender, audience, language and ideology, *Las aventuras de don Chipote* is at the opposite end of the spectrum from *The Squatter and the Don*. On the one hand, although both novels share a marked interest in stressing class issues, they are doing so from patently antithetical positions: that of landless workers versus that of land owners. As a consequence, their respective views on ethnicity also differ, since Ruiz de Burton's land owners must stress their aristocratic ("*Spano*-American") heritage, while Venegas' workers are clearly identified as working-class Chicanos/as, an identification that will later become predominant in the literature published after the 1960's Movement. In this sense, Venegas' novel is much closer to being a true antecedent of present-day protest literature than *The Squatter and the Don* could ever be, and *Las aventuras* was hailed as such an antecedent by its modern editor, Nicolás Kanellos. After contrasting it with Chicano novels from the 1970s, Kanellos concludes in his introduction: "esta novela augura la forma y el contenido de la novela chicana actual" (14) [this novel prefigures the form and content of the present day Chicana/o novel], and he salutes Venegas's work as the first Chicana/o novel (8).

From our current position in the midst of the essence vs. difference debate, further punctualization, that might not have been necessary when Kanellos first analyzed the novel, may now be in order. Indeed, Kanellos' reading works very adequately when relating *Las aventuras* to the predominantly militant fiction of the 1970s. But the 1980s and the 1990s have taught us to be more careful not to define any one artistic or social trend as defining "the" Chicana/o literary experience. It is to be expected, then, that some readers will not be as enthusiastic today about Venegas' work as Kanellos was only a decade ago. Undoubtedly, there are some aspects in *Las aventuras* that would make it a very problematic text for many readers in our day, as I suggested when examining gender-related issues. The reclamation of this text for a new history of the Chicana/o literature (or the reclamation of Ruiz de Burton's text, for that matter) can no longer be a matter of positing it as the ultimate definition of what Chicana/o literature was, is, will, or should be since, as we understand it now, both the historical and literary experiences of Chicanos/as have been multifold, thus precluding essentialist or reductive definitions.

In spite of these many differences, both novels do have some important elements in common. The most salient is probably the fact that both authors felt it necessary to respond to societal pressures by documenting their own stories and those of their communities. In this sense, these autobiographical novels constitute a history of early California as seen by the displaced Mexican American population. In the face of a serious threat of marginalization (a historical process which has kept both texts neglected for decades), Ruiz de Burton and Venegas managed to record in literature the experience of two segments of the population which had to adjust to a new and changed environment. Both novels are therefore testimonies of a rich cultural production in writing which flourished against all odds. Seen in this light, the differences between the two novels work to our advantage by enriching the perspectives from which that experience is addressed. They help us to demystify the previously posited homogeneity of a group which actually reveals internal differences from the outset of its history.

It should be apparent by now that differences among the Mexican American population, as well as among its intellectuals, antedates both the current debate on diversity and the Chicano Movement. As these two early novels show, the Chicana/o experience has been marked all along by variations determined by class, gender and even individual perceptions of ethnicity. When taking into consideration land ownership and labor relations, one also notes that the issues were addressed from very different ideological and aesthetic positions, depending on where a particular intellectual stood with regard to those matters. Read from our present social and theoretical frame of reference, these two novels also remind us once and for all that critical and rhetorical notions such as "reclaiming the Americas" and "literary recovery" must be carefully employed and historically based in order to be effective. In the recent past, crusades to reclaim the land at times overlooked the fact that large segments of it belonged to rich landowners who were granted their rights only at the expense of the indigenous population of the region. This in turn implied labor subordination for the majority of the Chicana/o and Native American population.[33] Therefore, the notion of "reclaiming the Americas," if we expect it to be fruitful and free of essentialist simplifications, must be addressed from a critical position that carefully takes into account not just ethnic considerations, but factors of class and gender as well.

Likewise, the most necessary and praiseworthy task of recuperating lost texts—which Kanellos, Sánchez and Pita, and others have begun—should also be approached carefully in order to avoid the perpetuation of reductionist generalizations about Chicana/o literary history, past and present. Both Kanellos, on the one hand, and Sánchez and Pita, on the other, seem to have read the texts they introduce from a homogenizing view of what Chicana/o literature is.[34] Their interest is, then, in tracing Chicana/o literature's genealogy by smoothing the differences found along the way and by concentrating on similarities between old texts and modern ones. They are able to do so as long as they concentrate on single texts from the past and a selective corpus of modern texts. When we actually contrast early texts as diverse as *The Squatter and the Don* and *Las aventuras de don Chipote*, we find very dissimilar sets of experiences, radically different class status on the part of their authors and characters, and totally divergent ideological positions on issues such as land and labor, language attitudes, social relations, etc. This, by the way, does not make any of the two texts more or less Chicana/o: it reminds us that there is not just one definition of Chicana/o that fits every text or every person of that ethnicity. My position, therefore, is closer to that suggested by Erlinda Gonzales-Berry who, in an article about early New Mexican literature, warns us against the dangers of overlooking differences when creating a new literary canon from recovered texts (129-30).

The unifying nationalistic rhetoric that sprang from the Chicano Movement and dominated much of the criticism written from that moment on, albeit politically useful, proves itself to be of little accuracy when confronted with past and present differences in the Chicana/o experiences. Therefore, if they are to be operative in the 1990s, notions such as land or textual reclamation need to be employed with enough flexibility to account for those differences. In our current evaluation of past texts, differences should not be overlooked for the sake of outlining a homogeneous literary history. - texts from the past need to be reclaimed and reprinted, but they must be read for what they are: diverse accounts of a diverse experience.

Notes

[1]This is the third and longest version of an essay originally written in 1992 and presented at the 1992 MLA Convention, on one of three panels entitled "Reclaiming the Americas." Part of the essay was intended to be a critical elaboration of the notion of land reclamation. After that version was written, a critical edition of *The Squatter and the Don* was published with an excellent introduction by Rosaura Sánchez and Beatrice Pita. The essay was then revised to incorporate my reading of Sánchez's and Pita's critical work and the results were presented as a lecture at the University of Washington. A discussion of the implications of textual recovery/reclamation was incorporated to that new version. This final version has been amended to account for recent publications relevant to the subject, mainly those by Erlinda Gonzales-Berry, and Genaro Padilla. Thanks to Elizabeth Small for her careful reading of the manuscript, and to Erlinda Gonzales-Berry for her suggestions while editing this volume.

[2]For some of the most recent revisionary stances, see the articles by Alex M. Saragoza, Norma Alarcón, Chela Sandoval, and Angie Chabram, cited in the bibliography.

[3]A somewhat similar revision of the myth of Aztlán had already been proposed by J. J. Klor de Alva (149-49), whom Daniel C. Alarcón follows to a certain extent.

[4]The reference here is to the volume edited by R. A. Anaya and F. Lomelí.

[5]The images cited refer, respectively, to the well-known books by Rodolfo Acuña, and by John R. Chávez.

[6]A useful review of works on population diversity can be found on Alex M. Saragoza's "Recent Chicano Historiography," particularly on pp. 11ff.

[7]All quotes from Ruiz de Burton's novel will be from the most recent (1993) edition of the text.

[8]All quotes of this novel will be taken from the most recent edition (Mexico: Secretaría de Educación Pública and Centro de Estudios de la Frontera Norte, 1985). All translations are mine. I would like to thank Kurt Westby and Elizabeth Small for their help in translating all quotes.

[9]An account of the fate of the Californios after the Anglo-American takeover can be found in the book by Leonard M. Pitt. For a detailed critique of Pitt's thesis, see Raymond V. Padilla.

[10]The letters are part of the George Davidson Correspondence, Manuscript Collection, Bancroft Library, University of California at Berkeley. I would like to thank a student of mine, Chelo Zepeda Carter, for providing me with copies of the letters. For a detailed discussion of Ruiz de Burton's life and trials, see Sánchez and Pita's introduction to the 1993 edition.

[11]Another fine example of this promotional literature is provided by the Southern California Bureau of Information's *Southern California: An Authentic Description of Its Natural Resources and Prospects Containing Reliable Information for the Homeseeker, Tourist, and Invalid*, from which I extract the following quotes: "Thus is Southern California distinguished as a land peculiarly favored by nature, a fitting counterpart of the Promised Land as it were ere the deserts were allowed to encroach upon its fertile plains" (7); "In hundreds of cases invalids make an entire recovery of health, and in other cases the disease is stayed and many years of life gained" (11).

[12]The only reservation that both the characters and narrator express against capitalism concerns the seemingly irreversible rise of the monopolies which, as it is well known, started to consolidate themselves around the 1880s. In accordance with her desire to write "a novel descriptive

of contemporary occurrences," Ruiz de Burton reveals here a keen sensibility for the latest economic developments.

[13]The same seems to be true of Ruiz de Burton. In a letter to Davidson (dated 12/4/1875), she writes about her hope for the U.S. annexing Lower California, since that will tremendously raise the value of her properties south of the border. She, as her characters, is quick to relinquish her Mexican citizenship in order to participate in the new state of affairs.

[14]This effort to somehow disguise the ethnicity of her characters is consistent with that of the real-life Ruiz de Burton in using the pseudonym C. Loyal: first, it conceals her ethnicity under the Anglo-sounding last name, and then it conceals her gender by using only an initial instead of a full first name. As noted by Sánchez and Pita, "ciudadano leal" ("loyal citizen") was "a common letter-closing practice used in official government correspondence in Mexico during the nineteenth century" (11). The fact that Ruiz de Burton uses a Mexican governmental formula in English reveals—I believe—a shift in allegiances similar to that of the Alamars; her loyalty is now to the newly arrived political powers.

[15]This position is also pointed out by Sánchez and Pita in their introduction to the novel. Their analysis, however, tends to privilege discourses of class at certain times (see p. 20), while downplaying their importance at others in favor of a classless vision of Californio society, as we shall see in discussing their conclusion.

[16]The only member of the family to resist refinement is William Darrell, as the following quote suggests: "The Darrell house was now finished, the furniture had arrived, been unpacked and distributed in the rooms, but the house seemed to old Darrell entirely too sumptuous for the plain folks that his family ought to be" (105).

[17]For a discussion of names in the novel see below.

[18]I am positing Ruiz de Burton's targeted audience as Anglo-American for several reasons. The most obvious include the language choice and the frequent narratorial explanation about the "Spano-Americans." A less obvious reason, but one that to me is equally revealing, is the fact that the novel seems to be a fictionalization of Ruiz de Burton's epistolary relation with G. Davidson. Nonetheless, as I shall immediately suggest, Ruiz de Burton is also writing her novel with a Californio audience in mind.

[19]In addition, as Mariano G. Vallejo attests in his "Recuerdos históricos y personales tocante a la Alta California," the commanding officers of the *presidios* were authorized to grant lands in California. An excerpt of Vallejo's memoirs can be found on Rosaura Sánchez's et al. *Nineteenth Century Californio Testimonials.*

[20]The play on names is constant throughout the novel and it serves as a symbolic guide to the characters' personalities. Names such as Clarence, Gasbang and (Judge) Lawlack speak for themselves. Less obvious manipulations include those already discussed within the Alamar family plus the maiden name of Mrs. Darrell, Moreneau, a French-looking name that would be pronounced "Moreno," meaning "brown" or "dark-haired" in Spanish; her sympathies for the Californios are in this way symbolically conveyed by her name.

[21]According to W. W. Robinson, railroads received title to 11.4% of the state of California's total area. For further discussion on railroads, see pp. 147-62 of his book. In particular p. 155 is of interest for our discussion, since it explains the switch from the coastal route to that of the interior, a switch strongly criticized throughout Ruiz de Burton's novel.

[22]I emphasize "their" as an example of how carefully Ruiz de Burton and her narrator mask their own ethnic identity.

[23]More so if one bears in mind the recent defeat of the French invaders in Mexico, already mentioned. A similar ambiguity is found on p. 129, when the narrator describes a scene in which a steamboat ("she" in the following quote) departs from San Diego: "In a few minutes she had made up for lost time, and was heading for Ballast Point, leaving San Diego's shore to be merged

into the hills of Mexico beyond, as if obeying the immutable law which says that all things must revert to their original source."

[24]In discussing Mexican American autobiographies of the Nineteenth century, Genaro Padilla has also posited the "discursive duplicity" of the texts he studies in relation to a double audience (34, 38, 70).

[25]For a similar defense of subjective negotiation of the self in our days see Norma Alarcón, *passim*.

[26]It is also interesting—without my wanting to push the parallel too far—that Sánchez and Pita suggest that don Mariano Alamar is, in fact, modeled after Mariano Vallejo, a personal friend of Ruiz de Burton (376, note 27). They also describe how Ruiz de Burton's family opted to leave Baja California as refugees when the Treaty of Guadalupe-Hidalgo (1848) left that area under Mexican sovereignty. They were part of a number of Mexicans who, according to Sánchez and Pita, prior to 1848 "had signed articles of capitulation which granted them United States citizenship and allowed them the retention of their own officials and laws" (9).

[27]Notice that Pitacio's stories are, at a certain level, a counterpart of the promotional literature discussed earlier. Although Pitacio does not seem to be aware of it, his stories (and those of others like him) contributed to bringing to the U.S. a flood of unskilled workers. These migrant constituted a work force that was much needed at the time by both the monopolists and by the settlers who had been enticed, in their turn, by reports like those by Shew and by the Southern California Bureau of Information.

[28]An analysis of this boom is available in Kanellos, *A History of Hispanic Theatre in the United States*, 44-59.

[29]An accurate discussion of the term "Chicano" is found in Tino Villanueva. In my text, I am using and emphasizing the word "permanent" because the term Chicano was not used at that time to describe permanent residents, let alone citizens.

[30]The narrator, throughout the novel, suggests that he has gone through similar experiences to those of his characters. Kanellos goes one step further by suggesting that it is also probably true of Venegas himself (see p. 14 of his introduction to the novel).

[31]In his entry on Daniel Venegas for the *Dictionary of Literary Biography*, Kanellos analyzes Venegas's success as a playwright, as well as the censures that his "liberties taken with language" brought him from elitist critics of the time (271). As for his popularity among working-class audience, see this quote from *La Opinión* (Jan. 8, 1930), reproduced in Kanellos's "Introducción" to *Las aventuras*: "el autor [Venegas] cuenta con muchas simpatías entre el elemento obrero mexicano de Los Angeles, por lo que seguramente tendrá casa llena esta noche." (15) [the author is very popular among Mexican workers in Los Angeles; therefore, he will surely have a full house tonight]. The occasion was the opening of Venegas's play "Esclavos" [Slaves].

[32]For a literary contextualization of Ruiz de Burton's novel, see the introduction by Sánchez and Pita (pp. 7-8). In contrasting Venegas' and Ruiz de Burton's literary references, I am referring to the former's as "popular" because the books and the literary characters he alludes to are known by many more people than those who have actually read them or about them. It was not necessary to have read Cervantes' *Don Quijote* or *Pedro de Urdemalas*, nor the anonymous *Lazarillo de Tormes*, in order to be sufficiently acquainted with their protagonists.

[33]It is only recently that revisionist critics have stressed the need to retrace the ties among Chicanos/as (as partly of Native American descent) and Native Americans. The focus of these scholars and writers has shifted, therefore, from claims of Aztec and Mayan descent to that of the Southwestern and Northern Mexican Native peoples. For an anthology which reflects in part that approach see Ray Gonzales, ed., *Without Discovery*.

[34]A similar homogenizing attitude is adopted by Genaro Padilla in relation to autobiographical texts of the past century: "Although there were class stratifications, regional differences, and

gender distinctions that nuanced literary discourse in important ways and that must be more finely examined in subsequent scholarship, I will argue that in the period after the American conquest, the life histories of Mexican American women and men articulate an interregional and even interclass sense of individual and communal disjuncture" (10).

Works Cited

Acuña, Rodolfo. *Occupied America: A History of Chicanos.* 1972. Cambridge: Harper & Row, 1988. 3rd. ed.

Alarcón, Daniel Cooper. "The Aztec Palimpsest: Toward a New Understanding of Aztlán." *Aztlán* 19.2 (Fall 1988-90): 33-68.

Alarcón, Norma. "The Theoretical Subject(s) of *This Bridge Called My Back* and Anglo-American Feminism." *Making Face, Making Soul.* Ed. G. Anzaldúa. 356-69.

Anaya, Rudolfo A., and Francisco A. Lomelí, eds. *Aztlán: Essays on the Chicano Homeland.* Albuquerque: El Norte Publications, 1989.

Anzaldúa, Gloria, ed. *Making Face, Making Soul. Haciendo Caras: Creative and Critical Perspectives by Women of Color.* San Francisco: Aunt Lute Foundation, 1990.

Calderón, Héctor, and José David Saldívar, eds. *Criticism in the Borderlands: Studies in Chicano Literature, Culture, and Ideology.* Durham and London: Duke UP, 1991.

Chávez, John R. *The Lost Land: The Chicano Image of the Southwest.* Albuquerque: U of New Mexico P, 1984.

Gonzales-Berry, Erlinda. "Two Texts for a New Canon: Vicente Bernal's *Las Primicias* and Felipe Maximiliano Chacón's *Poesía y prosa.*" Eds. Ramón A. Gutiérrez and Genaro M. Padilla. 129-51.

González, Ray, ed. *Without Discovery: A Native Response to Columbus.* Seattle: Broken Moon, 1991.

Gutiérrez, Ramón, and Genaro Padilla, eds. *Recovering the U. S. Hispanic Literary Heritage.* Houston, TX: Arte Público, 1993.

Kanellos, Nicolás. "Daniel Venegas." *Dictionary of Literary Biography.* Eds. Francisco A. Lomelí and Carl R. Shirley. Vol. 82. Detroit: Bruccoli Clark Layman, 1989. 271-74.

_____. *A History of Hispanic Theatre in the United States: Origins to 1940.* Austin: U of Texas P, 1989.

_____. "Introducción." D. Venegas, *Las aventuras de don Chipote.* 7-15.

Klor de Alva, J. Jorge. "Aztlán, Borinquen and Hispanic Nationalism in the United States." Eds. Anaya and Lomelí. *Aztlán*: 135-71.

Padilla, Genaro M. *My History, Not Yours: The Formation of Mexican American Autobiography.* Madison, WI: U of Wisconsin P, 1993.

Padilla, Raymond V. "A Critique of Pittian History." *El Grito* 6.1 (Fall 1972): 3-44.

Pitt, Leonard M. *The Decline of the Californios: A Social History of the Spanish-Speaking Californians, 1846-1890.* Berkeley: U. of California P, 1966.

Robinson, W. W. *Land in California: The Story of Mission Lands, Ranchos, Squatters, Mining Claims, Railroad Grants, Land Scrip, Homesteads.* 1948. Berkeley and Los Angeles: U of California, 1979.

Ruiz de Burton, María Amparo. 1885. *The Squatter and the Don: A Novel Descriptive of Contemporary Occurrences in California.* Houston: Arte Público, 1993.

Sánchez, Rosaura, and Beatrice Pita. "Introduction." M.A. Ruiz de Burton, *The Squatter and the Don.* 5-51.

_____, and Bárbara Reyes, eds. *Nineteenth Century Californio Testimonials.* San Diego, CA: U of California P, CRITICA Monograph Series, 1994.

Sandoval, Chela. "A Report on the 1981 Women's Studies Association Conference." 1982. Ed. G. Anzaldúa. *Making Face, Making Soul*. 55-71.

Saragoza, Alex M. "Recent Chicano Historiography: An Interpretive Essay." *Aztlán* 19.1 (Spring 1988-90): 1-77.

Shew, A.M. *California as a Health Resort*. Boston: James S. Adams Printer, 1885.

Southern California Bureau of Information. *Southern California: An Authentic Description of Its Natural Resources and Prospects Containing Reliable Information for the Homeseeker, Tourist, and Invalid*. Los Angeles: Bureau of Information Print, 1892.

Venegas, Daniel. *Las aventuras de don Chipote o cuando los pericos mamen*. 1928. México: Secretaría de Educación Pública and Centro de Estudios de la Frontera Norte, 1985.

Villanueva, Tino. "Sobre el término chicano." *Chicanos: Antología histórica y literaria*. México: Fondo de Cultura Económica, 1980. 7-34.

"Who ever heard of a blue-eyed Mexican?":
Satire and Sentimentality in
María Amparo Ruiz de Burton's
Who Would Have Thought It?

Anne E. Goldman

We went over the vast field of Mrs. Norval's virtues, and the vaster one of the doctor's errors, all of which have their root in the doctor's most unnatural liking for foreigners.... That liking was...the cause of the doctor's sending Isaac to be a good-for-nothing clerk in sinful Washington, among foreigners, when he could have remained in virtuous New England to be a useful farmer. And finally, impelled by that liking, the doctor betook himself to California, which is yet full of '*natives.*' And as a just retribution for such perverse liking, the doctor was well-nigh 'roasted by the natives,' said the old lady. Whereupon, in behalf of truth, I said, 'Not by the natives, madam. The people called '*the natives*' are mostly of Spanish descent, and are not cannibals.... 'Perhaps so,' said the old lady, visibly disappointed. 'To me they are all alike,—Indians, Mexicans, or Californians,—they are all horrid. But my son Beau says that our just laws and smart lawyers will soon '*freeze them out.*' That as soon as we take their lands from them they will never be heard of any more, and then the Americans, with God's help, will have all the land that was so righteously acquired through a just war and a most liberal payment in money. (María Amparo Ruiz de Burton, *Who Would Have Thought It?* 1872)

I. "Yankee Popocatapetls": The American Scene

The opening of María Amparo Ruiz de Burton's 1872 novel *Who Would Have Thought It?* disorients readers expecting the California landscape of her

59

1885 historical romance, *The Squatter and the Don*. No *ranchos* [ranches] or railroads give altitude or breadth to its horizon line, no *vaqueros* [cowhands] or *patrones* [owners] people it, no cattle graze upon it, no miners speculate over it, no squatters apportion its choicest views for themselves, and, most importantly, no land grants await their inevitable unjust settlement within its borders. At first glance, this satire of New England mores is distinctly less far-reaching than the political critique the Californiana writer articulates in *The Squatter and the Don*. The story of a middle class New England family whose fortunes and fates are altered by the orphaned Mexican girl who comes to live with them on the eve of the Civil War, *Who Would Have Thought It?* seems preoccupied with social problems as thematically estranged from Ruiz de Burton's later historical romance as they are geographically distant from its West Coast setting.

Despite its confinement to the over-decorated drawing-rooms of the Puritan nouveau-riche, however, Ruiz de Burton develops the convoluted story of *Who Would Have Thought It?* in such a way as to remind us that the social corruption it exposes and the political tableaux it depicts are not idiosyncratic to either the Boston coastline or the Washington scene, but instead are iconographic of national problems. The familial battles described in *Who Would Have Thought It?* are metonyms for the mid-century rupture in American domestic politics which during the course of the novel will take shape as the Civil War ensues. When she links the genealogy of Lola (rescued out of an Indian captivity during one of Dr. Norval's travels to California) with the history of abolitionist New England, she radically questions nationalist reconstructions of American history. Yoking two military ventures together—the Mexican-U.S. War of 1846-48 and the Civil War of 1861-1865—she advertises to readers the way in which these two conflicts are conventionally quarantined despite their historical contingency. Ruiz de Burton's satire collapses distinctions between two languages of war and demystifies both the swashbuckling romance of Manifest Destiny at the Alamo, and the epic sweep with which the U.S.'s domestic breach is traditionally depicted. As the passage I have excerpted above suggests, Lola's place in the Norval household warns smug readers that, thanks to the Treaty of Guadalupe Hidalgo, "the natives" of California are not so removed from the natives of New England as many of the latter might wish to believe.

Lola's presence on this New England scene affirms the social authority of "*the natives*," those who "are mostly of Spanish descent" (if at the cost of the Indian populations of America, the "cannibals" of Mrs. Norval's inflamed imagination) and in so doing anticipates the more exhaustive treatment of federally-condoned land seizure in California the author develops in *The Squatter and the Don*. Her regional transplantation calls into question the North-South axis which conventional narrative uses to locate the Civil War and the East-West dichotomy which pushes Mexicanos and Native Americans to the geographical margins of a country depicted with its center skewed at the Eastern limits of its territory. As I will argue later in this paper, the author's topographical overlay not only complicates the ethnic dichotomies written into the history of the United States but stands as a metaphor for its gendered polarities. The book's sentimental battleground—the family schism occasioned by disagreement over what to do about Lola—is Ruiz de Burton's camouflage, an appropriately feminized narrative space from within which she can deliver the most scathing and sustained critiques of American political opportunism. Through Lola as well as the Norval ladies, she will parody the masculine war theatre and conflate two spheres meant to be kept separate, namely, the domain of political event and action and the private, feminized world of marriage and family life. Ultimately, her insertion of a Mexican heroine into the social space of New England carries a political charge far in excess of reader's expectations about the work of the sentimental novel.

II. A *"most unnatural liking for foreigners"*:
The Perverse Piety of Puritan New England

> ...la clase ignorante americana tiene mayores vicios que los mexicanos de la misma escala social. Que el color moreno no es un indicio ni de ignorancia ni de desmoralización; que el cutis cobrizo americano cubre tan viles cuerpos como pueda cubrirlo un cutis azabachado.

> [...the uneducated class of Americans has greater vices than do Mexicans of the same social class. That the color brown is neither an indication of ignorance nor of corruption; that the copper-colored American skin covers bodies as vile as a black skin may cover.] ("Gringos y Greasers," *La Gaceta* [The Gazette] 27 September 1879)

From Francisco Ramírez's famous editorials in Los Angeles' daily *El Clamor Público* [The Public Clamor] in the late 1850s through poems honoring the heroes of Cinco de Mayo and essays celebrating the social and political activities of Mexicanos in the weekly *La República* [The Republic] circulating in San Francisco three decades later, the project of Spanish-language newspapers in California and the Western states was not only to provide Spanish speakers with information about what became in 1848 *el otro lado* [the other side] but also in part to counter the systematically racist representation of Mexicans and Mexican Americans produced in English throughout this period. In affirming the moral superiority of the Mexican working class in the face of its Anglo American social equivalents, the anonymous author of the editorial excerpted above also attests to the frequency with which Mexicans of all classes were scapegoated (then as now) as the source of a variety of regional and national problems. If a Spanish language newspaper like Santa Barbara's *La Gaceta* could publish articles which, under cover of humor, critique the *"green go"* as a "Judas" figure,[1] those writing in English were far more liable to risk censure by English-only readers for any remarks critical of anti-Mexican sentiment. All the more remarkable, then, to come across Ruiz de Burton's acerbic rereading of Yankee prejudice.

From the outset of her comedy of manners, Ruiz de Burton recirculates all of the stereotypical traits of the Yankee, using parody to turn the Anglo American racial aesthetic on its head. The virtues of true New Englanders, who are "sober-minded," "economical" and "thrifty," are gleefully unmasked as hidden vices in comparison with unsuccessful Puritans like Mrs. Norval's brother Isaac, whose sympathy for foreigners leads him to sojourn in Mexico, to be "free with his money" (that is, generous) and to have "a most lamentable penchant for gallantry" (72). As epitomized by Mrs. Norval, who discards her principles more quickly than her corset when she falls in love with the smooth-talking Reverend Hackwell, the Yankee is first and foremost a hypocrite. Likewise, Reverend Hackwell, whose preaching originates not from piety but an awareness of what amorous possibilities this order opens up for him. Responding to his colleague Reverend Hammerhard's question "…why didn't you become a Methodist or an Episcopalian,—anything more human than a blue Presbyterian?" (55), he reveals "If I had left the practice of law to become an Episcopalian preacher, I would not have stopped there—I would have ended by being a Catholic priest. Then I could not have married; and imagine what a loss that would have been to the ladies!" (56). The Reverend's adventures in love, which the novel spends much time in chronicling—his seduction of the hapless doctor's wife and his thwarted passion for Lola— demonstrate the veracity of this statement, if of none of his others. Like Cotton Mather with a sense of humor, Ruiz de Burton delights in exposing the concealed moral decrepitude of the *"cutis cobrizo americano."*

The author develops one of her most scathing indictments of Puritan hypocrisy through Mrs. Norval's spinster sister Lavinia, whose indefatigable nursing and intrepid efforts at the Capitol building to gain Isaac's release from a rebel prison eventually earn the respect of the narrator. If the author grants "Lavvy" "good-heartedness," (a quality she retains a virtual monopoly on amidst the reptilian Puritans), she nonetheless satirizes the nurse's efforts as engineered by duty, not passion:

> …as Lavinia had been properly brought up, she loved her patients…. The more groans and sighs and lamentations she heard, the more cheerful she became in the sublime sense of *duty*. And when the amputating-knife had to be used unsparingly, then Lavvy was…*"jolly"* in the midst of surrounding misery. I do not mean that

> the good-hearted Lavvy could rejoice in the sufferings of others, but she rejoiced
> in the thought that she could alleviate them." (143)

Such exuberant Dickensian satire is not an end in itself, however, but the means by which Burton undermines ideological equations that link "America" with the Puritans who controlled its Northeasternmost territories, in order to expose the regional agenda which underlies this nationalist rhetoric. Connecting the pretentious Misses Norval and their mother with the sententious oratory of Capitol Hill, she exposes the nation's verbal currency as a self-interested, morally impoverished language which only fools suffer gladly:

> It was the anniversary of some great day in New England when the Misses Norval
> were to make their farewell appearance in church before leaving for Europe—
> some great day in which the Pilgrim fathers had done some one of their wonderful
> deeds. They had either embarked, or landed, or burnt a witch, or whipped a
> woman at the pillory, on just such a day. (83)

In implicit contrast to the faith in prayer which makes of Lavinia a Catholic in sentiment[2] and Lola one in fact, the eyes of those occupying the pews of the Presbyterian church are not cast heavenward, but instead are directed more modestly towards the upper reaches of society. Ruiz de Burton strips the embarcation and landing of the Pilgrim fathers of its spiritual investiture and shows up these political entrepreneurs as the logical forerunners of the Norval sisters whose own scrambles up the social ladder she parallels with the much lauded entrance of their predecessors onto the American continent. One of the most rhetorically deft critiques in the novel is embedded in the sentence I have just cited, which deglamorizes the activities of the first of America's politicians through a list structure whose unhierarchized syntax mirrors its levelling theme: here the grandiose landing on Plymouth Rock is the prelude not to the foundation of good government but the scapegoating of its citizens (distinctly feminine) who are maimed and murdered via a series of violent punishments which rival the author's own ethnocentric description of West Coast "savages."

Parodying representation which is stuck like a broken record on the first Thanksgiving, she critiques the way in which the Pilgrims have remained icons for national identity by comparing the venality of the current crop of Congressmen and churchmen with the founding politicians of the United States. Mrs. Norval's heart first thrills to the words of Reverend Hackwell when she listens approvingly to a sermon whose theme "was the hackneyed one of the sublime love of religious freedom, which made the Pilgrim fathers abandon home, civilization, friends, to come to a comfortless wilderness" just at the moment when this good matron herself, in defiance of Doña Theresa's dying words to Dr. Norval to have Lola "baptized and brought up a Roman

Catholic" (46) is ensuring her step-daughter remain a member of the "blue" school of churches. When Lavinia arrives at the seat of government to ask for Isaac's release from prison, she encounters a similar vision of hypocritical self-interest in the person of Mr. Cackle whose dull sons have profited enough from the war business to insert themselves into the Washington political elite. Appropriately enough, she finds her old neighbor "before the painting representing 'the embarking of the Pilgrims,' discoursing upon the merits of it to a large number of admirers, who listened to his words in silent respect"(149).

III. "Who would have supposed such a Vesuvius covered over with New England snows?": Sexuality and Feminine Agency

> ...he would contrive to induce Lola to go on board of a steamer, and take her to Cuba and there force her to marry him. And, wild and absurd as this idea was, to the heated brain of the major it seemed quite practicable. (360)

Countering Anglo American depictions of the passionate Mexican ever ready "to put the dagger to the throat" (257) to end a love-quarrel, Ruiz de Burton entertains readers with this image of the wild-eyed Presbyterian divine. In this revision of the captivity narrative, it is the preacher who goes native and threatens the good name not of a Puritan blue-blood like Mary Rowlandson, but of an aristocratic "Spanish" Mexican. Her own treatment of the captivity narrative, which works off of both Californio and New England versions of this genre, spotlights neither the savagery of an othered people nor the miracle of divine wisdom but the much maligned chastity of Mexicanas in particular and the beleaguered sexuality of women in general. Rowlandson's *Narrative* stages the Christian captive's fraught relationship with her godless tribal captors as a locus for divine instruction; in Rowlandson's story, that is, Puritans can read a message from the deity. Ruiz de Burton's revision is less interested in foregrounding the relationship between Lola's ever-civil mother and her savage captors (although indeed, Native Americans are throughout Ruiz de Burton's writings demeaned as such) than in using it to critique the uncivil behavior of Major Hackwell, the ex-Presbyterian divine who in attempting to carry off Lola demonstrates a licentiousness in excess of Doña Theresa's Indian captors. The unravelling of Major Hackwell through the instrument of Lola places him in the same position as the besotted Mrs. Norval, who has turned a blind eye to reports of her lost husband's continued existence in order to "marry" her lover, but it is the "savagery" with which the Major exploits Mrs. Norval's amorousness, more than the madam's fevered state itself, which is most seriously indicted.

The feminine analogue to this parody of Anglo American masculinity, appropriately enough, is the prim and parsimonious madam herself: "Who would have supposed such a Vesuvius covered over with New England snows, eh?" the ex-divine murmurs about her in mock wonderment. Not to be outdone by his colleague, Hackwell embellishes the Reverend Hammerhard's description of this "'Yankee Popocatepetl'":[3]

> ...she is a Clytemnestra, a Medea, a Sappho! She is so earnest, and her love for me so fervid, that she almost makes me forget that she is thirteen years my senior, and compels me to love her; yes, just kind of sucks me into her furious love maelstrom! Whew!... If those superb eyes of Lola were not here maddening me...if I did not think of that girl night and day, I believe the old woman would succeed in kindling me with her conflagration... (251-2)

Not the less remarkable for its exuberant critique of the sentimental prose which was the order of the day in both Anglo American serials like *The Century* and *The Overland Monthly* and the Spanish language press, this overblown rhetoric undermines conventional representations of sexuality which maintained the purity of white womanhood by slandering everyone else. Mid and late nineteenth-century Anglo American western texts often affirmed feminine "spotlessness" not by denying the existence of feminine sexuality but by racially quarantining such expression; white gentility is represented as sexless because it is juxtaposed against the carnality of women of color. Ruiz de Burton turns this racialized representation on its head. Thus Lola's triumph is that she can inspire passion without being moved by it. Mrs. Norval, on the other hand, is ignited by a few flowery compliments cast in her general direction. Nor is the author's critique limited to Mrs. Norval; even the good hearted "Lavvy," whose hysterical attachment to her canary birds substitutes for the proffered and then reclaimed attentions of the Reverend Hackwell, chastises her own failure in modesty in language which slights Puritan purity and masculine integrity simultaneously: "'How very wrong girls are in permitting any liberties to men to whom they are engaged! How foolish! How silly! Who can tell what miserable liars they may not turn out to be?'" (48-49).

Ruiz de Burton's volcanic metaphors simultaneously avenge literary and political wrongs and open a space for feminine sexuality. Mrs. Norval's shift from beguilement into madness (she lapses into brain fever upon her husband's return) suggests that this representation is ultimately foreclosed upon. But however transient, however ironized, Ruiz de Burton's explicitly sexualized representation of female passion defies the contemporary literary standard that ruled against its display. While Ruiz de Burton's defensive representation of Mexican womanhood allows for no blemishes upon Lola's chastity and punishes Doña Theresa's involuntary humiliation at the hands of her Indian captors with death, she remains through the latter half of *Who Would Have Thought It?* surprisingly sympathetic with Mrs. Norval's own fall from grace. The single embrace Lola gives to Mrs. Norval's son Julian, when she sees her gravely wounded fiancé lying in bed "so pale, so very weak" (206) is countered by the author with this lengthy apology:

> ...if those arms had been strong, she would certainly have kept away from them, no matter how lovingly they had been extended to her.... In justice to Lola, it must be stated that she had passed the greater part of the night tracing for herself a 'prospectus' of her future conduct towards Julian, which was so strict and circumspect that Mrs. Norval herself could not have found a single fault with it. (206)

Lola's spotlessness must be defended with this gentle reproof, yet the author's remonstrance of Mrs. Norval concludes on a forgiving note. The hapless matron "had so far degenerated that she regarded her youth as misspent, her life a blank, until she loved Hackwell, until she was past forty. Poor woman! to have been a chrysalis all her days! Who would not excuse this avalanche of the snows of forty years?" (247). A curious mixture of revenge and compassion, this passage ridicules Mrs. Norval's less-than decorous passion and then, having accomplished redress, forgives it.

Such ambivalent satire remains the rule in the author's representation of Mrs. Norval. The following passage, for example, closes with a similar appeal to the understanding hearts of her readers:

> When that one passion—her love for Hackwell—was beyond her mastery, all her imps ran riot in bacchanalian freedom, and she was jealous of her sister and hated her, and she forgot her dying son, and she did not mourn for her lost husband.... All she now thought of and longed for, was to see Hackwell, to be near him. That was the all-absorbing, uncontrollable impulse.... Cast not a stone—no, not a little pebble—at the madam, for, after all, she was very womanly when she was so absurdly silly. And who is not silly when truly in love? (188-90)

The Reverend's description of Mrs. Norval as "compelling" his love provides her with a source of power, however tongue-in-cheek, that celebrates mature femininity and affirms its sexual nature.

I would argue that it is her own authorial remove from the Presbyterian matron that allows Ruiz de Burton to raise this erotic possibility for women. If it is qualified by the narrator and racially contained by the writer, this kind of representation is nonetheless pointed when we read it against her English- and Spanish-speaking contemporaries who position the forty-year old woman as a contradiction in terms. "La Mujer" [Woman], a vignette from Santa Barbara's *La Gaceta*, for instance, describes the teenage girl as beguiling (from 15 to 20 she is an "ave del paraíso" [bird of paradise]), but by thirty, she is already a "cotorra" [parrot][4] (whilst her masculine counterpart is a "gallo" [rooster] at the height of his power), and at forty, a "lechuza" [owl]. "Una Madre" [A Mother], an essay in *El Clamor Público*, sanctifies maternity as the condition closest to that of the angels, because as mother, woman sacrifices for her child both "su tranquilidad y sus placeres" [her peace of mind and her pleasures]. This celebration of motherhood as the only (earthly) disinterested love ("Una madre en fin es el único ser en la tierra que ama desinteresadamente" [A mother, in short, is the only earthly being who loves disinterestedly])[5] is certainly a stunning contrast to the description of maternity we are treated to in *Who Would Have Thought It?*

In an era distinguished by lachrymose complaining, where femininity is "invariable" [constant], "fiel" [faithful], "cariñosa" [loving] and "generosa" [generous] but ultimately, "Sumisa," [Obedient],[6] Ruiz de Burton's satire, sustained virtually without break over 443 pages, and her portraits of strong-willed, stubborn women disclose themselves as highly oppositional strategies, devices which critique gender and genre as these are imbricated in sentimental literature. Ultimately, the compelling—if ridiculous—figure of Mrs. Norval allows the writer to open a space for feminine authority where no such space is permitted. Just as her daughter Ruth "liked to *manage* her mother, because she was the *power* of the family" (66), so the repressed sexuality of the much-scorned Lavinia is a figure for the spinster's independent will: "...Lavvy wanted nothing better than plenty of employment for her exuberant moral energies and redundant force of will. The prospect of a tussle with a cabinet member or two, and plenty of skirmishes with delegations, did not terrify the strong soul of Lavvy" (142).

Lola's own tussles with the Norval family and its satellites may appear histrionic to contemporary readers, but situated within a discursive context which consigns woman to characterlessness, her defiance of Mrs. Norval's injunctions to come to Julian when he is wounded, and her open denunciation and advertisement of Major Hackwell's attentions towards her demonstrate an equally exceptional presence.

IV. "I come to demand a right": Lavinia's Siege of Washington and the Dissolution of Separate Spheres

> I think the sooner we give over to women the management of public business, the better it will be. If we did not have such brute arrogance and unblushing conceit, we would long ago have seen the justice and propriety of hiding our diminished heads. But no. Because we have the physical force to beat women at the polls with our fists, we maintain that they have no right there as thinking beings.... Glorious! Behold the result! How well the world is governed! (395)

If Major Hackwell's bitter denunciation of his sex's political and moral failure is less philosophic than self-pitying, following as it does so closely upon the heels of his own ignominious defeat—his botched abduction of Lola and her safe return to Mexico, the exposure of his schemes to defraud the government of funds meant for the war effort, the temporary insanity of his "wife" who has succumbed to brain fever following the return of the husband she presumed dead—the critique of masculine tyranny it exposes resonates all the more strongly. What better mouthpiece for systemic despotism than this petty tyrant? Just as Ruiz de Burton articulates her most radical ideas about feminine sexuality through a woman most distanced from her own position as author, her most stunning indictment of masculine self-centeredness proceeds from the mouth of the male figure least likely to be associated with the narrative's values. Yet this sardonic rhapsody is in fact only the latest and most explicitly gendered censure of the Anglo American political system the writer provides us with in the novel. While Hackwell's allusion to masculine battery strikes a chord with Ruiz de Burton's earlier invocation of the New England punishments meted out to dissenting women, it is through Lavinia's siege of Washington and her wondering appraisal of its malign political workings that the author develops one of her most scathing critiques of the federal government's corruption, a corruption that simultaneously burlesques Anglo American despotism and satirizes gender tyranny.

Ruiz de Burton justifies Lavinia's transgression onto the masculine domain of party politics by suggesting that her fearful encroachment of the public sphere is in fact an effort to right the private sector; that is, her sisterly efforts to locate Isaac stem from a desire to reestablish familial harmony rather than any impulse to find fault with government. In championing her brother's rights, however, she exposes the petty self-interest of bureaucrats which masquerades as federal policy. Washington, as Lavinia soon finds, is in truth "a city very congenial to all unbottled little imps" (208), and it is none other than Mrs. Cackle, social competitor of Mrs. Norval and proud mother of two "distinguished Congressmen" and "two renowned generals" (225), who personifies this statement when she affirms "A long war was good for the Cackle family" (234). Through this smug matron and her mock-heroic sons, Ruiz de Burton shows up American politics as a theatre not so much of the absurd as of the ridiculous. By contrast to the hasty retreats beat by these generals at the scene of battle, Lavvy's hesitant advancements on Capitol Hill at least move in a forward direction.

Of course all of this reorganization is tongue-in-cheek, its object not only to reorder a gendered and racialized hierarchy of space but to satirize both male and female actors in the process. But the writer's consistently ironical voice has a double purpose, sustaining this novel of manners and undermining the authority of sentimental convention at the same time. Such comic deflation of both the sententious rhetoric of political life and the high moral tone affected by the sentimental novel is never more successfully achieved than when Ruiz de Burton transports the language of war across generic lines in order to blur distinctions between the public and private spheres. Her personal correspondence plunders military vocabulary to give her struggles the dignity and valor reserved for masculine endeavor. The December 1875 letter to George Davidson, for instance, chronicles her conflicts with the legal system as a "contest with hard fortune" and transforms the war widow into a soldier under siege: "Even now surrounded by difficulties and discouragements of all sorts, I persevere and fight the fearful odds against me." In her fiction, however, such lexical borrowings are comic rather than epic. Consider how the following images of war circulate in this description of feminine service, a paragraph all the more resonant because it follows a battle scene:

> Lavinia's heart pranced like a war-horse at the sound of martial music, making the chest of the maiden resound with its galloping. Her patriotic fire spread to the Misses Cackle, until nothing but making sacrifices for their country's cause would satisfy them.... They made underclothes, and large, very large night-shirts; for these patriotic ladies seemed to take measure by their enthusiasm, and very possibly imagined that the heroes for whom the shirts were made must all be as large in size as in deeds. (105)

In a few phrases Ruiz de Burton shells the willful naiveté of women kept so far removed from public life they transform boorish neighbors into "heroes," the tedium of a middle-class existence spent pickling vegetables and tailoring shirts, the facility with which the brutality of war is obscured through the smoke and haze of nationalist rhetoric, and finally, the small minds—not to mention small body parts—of the cavaliers themselves, arrested through the prose of *Who Would Have Thought It?* in mid-flight as they canter towards their own trenches.

This lexical transplantation is exploited over and over throughout the novel, in one instance to lampoon the social pretensions of the Norval sisters ("...several Saratoga trunks...stood there, all packed full of the dry-goods which composed the elegant costly outfits of the Misses Norval for their summer campaign. Julian, though weak yet and very pale, had left the day before, just in time to arrive at Gettysburg before the firing commenced" (217) at another to ridicule both the Civil War and its domestic parallel, the family battle over the courtship of Julian and Lola which constitutes the sentimental plot of the novel itself ("Julian saw [Lola] politely received in her house before he returned to camp. Mattie was an ally of theirs, Ruth a neutral power, acting occasionally as spy, and the madam, flanked by Hack and Em, was at present in *status quo*") 259.

This oblique but merciless exposure of Anglo American policy makers and their feminine satellites is accompanied by more direct assaults as well. In ventriloquizing Ruiz de Burton's own critique of antifeminist policy makers, Major Hackwell's denunciation preempts rhetoric like that of Father Gasparri, who in 1877 wrote an editorial in *La revista católica* [The Catholic Review] anticipating a social meltdown should female suffrage be granted: "'the family will be destroyed, it will lead to juvenile delinquency, and increased abortions and eventually the destruction of the human race'"[7] Ruiz de Burton satirizes predictions like these through an ensemble of Cackles and Blowers, the former elder an ineffectual sycophant who disparages a like ability in the female sex ("'Women are so foolish! They never know how to make a good use of their capital, either in money or influence. Bah! and they want to vote!'" 152), the latter a pretentious sophist who in condescending to instruct Lavinia in the fine art of diplomacy exposes the moral vacuum at the heart of government. Prisoners are not exchanged, he explains, because by remaining in the South they hasten the anticipated starvation of their rebel captors along with themselves. When Lavinia stares "in silent amazement" (157) at this policy, the diplomat can only retrench, citing the incapacity of ladies who "can't well grasp great ideas, or understand the reasons that impel men in power to act at times in a manner apparently contrary to humanity, to mercy, to justice" (157). Ruiz de Burton's irony deflates the puffed-up rhetoric of the Washington policy maker to disclose him performing puppet theatre behind a curtain, gendering his disguise in the process. Lamenting "how little woman was appreciated, how unjustly underrated" (179) Lavvy reflects that "no matter how much a woman, in her unostentatious sphere, may do…after all she is but an insignificant creature" (145-6). Through Lavinia's reproach Ruiz de Burton not only provides a lesson in the gender of geography but opens the possibility of its remapping as well. Thus Lavvy mourns female powerlessness in order to correct it, transforming plea into command: "for the first time I come to ask a favor,—a *favor*, do I say? No. I come to demand a right,—" (146).

But what of Lola? Ruiz de Burton's experiments with transgressive feminine authority are sustained at the cost of her Mexican heroine, whose behavior she restrains, lest it risk the censure even the reformable Yankee women are treated to. Where Lavvy can work in a hospital with relative impunity, Lola's own nursing service remains restricted at home. This racially-inflected brave new world is qualified still further when Ruiz de Burton reminds us, through Lavinia, that it is "*ladies* with hearts and brains" who "were absolutely necessary to her country's cause. Not merely *paid menials* should attend the sick and wounded, but thoughtful women, who could judiciously order as well as obey" (179).[8] If the author widens the sphere traditionally allotted to

(Anglo) "ladies" by sanctioning activity outside the home," this restructuring of gendered spaces is sustained at the cost of (all) working women, with whom the genteel are now in danger of rubbing elbows. What alleviates this risk is the censure appended to Lavvy's argument, in which the work of the feminine masses is demeaned as mindless labor.

Ruiz de Burton's refusal to provide Lola with the same access to public space that Lola demands is a defensive response, hardly surprising when one considers the extent to which Anglo texts single-mindedly position all Mexicanas as maids. Still, within the confined space of the drawing room, Lola's superiority is unquestionable. If Lavinia becomes genteel through her goodness, Lola is a born aristocrat, "her mother being of pure Spanish descent," as Dr. Norval notes, "and her father the same, though an Austrian by birth, he having been born in Vienna" (33). However unpalatable to late twentieth-century readers, such class bound representation defends against the discriminatory language of Anglo America, that, as the Spanish language press often noted, typed all Mexicanos as working class; that is, crude and licentious. "Cuantas veces oímos hablar a un americano, de que tal o cual sujeto no era mexicano sino que era white man (hombre blanco) como si el color blanco fuese desconocido entre la raza latina" [How many times do we hear talk by an American, that this or that person was not a Mexican but a white man, as if the color white were unknown among the latin race] Santa Barbara's *La Gaceta* complained in "Gringos y Greasers," as if in response to ethnographic representations like the following, from Susan Shelby Magoffin's 1846 diary chronicling the Santa Fe Trail: "The women slap about with their arms and necks bare, perhaps their bosom exposed (and they are none of the prettiest or whitest)."[9] Ruiz de Burton uses her own Anglo American characters to exact literary recompense. "Talk of Spanish women being dark!" Mattie Norval exclaims, "Can anything be whiter than Lola's neck and shoulders?" (333). Even Mattie's sister Ruth makes grudging concession to Mexican refinement after Lola's money frees her from the monotony of the Yankee middle classes; her "new elegance" allows her to see "that the reason why Spanish ladies have small feet and delicate ankles is because they walk so very little" (70).

By flying in the face of Anglo American discourse that situates high culture between Boston's Old North Church and Washington's Capitol steps, this apparently inconsequential observation contributes to the novel's most important ideological work, which is to remap American political geography using a less provincial longitude. A conventional grid of class markers becomes the "stable" reference point for Ruiz de Burton's reorganization of the skewed racial axes through which Yankees have surveyed the United States and maintained their political title. By sending Civil War veteran Isaac to Mexico, she dismantles the North-South meridian that generally defines it. When, having become disenchanted with the federal policy he learns is the root cause of his imprisonment, he chooses Mexico over the Northeast, we understand that what looks like a sectional corruption—the secession of the South—is in fact a more systemic moral failing.

V. "blue-eyed Mexican[s]": Into Mexico

¡Pedir reclamaciones al gobierno mexicano! No faltaba otra cosa. Este país ha sido el teatro donde han sufrido los ciudadanos mexicanos toda suerte de ultrajes, atropellamientos e injusticias. Nuestras columnas serían muy limitadas si nos pusiéramos a dar una lista de las injurias sufridas por los mexicanos, desde '49, en California. ¿Cuántas víctimas inocentes de entre ellos, no han sido sacrificadas ya por el furor brutal del populacho?...puede ser que en la opinión del diario citado la sangre mexicana no vale.... El gobierno americano ve la paja en el ojo de su vecino pero no mira la viga que tiene en el suyo.

[To request reclamations from the Mexican government! That's the last straw! This country has been the theater where Mexican citizens have suffered all manner of outrages, abuses and injustices. Our columns would be very restricted if we were to give a list of the injuries suffered by Mexicans, since '49, in California. How many innocent victims among us, have not already been sacrificed to the brutal fury of the crowd?...it could be that in the opinion of the newspapers cited Mexican blood has no value.... The American government sees the mote in the eye of its neighbor but it doesn't see the beam that it has in its own.]

—*El Clamor Público*, 12 April, 1856, responding to an essay from the *Alta California* asking for financial compensation from the Mexican government for grievances against Anglo Americans in Mexico following the War.

He was disenchanted. He...felt that it would take a long time before he should again believe that in America there is not as much despotism as in Europe,— "despotism of a worse kind, because we pretend so loudly the contrary. If we didn't say so much about the freedom, the thing wouldn't be so bad. We are hypocrites and imposters besides..." (351)

When we cross along with Isaac to the other side in this novel, the geography shifts entirely: philosophically, morally, socially, and culturally, Mexico and the United States are distinct and at odds. Even their relation under imperialism, a relation that Ruiz de Burton insists upon and that might tempt contemporary critics to read them as two sides of the same post-nationalist coin, does not alter their essential opposition. Now we work hard to refocus attention on a border that has for many Americans been naturalized over the course of the last hundred and fifty years. In the 1970s and 1980s this attention to the border zone meant exploring its metaphysics via Aztlán; more recently, it is the material obstacles to crossing that are themselves dismantled, through language that assails the steel fences trespassing on desert country, words that point to the ugly visual redundancy of cement barriers separating one side's fenced compounds from the other's gateless, wall-less, often roofless squats, essays that indict the undocumented and documented border "officials" who share the job of picking people off the landscape. But Ruiz de Burton's chronological intimacy with the forcible remapping of 1848 prevented her from taking such geopolitical surgery for granted. Her own critical efforts, like many of her American contemporaries writing for the Spanish language press, are directed farther south and farther north, both to call attention to the unjust treatment of Mexican citizens of the United States (about whom *El Clamor Público*'s Francisco Ramírez would rhetorically question in "Americanos! Californios!" [Americans! Californians!]: "¿No tenemos todos los mismos derechos iguales a la protección de las leyes?" [Don't we have equal rights under the law?] and answer in "Los Mexicanos en la Alta California" [Mexicans in Alta California]: "No se les administra justicia, no se les respeta su propiedad, no se les deja libertad en el ejercicio de su industria…un ataque flagrante a los principios del derecho de gentes, una triste contradicción con los principios de que hace alarde el gobierno americano," [They do not administer justice to us, they do not respect their property, they do not permit them freedom in the exercise of their industry…a flagrant attack on the principles of peoples' rights, a sad contradiction with the principles that the American government boasts of] to reaffirm the cultural and political authority of Mexico.

The Squatter and the Don recuperates the downward political slide of the *gente de razón* by demonstrating their high moral character, but *Who Would Have Thought It?* literalizes this redress through representation whose oppositions turn the "contradicciones" of racist discourse on its head. "America" in this text parodies Anglo American versions of "Mexico"; it is crude and uncouth. America is peopled by barbarians who don't care when they miss the spittoon bucket and social climbers whose first contact with high culture sends them into a tailspin of uncontrolled sensuality. In Ruiz de Burton's novel, aesthetes belong in Mexico; New England, by contrast, is home for the vulgar. Isaac's crime is really that he has taste. Like Lola's father, with whom he stays in Mexico, he prefers "Havana cigars to a pipe or a chaw of tobacco, and those miserable sour wines to a good drink of whisky" (73). No less a person than the President is pictured as a rowdy who prefers band music to ballroom dancing; when Julian first encounters him, this venerable official is keeping time with the beat of the bass drum by tapping his teeth against "a gold-headed cane, which had just been sent to him by a lady in token of gratitude," whilst his leg, "a ballistic pendulum," "oscillated up and down, and dropped with the emphasis of a pile-driver,—for the foot of the lamented President was not small" (306-7).

But America's chief failing is hypocrisy, that fatal Yankee flaw. While Mexicans, if not for the American influence that prevails "with such despotic sway over minds of the leading men of the Hispano-American republics") "would be proud to hail...a good and just prince...who...has some sort of claim to this land, and who will cut us loose from the leading-strings of the United States" (281, 283), Americans espouse the virtues of liberty without appearing to recognize that they are largely deprived of them. In paragraph after paragraph, Ruiz de Burton satirizes American nationalist language, skewering its pretentious homilies as neatly as she censures Hackwell, whose smug sermons eulogizing Pilgrim forefathers are in fact epigrammatic of it. Democracy in the United States is the rhetorical national umbrella that doesn't keep the rain out; the narrator reflects of Julian, waiting in a storm, that he

> had to submit to the infliction, as everybody else does, will do, and has done. He was drenched and bespattered, with the rest of the traveling community, and, like everybody else, submitted silently, meekly; for in this free country we are the subjects of railroad kings and other princes of monopolies; we obey their wishes, and pay our money. (382)

If she indicts American nationalism, she celebrates Mexican patriotism. In a passage which declares her sympathies as decisively as the odes and paeans honoring Mexican military triumphs so numerous in the Spanish language newspapers, Ruiz de Burton suggests that "in some countries certain kinds of evil are impossible" (288).[10] If Mexico were "well governed," it could "avoid the majority of those misfortunes which we now call *unavoidable* human sorrows" (288). Through her description of the Medina household, the author provides readers with a model of such "good government" in microcosm. In keeping with the gendered strategy she develops at the novel's outset, this comparative political commentary is oblique. Anticipating the tone and language of *The Squatter and the Don*, she blames these troubles on "their veritable source...our lawgivers," then closes with a conventionally gendered disclaimer whose disingenuosness mocks efforts to keep women out of (literary) politics: "But I am no political philosopher. I am wandering away from my humble path" (288). If she focuses on domestic interiors, however, the implicit comparison between the spacious library and elegant dining room of the Medina country estate and the overdecorated ostentatiousness of the Norval drawing room is as pointed a critique as any assessment of military maneuvers could be. The Medina rancho, like Mexico generally, is home to "civilized citizens" (278), an aristocracy beleaguered by a "free and independent government" (278) bent on undermining its class privileges, but one that sustains its gentlemanly traditions nevertheless. In Lola's relatives we see Mexico's finest, learned men who, like Ruiz de Burton, are willing to defend

Puebla against imperialism but who are nostalgic for monarchy nonetheless; men who read the latest news from Europe in a library replete with "papers, books, reviews, pamphlets, etc" (279), who speak at least three languages and from whose table the newly arrived Isaac enjoys "the best wine he had ever tasted in his life" (286).

Granted, this picture of the sporting life may seem less than inviting to those of us whose civility does not depend on the cooperation of a houseful of servants. Abandoning the sustained irony that has characterized her send-up of American manners, she substitutes in its place a celebration of *mexicanidad* [Mexican culture] that admits only a select company, relegating the majority to the representational equivalent of no-man's land. Before we dismiss it as unalterably ideologically compromised, however, we need to read it not only against contemporary theorizing about ethnic, class and gender differences, but the languages of nationalism and sentimentalism her contemporaries were circulating on both sides of the border. When we begin to do this, we can appreciate how the author uses the drawing room as much to show up American savagery as to show off Mexico's *sangre azul* [blue bloods]; to correct, that is, that literary cartography which fetishized New England and pushed the rest of the Americas off the cultural map altogether. The hospitality Isaac enjoys in Mexico reproaches the hostile treatment Lola suffers in New England, just as the worldliness of the "two Mexican gentlemen" (284) indicts the provincialism of their counterparts in Washington—not to mention the parochialism of American letters.

Polite society in this book is not only an end but a means—a means to criticize, implicitly and explicitly, the barbarism of United States soldiers, the venality of their superiors, and the crass upward groping of people like the Norvals and the Cackles, who could not be polite if their lives depended on it.[11] And if it lacks the sardonic edge the novel sustains as a whole, the concluding portion introduces us to characters who, in moving comfortably between Sonora *ranchos* and Washington drawing rooms, undermine conventional Anglo American representations of Mexicanos on both sides of the newly defined border. Their very genteel professionalism, that is, is as far removed from the slovenly servants of Anglo American fictions of the Southwest as it is the "sad Indian Queens" and "Aztec pirogues" (*The Century*, 2) who invariably flit across the pages of imperialist romances about Mexico. Historicizing the novel this way does not mean we should either discard it because of its sustained classism nor romanticize it as the Movimiento's originary text. It does lead us, though, to appreciate the extent to which the book's rhetorical strategies are dissonant with the discursive practices of its period, and in so doing, to work towards a more nuanced picture of nineteenth-century Mexican American literature.

Notes

[1]See for instance this anecdote on the "Origen de la palabra 'Gringo'" reprinted in *La Gaceta* from the Mexican newspaper *La Revista del Norte de Matamoros*: "con todo el respeto a nuestros vecinos del otro lado, sometemos [el siguiente] al juicio de algunos amigos.... ¿Pues que te dijeron? —Me dijeron *green go*. —¿Y qué es eso? —Sepa Judas. —Pues déjalo, él lo será, o tal vez quizo decir, como entre nosotros, no hay pan, muchachito, vete."

[2]See for instance the following passage: "Lavinia's prayers were always extemporaneous and multifarious, shaped by passing incidents,—for Lavvy had the faith in prayer of a strict Roman Catholic" (163).

[3]Given its representation in the California newspapers, Popocatapetl was a particularly pregnant metaphor with which to undermine racialized conceptions of feminine sexuality because it resonated with discourses of commerce and imperialism as well. See this note in *El Clamor Público*, titled, portentously, "Riqueza Durmiente": "Los papeles de México anuncian que el volcán de Popocatapetl está cubierto por la parte interior de una capa sólida de azufre puro de unos hasta diez pies de profundidad. El comercio de azufre y ácido sulfúrico en los Estados Unidos, sola producirá treinta millones de pesos anualmente" 18 October, 1856. Appropriately enough for Mrs. Norval, whose guilty conscience and immoral behavior are personified by Ruiz de Burton as a series of "imps," the "slumbering" giant conceals an explosive substance (sulfur) which will be a boon for Mexico's balance of trade with the United States. Just so the metaphorical "conflagration" of the New England matron provides the Californiana writer with a means of redressing a representational imbalance.

[4]This passage not only maintains the bird metaphor but plays upon its colloquial expression, that of a chatterer.

[5]At greater length this passage reads as follows: "Bella es la muger (sic) en su infancia, porque es la imagen de un ángel que sonríe a la tierra, porque forma el encanto del hogar doméstico;... bella y querida como hija, interesante como esposa y como hermana, de valor inmenso como amiga, hay tadavía (sic) un estado en que a su belleza añade la santidad de su carácter, en que es casi una imagen viva de la inmensa Providencia; ese estado es el de la maternidad.... La muger ama a su hijo desde el momento en que lo concibe, lo lleva en su seno, y desde entonces lo sacrifica su tranquilidad y sus placeres.... la muger sacrifica su vida a la familia.... Para una madre consiste la felicidad en la dicha de sus hijos.... Una madre en fin es el único ser en la tierra que ama desinteresadamente."

[6]Note the following rather disingenuous tribute to "mugeres" (sic) called "Pobres Hombres!... ¿Será Verdad? —mugeres" part of which I excerpt here: "Es la muger invariable,/ Sumisa, fiel, cariñosa,/ Compasiva, generosa,/ Hospitalaria y amable. El hombre, egoísta, variable/ Y altivo con su poder,/ Sin llegar conocer/ Que teniendo cualquier nombre,/ Entre todos, no hay un hombre/ Que merezca una muger" (*El Clamor Público*, 2 Aug. 1856).

[7]I am indebted to Vicki Ruiz for bringing this quotation to my attention; it is cited from the first chapter draft of her book in progress, *From Out of the Shadows: A History of Mexican Women in the Southwest*.

[8]Since Lavinia (in her role as repressed spinster if not as competent nurse) is as much condescended to as lauded by Ruiz de Burton, it is possible to distance this ordering of labor and leisure from authorial vantage point. Ruiz de Burton's own class standing as the descendent and legatee of several very prominent Californio families, her insistently hierarchical portrait of "Spanish Californians" as the true "natives" of the state in *The Squatter and the Don*, and her self positioning in her personal correspondence all militate against this reading, however. Besides her historical romance, see the following defensive representation in this letter to George Davidson: "...for six weeks after coming here I did not even have a cook! I had to be nurse night and day,

and cook every thing else besides! and finances! Oh! the sick finances! how they did sicken me! They aren't any healthier, but now at least I have a cook, a Chinaman, a 'celestial' truly, for he is heavenly to me doing the cooking in this hot weather. So, though my hands are brown yet, and rough, I don't have to get up at 6 am to cook breakfast after being up all night taking care of my sick darling…" (26 July, 1880).

[9]Vicki Ruiz also cites this passage. Magoffin's other mention of Mexicanas is also worth quoting, if only to demonstrate how fully racist representation is contingent upon the well-being of the person circulating it: "…I did think the Mexicans were as void of refinement, judgement etc., as the dumb animals till I heard one of them say *'bonita muchacha!'* And now I have reason and certainly a good one for changing my opinion; they are certainly a very *quick and intelligent people*" (98). So vanity erases, momentarily, the racial hierarchy! Such openly dismissive and derogatory representation remained the rule for decades. Genaro Padilla calls attention to this letter from Sir James Douglas, quoted by Hubert Howe Bancroft in his 1888 *California Pastoral*: "the ladies in California are not in general very refined or delicate in their conversation…indulging in broad remarks which would make modest women blush. It is also said that many, even of the respectable classes, prostitute their wives for hire; that is they wink at the familiarity of a wealthy neighbor who pays handsomely for his entertainment" (115-6).

[10]Patriotic verses, together with sentimental lyrics, comprised the vast majority of literary contributions to the Spanish language press, both mid-century and towards the close of the nineteenth century. In tone and language, the following introduction to an "Oda Patriótica" published in *El Nuevo Mundo* on June 28, 1864, is characteristic of such literature, which insists on Mexican identity for citizens of Alta California post 1848: "Leída en la función con que los mejicanos residentes en San Francisco celebraron el glorioso aniversario del triunfo alcanzado sobre los franceses por el ejército mejicano a los órdenes del intrépido general Zaragosa, el 5 de Mayo de 1862." As late as the turn of the century, Mexican Americans writing for the newspapers often situated themselves as Mexican enclaves ("colonias") in a foreign land.

[11]Ruiz de Burton's celebration of the "leading men" of Mexican politics and letters responds as well to contemporary Anglo American representations that orientalized Mexico and romanticized it as a kind of American Egypt. Nine years after *Who Would Have Thought It?*, for instance, *The Century* featured a travel piece that beckoned Anglo tourists to a Mexico that would become familiar to early twentieth-century readers of Lummis, Austin and Lawrence. In this piece, as in scores of other essays, Mexico is a somnolent Lotus Land complete with "an interior full of indefinite promise" and "strange figures…who had come over the mountains on their sandal-shod feet from a country of which travelers said 'There is nothing stranger out of Egypt'" (1). As with ethnographic representation more generally, Mexico is an anachronism, titillating "modern" visitors with its "moving pictures out of another century; the silence of the streets, the air of suspended activity" (321). What follows is a particularly stunning example of this exoticizing, enfeebling language: "The houses repose…with a dull, slumbrous dignity which ignores the pathetic look of social decadence general discomfort creeping over them…. The gardens look weedy and wild; the strong sunlight spares no detail of decrepit woodwork, or faded paint, broken tile, or stain of leaking spout meandering down the stuccoed wall with a grotesque suggestion of unwiped tears on unwashed cheeks" (1-2).

Works Cited

"A Diligence Journey in Mexico." *The Century Magazine* (November 1881): 1-14.
"A Provincial Capital of Mexico." *The Century Magazine* (January 1882): 321-33.
Bancroft, Hubert Howe. *California Pastoral*. San Francisco: The History Company, 1888.
Gallardo, Aurelio Luis. "Oda Patriótica." *El Nuevo Mundo* 28 June 1864.

"Gringos y Greasers." *La Gaceta* 27 September 1879.

"La Mujer." *La Gaceta* 27 December 1879.

Magoffin, Susan Shelby. *Down the Santa Fe Trail and into Mexico: The Diary of Susan Shelby Magoffin, 1846-47.* Ed. Stella M. Drumm. Lincoln: U of Nebraska P, 1962.

"Origen de la palabra 'Gringo.'" *La Gaceta* 27 March 1880.

Padilla, Genaro. *My History, Not Yours: The Formation of Mexican American Autobiography.* Madison: U of Wisconsin P, 1993.

"Pobres Hombres!... ¿Será Verdad? *El Clamor Público* 2 August 1856.

Ramírez, Francisco. "¡Americanos! ¡Californios!" *El Clamor Público* 21 February 1857.

_____. "Los Mexicanos en la Alta California." *El Clamor Público* 7 August 1855.

Rowlandson, Mary White. *The Sovereignty and Goodness of God, together with the Faithfulness of His Promises Displayed; Being a Narrative of the Captivity and restoration of Mrs. Mary Rowlandson. 1682.* Rpt. in *So Dreadful a Judgement: Puritan Responses to King Philip's War, 1676-1677.* Eds. Richard Slotkin and James K. Folsom. Middletown: Wesleyan UP, 1978.

Ruiz, Vicki. "From Out of the Shadows: A History of Mexican Women in the Southwest." Unpublished essay, 1994. 8.

Ruiz de Burton, María Amparo. Letter to George Davidson. 4 December 1875. Ruiz de Burton papers, Bancroft Library, University of California at Berkeley.

_____. Letter to George Davidson. 26 July 1880. Ruiz de Burton papers, Bancroft Library, University of California at Berkeley.

_____. *The Squatter and the Don.* 1885. Eds. Rosaura Sánchez and Beatrice Pita. Houston: Arte Público, 1993.

_____. *Who Would Have Thought It?* Philadelphia: J.B. Lippincott, 1872.

"Una Madre." *El Clamor Público* 18 October 1856.

PART II

Assimilation, Accommodation or Resistance?

"Fantasy Heritage" Reexamined: Race and Class in the Writings of the Bandini Family Authors and Other Californios, 1828-1965

F. Arturo Rosales

This study reassesses the "Fantasy Heritage" as applied to Californios [original Spanish-Mexican settlers in California]. The myth as defined by a number of radical California writers in the 1940s, such as Carey McWilliams, Louis Adamic and Ruth Tuck, assumes that the descendants of Californios falsely believe that they were of pure Spanish descent and that California during the pre-Anglo period, unlike *mestizo* Mexico, was a cultural bulwark of Spain. The myth then became for interlocking agribusiness monopolies and developers, a symbol of California culture used to promote real estate, tourism and California agricultural products. The "Fantasy Heritage," according to McWilliams, who was the myth's foremost debunker, set up an "absurd dichotomy" between contemporary Mexican Americans in the Southwest and the mythical California "Spanish" (McWilliams 37).

Mexican American intellectuals such as Arthur Campa, Ramón Ruiz, Manuel P. Servín derided the myth. By the time of the Chicano Movement in the 1960s, the "Fantasy Heritage" was thoroughly discredited through a critique based largely on the earlier Anglo radical definition. Inspired also by Mexican *indigenismo*, an ideology that gives dignity to Mexico's Indian heritage, the Chicano Movement extolled "brown pride," a credo diametrically opposed to the "Fantasy Heritage." Regardless of the approach taken, all critics have been consistent; the "Fantasy Heritage" is myth because the original settlers to what became the Southwest had admixtures of European, Indian, and African genes. The passion with which detractors attacked the myth, however, has resulted in an impression that pre-Anglo Southwest Mexican culture had little to do with Spain and was revamped by a subscription to a false cultural identity. The most damning feature of this assertion is that Southwest Mexicans, consciously and unconsciously, constructed a synthetic history in order to ingratiate themselves with Anglos who did not like the real Mexicans (Robinson 155; Ruiz 15-17).

This essay, however, demonstrates that if Californios adhered to "Spanishness" they did so following their own agenda—one that predated the Anglo takeover. I argue that Eurocentrism, which was certainly embraced by Southwest Hispanics, is part of a general identity which a substantial portion of the Mexican population has insisted on, notwithstanding the rise of Mexican *indigenismo* in this century. Moreover, this disposition existed regardless of Anglo domination. Certainly, those mixed-bloods who considered themselves non-Indian were aware of their indigenous or African blood. But for better or worse, they put more stock, as willing agents, in their more obvious European background—filtered through a Mexican-*criollo* sieve, that is. In essence, discreditors of the myth have fallen into the quintessential race trap of trying to define Spanish American ethnicity by insisting on a rather strict correlation between culture and genetic pool content. Jack Forbes argues that Mexicans in the U.S. have been manipulated into using the term Hispanic thus acquiring a false sense of identity. After all, he indicates, Mexico's gene pool is over 80 percent Indian (59-62). Debunkers have also confused Californio eagerness to establish regional Hispanic superiority with their embracing the commercial Anglo-inspired myth. Regional chauvinism based on claims of having more Spanish blood, as shall be shown below, is also a time-honored habit in many parts of Mexico.

Origins of the Fantasy Heritage

To be sure, a unique fantasy notion was concocted by Anglos, as McWilliams and others have indicated. During the early nineteenth century, Anglo-Hispanic contact in the Spanish-Mexican north resulted in the negative casting of Hispanic culture. Nonetheless, by the second half of the nineteenth century, an Anglo-led hispanophilic movement, centered primarily in California and New Mexico, sanitized the unfavorable image. Influential Anglo authors such as Charles Lummis, Bret Harte, Helen Hunt Jackson and Gertrude Atherton perpetuated and manipulated a myth that depicted early California history in sentimental, bucolic terms—also as an extension of Castilian Spain. The view was embraced by Anglos in reaction to "crass materialism, vulgarity, and rootlessness" characterizing nineteenth century, industrializing America (Weber 1987: 11).

Accompanying the construction of pure Castilian origin in this century was "mission revival" architecture based on Mediterranean images—large houses and missions bolstered by thick adobe walls, roofed with red tiles, graced by wide arches, and adorned by elegantly carved wood furnishings. In typical "Ramona" fashion, Franciscan missionaries, originally renounced by Anglo bigots, were now seen as kindly pastors looking after their flock of Indian neophytes. The ideological mission revival movement was fueled also by economic motives. To Charles Lummis, for example, the Californio romantic image was worth more in tourism and publishing profits than California oil and agriculture.

Unfortunately, this romantic thrust clearly promoted the dichotomy identified by McWilliams. In this century the Eugene Bolton border-lands historical school gave the "Fantasy Heritage" scholarly respect and the dichotomy achieved intellectual credibility. Bolton himself, for example, saw the *mestizo* as savage and unequal to the Spaniards (Weber 1987: 5-25). More recently the myth was bolstered by the popular media and during the Great Depression it served as a form of escapism in California. Los Angeles boosters even endowed the "Fantasy Heritage," with its aura of "history and romance," the ability to draw more tourists than sunny weather or "movie-industry glamour" (Davis 27). Still the foundation for the creation of the lore was real. It cannot be denied that the people of Spain and their descendants, greatly influenced not only the Southwest, but all of Spanish America with both culture and genes. It can be said that fantasy manufacturers elaborated or distorted from a real foundation.

Historians and the Fantasy Heritage

Before actually discussing heretofore unanalyzed writings of Californios, further query on how recent historians have charged Southwest Mexican with claiming a fantasy heritage is necessary. Carey Williams, active as a journalist and crusader in the 1930s and 1940s, saw something pitiful and perverse in the excesses of this posturing. He was particularly offended by the pleasure derived from romanticizing nineteenth century Hispanic society and simultaneously denigrating contemporary California immigrant Mexican society. He dismissed the alleged Californio participants in this process as gudgeons. Similarly David Weber, writing over twenty years ago, indicated "Mexican Americans who prefer to be called Spanish, Hispano, or Latin American in order to disassociate themselves from more recent arrivals from Mexico are deluded by the fantasy that their ancestors are Spanish" (Weber 1972: 22). More recently Weber has modified his stance somewhat, assuring us that the Southwest Hispanic culture remained vigorous until the Anglo conquest. In spite of the toll taken by rigorous frontier conditions and miscegenation "the core of Hispanic frontier culture and society remained recognizably Hispanic and clearly intact" (Weber, *Spanish* 333). Rodolfo Acuña, in another dated piece, strips Southwest Hispanics of all agency in regards to the myth by interpreting its rise as a sequitur to the colonizing state's monopoly of ideas. Discussing Hispanic New Mexicans he indicates, "In a colonial society, social control is facilitated by erasing the historical memory of the colonized...." As a consequence, "In order to survive economically, many descendants of the original New Mexicans [read Californios] have found it convenient to separate themselves from Mexicans.... They rationalized they were the descendants of...Spanish conquistadores" (55-56).

But the critique has survived into recent years. The most extensive synthesis of the "Fantasy Heritage" and Southwest Hispanics to date appeared in John R. Chávez's *The Lost Land*. In this assessment, the myth is inexorably linked to Anglo subordination; Southwest Mexicans quickly internalized it, grateful they were no longer subject to earlier, more hostile views. By promoting the image to distinguish themselves from "Indian peon" immigrants in the twentieth century, they became more acceptable to Anglos. But while some Southwest Hispanics accepted the "Fantasy Heritage," Mexican immigrants ignored it. "The Mexicans who arrived in the Southwest after 1900, and especially after 1910...had a renewed pride in their Indian heritage," Chávez states. Southwestern Hispanics, on the other hand, allowed the myth to be foisted on them. Chávez also asserts that because the "Fantasy Heritage" was inclusive to "Spanish" southwesterners, it denied immigrant Mexicans an identification with the Southwest—an idea offered by Weber some years before. As Chávez puts it, the myth was "an attitude that made the new arrivals feel alien in the Southwest despite the familiar geography and Mexican culture of the region." Furthermore, Anglos appreciated the romantic, pastoral image of Californios, a portrayal which divested them of ruggedness—a trait Anglos reserved for themselves (86).

The first Hispanic writer considered to invoke the myth according to both Weber and Chávez was Guadalupe Vallejo, a member of an old Californio family. She was the niece of Mariano Guadalupe Vallejo a California notable and large land owner in the Sonoma Valley. Guadalupe's gender was erroneously presented as male, but she is very definitely a female, born in 1844, to Jesús Vallejo, Mariano's brother and Soledad Sánchez.[1] In 1890 she wrote a piece for *Century Magazine* in which Chávez assumes she adhered to the Anglo-created myth because the essay confined the use of "'Mexican' strictly to the lower class and to articles and customs that came from Mexico. Otherwise his [read her] article was a litany of hispanizations..." (91). But as shall be seen below, Guadalupe's ideological framework transcended this genre of following the lead of Anglo romanticists.

Alfonso Yorba, a descendant of the Californio elite, wrote a 1935 article for the *Southern California Quarterly* maintained that San Juan Capistrano was one of the few areas where "Spanish" culture survived. Like Guadalupe's essay, this too has been offered as evidence of Californio adherence to the myth.

> The last of the Spanish Pueblo towns sleeps on into 1935 almost untouched by the modern world. A long row of old adobe houses lines the main street—U.S. Highway 101—and all the corners of the little town one finds the crumbling adobes of yesterday. (Chávez 96)

Here similarities to Anglo myth makers are more evident than in Guadalupe's piece. A content analysis of both Vallejo's and Yorba's essays demonstrates a desire to a establish superior, albeit romantic, regional Hispanic identity, more than a desire to succumb to a pathological denial of kinship to Mexico. Moreover, popular culture in Mexico, when Yorba wrote, was also undergoing a bucolic fantasy period—witness the surge of *rancho* [ranch] films that emerged during this period. The contours of these productions had much in common with the California fantasy promotion.

In fact, in the 1930s and 1940s, boosters of the California "Fantasy Heritage" often endowed "Old Mexico" with images of a romantic Hispanic present, a conceit often alluded to by Mexican Americans who were not descendants of the Californios, as well as by promoters of Mexican tourism, both in Mexico and California. The Padua Institute located in Claremont, California romanticized and commercialized California Mexican culture. The Institute cast dramas using Mexican American entertainers in a dinner-theater setting, portraying "Spanish" California themes. But the pastoral, bucolic images generated by this business extended to Mexico as well. For example, one such play entitled "Calle del Beso" was based on the tragic love story engendered by a quaint legend from Guanajuato, Mexico. In essence, this process was not exclusive to native Southwest Mexicans.[2] Interestingly, during this same period, Mexican towns retaining colonial characteristics such as Guanajuato, Querétaro, and Morelia attracted Mexican tourists by staging "Spanish" *zarzuelas* and forming *estudiantinas* [minstrels who employ mandolins and guitars and perform Spanish American and peninsular ballads]. The young musicians dress in capes and daggers, just like characters in *Siglo de Oro* dramas.

The Bandini Family Writers

To determine further if indeed Southwest Hispanics adhered to the "Fantasy Heritage" myth, the writings of one family, the Bandinis of southern California, will be assessed here in some detail. A well-known Hispanic family in nineteenth and twentieth-century California, the Bandinis were well integrated into elite Californio society. The choice of the Bandini family was made because their essays span over one hundred and thirty years and are available as published sources. In addition, no scholars have ever analyzed their works either as a collective group or as individual authors.

The Bandini works examined here reflect attitudes and ideological viewpoints held by many other Californios. The works are racially exclusive, elitist, and written predominantly from a male perspective. With the exception of the works of José and his son Juan, they are written in English, but their cultural derivation is Hispanic. In California, nineteenth-century Hispanic elites were probably more democratic in their outlook to subordinate classes than their compatriots in the interior of Mexico with which they could not compare either in wealth, or Spanish "pedigree." Therefore, class differences within the *gente de razón* [merchants, artisans and small and large ranchers] were not as great as in central Mexico. Indians, of course, were excluded from any notion of equality in both areas.[3]

The patriarch of the family was José Bandini. A Spanish navy officer born in Cádiz, Spain, he was sent briefly to Monterrey, California from Peru in 1818. After Mexican independence in 1821, José decided to make his home in San Diego. In Peru he had been married twice and although the father of many children only his son Juan accompanied him when he first decided to make California his home (*Description* vi-vii). José Bandini's interests centered on commerce and in 1828 he wrote *A Description of California in 1828*. Originally it was a letter to the British Consul in Nayarit, Mexico. Among other things, the letter emphasized the neglect of California by the central Mexican government. Obviously, José did not engage in posturing a heritage vis-à-vis Anglo dominance, since he had no inkling of California's fate in 1828. He paid some attention to questions of race, however. "The inhabitants of these pueblos are white people, and in order to distinguish them from the Indians they are commonly called *gente de razón*." There is no evidence in his letter of the future "Fantasy Heritage" notion that Californios by-passed Mexico when they settled California. As he put it, "Almost all are descendants of a small number of individuals who came with their wives from the Mexican mainland." Assessment of these *pobladores* [settlers] was not very positive, however. After indicating that they seemed healthy, robust and well-built, he complains of their idleness and lack of learning, indicating that, "They exert themselves only in dancing, horsemanship, and gambling, with which they fill their days." The observation that the inhabitants were white is objective rather than a guise to distract future historians and observers from the fact that early California pioneers were racially mixed. Using racial classifications which have risen primarily in Anglo America, these early Californios were probably not white. But the reasons for José's classification will become apparent below.

Bandini described the Indians less favorably—lazy and not very intelligent—but the assessment is definitely not fodder for the "noble savage" characterizations of Helen Hunt Jackson and other authors later in the century. "As their true character is one of vengeance and timidity, they are inclined towards treachery. They do not recognize kindness, and ingratitude is common among them" (7, 9).

Juan Bandini, José's son, wrote a manuscript of the history of California for the 1796-1845 period. In this short work, his assessment of race and class echoed that of his father's and did not contain romantic notions of early California life. It was designed instead to justify his turning his back on Mexico at the time of the Anglo invasion in 1846. As a consequence, his work contained the same complaints about the neglect of California by the Mexican government (*Historia*).

Juan's son Arturo Bandini, was the most talented of all the Bandini clan of writers. He lived in a "simple Los Angeles home filed [sic] with books and manuscripts—the quiet life of a scholar and collector" (Baker 25). His passions were big game hunting and deep sea fishing and it is to these pastimes that he devoted much of his literary works. Arturo married an Anglo, Helen Elliot of Indiana, who wrote a history of California that attributes to Californios race and class distinctions. Accordingly, she wrote "Many of those who came up from Mexico to live in the Pueblos were idle or dissipated, and nearly all uneducated." In time, however, "a much better class of people came into the country—men of education, brave, hardy members of good Spanish families..." (*History* 118-19). By this she did not deny the Mexican origins of good families. She was distinguishing their class and their race. Moreover, some of these latecomers did come from Spain as did her father-in-law.

Elsewhere, in discussing Anglo mistreatment of Californios as they lost land and were expelled from gold mines, she states: "The American miners seemed to feel that the Californian had no right to be there. Of course there were some of the lower class, many who were part Indian, who would lie, steal, or if they had an opportunity murder." However, Helen remained frank in describing the rising enmity between Anglos and Californios during the gold rush. She relates one incident where "a gentlemanly young Spaniard" was flogged after a race riot in the mines, and when released "he swore eternal vengeance on the American race" (183-184). Again, she proves to be a racist, but certainly she would not deny Hispanics in Mexico of wealth and status, the accolades she reserves for her Californios.

Her husband Arturo, born in 1855, on the other hand, does not claim a "Spanish" pedigree in his works. His most best known piece concerning California Hispanic life is *Navidad* [Christmas], published in 1892. Arturo describes a *pastorela* pageant held in Los Angeles when he was an adolescent.

Great detail is devoted to the dress of Californio horsemen and families but the pastorela takes up the bulk of the narrative. "Gaily decorated and festooned carretas, prancing horses, and splendid horsemen were a common enough sight for us, but the *Pastores*—Ah! That was something that occurred but once a year during Navidad—Christmas time" (13.) Arturo relates the roles played by some of the boys in the play, including his own. In describing the part in which the Devil and St. Michael engage in battle, Arturo reveals a patronizing view of Indians.

> As a matter of course the fiend was soon put hors de combat, much to the edification of the pious ones, but to the great chagrin of us boys who looked on him as the principal hero of the day. Our confidence and admiration were soon restored, however, for, on rising to his feet, the fiend, would select some young, active looking Indian in the crowd and rush him with a blood curdling screech. "Lo" could not stand this and would light out for dear life, superstitious fear adding wings to his feet. (14)

When discussing the typical food on Christmas he remembers, "*Buñuelos*—sweetened cakes fried in grease. *Buñuelos* are to my mind, always associated with old-time Christmas and *pastores*" (15). Then he describes the frankly Mexican character of the Los Angeles Christmas-time fiesta.

> confusion reigned supreme; shrill cries, expostulations and silvery Spanish oaths filled the air. Caterers—*tamale* men and women; candy and fruits vendors—*enchilada* and *tortilla* women; proprietors of musical taverns—all struggled and even fought for choice locations.... Above all the din could be heard the twangings of guitars, shrieking of violins and songs interspersed with blank verse. (17)

Only once in the text does Arturo refer to Californios as Spanish-Americans, and this he does rather fleetingly. His posture towards the lower classes is simply typical of the attitude held by members of his class in Mexico during the same period. To see this we will return to the setting of the street fiesta.

> If you wish to know the rank, wealth or social standing of each individual, watch the actions of any proprietor of a booth; see how deferential his smile to some, and with what humble but all-absorbing interest he listens to their conversation. But suddenly he straightens up, and stands on tip-toe, looks shocked and offended, but loud enough to be heard by his visitors. "Sh! sh!" What is the matter you wonder. Why, he is only rebuking and silencing the two *pelados* [impecunious ones] for daring to talk in such presence. (17)

Arturo deals with the issue of Anglo encroachment from a somewhat apologist perspective, but at the same time he acknowledges the demise of Californios at the hands of Anglo American aggression.

It has been asserted with good reason that many Americans profited by abusing the confidence or taking advantage of the simplicity of these people. This is undoubtedly true, but the record of the good old pioneers is quite clear on that score; the cloud overshadows some later comers. (16)

By "good old pioneers" he refers to the very first non-Hispanic Europeans who acculturated to Californio life. While writing from an elitist perspective, it is clear that Arturo's desire is to maintain the identity of Californios through the intimacy of personal narrative.

The works of Arturo and Helen's son, Ralph Bandini, born in Pasadena in 1885, are the most prolific. His renditions are based on imagination, California legends and historical events, some of which his mother included in her writings. But even he does not often subscribe to the "fantasy" notion. His stories are romantic but they could have been set in Mexico as well and some in fact have Mexican themes. In 1939, a series of his short stories appeared in the *Los Angeles Times* Sunday magazine. Few Hispanic fiction writers have received more exposition considering that in the 1930s the *Los Angeles Times* had a circulation of over 200,000.

One piece, which takes place in pre-Independence California and is treated by Bret Harte as well, is based on a true incident. Apart from its obvious romantic inclination, this story inexorably ties Californios to Royal Spain which of course they were at this point. The protagonists are "Count Nicolai Rezanof, emissary of his imperial majesty, Czar of Russia" and Concepción Arguello, a native Californian. At the story's beginning Rezanof negotiates a trade agreement with Don José Joaquín Arrillaga, "His most Catholic Majesty's Governor of the far-flung royal province of Alta California," and José Darío Arguello, "comandante of the presidio at San Francisco." During the Russian's visit, Concepción, the daughter of Arguello, falls madly in love with the Russian but permission to marry is denied them because "he is of alien faith and race." Tragically he is killed in a shipwreck, never to return. She is heartbroken, never marries, and becomes a nun. "Then came a day when sleepy Monterey stirred into life." The British fleet was anchored off-shore and its Captain, Sir George Simpson, was invited to a banquet in his honor. At the gathering, the Englishman mentioned casually that Rezanof had died. He then inquires about the woman the Russian had loved.

"Tell me does she live?" With his words there was a deathly silence. No one answered. The eyes of all Californians present dropped to the table. Then, far down the board a woman slowly rose; a woman garbed in the habiliments of a nun. For an instant her hands seemed to clutch at the cloth. Then hardly more than a whisper came her answer. "No señor. She too is dead." (Ralph Bandini, "Concepción" 3,12)

"Grandmother Made a Flag" is the story of how Doña Refugio Arguello de Bandini, Ralph's grandmother, made the first American flag in California out of bits and pieces from dresses and petticoats. The event supposedly connects his family to a "Betsy Ross" image of the beginning of California. As indicated above, Juan Bandini, Refugio's husband, actually sided with the Americans during the Mexican-American War and was considered a traitor by many other Californios. Ralph rationalizes his grandfather's role in siding with the *americanos* because of the bad government of Mexico, a theme which Juan Bandini himself harped on throughout the rest of his life. But here there is also a hint of regret that the Americans took over.

> Doña Refugio did not know it, with the making of that flag came the beginning of the end—an end that saw the sprawling adobes crumble back into the dust; that swept off our old Camino Real the jogging Vaqueros; that stilled forever the reedy tenors, the tilting love songs, the tinkling guitars. Those days are gone. Nothing can bring them back, for good or bad, they are gone, but in their going they left their mark, a mark that neither man nor time can ever erase. (12)

Ralph, like other Californio writers, alluded to cultural misunderstandings. This is seen in "Ranchero" a story about Abel Stearns' experience in acquiring a rancho. Stearns, Ralph's uncle by marriage, was married to Arcadia, Arturo's sister. In the story Abel Stearns negotiates the purchase of Los Lobos ranch from Ygnacio Valencia who at first was not too eager to sell. In spite of the Yankee's brusque manner, Don Ygnacio eventually gives in. The transaction completed, Stearns rides out to his new acquisition, making mental notes on changes necessary to make the ranch pay. Juan López, the *mayordomo* [foreman] appears and announces to Stearns that his people are waiting at the large ranch house. "'My people?' he echoed, his voice betraying his bewilderment. 'I don't understand! What do you mean?'" López answers Stearns, "The people of the *rancho*, señor Patrón. The people of Los Lobos. The *vaqueros*, the *trabajadores*, the women, the children, the Indios, the pobres, they all desire to welcome you señor." Obviously, Ralph subscribes to the old precept that landowners in Spanish America, are not driven by the same capitalist orientation as Anglos. In his story the *hacendado* [landowner] has the responsibility, not just for physical property, but for the people as well, which are somehow organically attached to the landholding (6).

Race and class issues are poignantly portrayed in "There Were Two Roads." Felipe and José, two Indian boys from San Juan Capistrano, wanted to be *vaqueros* [ranchers]. Ralph's characterization of them is patronizing, but he also seems to envy them saying that life "For Indios, and for a subjected people…was pleasant…. There was little schooling—but not too much.

There were rules to obeyed, but they were not too burdensome." But in spite of this freedom they look at the *rancheros* with awe.

> In the Spring came the rodeos—days of tumult; bellowing of angry cows, shrilling calves; struggling, wrestling, swearing vaqueros; the sing-song chant of tally men; the acrid swirling clouds of dust and smoke…. They joined the vaqueros and swore that they would some day be vaqueros….

On these occasions, "Felipe and José laughed as much as an Indian can…" In telling of the round-up Ralph takes the occasion to describe the life of the Californios who have gathered at the mission church of Father Peyri.

> The "great people" would come into the village from the ranchos and the rodeo would turn into a fiesta atmosphere inside the mission gates. Pressing as close as they dared, Felipe and José watched with wide, respectful eyes as the great land barons jingled up to the mission gates, creaking carretas of their women folk jolting in their wake. As they heard the sonorous Spanish phrases of greeting, the whir and jingle of spurs; saw the brilliant clothes, the palefaced women of the white men, strange pulses leaped within their half-barbaric veins.

But instead of the two Indian boys becoming like the *rancheros* and jingling up to receive Father Peyri's advice and blessings at rodeo time, Felipe becomes a lay brother. He is killed, however, in a December 1812 earthquake.

In "Ashes of Romance," which treats racial mixture, Ralph's attitude seems equivocal. It features Don Agustín, a small rancher and his family who are poor, but white and proud. Doña María is the wife, Francisco and Alejandro are the two sons, and Josefa is a budding beautiful daughter. Agustín was not rich but he knew that there was no need to worry about the future of Josefa who grew more "beautiful with every change."

> Sons of the greatest families in the Californias would be at her feet. Bueno, why not? Her blood was as good as any—her beauty beyond compare. Bien, one of these days…she would leave La Boca and become a patrona in her own right. (6, 8)

Living with them is a handsome *mestizo* named Felipe who was brought up as part of the extended family. Felipe was the son of an Indian woman, who had been Josefa's servant, and his father was "a soldier of Spain." Both parents died when Felipe was only a baby. Inevitably "the spell of love" came to La Boca de San Martín.

> Perhaps it was the golden California moon, bathing the valley in milky haze: perhaps the velvet nights and the stars so close above; or the chanting colors of sunset on the brooding guardian mountains; the tinkle of a guitar and a love song of the land; the voice of California—coyotes wailing at night. (6, 8)

When Felipe went to Don Agustín to declare his love for Josefa he was rejected. Agustín tells him that because he is a *mestizo*, he could not marry Josefa, "you are neither cow or bull...." Elsewhere in the same conversation Josefa's bigoted father tells Felipe, "In my daughter's veins...runs the blood that has been kept pure for 1000 years. God willing, it will be kept pure for 1000 years to come." Don Agustín expels Felipe warning him never to come near Los Lobos again but Felipe and the fetching Josefa run off to elope. An angry Agustín exhorts his two sons to track them down. When captured, Felipe is allowed to escape by Alejandro and Francisco because it is certain that their father would kill the *mestizo* if they were to take him to the *rancho*. While Ralph shows some sympathy for Felipe's and Josefa's plight, he seems to imply that the bigoted father has a right object because of the sacred precedence of one thousand years of *limpieza de sangre* [purity of the bloodline]. On the other hand, he also implies *que lo castigó Dios* [God punished him] for his obsessive racial pride (6, 8).

But does Ralph write from an Anglo "Fantasy Heritage" perspective? On the surface he appears totally assimilated into Anglo society. He was a Republican, for instance, at a time in which the majority of Hispanics in California were supporters of the New Deal. In addition he was a Mason, a lifetime member of the Skull and Snake Society of Stanford University, and an officer in both the Casa del Mar Beach Club and the Catalina Island Tuna Club. Even though Ralph was a lawyer by training, (Stanford, 1908), he did not practice very much because he lived on an inheritance (Spalding 12). The Baker-Bandini estate was partially left to Arturo's sons by his sister Arcadia Bandini de Baker. When this widow of two very successful Anglo entrepreneurs died childless in 1897, Arturo managed the estate until he himself died in 1912 (Baker 27). His son Ralph, however, "was charming, likeable and sympathetic but not a hard worker. He made unwise investments and lost all his inheritance...."[4]

Then was Ralph like Charles Lummis, interested in profiting from an Anglo market hungry for California lore? By 1939, he was trying to make a living off writing, certainly exploiting the contemporary mission-past vogue in California. Like his father he also wrote wild-life adventures. In *Tight Lines*, a book about deep-sea fishing, he employed the same romantic constructions in depicting professional fishermen that he used in his Californio stories. His stories in the *Times* (not all have been analyzed here) demonstrate great nostalgia for old Hispanic California, some of which he remembered from boyhood, and a great amount of disenchantment with modern Los Angeles.

Ralph was part Anglo—how does this effect his work? Most offspring of mixed marriages in California had an Hispanic mother but Frank and his brother Elliot did not. According to Elliot's wife, they spoke Spanish but were Anglicized because of Helen's influence. Ralph, however, never showed literary interest in his Mother's roots in the state of Indiana. Perhaps there was no romance there, and besides Helen wrote of nothing else except the Californio past. Frank identified deeply with her stories as he did with his father's, according to his sister-in-law, although "he made up a lot, and was a first-class spinner of yarns."[8] Moreover, in relating the star-crossed love story of Concepción Arguello he offers "she is of my blood." Such familial links are made with many of the Californio subjects in his works.

One of the most recent Bandini writers, in the 1960s, is Arturo's grand niece Arcadia Bandini de Brennen. Ostensibly she had less of an Hispanic background than Ralph since her mother María Antonia Couts was half-Anglo and her father was Chalmers Scott. María Antonia and Chalmers, living in rather modest circumstances, had eleven children. Arcadia, in a custom often followed in Mexico during this time, was raised by her namesake great-aunt Arcadia Bandini de Baker, the childless but wealthy daughter of Juan Bandini. This seems to have resulted in the younger Arcadia retaining a good dose of Californio culture. But because of the Baker wealth, she received an expensive education, including a stint in Paris where she studied piano.

Like Ralph, her essays invoke romantic California images. In telling of the ship journey taking the Bandini family from Peru to California in 1820 she declares "all the household furniture and belongings were bought, since the Bandini family were of the Princely Bandini family of Florence. One may imagine how wonderful, rare and beautiful their household furnishings were!" (Bandini Brennen 3, 14).

Nonetheless, as Arturo Bandini's *Navidad* demonstrates, when Californios revealed evidence of past material culture it was inevitably Mexican. In ladling for traditions to recount from immediate past, Arcadia launches into a detailed description on the making of tamales, Sonoran-style flour tortillas and California *frijoles*. The memories of freshly made tortillas she said "makes me hungry for one, just to write this...and these I never had sense enough to learn to make" (4-5, 14). This at least demonstrates that Arcadia was not hiding a Mexican connection. In five generations after the first Bandini wrote it can be said that while they unabashedly espoused an elite family background, they did not go out of their way to deny ties to Mexican Hispanicism.

Adjusting "Fantasy Heritage" Application

The myth as constructed and used by Anglos is historically very clear but as shown above, it must be tempered with the knowledge that a similar process took place in Mexico. What requires further attention than what has been given by scholars thus far is how it applies to Californios and other Southwest Mexicans. For example, the most potent feature of the "Fantasy Heritage" is a desire to be a descendent of Spain. But critics have ascribed this wish to Southwest Hispanics as a unique process. Nonetheless, the seed of this racial aesthetic germinated in a larger continental context and was carried by settlers to California and elsewhere in northern New Spain/ Mexico. Consequently, the explanation that it emerged as an avenue to integrate with Anglos should be given more careful thought. As early as 1813, for example, a priest at the Santa Barbara Mission noted it was common knowledge that the residents of the local *presidio* were not "genuine Spaniards," but "if they were told to the contrary they would consider it an affront" (Weber *Spanish Frontier*, 328). Undoubtedly, pursuing Spanish cultural identity in California acquired a peculiar character in response to conditions imposed by the Anglo conquest—the point here is that Californios were predisposed to its guiles because of an earlier orientation.[5]

While scholars like John Chávez and David Weber consider that the adherence to a Spanish heritage has played a role in resisting Anglo dominance and cultural decline, their works are more emphatic about casting Hispanic adherents to the myth as victims of Anglo manipulation. Additionally, the documents used as a measure of "Fantasy Heritage" which they employed for California to discuss this process were too few to offer any definitive conclusions.[6] Genaro M. Padilla, on the other hand, by viewing autobiographies of Southwest Mexicans, developed a methodology that probes more deeply into how subordination affected Southwest Mexicans. Moreover, his interpretation is not as intent on reading "fantasy heritage" intentions into their testimony. In one study, he focuses on Mariano Guadalupe Vallejo, a wealthy California landowner who lost his entire fortune after the Anglo conquest (Padilla). Initially, Vallejo welcomed the Anglos, but later he bitterly lamented California economic subordination and cultural decline. "No sooner had they arrived than they assumed the title of attorney and began to seek means of depriving the Californians of their farms and other properties," he is quoted as saying (45). In another observation, Mariano is highly resentful that French and German were promoted in the schools of San Francisco while Spanish was disdained (Padilla).

Through such commentary, Vallejo maintained cultural dignity although losing out on wealth and property. It also assured him that Anglos like Hubert H. Bancroft would not tell the story of Californios without their involvement. Felipe Fierro, a contemporary of Vallejo and editor of *La Voz del Nuevo Mundo* [The Voice of the New World] also encouraged Californios to resist cultural annihilation through writing. There is little in Mariano's exposition that inspired "Fantasy Heritage" visions, however. It limited itself to personal observations on politics, California culture, and insights on the personal lives of contemporaries (Padilla) This does not mean that later writers, faulted for falling prey to "Fantasy Heritage," such as Alfonso Yorba did not conform to the Vallejo tradition. While Vallejo and Fierro both counseled others to follow their lead, they did not insist on acknowledging a *mestizo* identity.

Further inquiry into Guadalupe Vallejo's life (the female), who has been presented as the quintessential Californio purveyor of the "Fantasy Heritage," reveals she was not a propagandist for such a myth. For example, she stated her purpose was to record "details and illustrations of the past that no modern writer can possibly obtain except…from hearsay, since they exist in no manuscript, but only in the memories of a generation that is fast passing away" (Weber 1972: 46). In 1890, her piece in *Century Magazine*, caught the attention of a reporter for the *San Francisco Morning Call*, who then sought her out. She was found in Oakland "after some difficulty" in a "modest domicile." There "a little sign, bearing the legend 'Spanish Taught' is the only outward appearance that here a daughter of one of the oldest and proudest Spanish families…now dwells." Nothing in the interview portrays Anglos in a favorable light, nor does she demonstrate a desire to ingratiate herself. She remembers that as a child she was terrified of the "terrible Americans" and during the 1846 invasion (when her uncle Mariano was jailed) they came to search her father Jesús' house. "We younger ones were terribly afraid of Americans then.…" She would have jumped into bed of burning coals, Guadalupe added "had not my father's barber put out his arm and saved me." The reporter found it highly ironic that she was supporting herself and her aging Mother through "teaching her mother tongue to the invading Americans."

The Fantasy Heritage and Mexico

John Chávez's assertion that many Mexican immigrants expressed pride in their *mestizo* background is correct. The notion that rejection of Mexican immigrants by Southwest Hispanics resulted in their inability to identify with the Southwest requires a more careful assessment, however. By the time of large-scale immigration early in this century, the old Southwest heritage was not visible to newcomers because urbanization, industrialization and the development of commercial agriculture inundated the old Hispanic characteristics—especially in California. Very few immigrants went to northern New Mexico, for example, where southwestern Mexican culture was most vibrant. Besides, immigrants identified deeply with their *patrias chicas* [regions] in Mexico, an affiliation that they would not have given up easily.

Large-scale Mexican immigration brought a small, but expressive group of exile intellectuals who through newspapers and cultural activity promoted an adherence to Mexican identity. Living in an alien environment and rejected by Anglos, other immigrants followed the lead of these more educated compatriots. They shed provincialism and developed an orientation based on emerging nationalism in Mexico. Diametrically opposed to the "Fantasy Heritage, they paid homage to their Indian past, an important feature of twentieth century Mexican nationalism (Rosales 1990).

The Los Angeles immigrant leader Juan B. Ruiz, for example, when compared to his contemporary Ralph Bandini, differs sharply in racial ideology. In 1937, Ruiz, a pharmacist known as the "Mayor of Little Mexico," was interviewed by a Federal Writer's Project worker. In describing him, Eustace L. Williams says, "His profile is reminiscent of one of the old Spanish Conquerors. Expression, complexion, coloring of hair and eyes show that he is evidently descended from pure stock of the Old Country. *In this, however, he takes no interest. Says with a shrug that he is a native of Mexico, nothing more* [emphasis mine]." Ruiz' reaction was typical of other immigrant leaders of the 1920s who could have claimed both racial and class exclusiveness. He was born in Culiacán, Sinaloa in 1896 of a wealthy family who lost everything during the revolution. He studied chemistry, but by 1920, weary of violence and instability in Mexico, he crossed the border. First he came to Arizona and then left for California, the whole time relying on menial jobs and on selling dry-goods to earn a living. Finally, with a partner, he entered the drugstore business.

Why did he not still carry in 1937, a race consciousness provoked by his being white and from an elite Mexican family? Certainly in nineteenth century Sinaloa, the ethnic ideology of his class differed little from that of elite Californios. Perhaps the humbling experience of having to emigrate and work in menial labor forced Ruiz to relate more to Mexican immigrants who in Porfirian Mexico would have been below his station. During the years of repatriation, for example, Ruiz energetically worked with the Mexican Consul in helping his destitute countrymen (Balderrama 40). Besides, as a pharmacist, his customers were mainly Mexican laborers, a factor which probably influenced his identification with working class compatriots.

There is another reason why white Mexican immigrant leaders did not parade their racial pedigree, a practice common in Latin America, and certainly among the Californios. In Mexico such a racial aesthetic was modified after the Revolution of 1910, resulting in an intellectual and official acceptance of Mexico's Indian background. As a consequence, much prestige was given to that position and many middle class Mexicans and intellectuals adopted the new consciousness—or at least paid it lip service. In this milieu, to deny one's Indian background, or inversely to flaunt European racial characteristics, was considered inappropriate. Many upper class immigrants who came to the

United States, were among those affected by the new ideology. Certainly Ruiz was one of those. He was a close friend and political supporter in the 1920s of José Vasconcelos, foremost among the promoters of a unique form of *mestizo* identity in Mexico.

Roots of the Spanish Heritage Desire in Mexico

Prior to the Revolution, an *indigenista* perspective was limited in Mexico and race consciousness favored a European aesthetic, as was the case in the rest of Latin America. The formation of the exclusionary cultural politics of southwestern Mexicans vis-à-vis immigrants from Mexico should be viewed within this larger framework.[7] In Mexico, as elsewhere in Spanish America *la gente de razón* did not have to be purely European to be considered white. Rather, class status served as a determinant in racial classification and in California, members of the non-Indian castes, many who were obviously racially mixed, were considered by José Bandini as *blancos* (see above) using such a criteria.

Within the colonial corporate structure, racial branding was more rigid in the centers of power, around Mexico City, where the largest surviving native American populations continued to live. There, Spanish colonial officials vigorously applied racial identifiers to the newborn—this determined caste ranking. Next to a peninsular—born in Spain—a criollo [a Spaniard born in Mexico] was the most desirable ranking. Then came *castizos* who were three quarters Spanish but officially they were *españoles*. At the other end of the spectrum were *indios*, categorized because of parents who were culturally identifiable as Indians and because of racial characteristics. Over sixteen categories—*mulatos*, *chinos*, *zambizos* to name but a few—represented the offspring of multiple European, African and Indian miscegenation. Finally all nonwhites were classified as *castas* [mixed bloods].

Since racial ranking conferred either superiority or subordination, northward bound settlers took advantage of their remoteness from central Mexico to shed despised racial categories and accrue the desired ones. Northern migration started soon after the conquest. In 1546, silver was discovered in Zacatecas, the first of a series of finds in *el gran chichimeca* as this vast region north of Querétaro was called. The area was sparsely populated by hostile Indian tribes who challenged mining operations. By the century's end, Chichimeca-nomads were brought under control through a combination of military and religious campaigns. Sedentary Indians from the central highlands were forced to work the mines, but obliged to travel hundreds of miles on foot from their homes. This unwilling source proved inadequate. Within a generation the mine operators turned to wage labor. From the central high-

lands, hundreds of thousands of *mestizos*, born soon after the conquest, acculturated sedentary Indians, blacks and Spaniards migrated to the *reales* [mining
centers] settling permanently. Not all new arrivals became miners. Many were
artisans, petty merchants, or bandits. The majority who did not enter the
mines labored in agricultural production and livestock raising, an important
corollary to mining, as peons on haciendas or peasant owners of small farms.
Within a few decades, these activities determined the social and racial-cultural
arrangements of the region.

The process was carried north as the mining frontier moved in that direction in the seventeenth and eighteenth centuries. By the time Mexico acquired
its independence from Spain in 1821, permanent colonies existed in coastal
California, southern Arizona, south Texas and in New Mexico and southern
Colorado. Leaders of most colonizing expeditions were persons born in Spain,
but the rank and file soldiers artisans and the workers in general were *castas*
or *criollos*. In some cases, Indians with a defined separate identity, such as
tlaxcaltecos, accompanied the settlers. In spite of this racial diversity all colonizers had Hispanic cultural traits.[8]

In time, however, as racial mixing stabilized in many parts of New Spain,
the term *español* was applied to persons in a social position to demand that
classification—even though not meeting all racial requisites. This was especially true in the extreme north where a more dynamic social and racial mixing took place than in Central Mexico. This provided opportunity to settlers to
reject the *indio* or nonwhite status (Weber, *Frontier* 328-29). For example, in
a 1793 census, 74 percent of the population in Bexar (present-day San Antonio) was *español*, only 26 percent were declared *indio* or *casta*. By then considerable racial mixing had occurred between Bexar's *mestizo* founders and
European Canary Islanders who were also earlier settlers. Nonetheless, economic status and community prestige determined a person's cultural-racial
category. Once a person was elevated into the *español* category, the family
attempted to stay at that level in subsequent generations through political and
economic influence and by marrying "white," called *mejorando la raza*
[improving the bloodline] (Poyo 86-87). Mexican independence led to official
blurring of all these distinctions but throughout the nineteenth century they
were maintained informally at local levels of social interaction.

This was true in West Central Mexico, for example, the initial northern
frontier in the sixteenth and early seventeenth centuries. In the 1930s, Paul S.
Taylor studied the village of Arandas, Jalisco, which is located in Los Altos,
an area also known as El Tapatío famous for people with a great amount of
Spanish blood.

> In the heart of the Mexican Republic is a region inhabited by people who are over-
> whelmingly of Spanish stock. Living in comparative isolation, these people have

retained to a high degree their Spanish heritage...mingling very little with the large numbers of *indígenas* [indigenous population] who inhabit adjoining regions. (Taylor 1)

Taylor acknowledged that racial mixture had taken place because he studied the marriage records of very early Arandas inhabitants. However, once the mixture took place, the villagers consciously maintained whiteness and Taylor observed that the majority looked more European than Indian. In essence, as probably happened in many southwestern communities, Arandas villagers attempted to stem further race mixture once a society of acceptable insiders was established. As Poyo has shown in the Bexar study, the insider status was based on economic and political criteria as well.

Even though Taylor knew they had mixed he concluded matter-of-factly, "The people of Arandas are generally regarded, and they so regard themselves, as of Spanish stock...persons who know the region indicated that their ancestors were from northern Spain." Statements made by Arandas inhabitants regarding race show remarkable parallels to the posturing in Frank Bandini's stories discussed above. "The señoritas do not want to marry *mestizos* or *indígenas*. They do not want to mix," said a business man. "A young woman who had been in the United States "of whitest Spanish type" said, "Parents don't want their daughters to marry Indians; they want them to marry white blood. Of course they're proud, proud of clean blood and old customs!" Many of these respondents had lived in the United States where contact with Anglos might have heightened race consciousness. But as Taylor concludes, "These attitudes probably were but slightly, if at all influenced by dominant race attitudes in the United States; rather they are of local, or of European origin" (18-19)[9]

As in Arandas, studies of other local communities in Mexico, such as San José de Gracia and Chavinda, both in Michoacan, or Sonora, yielded similar conclusions. Speaking of peasants who joined the independence movements from northern Michoacán, the Mexican historian, Luis González states "the criollo ranchers from the Sahuayo parish, more concretely from Jucumatlan, did not deny their Spanish background, on the contrary they claimed it with pride...at the same time they were culturally *mestizo* and *anti-gachupín* [anti-Spanish]" (70).

In nineteenth century Sonora, rejection of Mexicans from central Mexico called *guachos*, was very strong. The reasons, rooted in political and economic causes was also expressed in racial and regional terms. It was a disgrace for daughters of Sonoran notables not to marry white and as a consequence, like in California, "significant numbers of upper class women married foreigners." The racial attitude permeated down to the lower classes as well. In the 1860s in the small town of Baroyeca, for example, "the son of a Spanish father and

Indian mother expressed great pride in his European ancestry, proclaiming to be 'white' even though he lived a rather destitute existence" (Tinker Salas 18)[10] According to Miguel Tinker Salas, a social historian of Sonora, "being European did not simply imply physical appearance, but rather, it stressed preservation of a particular lifestyle and customs" (20)[10]

Conclusion

Southwest Hispanic writers, usually depicted as endorsers of the Anglo fantasy, did not always conform to the notions established by Lummis, Harte and Hunt Jackson. Many Southwest Hispanic elites were white or passed for white by using Mexican, not Anglo criteria. Lesser ranking subordinates who were of mixed races simply followed their lead and claimed whiteness as well. Undoubtedly, domination of Anglo Americans altered racial thinking but a colonized mentality did not result in claims to racial exclusiveness. Thus the "Fantasy Heritage" as invented by Anglo American writers did not drastically alter the race consciousness of Californios. That they and other Southwest Hispanics did not evolve a *mestizo* cultural heritage is a pre-Anglo contact phenomenon that should be viewed within a larger Mexican context.

It has only been in this century that Mexican political leaders and intellectuals have applied a catharsis to remind Mexicans of their Indian genes. Some Mexican immigrants brought this ideology early in this century but pressures of Anglo American racism did not allow it to take root among the Mexican American generation who were mostly children of the immigrants. They were more influenced by a preexisting desire to claim Spanish background than by *indigenismo,* which in Mexico probably took hold only among select but influential groups—i.e., those in a position to enforce politically correct canons (note reference to *estudiantinas* above). With the Chicano Movement, acceptance of *mestizo*, Indian origins has been resurrected among the general Mexican American population and probably among many descendents of Californios.

A major reason why elite Californios adhered to the what has appeared to some as "Fantasy Heritage" posturing was to resist the annihilation of their own class. Descendants of lower class Californios probably took their cues from the upper classes, also claiming racial exclusiveness. For the elites, however, resistance took the form of a collaboration similar to postures of other conquered noble or elite classes throughout history. The Irish aristocracy, for example, collaborated with their English conquerors in order to maintain some privilege. With economic domination, modernization and industrialization, many were anglicized and subordinated but remained mindful of their identity. The indigenous nobility of Mexico attempted a similar effort that allowed them the ability to maintain some customs and positions of privilege, at least during their own lifetime.[11]

Furthermore, as was shown above in the case of Arturo Bandini, his grandfather, his father, Mariano Vallejo, his niece, Guadalupe Vallejo, literary portraits of California were not compulsive about projecting an image of "Castilian purity" as we have been led to believe by recent writers. In addition, all the Californios discussed here, lamented the decline of their culture and in some cases were critical of Anglo oppression. A more thorough recovery of manuscripts and forgotten publications written by Hispanic California writers will allow us to make the assessment with more precision, however. One that will hopefully refrain from a presentist scolding of dead historical figures.

Notes

[1]That Guadalupe Vallejo is female can be seen in the *San Francisco Examiner*, August 6, 1904, Obituary. For a portrayal of her see Helen Elliot Bandini, *History of California* passim and index, p. 302.

[2]Clippings, unnamed Works Progress Administration (WPA), Federal Writers Project Files (FWPL), Special Collections, University of California, Los Angeles, Box 29. Brochures and programs of the Padua Institute, Box 85; Ibid., Mexican travel pamphlets, Box 86; See Rosales, "Shifting Self Perceptions," 71-94 and García, "Mexican Americans," 187-204, for discussions on this ideology in Texas; For Mexican American Generation adherence to bucolic "Old Mexico" imagery in Arizona and Texas, see Rosales, "Chicano Art," 65-66. In fact, early Mexican films such as the 1935 classic "Bajo el sol del cielo" depicted Mexico within this romantic genre.

[3]See Griswold del Castillo, 10-12, for a discussion of egalitarian features of California society during the Spanish and Mexican periods. For an appraisal of literature which discusses egalitarianism on the frontier, see Weber, *Myth and History*, 33-54.

[4]Mrs. Elliot Bandini to Author, January 1993.

[5]Miranda, 265-278; For antecedents in Mexico see Knight, 71-114.

[6]To be sure, attributing resistance to a society that left a legacy of racial denial makes this a rather thorny task. This point is made in Genaro M. Padilla in "Learning to Live."

[7]John Chávez admits that "The upper class in New Mexico, as in California and *Latin America as a whole*, was conscious of its 'Spanish' ancestry [emphasis mine]." This is somewhat contradictory, considering that in other parts of his book, the claim to a Spanish background is explained as a response to the Anglo takeover (Chávez, 93).

[8]See the following authors for an assessment of race mixing and race consciousness in Mexico: Simpson, Morner, Gibson, Palmer, and Weber, *Myth and History*.

[9]For Chavinda Michoacán, see Armstrong.

[10]For race consciousness in Colonial Sonora see Pfefferkorn. Quotes from Tinker Salas, 18-20.

[11]See Miller, 1-25. For similar developments in Mexico, see López Sarrelangue, passim.

Works Cited

Secondary Materials Unpublished

Telephone interview with Mrs. Elliot Bandini, November 15, 1992.
Letter from Mrs. Elliot Bandini to Author, January 1993.

Newspapers

San Francisco Call 14 December 1890.
San Francisco Examiner 6 August 1904.

Archival Material

Works Progress Administration, Federal Writers Project Files. Boxes 29, 46, 85, 86. Special Collections. University of California, Los Angeles.

Secondary Sources

Acuña, Rodolfo. *Occupied America: A History of Chicanos.* New York: Harper and Row, 1988.

Armstrong, John Milton. *A Mexican Community: A Study of Cultural Determinants of Migration.* Ann Arbor: University Microfilms, 1949.

Baker, Patricia. "The Bandini Family." *Journal of San Diego History* 15 (1969): 25-27.

Balderrama, Francisco E. *In Defense of La Raza: The Los Angeles Mexican Consulate and the Mexican Community, 1929-1936.* Tucson: U of Arizona P, 1982.

Bandini, Arturo. *Navidad.* San Francisco: California Historical Society, 1958.

Bandini Brennen, Arcadia. "Arcadian Memories." *California Herald* 10 (1963): 3, continued on 14.

_____. 1965. "Arcadian Memories," *California Herald* 12 (1965): 4-5, continued on 14.

Bandini, Helen Elliot. *History of California.* New York: American Book Company, 1908.

Bandini, José. *A Description of California in 1828.* Trans. Doris Marion Wright. Berkeley: Friends of the Bancroft Library, 1951.

Bandini Juan. *Historia de la Alta California, 1796-1849.* Berkeley: University of California, Bancroft Library, n.d.

Bandini, Ralph. 1939. "Ashes of Romance." *Los Angeles Times Sunday Magazine and Southland Home and Gardens* (July 16, 1939): 6, continued on 8.

_____. "Concepción Arguello." *Los Angeles Times Sunday Magazine and Southland Home and Gardens* (March 26, 1939): 3, continued on 12.

_____. "Grandmother Made a Flag." *Los Angeles Times Sunday Magazine and Southland Home and Gardens* (March 5. 1939): 12.

Bandini, Ralph. "Ranchero." *Los Angeles Times Sunday Magazine and Southland Home and Gardens* (July 23, 1939): 6, continued on 14.

_____. "There Were Two Roads." *Los Angeles Times Sunday Magazine and Southland Home and Gardens* (August 20, 1939): 10, continued on 21.

Chávez, John R. *The Lost Land: The Chicano Image of the Southwest.* Albuquerque: U of New Mexico P, 1984.

Davis, Mike. *City of Quartz.* New York: Vintage Books, 1992.

Forbes, Jack D. 1992. "The Hispanic Spin: Party Politics and Government Manipulation of Ethnic Identity." *Latin American Perspectives* 19 (1992): 59-62.

García, Mario T. "Mexican Americans and the Politics of Citizenship: The Case of El Paso, 1936." *New Mexico Historical Review* 59 (1984): 187-204.

Gibson, Charles. *The Aztecs Under Spanish Rule: A History of the Indians of the Valley of Mexico.* Stanford: Stanford UP, 1976.

González, Luis. *Pueblo en vilo: microhistoria de San José de Gracia.* México: El Colegio de México, 1968.

Griswold del Castillo, Richard. *The Los Angeles Barrios, 1850-1890: A Social History.* Berkeley: U of California P, 1979.

Knight, Alan. "Racism, Revolution, and Indigenismo, Mexico, 1910-1940." *The Idea of Race in Latin America.* Ed. Richard Graham. Austin: U of Texas P. 1990. 71-114.

McWilliams, Carey. *North From Mexico: The Spanish Speaking People of the United States.* Philadelphia: J.B. Lippincott Company, 1949.

Miller, Kerby A. *Emigrants and Exiles: Ireland and the Irish Exodus to North America.* New York: Oxford UP, 1985.

Miranda, Gloria. "Racial and Cultural Dimensions of *Gente de Razón* Status in Spanish and Mexican California." *Southern California Quarterly* 70 (1990): 265-78.

Morner, Magnus. *Race Mixture in the History of Latin America.* Boston: Little Brown, 1965.

Padilla Genaro M. "Learning to Live with (not necessarily like) the Past: Reading Spanish Colonial Narrative." Ms.

———. "The Recovery of Nineteenth-Century Autobiography." *American Quarterly* 40 (1988): 286-306.

Palmer, Colin A. *Slaves of White Gods: Blacks in Mexico.* Cambridge: Cambridge UP, 1976.

Pfefferkorn, Ignaz. *Sonora: A Description of the Province.* Albuquerque: U of New Mexico P, 1949.

Poyo, Gerald. "Immigrants and Integration in Late Eighteenth-Century Bexar." *Tejano Origins in Eighteenth Century San Antonio.* Eds. Gerald Poyo and Gilberto Hinojosa. Austin: U of Texas P, 1991.

Tinker Salas, Miguel. "In the Shadow of the Eagle, the Transformation of the Northern Frontier and the Evolution of the Border." Ms.

Robinson, Cecil. *Mexico and the Hispanic Southwest in American Literature.* Tucson: The U of Arizona P, 1977.

Rosales, Arturo F. "Chicano Art: A Reflection of the Community." *The Americas Review* 18 (1990): 65-66.

———. "Shifting Self Perceptions and Ethnic Consciousness Among Mexicans in Houston 1908-1946." *Aztlán* 16 (1985): 71-94.

Ruiz, Ramón E. "Spain in California: Facts and Fantasy in the State's History," *Frontier* 8 (1964): 15-17.

Sarrelangue López, Delfina Esmeralda. *La nobleza indígena de Pátzcuaro en la época virreinal.* México: UNAM, Instituto de Investigaciones Históricas, 1965.

Servin, Manuel Patricio. "The Beginnings of California's Anti-Mexican Prejudice." *An Awakened Minority: The Mexican Americans.* Ed. Manuel Patricio Servin. Beverly Hills, CA: Glencoe, 1974.

Simpson, Lesley Byrd. *The Ecomienda in New Spain: The Beginning of Spanish Mexico.* Berkeley: U of California P, 1950.

Spalding, William S. *History of Los Angeles City and County, Biographical, Vol. 2.* Los Angeles: J. R. Finnel & Sons, 1931

Taylor, Paul S. *A Spanish-Mexican Peasant Community: Arandas in Jalisco, Mexico.* Berkeley: U of California P, 1933.

Vallejo, Guadalupe. "An Indian Legend," *California Illustrated Magazine* 3 (1893): 783.

Weber, David J. *Foreigners in their Native Land: Historical Roots of Mexican Americans*. Albu-
    querque: U of New Mexico P, 1973.
_____. *The Spanish Frontier in North America*. New Haven: Yale UP, 1992.
_____. "The Spanish Legacy in North America and the Historical Imagination." *Western His-
    torical Quarterly* 23 (1992): 5-25.
_____. *Myth and History in the Hispanic Southwest*. Albuquerque: U of New Mexico P, 1987.

Outlaws or Religious Mystics? Public Identity and Los Penitentes in Mexican-American Autobiography

Margaret García Davidson

Miguel Antonio Otero and Nina Otero-Warren should occupy an important position in the recovery of an Hispanic literary tradition in the United States. They are certainly not obscure historical figures: both writers maintained active political careers and public lives in various positions of community service—Miguel Otero as governor of the New Mexico territory and Nina Otero as Superintendent of Schools for Santa Fe County. And, their major works—autobiographies written in English within a year of each other, 1935 and 1936 respectively—received relatively wide national circulation and were frequently reprinted.[1] Currently, selections from both books do appear in various new anthologies of Mexican-American literature. Yet these two writers stand at the margins of Mexican-American literary history, their works either ignored, dismissed, or distorted.

The explanation of this marginalization is clear: most critics of Chicano literature work within a tradition which focuses on cultural conflict as the defining element of Mexican-American literature. Early assessments by Luis Leal and Raymund Paredes perceive the Oteros as elitist, either favoring assimilation and a denial of ethnic identity or over-romanticizing a Spanish European heritage. Both Leal and Raymund Paredes demonstrate a profound discomfort with the Oteros for several reasons, but primarily because of what they perceive as a clear absence of any violent struggle, overt resistance, or opposition to American culture. As male critics, their discomfort appears distinctly gendered. They have offered a grudging acknowledgment of Miguel Otero's historical prominence and the subsequent value of his autobiography, while dismissing with disparaging haste Nina Otero's work. Nina Otero's *Old Spain in Our Southwest* discomfits these early critics for two related reasons:

a tone of "excessive romantic nostalgia" and the attendant privileging of an upper class way of life.

Any critic, looking for cultural conflict or social resistance in *Old Spain in Our Southwest* or *My Life on the Frontier*, is likely ultimately to be disappointed. I want to argue that in judging these early biographies in the contemporary terms of cultural conflict and social resistance, Chicano literary critics have failed to recover the works on their own terms and have, in effect dictated Chicano theory. In considering the broad historical context and the details of their respective lives, the Oteros' autobiographies may be seen as much more vexed, not so easily cast as favoring assimilation into (or resistance against) American culture or romanticizing a Spanish European ethnicity. The fact that the Oteros share a close family relationship as cousins a generation apart is little known outside New Mexico and is only one of many ways in which historical context complicates the reading of these texts. This complex family interaction is evident in the fact that Nina Otero referred to Miguel Otero as "uncle" and was frequently found at the governor's mansion while he was in office. In his autobiography, Miguel Otero often refers to Nina Otero, her mother, and stepfather without ever clarifying that these people are indeed his extended family. Knowledge of this family connection immediately enriches the complexity of intersections between the two texts and the two writers.

The autobiographies reflect a distinct border positioning; they are a product of "mixed blood, mixed marriages, and constantly intersecting cultures across private and public spheres of the Oteros' lives. Once again, attention to biographical detail enriches the reading of these texts. Miguel Otero represents a common phenomenon in the southwest border region: a mixture of races. The Oteros were a Spanish/Mexican family of several generations in New Mexico.[2] His mother's family was a prominent Southern family, the Blackwoods, of Charleston, South Carolina. As his autobiography describes, Otero came of age frequently traversing the eastern United States and the southwestern territory—experiencing not only geographic crossings, but cultural crossings as well. While Nina Otero is not literally a product of mixed blood, she grew up in a household with mixed cultures. Her father, Manuel B. Otero, was killed when she was two years old. Not long afterwards, her mother married an American, Alfred Bergere (a recent immigrant from Italy via a long stay in England), and hired an Irish nanny to help care for the children. Clearly, from childhood forward, both Oteros experienced a diverse mixture of cultures and languages.

Both autobiographies attempt to recapture life on a geographic border, that area of contested land between the United States and Mexico (now the southwestern United States, formerly Mexico's northern frontier). Not only is the setting a physical border landscape, but the texts reflect a border position in their use of time and language, in genre, and in their recent critical evaluation.

More recently, Genaro Padilla and Tey Diana Rebolledo read these texts somewhat differently, more positively. They emphasize the historical context of these works and point to certain ruptures and contradictions which read as strong evidence of a subtle cultural resistance written into the texts. Suggesting that many of these writers, especially the women (such as Nina Otero), wrote communal autobiographies rather than the more traditional history of the individual self, both Padilla and Rebolledo propose a broader definition of autobiography to include non-traditional texts, such as recipe books and family romances. Recalling a communal past through family and personal reminiscences suggests nostalgia not as a sign of submission but as an act of cultural resistance. Still, despite broadening the discussion of Chicana/o autobiography and thus revaluing the early texts, Padilla's theoretical position continues to reflect the discomfort of earlier critics and persists in defining these writers in terms of the social resistance and cultural conflict encoded within the texts.[3] Using feminist theory to take issue with these male critics and their easy dismissal of female writers, Rebolledo addresses class status as a necessary precursor providing these women the opportunity to write rather than engaging class status as a point of elitist political/cultural positioning. Like Padilla, Rebolledo's recent work continues to focus on the covert traces of resistance to both American culture and the Mexican American patriarchal system within which female writers and critics, alike, work.

The literal and metaphorical use of the border as a site of multiple intersections provides a more appropriate means for understanding and critically evaluating these autobiographies. The border is the site of intersections resulting in cultural conflict and social resistance—often literally, violently, and sometimes silently, figuratively. The border, however, is also the space of permeable boundaries where intersections result in mixtures, literally and figuratively: mixed blood, *mestizaje*; mixed language, *caló* or code switching between English and Spanish, adding English suffixes to Spanish verbs; mixed cultures—green chili on hamburgers, breakfast burritos at McDonald's. The border is often a space where intersecting cultures produce a *mestizaje*, in the sense that Gloria Anzaldúa proposes, wholly different from what occurs on either side of the border.[4] Critical emphasis on the politics of resistance tends to overlook the complexity and richness of these other various border intersections and the imaginative products of those intersections. I would argue in this paper that, while cultural conflict often plays an important role in defining Chicano literature, it is not always the primary feature of such early border texts as these autobiographies written by the Oteros.

Miguel Otero and Nina Otero-Warren reflect their roles as public representatives of their community and their ethnic group as Spanish/Mexican Americans. With an acute awareness of the complex public nature of their lives, both Oteros self-consciously negotiate the duality of being both Spanish/Mexican and American in their autobiographies. The intense socio-cultural focus of Americanization and nationalism during the early twentieth century further complicates their efforts to relate the multiple stories of intersecting cultures. As public figures, their ethnic identities become complex subtexts written against negative stereotypes of the Mexican and the Spanish. For the Oteros, culture and ethnicity become an unspoken private element of a written public self: the tension between public and private shapes the ways in which culture and ethnicity are inscribed when writing the self.

Consider one such point of intersection between the two Otero texts: their very separate and divergent treatments of a well-publicized religious ceremony specific to the Spanish/Mexican population of northern New Mexico and southern Colorado—the Penitente ritual during Holy Week. The Penitente ritual is an often literal re-enactment of Christ's crucifixion, complete with self-flagellation, cross-bearing, and other severe forms of penance, as a deeply spiritual expression of faith and not simply a dramatic art form.[5] The Penitentes themselves are a strictly male brotherhood often known as Los Hermanos de Sangre [the Brothers of Blood] or Los Hermanos de Luz [the Brothers of Light]. Los Hermanos eventually went underground and became a closed secret fraternity at some point after the U.S./Mexico War in 1848 when the southwest became U.S. territory. While mostly known for their religious ceremonies during Holy Week, the brotherhood also played an integral role in the daily self-governing of their respective communities, both in meting out justice when necessary and in caring for families in need. Most male members of the community belonged to the brotherhood, a de facto form of community self-reliance due to their geographic isolation and relatively small numbers.

Between the 1850s and the 1930s when the Oteros describe the Penitentes, much misinformation and confusion surrounded the group, centering specifically on the Holy Week ritual. According to Marta Weigle, by the 1930s and continuing through the present, the exact origin of the Penitentes remains vague with strong arguments to refute both the theory grounded in medieval Spanish Catholicism as well as the theory based on the ancient Aztec blood ceremonies. Membership in the Penitentes often remains uncertain in some communities and the brotherhood continues to resist complete documentation by either themselves or the ubiquitous cultural anthropologists who study the southwest.

Historically, as Americans moved westward into this territory and encountered the Penitentes they were both horrified and fascinated by the religious expression demonstrated in the ritual. Predominantly Protestants with a long history of mistrusting Roman Catholicism, these newcomers sometimes developed a virulent anti-Catholic sentiment due to a misunderstanding of the way in which religion permeated daily life in these communities. The first descriptions of the Penitente rituals fed an insatiable American taste for any romantic and/or exotic tale of the West, thus becoming popular material for endless newspaper articles and some romance novels—all of which were written by Anglo Americans, outsiders to the communities they described. Frequent newspaper accounts easily contributed to the perception of the ritual as spectacle. Most reports exaggerated and sensationalized the Penitente ceremony despite claims to being "eye-witness" accounts. In these descriptions of the Penitentes, a curious split occurs according to the gender of the particular author.

The two earliest Anglo American recorders were Charles F. Lummis in *The Land of Poco Tiempo* (1889) and Alexander M. Darley in *The Passionates of the Southwest, or The Holy Brotherhood: A Revelation of the Penitentes* (1893). A Presbyterian minister, Darley is especially vituperative and anti-Catholic in his portrayal of a ritual he terms "barbaric" while exaggerating in great detail (complete with drawings) a bloody violence in the penitential rites. Lummis, a newspaper reporter turned western travel writer, describes the Penitentes in more circumspect but equally critical terms. His account of the Penitentes becomes particularly famous for the photographs, the first of their kind, he was able to take during the Holy Week rites at San Mateo, New Mexico, in 1888. For Lummis, the Penitentes, as much as the southwest generally, were a romantic, exotic landscape both harsh and primitive, sometimes questionably beautiful.[6]

With the women writers, Mary Austin, Alice Corbin Henderson, and Dorothy Woodward, the Penitentes and their rituals receive a more sympathetic and complete portrayal in keeping with an historical religious context of Christianity. Mary Austin, the earliest of these writers, publishes her description of the Penitentes in her book, *The Land of Journeys' Ending*.[7] Though clearly a more accurate, respectful portrayal, the title, "The Trail of the Blood," continues to play on the American appetite for the sensational. Both Henderson and Woodward write their descriptions in the 1930s, contemporaneous with the Oteros. Woodward's *The Penitentes of New Mexico* was an unpublished scholarly study of the religious and social context of the brotherhood, submitted as her Ph.D. thesis to Yale in 1935. Henderson's *Brothers of the Light* (1937) provided a more general, secular approach to the Penitentes, finding a certain mystical beauty in their religious expressions.[8] Both Austin's and Woodward's descriptions become the basis for further scholarship on the Penitentes during the 1970s by Marta Weigle. While providing a necessary corrective, these female voices arrive on the scene much later and must work against a voluminous journalistic record sensationalizing the Penitente ritual.

The published material on the Penitentes received wide circulation and became inscribed on the American public consciousness, inextricably linked to New Mexico and identified as a cultural marker for Mexican-Americans. Significantly, Mexican-American writers maintained a curious silence on the subject of the Penitentes. By describing the Penitentes in their autobiographies, the Oteros become two of the first known Mexican-Americans to approach the subject in a national forum.[9] Given this background regarding the widespread public awareness of the Penitentes filtered through (Protestant) Anglo American consciousness, the Oteros' inclusion of this religious ceremony complicates the issue of ethnicity in their individual texts. The Oteros' description of the Penitente ritual bears closer examination for the ways in which it reveals construction of an ethnic identity for the community as well as for the individual writers. Because these descriptions are contemporaneous, written within a close extended family context, and represent both male and female perceptions, the Oteros' attention to the Penitentes also provides an especially rich and complex reading of gender differences and the overlapping intersection of private and public lives.

A striking comparison of issues of gender and ethnic identity within autobiography can be made when we compare Miguel Otero's brief description of the Penitentes with Nina Otero's description of the Holy Week Processional. Writing styles aside, the approach and information provided (or selectively omitted) radically differ between the two narratives. Nevertheless, both Oteros seem to share a common goal in their explanation of the Penitentes: to correct the stereotypical image that linked this negative and frequently sensationalized public portrayal of the Penitente ritual to the ethnic identity of their community and thus by extension to themselves, as public representatives of that community. While employing broadly different writing strategies and playing off the expectation of the sensational, both Oteros distance themselves from and write against this ritual as the exotic. In attempting to correct the negative public perception linking the Penitente ritual as a cultural marker to the Mexican American ethnic identity, both Oteros reflect the complexity of intersecting cultures. Such complexity includes a certain degree of social resistance and much more that is not resistance but perhaps an example of cultural identity in transition—an imaginative weaving of multiple private and public roles as borders are crossed and re-crossed.

Miguel Otero writes within the traditional boundaries of autobiography, producing a three-volume work charting his boyhood from 1864 through adulthood to the end of his term as governor in 1906. He purposely attempts to write the history of the southwest as national public autobiography and, consequently, the development of the self shrinks in direct relation to the broad frontier landscape and the immensity of U.S. westward expansion. He writes the story of both his own coming of age and that of the southwest. The autobiographical self-portrait only begins to catch up with this larger-than-life view of the southwest in his third volume, when Otero himself becomes a larger-than-life public figure as the territorial governor of New Mexico, the first Mexican-American in such a position of power. From this position of public authority, bridging two cultures and two centuries, Otero looks backward to re-create his own coming of age and the "coming of age" of both a people and a geographic area.

In *My Life on the Frontier: 1882-1897*, the second volume of this autobiography, Miguel Otero deliberately confronts the sensationalization of the Penitente ritual by acknowledging "the widespread publicity such events have had for the last fifty years" (46). In fact, he clearly states that he is writing about them because he has been asked to, because this is a topic people are intensely curious about, and because his own personal history has been inextricably tied to that of New Mexico, and thus he is by default linked to any event related to the state's history. Otero does not present himself as an active participant in the Penitente ritual. In fact, the source of his knowledge remains vague and with good reason, considering his emphasis on the sensationalized, negative image of the Penitente ritual. Miguel Otero deliberately exaggerates the negative perception of the Penitente ritual by emphasizing its lawlessness and deconstructing its religious implications. With such a strategy, he creates a distance between the Penitentes and himself—effectively disassociating the Penitentes from the general Mexican American community.

He first identifies the Penitentes as a vague group—"those classes of natives where ignorance predominates" which includes "some of the lowest and meanest of the natives," whose secretive ritual has more to do with cattle rustling than religion (46-7). Thus he splits the community and creates a sense of difference, an "Other" within his own ethnic group. But even this attempt to split the group and rupture the link between the Penitentes and ethnic identification doesn't quite work. He has to qualify his statement about "those classes of natives" by acknowledging that while "many of the most prominent native New Mexicans were Penitentes" that was *in the past*. This particular qualification creates a problematic space for several reasons. First, "prominent native New Mexicans" as a group elides any direct mention of his own or his family's participation in the Penitente group, but also suggests that as prominent New Mexicans themselves the possibility exists, especially considering the detailed information on the ritual which follows and which evades any direct reference to the source of such information. Otero hastens to explain that in the past the reasons for belonging to the Penitentes were predominantly political, inferring that membership had more to do with campaigning for office rather than with religious beliefs. Once again he emphasizes an alternate reason for the existence of the Penitentes: maybe it's politics or maybe it's cattle rustling, but it isn't religion.[10]

In fact, his very next disclaimer has to do with the relationship of the Catholic Church to the Penitentes. He takes great pains to separate the Church from the Penitente rituals, pointing out that both the Pope and Archbishop Lamy had long since officially ordered their disbandment.[11] With Catholicism so obviously a cultural marker of ethnicity for Mexican Americans, it is apparent that Otero's effort to distance the church from the Penitentes is also an effort to weaken that link between the Penitentes and ethnic identity. The distancing is only partially successful and Otero retains some discomfort in reiterating that the group still exists, that New Mexico is the "only place that can still boast (or rather lament)" their existence among its inhabitants. Otero's discomfort is evident in his choice of words—the "boast" that is more properly a "lament."

Curiously, after so many qualifications, attempts at disassociation and efforts to disparage the religious thrust of the ritual, Miguel Otero then proceeds to describe the Penitentes in great detail. Otero's description emphasizes the blood and pain of the ritual in much the same manner as earlier American journalistic reports. Not only does he go into great detail in his own narrative, but he repeats the description with a first-hand account of the ritual quoted at length from a local newspaper. The gender difference is particularly strident: while the female autobiography is twice-silenced on this male ritual, the male autobiography shouts from the page with excessive attention to particulars of the violent self-flagellation and other severe penitential rites. Such exaggerated attention to this ritual, already widely sensationalized, effectively disrupts its association as a marker of ethnic identity for Miguel Otero. However, it also has the dubious consequence of allowing the negative stereotype to continue unchecked.

In contrast, Nina Otero-Warren confronts the negative stereotype of the Spanish/Mexican American Penitente ritual by indirectly describing it within the context of daily life events. The chapter entitled "Holy Week Processional" is just one in a series of efforts to explain and demystify Catholicism as practiced by Mexican Americans for a distinctly Anglo American and non-Catholic audience. She attempts to show Catholicism as a lived communal religion, not casually or esoterically practiced, but deeply saturating the social and economic fabric of everyday life. In this larger context, the Penitentes are shown as part of the seasonal rhythmic expression of religion. Thus, Otero-Warren shifts the emphasis and frustrates expectations by focusing on "Holy Week" and Lenten ceremonies generally, rather than the Penitentes as a particular, secret group. Her description of the prayer service, however, avoids any direct description of the Penitentes or their active participation in the ritual other than as the disembodied chant of voices, focusing instead on the ambiance of ritual spirituality.

The autobiographical I (both self and eye) emerges as the central participant in and observer of the Penitente ritual. The self and not the Penitentes becomes the focus of the description as she writes:

> *I went* to a small village on this day to pray with the Penitentes... *My heart* was beating fast in anticipation of what was to follow... *I knelt* in front of the candles... *I had a feeling* that the church was crowded... *I joined* in the response... *I was* the only woman in the midst of the group [emphasis added]. (81)

The descriptive emphasis in this chapter shifts from observation to the narrator's direct emotional experience of the prayer service, omitting any significant details about the actual cause of their emotions. As the only woman present, her casual acknowledgment of this fact opens the text to speculation that this is not an ordinary religious service with full community participation. Still, Otero-Warren remains silent about the secrecy surrounding this all-male ritual, concentrating instead on the chants, the music, the processional walk in the dark, rather than providing any information about the presence of the Penitentes themselves or their participation in the ceremony.

Her description of the cross also opens the text to ambiguity by the things expected but left unsaid:

> Suddenly, the light of a lantern reflected an object—the *Calvario*. The senses around me became distinct. The moon was coming up, shedding a yellow glow over the canyons. The cross at the foot of the moonlit mountains; the arms outstretched in prayer! (81)

The lantern and the moon cast light, revealing the scene, the cross, in detail, but it is a detail known only to the narrator and not revealed to the reader.

So much of the sensationalism regarding the Penitentes hinges on the rituals surrounding their re-enactment of Christ's crucifixion, that the deliberate omission of that part of the ritual provides some interesting insight regarding both issues of ethnic identity and gender. Unlike her cousin's detailed description of the ritual itself, Nina Otero chooses to focus her description on the atmosphere surrounding the ritual, the sounds of the music and the night, the effects of the lighting and the landscape, and her own emotions, not the actual Penitente rites. By focusing on the atmosphere and her own reactions, she removes from the public eye those acts misperceived as spectacle. She creates a more familiar sense of spirituality and religious worship out of a ritual where many readers would expect the extraordinary, the unfamiliar, the exotic. In part, this approach reflects a woman twice silenced because she is participating in both a secret and a particularly all-male ritual. As a secret ritual, despite the many "eye-witness" newspaper accounts, participants and guests were expected to maintain a silence about the actual events of the ritual. As the only woman participant in this particular ritual, her silence suggests that her very presence was illicit in the group and necessarily secret to the male participants. In fact, as she describes her presence in the chapel, she implies a certain invisibility—she does not actually see the Penitentes; she "feels" their presence; she "has a feeling that the church was crowded." The implied invisibility works both ways: she does not see the Penitentes and they do not see her. Thus, the strategy of invisibility only works with an agreement to silence; she can write about her participation in the prayer service but she may not write about the service itself.

Her silence and emphasis on atmosphere rather than actual acts also suggests a deliberate feminine strategy in writing against violent, negative stereotypes through their omission and replacement with an attention to the aesthetic in much the same vein as the Anglo American women writers—Austin, Henderson, and to some extent, Woodward. She uses autobiographical experience, her participation in the prayer service, to distance herself and the community from the violence, inverting the perception of the ritual and maintaining silence regarding the matter of self-punishment. The result is a Penitente ritual transformed from the exotic and sensational to the unadorned Gregorian chant, to prayer and singing, music and moonlight, an expression of devotion more understandable and less horrifying to her audience.

Given the controversial perception of the Penitentes from within their own communities and the clearly outrageous public perception of the Penitentes from without, it is remarkable that the Oteros confront those perceptions, acknowledging the implicit negative connotations associated with the brotherhood and by extension to all Spanish/Mexican Americans. Their willingness to re-write the Penitente ritual, thereby defusing those negative perceptions, suggests a complex negotiation between cultural conflict and accommodation. Writing on and from the border, neither Otero commits to a definable or overwhelming resistance to American culture. Nina Otero-Warren provides an undeniably romantic vision of the Penitente ritual, aligning herself with the brotherhood as a personal expression of faith while very nearly creating an unrecognizable portrait of the Penitentes. Conversely, Miguel Otero attempts to distance himself as much as possible from the Penitentes, and often sounds remarkably like the earlier American reporters of the ritual. Regardless of his vigorous dismissal of the Penitentes as a cultural marker for his ethnic group, Miguel Otero appears to further implicate himself with his intimate knowledge of the ritual simultaneously with his efforts to clearly disassociate himself, and Mexican Americans generally, from the brotherhood. In their texts, both Oteros reflect an acute awareness of public positions which both separate them from and connect them to the Penitentes. Neither Otero would be read comfortably (or seriously) by those Chicano historians who view the Penitentes themselves as one of the strongest, earliest examples of active social resistance in the southwest. The Oteros do provide a complex view of the intersecting cultures by acknowledging and trying to negotiate the various perceptions and misperceptions of the Spanish/Mexican American community.

Both Oteros are deeply concerned with clarifying those cultural or religious markers which reflect ethnicity, such as the Penitente ritual. Their strategies for dealing with those markers of ethnicity ultimately irritate and annoy critics of this literature; yet, those same "irritants" complicate and enrich their autobiographies. The resulting ambivalence of narrative strategies which draw from mixed cultures (i.e., Spanish, and Mexican, and American) to explain markers specific to one culture (Spanish/Mexican) can suggest denial of ethnic identity—a politics very much at odds with current ideologies of cultural resistance. Or, such strategies can suggest, perhaps at best, some combination of an encoded resistance and accommodation—a problematic, but necessary, politics of survival, an example of cultural identity in transition. How an audience reads this ambivalence very much depends on a willingness to allow space for contradictory impulses, acknowledging resistance as one element among many within a border geography. The conflicting tensions between accommodation and resistance are not only inscribed into these autobiographies as an act of writing the self, but these tensions are also inscribed into the act of reading as literary critics evaluate the texts. If we are to recover the Hispanic literary tradition, we must come to terms with these writers who resist our resistance.

Notes

[1]Miguel Antonio Otero published the first volume of his autobiography, *My Life on the Frontier: 1864-1882* in 1935, followed by two more volumes, *My Life on the Frontier: 1882-1897* (1939) and *My Nine Years as Governor of the Territory of New Mexico: 1897-1906* (1940). While Miguel Otero's autobiography fits within the traditional definition of this genre, Nina Otero's only book, *Old Spain in Our Southwest*, borrows from many genres, but is firmly anchored in autobiography, although in a non-traditional sense, as I argue in my dissertation.

[2]I use the term "Spanish/Mexican" in describing both Oteros to accurately reflect their own usage of terms in self-identification (most frequently as "Spanish American") as well as the historical usage of "Mexican American" to generally identify the native population of New Mexico and the Southwest after 1848.

[3]While Padilla continues to demonstrate some discomfort with the class issues presented by these early writers, he also self-consciously examines his own aversion. In a recent conversation,

he has suggested that "by acknowledging them as 'antepasados' [forebears], I assent my affiliation with them."

[4]In *Culture and Truth*, Renato Rosaldo describes the border as those "blurred zones in between" where mixtures occur as a "little of this and a little of that, and not quite one or the other," resulting in something he terms "hybrid invisibility" (209). It would seem that critics of Chicano literature, in focusing exclusively on social resistance, frequently prove Rosaldo's point that the hybrid, or *mestizaje*, is indeed an invisible element in the border landscape.

[5]Marta Weigle describes the "supervised expressions of the penitential spirit" in *Brothers of Light, Brothers of Blood: The Penitentes of the Southwest* (xi). Although somewhat problematic because of its reliance on these earlier studies, at present her research remains the most scholarly and detailed source of information on the history of the Penitente brotherhood and their ceremonial rituals.

[6]Weigle cites the beginning of outside interest in the Penitentes with the "highly emotional and inaccurate accounts" written by Lummis and Darley (282).

[7]Austin first published this description of the Penitentes in *Century Magazine* in 1924.

[8]Weigle finds Henderson's text "the most sensitive and beautiful outsider's account" of the Penitente ritual but "less sound historically" than Austin or Woodward (283).

[9]The only other currently known Mexican-American writers to describe the Penitentes early in this century are Aurelio M. Espinosa and Ely Leyba, who published articles in magazines with specific and limited readerships, i.e., *The Catholic Encyclopedia* (1911) and *New Mexico Magazine* (1932), respectively.

[10]The effect of class status on markers of ethnic identity is clearly present in Otero's discussion of who the Penitente members were and their subsequent identification as either politicians or cattle thieves. The negative tone associated with the lower class is a factor which continually disconcerts literary critics because it suggests an elitist attitude and a denial of ethnic identity—a politics directly at odds with an ideology of social resistance.

[11]While the Catholic Church officially denounced and disassociated themselves with Los Hermanos publicly, Woodward and Weigle document a very ambivalent relationship between the Church and the Penitentes. In practice, local priests often privately supported and participated in the Penitente ritual. Furthermore, since the 1850s the Church at various times attempted to recognize the Penitentes' affiliation with Catholicism.

Works Cited

Anzaldúa, Gloria. *Borderlands/La Frontera: The New Mestiza*. San Francisco: Spinsters/Aunt Lute, 1987.

Austin, Mary. "The Trail of the Blood." *The Land of Journeys' Ending*. Tucson: UA, 1983, c1924. 349-72.

Darley, Alexander M. *The Passionates of the Southwest, or, The Holy Brotherhood*. Pueblo, CO: 1893.

Henderson, Alice Corbin. *Brothers of Light: The Penitentes of the Southwest*. New York: Harcourt, Brace, 1937.

Leal, Luis. Mexican American Literature: A Historical Perspective," *Modern Chicano Writers: A Collection of Critical Essays*. Eds. Joseph Sommers and Tomás Ybarra-Frausto. Englewood Cliffs: Prentice Hall, 1979. 18-30.

Otero, Miguel Antonio. *My Life on the Frontier: 1864-1882*. New York: Press of the Pioneers, 1935.

_____. *My Life on the Frontier: 1882-1897*. Albuquerque: U of New Mexico P, 1939.

Otero, Miguel Antonio. *My Nine Years as Governor of the Territory of New Mexico: 1897-1906.* Albuquerque: U of New Mexico P, 1940.

Otero-Warren, Nina. *Old Spain in Our Southwest.* New York: Harcourt Brace, 1936.

Padilla, Genaro. "Recovering Mexican-American Autobiography," *Recovering the U.S. Hispanic Literary Heritage.* Eds. Ramón Gutiérrez and Genaro Padilla. Houston: Arte Público, 1993. 153-78.

Paredes, Raymund A. "The Evolution of Chicano Literature," *Three American Literatures: Essays in Chicano, Native American, and Asian-American Literature for Teachers of American Literature.* Ed. Houston A. Baker, Jr. New York: MLA, 1982. 33-79.

Rebolledo, Tey Diana. "Narrative Strategies of Resistance in Hispana Writing." *The Journal of Narrative Technique* 20 (Spring 1990) 2: 134-46.

Rosaldo, Renato. *Culture and Truth: The Remaking of Social Analysis.* Boston: Beacon, 1989.

Weigle, Marta. Brothers of Light, *Brothers of Blood: The Penitentes of the Southwest.* Albuquerque: U of New Mexico P, 1976.

Woodward, Dorothy. *The Penitentes of New Mexico.* New Haven: Yale UP, 1935.

"We can starve too": Américo Paredes' *George Washington Gómez* and the Proletarian *Corrido*

Tim Libretti

In analyzing the folk base of contemporary Chicano narrative and its relation to the corrido tradition, Ramón Saldívar argues "that contemporary Chicano narratives and other forms of novelistic discourse are to problematic mid-twentieth-century society what the epic heroic corrido was to the integrated world of the late nineteenth and early twentieth centuries: self-consciously crafted acts of social resistance" (42). Chicano narrative emerged for Saldívar as a transitional form historically situated "between an integrated but distant heroic past and a fragmented and all-too-present reality" (47). This "shift from one symbolic form to another" demarcates, he argues, "the end of one historical experience and the beginning of another historical stage" (42). This shift or transition, however, should not be understood as an historical or cultural discontinuity, for the emergent practice of Chicano narrative still finds its conditions of production, its informing cultural politics, within the residual form of the corrido. Indeed, for Saldívar, one must understand "the corrido as a vital item of Chicano cultural politics and as a substantial part of the folk base of Chicano narrative" in order to establish "the historical specificity of that narrative and its work of resistance to the conditions of advanced postmodern American capitalism" (42).

The recovery of Américo Paredes' 1930s novel *George Washington Gómez* offers new empirical ground and thus presents a unique opportunity for studying this shift as the novel dramatizes both the decline of the corrido in its traditional ballad form with the concomitant and tragic forgetfulness of its resistance politics, as well as the necessity for maintaining and transforming the corrido as a way of seeking a new form to meet and comprehend the changing political requirements of the 1930s. Indeed, it is precisely in response to the changes and crisis in the developing capitalist order that Paredes attempts to transform the corrido ballad into novelistic form and to reformulate resistance from the order of cultural struggle to a more overtly articulated program of class and anti-colonial nationalist struggle. In this paper, then, I want to look at the way in which Paredes uses and transforms the corrido in the novel as a way of rethinking resistance to Anglo domination or encroachment figured as a symptom of capitalist imperialist expansion. Specifically, I will argue that the novel reconceives the relation between race, class, culture, and nation, effectively rewriting the master narrative of class struggle to include the specific conditions of Chicanos and to highlight the agency of Chicanos in those struggles. Paredes accomplishes this political and cultural transformation through a synthesis or hybridization of the traditional corrido form with the then emergent form of literary class struggle, the proletarian novel.

Written against the backdrop of the Great Depression, *George Washington Gómez* can be read as responding to and negotiating between the political programs being forwarded by middle-class Mexican-American organizations such as the League of United Latin American Citizens (LULAC) and by the Left, mainly the Communist Party during the Popular Front era. The synthesis of the traditional form of Mexican-American resistance, the corrido, and the rapidly developing literary form of class struggle, the proletarian novel, provided the cultural solution to the complex political questions facing Mexican-Americans. Where do they fit in the class struggle? What is the role of nationalism or culture in the class struggle? How do racial minorities fit in with or assert themselves as members of the working class within the working class struggle? In *George Washington Gómez*, we see a hybrid of the typical thematics of Chicano literature (identity, anti-assimilation, historical memory) and the revolutionary thematics of the proletarian literary movement of the 1930s in the midst of which Paredes was writing. Indeed, the novel's proletarian milieu resembles that of the folkloric corrido and its socially symbolic acts of resistance. Thus, in thinking about the importance of the recovery of Paredes' novel, this paper will also explore the significance of the dual generic associations of the novel in terms of its potential for leading to the creation of new paradigms for organizing and rethinking the contemporary space of Chicano literature and for theorizing the intersection of Chicano literature with other resistance genres.

As with any moment of intense political, social, and cultural ferment, the Great Depression gave rise to liberating new paradigms for discussing and assessing literary practice, overthrowing previously dominant critical and literary tendencies. *George Washington Gómez* helps us rethink the thirties even further. Américo Paredes is already well-known for his scholarly and theoretical work on the corrido form *With His Pistol in His Hand*—as well as a host of essays on the corrido and the related subjects of folklore and culture on the Texas-Mexican border—which gave rise to what has been perhaps a central paradigm for discussing and assessing Chicano literary works as well as for organizing and defining the ideological determinants and limits of the Chicano literary field as a whole. The recovery of *George Washington Gómez*, however, allows us to measure the differences between Paredes' theoretical work on the corrido form against his creative practice of the corrido in this novel. What we see is that while his creative practice in part ratifies his associated critical tenets, the novel also outdistances those tenets as well in ways that call for a rethinking of the corrido tradition and form in Chicano narrative. Paredes plays the role of Fanon's native intellectual recuperating and modifying remnants of national culture as a way of reinvigorating and remolding national consciousness and also redefining the struggle that constitutes the task of the day. He is one of Fanon's storytellers,

> who used to relate inert episodes [but] now bring[s] them alive and introduce[s] into them modifications which are increasingly fundamental. There is a tendency to bring conflicts up to date and to modernize the kinds of struggle which the stories evoke, together with the names and heroes and types of weapons. The method of allusion is more and more widely used. The formula "This all happened long ago" is substituted with that of "What we are going to speak of happened somewhere else, but it might well have happened here today, and it might happen here tomorrow. (Fanon 240)

Paredes updates the struggle by dramatizing precisely the shift in historical stages that Saldívar mentions and by modifying the corrido to encode and express a program of class rather than border struggle, infusing a proletarian element into the traditional form.

The corrido, for Paredes, is an inherently political or confrontational form, but it is one that locates the site of political struggle in the sphere of culture. "Border conflict," Paredes argues, "a cultural clash between Mexican and American, gives rise to the Texas-Mexican corrido" (*Pistol* 140). Paredes actually identifies the outlaws against Porfirio Diaz's regime in the 1880s as "the first important corrido heroes of Greater Mexico" (*Pistol* 143). But, Paredes argues, "since these men symbolized a struggle between classes rather than cultural strife, the ballads about them were of a proletarian cast" (143). However, as the corrido becomes the dominant form of Lower Border Balladry, as it enters "its decadent period in the 1930s," it is evolving, Paredes argues, "toward one theme, border conflict; toward one concept of the hero, the man fighting for his right with his pistol in his hand" (149). The corridos portraying cultural strife on the border displace those of a proletarian cast:

Border conflict dominates as a theme. The old ballad subjects,dealing mostly with the everyday activities of the Rio Grande folk lose much of their interest. Ballads are received from Greater Mexico, from Cuba, and even from the United States, but their themes, mostly proletarian, are not imitated… The proletarian ballad's concept of the hero as an outlaw who robs the rich to give to the poor does not gain acceptance…." (149-150)

In *George Washington Gómez*, Paredes restores a proletarian content to the novelistic corrido and reimagines the conflict as centering not on the geopolitical borders between Mexico and America but on the borders between classes, in this sense anticipating Gloria Anzaldúa's assertion that "the border-lands are physically present wherever two or more cultures edge each other, where people of different races occupy the same territory, where under, lower, middle and upper classes touch…" (Preface). The dynamics of power on the border are not understood as simply cultural strife but as having a deeply class character that requires, in resistance, theorizing and engaging in class struggle. It is important to note that in the novel Paredes does not dismiss cultural struggle in favor of class struggle but rather adopts a more complex view that sees cultural struggle for colonized people as inherently political and a crucial aspect not only of class struggle as it is traditionally and narrowly defined but as an aspect of the national liberation struggle which the novel projects—in the spirit of Frantz Fanon and Amílcar Cabral—as a phase of the class struggle for colonized and internally colonized peoples. Paredes, then, effectively retheorizes the cultural practice of the corrido based on an interpretation of the relation between class and nation in his vision of cultural resistance.

The novel opens with a section titled "Los Sediciosos" [The Seditionists] in reference to an actual corrido written in 1915 by a group of Mexicans held prisoner in Monterrey, Mexico for their participation in the "Plan de San Diego," a campaign to set up a Spanish-speaking Republic of the Southwest, the event which the corrido commemorates. This history is somewhat fictionalized in Paredes account, as he changes names to protect the militant—the actual leader of the movement Aniceto Pizaña becomes in the novel Anicleto Peña. Beginning the novel this way, Paredes, with an almost painful and lamenting nostalgia, recovers this historical moment as well as the cultural form that contains, transmits, and, in a sense, bears witness to it. At the same time he dramatizes the loss of this historical and cultural tradition as a model of resistance for future generations. It is in the midst of these events that the title character George Washington Gómez is born. He is the son of Gumersindo, a character who looks white, who reads gringo newspapers, who believes the gringo pastor's preachings of brotherhood despite the advice of his militant brother Feliciano that "it was all very well for him, who came from up north to talk about love between all men and everybody being brothers. And it was all very well for Gumersindo who came from the interior of Mexico to be taken in by such talk. But a border Mexican knew there was no brotherhood of men" (19). Gumersindo refers to Texas as "their country," forfeiting all right and connection to the land and ceding to Anglo colonization. He has lost faith, he tells Feliciano, in the nationalist struggle. Ironically, it is Gumersindo who is murdered in a confrontation with the rinches [Rangers] who are looking for his militant brother-in-law Lupe. As Feliciano finds him on the brink of death, Gumersindo implores Feliciano not ever to tell his son how he died: "My son. Mustn't know. Ever. No hate, no hate" (21). Feliciano argues but reluctantly promises not to tell George Washington Gómez, in a sense repressing that history of resistance and confrontation that informs his identity, depriving him of that cultural and historical memory. For Paredes writing in the 1930s, this moment, this failure of cultural and historical transmission, constitutes the threat of the disappearance of the corrido and its politics of resistance.

The novel serves prophetic notice of the consequences of this loss and simultaneously registers the changing economic and political conditions that call for cultural models of resistance that comprehend the specific history of oppression and struggle informing the Mexican-American experience in Texas. In Part II titled "Jonesville-On the Grande," Paredes chronicles the colonization of the Southwest and the concomitant process of the proletarianization of the Mexicans divested of their land:

> Mexicans labored with axe and spade to clear away the brush where the cattle of their ancestors once had roamed. To make room for the truck farming and citrus groves. And the settlers poured in from the U.S. heartland, while Mexicans were pushed out of cattle raising into hard manual labor...the American had begun to "develop" the land. He had it cleared and made into cotton fields, into citrus orchards and towns. And it was the Mexicotexan's brown muscular arms that felled the trees. He wielded the machete against the smaller brush and strained his back pulling tree stumps out of the ground. For this he got enough to eat for the day and the promise of more of the same tomorrow. (36, 42)

Paredes registers here the building of the U.S. nation through the extraction of surplus value and labor from the Mexicotexans' bodies, invoking the shift from a precapitalist small agrarian land-based economy to capitalist economy based on a system of wage-labor. Moving from Part I, where Paredes rehearses the traditional corrido of border conflict in which the men with pistols in their hands attempt to recover the Southwest territory, to Part II, in which he represents the thorough displacement of the Mexicotexans from the land into wage labor, the novel suggests the need for an updated corrido.

In the spirit of Fanon's storyteller, Paredes updates this form thereby highlighting the class aspect of the Mexicotexan experience and constructing a novelistic class consciousness that will comprehend the racial patriarchal class system and, specifically, the positioning of the Chicano in relation to those economic, ideological, and cultural forces. He fosters this class consciousness in the narrative by setting the Chicano experience in the context of the broader depression era national economy as a way of highlighting the super-exploitation and poverty the Mexicotexans have endured in relation to other Americans. Indeed, conditions such as those that prevailed during the depression seemed unimaginable and a more impoverished situation impossible. Paredes writes in Part IV titled "La Chilla":

> For some time now, the newspapers had been telling of strange things happening in the North. Men were blowing out their brains in Chicago. In New York City they were jumping out of tall buildings and smearing themselves all over the pavement below. Businesses were going broke, and breadlines were coming into existence. But in Texas, especially its southern tip, things seemed to be normal, almost prosperous. The truck farmers and orchard owners still sold their produce, spent part of their earnings and banked the rest. For the Delta, the Great Depression still was far away. And to the Mexican laborer who tilled the American landowner's fields and orchards, such a thing as a depression was beyond his understanding. He could not imagine a state of things where he would be poorer than he already was. He heard about the people of Oklahoma, who were leaving their land, getting on their trucks and going west. To the Mexicotexan laborer, anybody who owned a truck was rich. He heard of some sharecropper families who had nothing but flour and bacon. The Mexican laborer, who had subsisted on tortillas most of his life, wondered how people who could afford biscuits and bacon could be poor. (194-5)

Representing typical literary depression scenes effected by the stock market crash of 1929—really the beginning of the 1930s proletarian literary tradition—and contrasting them with very different experience of the Mexican laborer in the Southwest, Paredes at once invokes his text's relation to the proletarian novel form but also marks its difference from that form. Working within the proletarian form, Paredes identifies the work as a narrative of class struggle; but by bringing to bear the specificity of the Mexican working class and national experience on the proletarian literary form, Paredes complicates and expands the parameters of the form and rewrites traditional narratives of class struggle to incorporate the national struggle of the internally colonized Texas Mexicans. This strategy allows Paredes to identify the Mexican laborer as part of and in solidarity with the working class—exemplified by the farmworkers complaint in the novel, "We can starve too" (199)—and also to highlight the unique circumstances of racial and class oppression the Mexican laborer endures. Indeed, Paredes even emphasizes the specificity of the Mexican racial experience in the U.S., writing:

> In the United States, he is not the only racial group that often finds the going hard. But while their are rich Negroes and poor Negroes, rich Jews and poor Jews, rich Italians and Poles, and poor Italians and Poles, there are in Texas only poor Mexicans. Spanish-speaking people in the Southwest are divided into two categories: poor Mexicans and rich Spaniards. So while rich Negroes often help poor Negroes and rich Jews help poor Jews, the Texas-Mexican has to shift for himself. (195-6)

Marking the difference of the class experience as lived through race, Paredes accentuates the need to find a race- or culture-specific form to register class consciousness which incorporates features of but establishes its difference from the dominant proletarian novel of the 1930s; for, as E.P. Thompson argues, "Class-consciousness is the way in which [class] experiences are handled in cultural terms: embodied in traditions, value-systems, ideas, and institutional forms"(10). Paredes's novel, representing the Texas-Mexican as one who must "shift for himself," underlines the national or colonial character of the Texas-Mexican struggle and asserts the centrality of cultural practice and struggle in the national/class struggle. Writing in 1930, Paredes takes up what would later be Amilcar Cabral's call to "return to the source"—to revitalize and learn the hidden and distorted and almost erased cultures that the colonizers have tried to wipe out as part of their struggle to dominate colonies in the Third World and, in the case of Mexicans, "internal colonies" in the U.S.

The theme of the "return to the source" is dramatized precariously through the development of the protagonist George Washington Gómez. The novel is essentially a bildungsroman that charts the ambiguous and ambivalent social development of Guálinto as he walks a tightrope between Anglo and Mexican culture. Although Guálinto has no knowledge of the true history of his father's death (and later when he does learn he wrongly blames Feliciano for his death, thus eschewing the radical past of resistance he represents), he does have some knowledge of Texas-Mexican folklore and an uncertain sense of the revolutionary past: "The Revolution was a household word, but half-understood by Guálinto. He had a confused picture of it as a tremendous tumult rolling along like a hurricane. A whirlwind of fire and smoke and shouting punctuated by shots and galloping horses and studded with scenes of firing squads. A storm without purpose or direction. No one could do anything about the Revolution" (102). Guálinto is similarly represented as a "storm without purpose or direction." Guálinto's family, for example, Paredes writes,

> take it for granted that he would grow up to be a great man as his dead father had wished. A great man who would help and lead his people to a better kind of life. How this would be accomplished they did not know. Sometimes they thought he would be a great lawyer who would get back the lands they had lost. At other times they were certain he would become a great orator who would convince even

the greatest of their enemies the rightness of his cause. Or perhaps he would be a great doctor who would go around healing the poor and thus create an immense following. (125)

What is lacking here is a clear vision of a cultural and political mission that tradition or historical memory can provide. Missing also is any sense of the political militance or resistance that Paredes nostalgically but also hopefully recuperates in Part I of the novel. The suspense of the novel resides in the crucial development of Guálinto's character as he vacillates between turning toward either Anglo or Mexican culture for direction, a tension in the novel represented as a conflict between home and school and between oral and written cultures: "In the schoolroom he was an American; at home and on the playground he was a Mexican... The boy nurtured these two selves within him, each radically different and antagonistic to the other, without realizing their separate existences"(147). Paredes makes clear the crucial consequences of the resolution of this divided identity in terms of the direction Guálinto will take in the future. Either he will choose as models figures from Mexican history who resisted Anglo conquest and colonization or he will identify with American cultural heroes who engaged in nation-building through genocidal conquest and colonization:

> George Washington Gómez secretly desired to be a full-fledged, complete American without the shameful encumberment of his Mexican race. He was the product of his Anglo teachers and the books he read in school, which were all in English. He felt a pleasant warmth when he heard "The Star-Spangled banner." It was he who fought the British with George Washington and Frances Marion the Swamp Fox, discovered pirate treasure with Long John Silver, and got lost in a cave with Tom Sawyer and Becky Thatcher. Books had made him so. He read everything he could lay his hands on. But he also heard from the lips of his elders songs and stories that were the history of his people, the Mexican people. And he also fought the Spaniards with Hidalgo, the French with Juárez and Zaragosa, and the Gringos with Blas María de la Garza Falcón and Juan Nepomuceno Cortina in his childish fancies. (148)

Guálinto's fate hangs in the balance most of the novel as he vacillates in determining his identity. At one point late in the novel, for example, "all the tales of hate and violence from his childhood came back to him from the half-consciousness in which they had been submerged. They came, they took away everything we had, they made us foreigners in our own land. He thought how there had always been an Anglo blocking his path to happiness, to success, even to plain dignity" (273). Finally the pressures of Americanization win out and in an ending full of tragic irony, George Washington Gómez ends up working for the U.S. government working in, of all things, border patrol along the Texas-Mexican border. His duties during World War II is to keep tabs on subversive Mexican political groups that might arise. He tells Feliciano that he sees no future for the Texas-Mexicans. "Mexicans will be Mexicans," he tells Feliciano, "A few of them, like some of those would-be politicos, could make something of themselves if they would just do like I did. Get out of this filthy Delta, as far away as they can, and get rid of their Mexican Greaser attitudes" (300). Just as early in the novel Feliciano's partners in the campaign for a Spanish-speaking Southwest Republic eventually betray the revolution in one way or another, so George Washington Gómez also betrays the revolution by rising individually within an American free market economy that racially and economically oppresses most Mexicans. The typical narrative of 1930s proletarian liberation would have called instead for his assent with his class and nation. As such he ends up detached from the communal Mexican culture epitomized for Paredes in the corrido: "in the corrido, a product of an integrated community sharing a working-class world view and values, there is no place for the idiosyncratic, for an individual perspective that stands totally outside of communal concerns. No individual life, even that of the hero, may be regarded as uniquely different from the fate of the community as a whole" (Saldívar 36).

But why does Paredes choose to tell this story as a tragedy? In part, through representing the dangers involved in the seduction of Americanization, Paredes is responding to two very different ways of approaching the Mexican condition in the U.S. in the 1930s: 1) that of such groups as The League of Latin American Citizens [LULAC], a middle-class reform organization that powerfully shaped the Mexican-American generation and endorsed Americanization; and 2) that of the left, particularly the Communist Party. The latter was active in Texas, particularly through El Congreso del Pueblo de Habla Española [Conference of the Spanish-Speaking People], and was forwarding its own brand of Americanization, albeit one seemingly much different from that of LULAC. Fundamental to LULAC's effort to assimilate American democratic ideals was the need to reinforce the idea among Mexican Americans that they were as American as anyone else in the United States. Mexican Americans should not reject Mexican cultural traditions, but they were cautioned by LULAC not to participate in organizations that stressed Mexicano nationalism. The "American character" in particular attracted LULAC. It believed that the "genius" and "quality" of Americans had made the United States great and that Mexican Americans should develop American virtues, particularly individualism. LULAC maintained that only in the United States could citizens progress and retain their individuality. Individualism was not foreign to the "Mexican character," but it could be refined and enhanced in an American context. Indeed, these values of individualism

and anti-Mexican nationalism are those very values Paredes diagnoses as tragic in the developing character of George Washington Gómez.[1]

On the other side of the political spectrum, Paredes' novel also stands as a critique of the Communist Party's theory of class struggle and its policy of Americanization during the Popular Front Period from 1935 through World War II. In foregoing its typically more radical working-class politics in the mid-1930s, the Communist Party instituted a more broadly defined anti-fascist democratic platform attempting to recruit sectors of the bourgeoisie into a popular democratic front. Seeking to make communism appeal to a broader range of people, the Party attempted to suggest an historical link between U.S. bourgeois democracy and communism and to assert communism as part of and continuous with the liberal democratic tradition in the U.S., arguing that communism carried "forward today the traditions of Jefferson, Paine, Jackson, and Lincoln, and of the Declaration of Independence." The General Secretary of the Communist Party of the United States at the time, Earl Browder, even declared, "Communism is the Americanism of the twentieth century" (Ottanelli 123).

For Paredes, however, culture and history have a weight such that they cannot simply be rewritten or refigured as one pleases. Similarly, even though George Washington Gómez's parents erroneously identify George Washington as he who drove out the English and freed the slaves, as a liberator, the name in the story seems to have an historical weight precluding its transformation into a radical meaning. Through the use of the figure of George Washington, Paredes seems to be critiquing the Communist Party for its lack of sophistication in recognizing the importance of culture and tradition to a political movement. Choosing a liberal tradition will yield a liberal politics, Paredes suggests. Moreover, this American culture does not comprehend the history and experiences of Mexicans in the U.S. and interpellates them into a racist cultural tradition.

Furthermore, concomitant with the policy of Americanization, the Communist Party also forewent its formulation that African Americans and Mexicans constituted oppressed nations within the U.S. in order to attempt to assert unity. Disregarding this earlier analysis (such as its theory of the Black Belt), the CPUSA viewed African Americans, like Mexican Americans, as part of the more expansive working class—downplaying the significance of racial differences constitutive of national consciousness—and called for their political unification with the progressive sectors of the black and white bourgeoisie. Indeed, in an essay titled "The Mexican Question in the Southwest," Emma Tenayuca and Homer Brooks, the state chairman and state secretary of the Communist Party in Texas, while acknowledging that "the Mexican people of the Southwest have a common historical background and are bound by a common culture, language, and communal life," also argue that "the Mexican communities exist side by side with Anglo-American communities within a territory where the populated districts are separated by large and thinly populated mountainous regions" (261-2). Given these conditions, they ask, "Should the conclusion, therefore, be drawn that the Mexican people in the Southwest constitute a nation—or that they form a segment of the Mexican nation (South of the Rio Grande)? Our view is no" (262). Tenayuca and Brooks conclude that because "their economic (and hence, their political) interests are welded to those of the Anglo-American people of the Southwest,"

> We must accordingly regard the Mexican people in the Southwest as part of the American nation, who, however, have not been accepted heretofore by the American bourgeoisie; the latter has continued to hinder the process of national unification of the American people by treating the Mexican and Spanish-Americans as a conquered people. (262)

This reading ignores the presence of racial/national conflict within the working class which precludes a genuine working class solidarity, instead figuring racism as informing only bourgeois thinking.

Countering this view of Mexicans in the Southwest, I have been suggesting, Paredes novel forwards a version of class struggle in which nationalism or the national struggle constitutes a key component. He foregoes those Stalinist terms which understand the nation in purely objective terms (territory, language, economic unit, etc.)—those endorsed by Tenayuca and Brooks— and instead sees the Mexican or Chicano nation as an imagined community (Benedict Anderson) or cultural creation (Eric Hobsbawm). Indeed, as Trotsky once noted with relation to the Black national question in the U.S., "on this matter an abstract criterion is not decisive, but the historical consciousness, the feelings and impulses of a group are more important"(28). Historically, Paredes' novel asserts, Chicanos have been treated as a conquered people, so that their response to this treatment should be a reaction against that conquest. That resistance should take the form of a nationalist anti-imperialist politics and not a politics that advocates assimilation into a culture informed by racialist norms and hierarchies which sanctioned and justified the conquest through its own racist principles initially. Paredes' national struggle takes place within the cultural arena but not with the goal of reclaiming lost territory. Instead he advocates the formulation of a political program in cultural terms, one that comprehends the distinct history and unique conditions of oppression and exploitation endured by Chicanos in the U.S. yet also allows for an alliance with the working class struggle. For Paredes, as for Fanon,

If man is known by his acts, then we will say that the most urgent thing today for the intellectual is to build up his nation. If this building up is true, that is to say if it interprets the manifest will of the people and reveals the eager...peoples, then the building of a nation is of necessity accompanied by the discovery and encouragement of universalizing values. Far from keeping aloof from other nations, therefore, it is national liberation which leads the nation to play its part on the stage of history. It is at heart of national consciousness that international consciousness lives and grows. (247-8)

In many ways, Paredes articulates in the novel a version of the internal colonialism theory that Robert Blauner would develop some thirty years later: "the colonial attack on culture is more than a matter of economic factors such as labor recruitment and special exploitation. The colonial situation differs from the class situation of capitalism precisely in the importance of culture as an instrument of domination. Colonialism depends on conquest, control, and the imposition of new institutions and ways of thought" (67). Paredes, however, also challenges and modifies this theory, suggesting that class oppression too has a cultural component such that any struggle for working-class liberation must develop a culture of resistance expressive of counter history, values, and interests.

Thus, the recovery of Paredes' novel *George Washington Gómez* is important on two fronts. First, it gives us the inauguration of a Chicano working-class literature that can provide a paradigm for highlighting the class content and narratives of class struggle of other Chicano genres. Additionally, however, Paredes intervenes in and rethinks the Marxist socio-cultural approach being developed in the Thirties and by synthesizing the corrido and the proletarian novel forms, he offers a version of a Chicano Marxism, so to speak (in the spirit of Cedric Robinson's *Black Marxism*) and provides models for the rethinking of class struggle today in the context of the multiracial, indeed, multinational U.S. working class.

It is from such texts as *George Washington Gómez* and others like Leslie Marmon Silko's *Almanac of the Dead*—each of which intervenes in, challenges, and deepens Marxist models or narratives of class struggle that a new left will finds its cultural sources for a new political agenda of resistance and liberation.

Note

[1]For a fuller discussion of the development of LULAC and of the relation between Mexican Americans and the Communist Party in Texas see Mario García's *Mexican Americans*, pp. 25-62 and 145-231.

Works Cited

Anzaldúa, Gloria. *Borderlands/La Frontera: The New Mestiza*. San Francisco: Aunt Lute, 1987.

Blauner, Robert. *Racial Oppression in America*. New York: Harper and Row, 1972.

Fanon, Frantz. *The Wretched of the Earth*. New York: Grove, 1963.

García, Mario. *Mexican Americans*. New Haven: Yale UP, 1989.

Ottanelli, Fraser. *The Communist Party of the United States From the Depression to World War II*. New Brunswick: Rutgers UP, 1991.

Paredes, Américo. *With His Pistol in His Hand*. Austin: U of Texas P, 1973.

_____. *George Washington Gómez*. Houston: Arte Público, 1990.

_____. "The Mexican Corrido: Its Rise and Fall". *Folklore and Culture on the Texas-Mexican Border*. Austin: Center for Mexican American Studies, 1993.

Saldívar, Ramón. *Chicano Narrative: The Dialectics of Difference*. Madison: The U of Wisconsin P, 1990.

Tenayuca, Emma and Brooks, Homer. "The Mexican Question in the Southwest." *The Communist* 18 (March 1939).

Thompson, E.P. *The Making of the English Working Class*. New York: Vintage Books, 1963.

Trotsky, Leon. *On Black Nationalism and Self-Determination*. New York: Pathfinder, 1967.

PART III

History in Literature/Literature in History

Having the Last Word: Recording the Cost of Conquest in *Los Comanches*

Sandra Dahlberg

Los Comanches, written in Santa Fe, New Mexico, in the late eighteenth-century, dramatizes the conflicts between the Comanche Indians and Spanish military forces on the New Mexican Northern Frontier during the last quarter of that century.[1] It is a work in which both parties, Spanish/New Mexican and Comanche, initially represent themselves as conquerors intending to eradicate the other's presence from the region, a move which effectively confuses the designations of conquering and conquered parties. This drama deviates from the traditional dramatic conventions of the era by complicating the Spanish/New Mexican "victory" with associations of sin, and by burying in the rhetorical debates a multi-vocal dialogue which, at its center, represents the human and cultural costs of conquest rather than justifying the actions or glorifying the outcome with religious conversion. *Los Comanches* is also important because through this drama we are introduced to a distinctly New Mexican identity that embraced regional rather than viceroyal loyalties and provided a prototype for a genre that greatly influenced American culture, the western.

One complication associated with *Los Comanches* is the inability to substantiate authorship, although there is much evidence to suggest that the author may have been Pedro Bautista de Pino of Santa Fe.[2] Pino was born in Santa Fe during the mid-eighteenth century to a family whose ties to New Mexico dated back to 1692. As a New Mexican Pino was required to serve in the militia which he described as the most successful provincial militia at maintaining the "span of land within [New Mexico's] old boundaries" (Carroll 67). However, Pino also criticized the economic impositions the militia system imposed upon the New Mexicans who were required to furnish their own arms, ammunitions, supplies and horses for campaigns that often kept them away from home for two to three months. This in an agricultural region that had a barter-based economy. In his *Exposición* to the Spanish Cortes in

Cadiz, Pino challenged this service as an "extremely heavy and unbearable burden, which ha[d] no parallel in any other province" (Carroll 68). He also questioned the appropriateness of a system that "ruined" many fine men who "[had] to sell their own clothing and that of their family in order to equip themselves with ammunition and supplies" (Carroll 68). Though mindful of the necessity for Spanish frontier controls, Pino's primary loyalty was with the New Mexicans who he felt were neglected by the viceroyal and gubernatorial policies. Of importance is that the text of *Los Comanches* complements Pino's *Exposición*, but the drama cloaks the severity of censure in the comedic and epic dramatic conventions. Also, one reason for the ambiguity of the author may lie in the realities of the era as it would have been socially and politically imprudent for any New Mexican to openly contest the viceroy or its policies.

Pino was a significant political figure as evidenced by his appointment as the New Mexican representative to the Spanish Cortes in 1812, for which he prepared a report of New Mexico (the *Exposición*). In this work, Pino astutely becomes both supplicant and critic by pleading for relief from the severity of militia duty, promoting the integrity of the Comanches and, at the same time, advocating for the economic and political support needed to ensure the viability of New Mexico. In doing so, the correlation between the tensions and issues presented in Pino's *Exposición* and those portrayed in *Los Comanches* is striking. Furthermore, it is important to remember that the format of *Los Comanches* is strongly grounded in the conventions exhibited in two works so widely accessible in the region that most New Mexicans, including Pino, were, in all probability, familiar with them: *Los moros y cristianos* (*The Moors and Christians*), and *La conquista de México* (*The Conquest of Mexico*).

When the Spanish began their conquest of the Americas, they brought with them the medieval Christian dramas that had effectively reinforced Catholic doctrine to the people of Europe for centuries. Personal journals and accounts written by contemporaries of Cortés record performances of the "miracle plays" in a newly conquered Mexico City. According to Arthur Campa, as the indigenous population was only gradually converting to Catholicism at this point, the strictly dogmatic elements of these plays were often compromised in an effort to appeal to a wider audience in the hopes of furthering conversion (7-11). At the same time, another Spanish transplant was introduced to Americas' peoples, *Los moros y cristianos*. This play, highly popular in Spain, not only celebrated the expulsion of the Moors from the Iberian Peninsula but, more importantly, the victory of Christianity over "heathenism." In its New World manifestation, the Moors were synonymous with Indians, and the repeated performances of this play often coincided with

Spanish military victories over resisting "heathen" tribes (Anderson 104). Spain believed that Indians who accepted Catholicism were far more likely to acquiesce to the "superiority" of the Spanish cause. And, aside from the doctrine, the play itself was entertaining.

The Spanish conquest of Mexico City produced the first New World drama, *La conquista de México*, which patterned after *Los moros y cristianos*, featured the encounter between Cortés and Moctesuma (Gillmor 18). This play, while upholding the veracity of Catholicism, was much more focused on the actual conflict between Spanish and Indian in the effort to control the environment in the name of religion than it was on facilitating religious conversion. The conquest was, however, presented as divinely ordained and the Spanish conquerors were portrayed as redeeming the Indians from bloody, paganistic rituals and cultures through the adoption of Spanish Catholic standards.

While the focus of *Los Comanches* is also conquest, the text of the play greatly problematizes the colonization and the proselytizing efforts of the Spanish in New Mexico. The author presents distinct Spanish, New Mexican and Comanche identities in order to examine the inter-relations of these cultural groups, all of whom were active participants in the historical events dramatized in *Los Comanches*. Curiously, most of the research on *Los Comanches* has focused on determining the play's historical accuracy rather than examining it as a literary construct whose characters and events gain significance only when analyzed in conjunction with the deliberate deviations from the historical record.

There are, in fact, three very important conflations created in his drama: three Spanish-Comanche battles become one; two Comanche leaders, both called Cuerno Verde, are synthesized; and the characterizations of Fernández and Anza, the Spanish military leaders involved in the battles are merged as well. In order to accurately interpret the import of these conflations, we must first establish the historical basis for *Los Comanches*.

During the eighteenth-century, the Comanche Indians were the most powerful and wealthiest of the Southern Plains tribes. Their wealth was partly attributable to their willingness to trade with both the Spanish and French between which they were strategically located. The Comanches were severe, however, in their intent to subjugate the other regional tribes and they waged a continuous war with rivals who infringed upon their territory, especially the Apaches. The Comanches were also one of the first tribes to recognize the political and economic benefits that accompanied treaties and alliances with the Spanish. New Mexican governor Tomás Vélez Cachupín determined that without a Comanche alliance, the remote settlements of the northern New Mexican frontier, which consisted of subsistence farmers poor in resources and arms, were indefensible rendering settlement tenuous at best. Under the governorship of Vélez, the Spanish and the Comanches not only established trade relations, they also formed a military alliance against their common Apache enemy. Sanctioned by the Spanish, the Comanche war machine was directed mercilessly on the Apache thereby relieving the frontier settlements from continuous Apache and Comanche onslaught which resulted in an increased population and added prosperity in these northern settlements for nearly three decades.

In 1767, however, with the appointment of Pedro Fermín de Mendinueta as governor, a punitive Indian policy was implemented without notification to the tribes involved. The Comanche learned of the new policy when Spanish forces inflicted harsh reprisals on the Comanches in response to their killing of five New Mexicans caught violating treaty laws within a Comanche camp. The Comanches felt that they had acted in accordance with the existing treaty, given the severity of the treaty violation, and did not expect Spanish rebuke much less attack in response. The Comanche re-countered the Spanish duplicity according to their custom by attacking one person at a remote settlement.[3] Vélez understood the need for each side to execute a token act of revenge in order to retain honor and mutual respect when these misunderstandings arose. Mendinueta's policy effectively left the Comanches no option but war, a move which endangered the northern frontier as settlers fled for the safety of larger communities such as Santa Fe. Decades of peace and prosperity disintegrated as Comanche and Spanish mounted increasingly hostile retaliatory campaigns (Simmons 87).

Acting as the New Mexican representative to the Spanish Cortes in 1812, Pino described in depth New Mexican relations with "the honorable Comanches." He described their government as republican in nature led by an "elected general chief [who] administer[ed] a military form of government" (Carroll 130). Pino attests to the Comanches' industriousness, superior "technical knowledge" and habits which he compared favorably to the rural people of Spain. Importantly, Pino stresses the moral fortitude of the Comanche people in terms designed to ensure European respect. Modesty was attributed to both genders and of the Comanche women he noted that they "wear a [long] tunic with a high neck and long sleeves; only the hands and face of a Comanche woman are displayed" (Carroll 129). The Comanche comparisons with Spanish and New Mexican criterion cannot be underemphasized. The passage clearly demonstrates Pino's high regard for the Comanche people to which he attributed European-Christian standards and customs.

The years of Comanche-Spanish alliance contributed to the republican nature of Comanche leadership. By 1769, during that first retaliatory Comanche raid on Ojo Caliente after the policy change, reports indicate that the Comanches were led by a "little king" who surrounded himself with bodyguard warriors and who stationed himself under a buffalo hide canopy (Thomas 167). The distinctive feature of this leader was the green horn (cuerno verde) which he wore on his forehead. The tribal veneration of Cuerno Verde is remarkable since the Comanche usually placed a higher value on youthful stamina rather than on aged wisdom, and this Cuerno Verde (the elder) was at least in his early forties at the time. By 1779, the date of the final Comanche-Spanish battle, Cuerno Verde the younger must have been in his thirties and his son at least in his teens. It is important to recognize the respective ages of the two historical Cuerno Verdes so that we can appreciate the implications of the conflation of these characters in *Los Comanches.*

The epic conflict represented in the play between Cuerno Verde and the Spanish under the command of Don Carlos Fernández began with the historical Fernández' 1774 raid on a Comanche camp. Fernández, a legendary Indian fighter, led a surprise attack on the Comanche which, according to the records of Governor Mendinueta, resulted in the capture or slaughter of eighty percent of the five hundred Comanche camped there. Only eighteen warriors and a few women and children escaped (Noyes 64, Thomas 174-175). Historians Alfred Thomas and Stanley Noyes concluded that Cuerno Verde the elder died during this battle. However, among those that escaped were Cuerno Verde's son and grandson. Enraged by his father's death, Cuerno Verde the younger assumed use of the notorious green horn, as well as the regal attributes accorded his father, and viciously and relentlessly terrorized the frontier settlements for the next five years. Cuerno Verde the younger, now widely feared as the "scourge" of the Northern Frontier, became the primary target of Spanish military efforts to conquer the Comanches (Simmons 86-87).

The second battle occurred in 1778 when newly appointed governor Don Juan Bautista de Anza, a successful Indian fighter and administrator whose successes in California included the establishment of San Francisco in 1776, took matters into his own hands and personally led a ruthless campaign against the Comanche in 1779. He had under his command 103 presidial soldiers, 225 militiamen, 259 Pueblo auxiliaries, and 200 Ute and Jicarilla warriors. Nearly 800 strong, Anza attacked a Comanche camp of approximately 400 men and 850 women and children. As Noyes notes:

> Soldiers made prisoners of thirty women and thirty-four children. In addition the Spaniards and their allies captured the entire enemy horse herd, more than five hundred head. They seized all of the [Comanche's] baggage and supplies. There was so much spoil it later took more than a hundred horses to carry it away. (76)

The magnitude of this battle's spoil appears unique in the historical records. No other battle emphasizes the quantity of spoil as does this battle and in all probability it is the one presented in the section of *Los Comanches* narrated by Barriga Dulce. However, Cuerno Verde was not present at this battle. He was raiding Taos at the time. Yet, the defeated camp was Cuerno Verde's and the Comanche culture required that he revenge the losses inflicted upon his people.

The third incident that contributed to the dramatized battle occurred directly after the above raid. Anza correctly surmised that Cuerno Verde would avenge the Spanish attack. Anza's forces tracked Cuerno Verde to Southern Colorado, near what today are the Greenhorn Mountains, so named in his honor, and established an ambush for Cuerno Verde and his small force of forty warriors. In this canyon, Cuerno Verde valiantly encountered the massive Spanish forces, riding in front of his small band as was his custom, in what he surely recognized as a suicidal act. Anza's reports of this battle boasted not only of Cuerno Verde's death, but that of his first born son, four captains and a medicine man (Noyes 78).

These three incidents, Fernández' battle of 1774, and the two Anza battles, all contribute to the drama depicted in *Los Comanches*. Why were these three battles and the depiction of both Cuerno Verdes conflated in the play and why is Anza absent in the drama? The answers to these questions are imbedded in the dialogue of the drama and they give us important insights into the author's intentions when he wrote *Los Comanches*.

Los Comanches begins with Cuerno Verde's posturing speech to Don Fernández.[4] This Cuerno Verde reminds the Spanish army of the Comanche's power on the *llano* and the Comanche intention to conquer all the people of the region including the Spanish by stating:

> For the most enraged I humble
> And the haughtiest I subdue
> Unrestrained and without fetter
> Knowing none who master me. (11-15)[5]

Confident in a Comanche victory, Cuerno Verde goes further by demanding that the Spanish reconsider the effects that this battle will have on the New Mexican settlements by adding the Spanish to the list of the various peoples with whom the Comanche successfully warred.

> Let [the Spanish] ask the many nations
> Who have felt my conquering heel,
> Let them ask my might and prestige,
> Learn the misery they now feel.
> Today they find their homes abandoned,
> And their homes in ruin see
> Let them ask the Caslana nation,
> What it is to war with me. (34-41)

The Caslana nation mentioned is actually the Apaches (Carlana) and the "ruin" was, under the Vélez treaty, sanctioned and encouraged by the Spanish.[6] Now, however, the thrust of the Comanche force is being directed against the former ally and the Comanches expect that the battle will force the Spanish to abandon the northern frontier. Interestingly, Cuerno Verde not only raises the issues of eradication and conquest, he also introduces charges of impiety, a remarkable move for a "heathen" character in a drama descended from the Catholic conversion genre. In addition, the response positioning of Fernández throughout the drama effectively renders him literarily subordinate to Cuerno Verde and the Comanches.

By all accounts, Don Carlos Fernández was a man "advanced in years" when he commanded the 1774 campaign.[7] *Los Comanches* acknowledges Fernández' elderly image by having that character assert "though I am advanced in years…Carlos Fernández has no fears" (131/133). Fernández rose to favor under the governorship of Vélez, whose Indian policies promoted reconciliation and fostered trade and military alliances with the powerful Comanches. In Los Comanches, the aged persona of Fernández is utilized to characterize the passing of Vélez' cooperative Indian policies. However, Fernández and the chauvinistic posture he presents are superseded by Barriga Dulce's solipsism. Both historically and literarily, Fernández represents political policies based on Christian rhetoric emphasizing loyalty to the Church and to Spain. In his first lengthy rebuttal to Cuerno Verde, the character of Fernández proclaims the futility of the Comanche efforts given the power and prestige of Spain:

> In the land across the waters,
> There reigns a prince of right
> Who rules the world from pole to pole
> Through his power and his might.
> Throughout this entire world you see
> His power reigns supreme
> Germans, Englishmen, Turks
> All peoples whomsoever they be
> When they hear the name of Spaniard
> Bend and tremble at the knee. (108-117)

The language in this speech invokes both religious and secular implications by referring to the Spanish king as the "prince of right" and by asserting his "supreme" power, terms usually attributed to Christ, especially in the dramatic conventions of late eighteenth-century. The vague references to conversion come much later and with substantially less fanfare as Fernández merely asserts the "valor of…Catholic arms" (142) and even then he is addressing his own troops rather than offering redemption to the Comanches. The religious emphasis is first forwarded by the character of Don José de la Peña as he prays to the Virgin Mother for aid. Fernández' only other reference to divinity is in his last speech, just before the final foray, in which he says: "Sound your trumpets, Santiago!/ Holy Virgin! Lend your aid!" (394-395). Yet, these lines are eclipsed by the earlier lines which provide lengthier and more explicit rhetoric concerning Spanish "might."

By placing the religious extollations at the end of Fernández' speeches, the author shows his audiences that the Spanish were more interested in invading lands "when it suited me [and Spain] that way" (135) than they were in upholding Christian standards in the province. Fernández' emphasis on conquest without an attempt at Catholic conversion gives us an indication of the perversion which the author attributed to the developing socio-political system, a direction he felt neglected the religious mission originally combined with settlement. Another schism is also worth noting: the character of Peña introduces the moral ethos behind the battle when he prays not for the aid of Santiago, the Spanish patron saint of warriors and an important referent in the Spanish-Moor conflict, but to Mary who, as *la Virgen de Guadalupe* [the Virgin of Guadalupe], had significant New World attributes.

The presence of Anza in the character of Fernández is evidenced by the focus on conquest in Fernández' speeches which are characteristic of Anza's punitive measures, especially when Fernández boasts: "Your lands I've always invaded, when it suited me that way" [134-135]. Fernández is not only personifying the Anza administration's lack of regard for the Comanche people and the Spanish intent to conquer the Indians rather than cooperate through treaties as a means to insure the success of the New Mexican settlements, he is also reflecting authorial disapproval of Anza's personal involvement in the war with Cuerno Verde's Comanches. The use of the personal pronoun rather than relying on the established empirical power, exposes Anza's self-pride, his need to flaunt his power, a tendency supported by Anza's own notes on the engagement.[8]

The conflation of Fernández and Anza effectively amounts to a literary censure of Anza's punitive policies by deliberately denying Anza the honorable recognition usually accorded a successful military leader. This censure is intensified when we consider that no triumphant speech is delivered by any of the victorious Spanish soldiers. Spanish advantage is proclaimed instead by a lowly Spanish camp follower, Barriga Dulce, whose lines at the end of the play present the most problematic evaluation of the event and further condemn the conspicuously eclipsed Anza by destabilizing the foundational rhetoric presented earlier in the drama.

Barriga Dulce describes the deaths of Cuerno Verde and many of his men, the triumph of the Spanish troops, and more importantly, he delineates the significance of the achievement to Spanish interests of which the author of the play was an uneasy party.

> Let [the Comanches] die, the more the better
> There will be more spoils for me.
> Soft tanned skins of elk and beaver,
> What a comfort they will be. (414-417)

For Barriga Dulce the conquest is grounded in mercenariness. Glory, for Barriga Dulce, is not associated with piety or military prowess. As he states, "My glory is measured by my girth" (437). He waits like a vulture for the battle to conclude, gloats about the bloodshed, and greedily anticipates the wealth that he will be able to confiscate as a result. When Barriga Dulce enters the abandoned Comanche camp in the last scene, his avarice becomes even more pronounced.

> Ah, at last I've reached their treasure,
> There is plenty here indeed.
> Sugars, fruits, and meats and jellies,
> What a life these heathens lead.
> Everything to tempt the palate,
> What a feast fit for a king.
> I shall eat and then I'll gather,
> I'll not leave a single thing.
> Let them fill themselves with glory,
> While I eat with joy and mirth. (426-435)

In a play which established the adversarial stances by masking Spanish motives in divine imagery, the assertion of avarice, gluttony, sloth, idle boasting and, worst of all, pride at the end of the play signal the extent of the writer's disapproval. Not only did the Spanish fail even to try to covert the Comanches, but the nature of the campaign corrupted the participating New Mexican Christians. The severity of these sins, especially in the more dogmatic Catholicism of the eighteenth-century, demonstrates that the author perceived Anza's military endeavor against Cuerno Verde as motivated by a personal desire to humiliate the Comanche leader and as an immoral pretense to confiscate substantial property. Since Barriga Dulce does not participate in the battle, this character can also be viewed as a rebuke to the New Mexican settlers who encouraged these punitive campaigns because of the material benefit settlers incurred as a result. The Anza battles occurred just after the summer hunts and the appropriated "spoils" provided the province the means for a more comfortable winter in this subsistence economy.

In addition, rather than describing the Comanche village as meager in this passage, thereby relegating it to savage status, the village is instead filled with treasure on a European standard and, as in Pino's *Exposición*, demands that the moral code of these people, by extension, be recognized as equivalent to although different than the Christian's. The Comanches were still "heathens" in the technical sense of the word, but Pino believed that with continued effort they would be converted (many of them already were) thereby re-fortifying the former alliance. The life led by "these heathens" was presented as far from rudimentary; they had standards and supplies which were "fit for a [Spanish] king." The allusion to kingly status also reinforced the social status and wealth of Cuerno Verde. He was not a solitary chieftain; he was the leader of a very successful people who tried to adjust to and accommodate the Spanish invaders even to the point of appropriating some social and cultural structures in what can be interpreted as an attempt to gain further favor and stability.

Barriga Dulce's speech cannot be dismissed as a retroactive attempt to empower or ennoble a conquered adversary because the greed with which the play concludes sharply contradicts Catholic virtues espoused by the Spanish militiamen in the play's dialogue. *Los Comanches* depicts a substantial rift between the Spanish military forces whose loyalties were to the viceroy in Mexico City and who used the frontier to advance personal political careers, and the New Mexican civilians required to support the governmental policies by providing supplementary manpower for these battles, the consequences with which the New Mexican people had to live. The play is also critical of the settlers, personified in Barriga Dulce, whose greed undermined the integrity of New Mexico by refusing to acknowledge the rights of the Comanche people and their losses when it was to their economic advantage.

Pino respected and understood the Comanche motivations in response to Anza's policies. In his *Exposición* Pino states that:

> The Comanches do not accept quarter but they give it to those they conquer. They prefer death to submitting to the least act of humiliation. In battle they never attack treacherously or with advantage; they always fight face to face after having given warning with their whistles. Although their principal weapon is the arrow (patca), they also use lances and firearms, as do our soldiers, and they vary their tactics in such a way as to demand respect in all their maneuvers.

> The battles that we have had with them have been long and bloody. They were hostile to this province until…Governor Don Juan Bautista de Anza decided to punish them. After having made preparations for a decisive campaign, he went out in person. He succeeded in defeating thirty chiefs (none of them accepted quarter). (Carroll 131)

Careful analysis of Pino's wording, when read against *Los Comanches*, clearly condemns Anza's use of "punishment" even while he recognizes the hostilities that existed between the province and the Comanches. Throughout his

Exposición Pino emphasized the successful treaties, instituted both before and after these encounters, which underscored Comanche honor. Pino also makes a clear distinction in his work between the persona of Cuerno Verde that was perpetuated in *Los Comanches* and the man he knew as Tabivo Naritgante (brave and handsome) who "refused quarter and died in this memorable campaign" (Carroll 132). That Pino specifically mentions Cuerno Verde and addresses the conquest issues in a manner similar to those depicted in *Los Comanches*, supports the possibility, though rather tenuously, that Pino was the play's author.[9]

The element of revenge was, and still is, a powerful frontier motif. Both historically and literarily Cuerno Verde was motivated by a cultural code which demanded personal revenge in response to direct attacks on his familial band. As governor, Anza was responsible for the precariousness of the frontier settlements, yet it was to the province's advantage to establish peace rather than commit personally to a savagely punitive operation. As a Comanche, Cuerno Verde was not expected to uphold the Christian value of forgiveness, however, his familial motivation for revenge, more Christian than Anza's in that it was directed by paternal love as his opening speech indicates.

> Today for certain blood will flow—
> Blood that means revenge for me.
> This recalls to my memory
> One of these, though brave and bold,
> He left his blood to stain the flowers
> On a battle field of old. (48-53)

This Cuerno Verde is asserting his willingness and need to honorably revenge his father's death, the one who "left his blood…on a battle field of old" as a justification for his present altercation with Fernández. Fernández/Anza acts to advance his military reputation, he wants to kill the renowned Cuerno Verde.

In the play, Cuerno Verde's honor is substantiated as he asserts the need to preserve his people by repelling the Spanish invaders by force if necessary if peace cannot be secured. In fact, the character that tries to resurrect the treaty is Tabaco, a chief who reminds his fellow Comanche that:

> Alone, unarmed, and fearing no one,
> To Taos I went, among these men,
> On a peaceful mission went I,
> And we signed a treaty then.
> I can say this of the Spaniard,
> He respects a worthy foe.
> Without fear I went amongst them,
> Mingled freely, and you may know, (334-341)

The Comanches are represented as reconciliatory, while the portrayed Spanish ignore Tabaco's offer. Whether or not the Comanche ever actually felt able to "mingle freely" in the Spanish settlements, the level of comfort depicted suggests that some New Mexicans were not threatened by the Comanche presence in the heart of their most important trading centers and towns.

The prolonged hostilities between the Comanches and the Spanish during this decade resulted in the deaths of three generations of Cuerno Verde's family. Ironically, the men who died were the individual Comanches who most emulated Spanish social hierarchies and who strenuously supported the treaties by strictly enforcing them among the Comanches. Cuerno Verde in the play personifies the severity of the region's human and cultural loss. *Los Comanches*' original audiences were undoubtedly familiar with the factual circumstances of both Cuerno Verdes given the magnitude of fear that the younger invoked among the settlers, and they were assuredly aware of the circumstances of each man's death. The play effectively propelled Cuerno Verde the younger from the role of "scourge" to that of the tragic hero. A standard explanation for this depiction is that the routing of Cuerno Verde decimated the Comanches so pitilessly that these people no longer posed a viable threat to the Spanish establishment and the Spanish could be "generous" and glorify the now dead enemy. This interpretation would also increase the perception of Spanish valor by strengthening the image of this noble foe's victors. This is not, however, what the author did. Instead, he used *Los Comanches* to condemn the direction of Spanish policies in New Mexico by demonstrating the slippery slope which led to the moral decline of the New Mexican settlers and resulted in the decimation of the Comanche as well. At the end of the play, not one Spanish soldier proclaims victory. We are left only with the death of Cuerno Verde and the callous defilement of the Comanche camp by the Spanish in the form of Barriga Dulce. It is conquest at its ugliest yet at its most honest depiction.

The play is an interesting vehicle problematizing the society that executed the Comanche conquest for profit and malice rather than for religious or even safety reasons, orders the New Mexican militiamen were compelled to obey regardless of their personal aversions to the actions. The drama shows that if safety was the main motivation for the military actions, rather than complete conquest and material gain, then treaties similar to those established by Vélez would have been sought. The comic gluttony of Barriga Dulce is biting and incredibly laced with sarcasm and his proclamation of "Santiago! You are with us" should be read as farcical if not blasphemous. That both Fernández and Barriga Dulce invoke Santiago's protection in the bloody endeavor, but both neglect to substantiate the sentiment with charitable acts, problematizes the absolute right of conquest that Fernández asserts and which is customarily justified in dramas of this genre.

In *Los Comanches*, there is no clear victor. Cuerno Verde, the play's heroic character, is dead, his Comanches defeated, and the only portrayed result of this carnage is that Barriga Dulce and others like him will appropriate the spoils for personal, not societal, gain. There is no strong re-assertion of Spanish/New Mexican integrity in the face of Barriga Dulce's boastings. Barriga Dulce is the last character to speak and he does so all too nonchalantly if not flippantly:

> See our brave and valiant comrades,
> How they cut and thrust and pierce.
> Like the autumn leaves they scatter,
> It is o'er. They all have fled.
> While upon the field of battle
> Lies Cuerno Verde, with his dead. (448-453)

The focus at the end of the play is redirected to Cuerno Verde and we are again reminded that something much more significant than a battle occurred. The reference to the autumn leaves signals the moral decline of the region as New Mexico moves toward the harshness of an unnatural, and unethical political winter. There is no secure ethos; the depiction of the settlers' greed encourages the audience of New Mexicans to re-evaluate the "victory" and analyze its cost. There were no winners. The Comanches lost their sovereignty, their leaders, their way of life. The settlers gained some property, the Spanish military fought a "good" battle, but the result was perverted by the settlers' greed and Anza's pride. There is no resolution. The visionary depictions in *Los Comanches* suggest that military pride and settler greed would continue to incite more battles over terrain and resources. Indeed, this very battle is with us today and it is waged in academia as we determine literary canons. During the emergence of this nation, which occurred at the same time that Cuerno Verde fought for his people's survival and *Los Comanches* recorded the loss, a revolution was in progress in New England that established another model for conquest that would soon supersede the Spanish in the Southwest, one which relegated Cuerno Verde to historical and literary obscurity.

The themes and issues presented in Southwestern literatures, and *Los Comanches* in particular, address and problematize the assumptions of conquest and survival that are inherent in all of American literature as are the characters, such as Cuerno Verde, that such histories produce. The literatures of the Spanish colonial era of the Southwest are as integral to our understanding of twentieth-century America as are those of New England, if not more so.

We, as a society, have just not been educated and acculturated to see those influences the way we have with English colonization myths. Though currently banished from the traditional literary canons, *Los Comanches* must be recognized as one of the first works in the distinctly American frontier genre representing ideologies that still pervade our American culture, greatly influencing current political policies. More importantly, *Los Comanches'* determined exploration of the complexities of violent cultural amalgamation and the consequences of conquest must be taught because our students, and our society, grapple with the reverberations on a daily basis.

Notes

[1]Aurelio M. Espinosa's 1907 edition of *Los Comanches* is based on a manuscript secured from Amado Chaves, believed to be dated from 1840-1850. A. Espinosa estimates that the play was written around 1780. Espinosa published his edition in the *University of New Mexico Bulletin Language Series*, I.1 (1907).

[2]Arthur Campa supports the assertion that the play was written by one of the New Mexican militiamen: "the drama of *Los Comanches* no doubt was written by some unknown soldier upon his return from the campaign, while the event was still fresh in his memory" (15) cited from Campa's "*Los Comanches*: A New Mexican Folk Drama." Aurelio Espinosa reports that the Chaves manuscript identifies Pedro Pino, Carlos Fernández and Don Juan de Padilla as commanders during the 1777 campaign against the Comanches, placing Pino in the position identified by Campa. In addition, Pino's *Exposición* testifies to both his literary skill and his inclination to address the issues presented in *Los Comanches*.

[3]An unsigned report to Mendinueta for the period between September 17 and November 9, 1769 reads as follows: "On September 26, a group of twenty-four Comanches arrived at the frontier pueblo of Ojo Caliente, killing there an incautious settler who was going about unarmed" qtd. in Thomas, *Plains Indians*, page 166.

[4]The *Los Comanches* quotations come from Gilberto Espinosa's poetic translation of Aurelio Espinosa's edition. G. Espinosa also published a prose translation in *Heroes, Hexes and Haunted Halls*, Albuquerque: Calvin Horn Press Inc., 1972.

[5]I took the liberty of numbering the lines in Gilberto Espinosa's translation of *Los Comanches*.

[6]Carlana was the name of an Apache chief who lived during the first few decades of the eighteenth-century and whose name afterward became associated, though in a limited fashion, with a particular band of Apaches. In *Los Comanches* Carlana becomes Caslana in a move explained by Aurelio Espinosa's seventh explanatory note for "Los Comanches": "in New Mexican Spanish the change, r to s is very common, and Caslana may be an error of the copyist for Carlana."

[7]There is no doubt that the literary Don Carlos Fernández is the very individual that Governor Mendinueta appointed to lead the 1774 battle. Thomas includes in *Plains Indians* a letter dated October 20, 1774 in which Mendinueta identifies Fernández and provides details of the strength of his force which support the depiction in *Los Comanches*. "Their march began on the 19th of last September with a command of six hundred men, among them soldiers, militia, and Indians, over whom I appointed as commander, Don Carlos Fernández. In spite of his advanced years, he is well known for his valor and capacity" (174).

[8]In his book *Los Comanches: The Horse People, 1751-1845*, Stanley Noyes assimilates the historical material on Anza and his interactions with the Comanches and other Indians and concludes that "by 1779 the new governor of Nuevo México found that this 'cruel scourge' had 'exterminated many pueblos,' or villages. De Anza accused him of 'killing hundreds and taking as many prisoners whom he afterward sacrificed in cold blood.' Even if Cuerno Verde II refrained from torturing his Spanish captives, their deaths surely could not have been pleasant. It was for that reason, in part, that Lieutenant Colonel Juan Bautista de Anza, that very year, 'determined to take his life' (73)." Noyes appears to be quoting from Thomas, who, along with Simmons, depict an Anza that was at times obsessed with Cuerno Verde.

[9]Aurelio Espinosa's examination of the Chávez manuscript, determined that the author of *Los Comanches* was "not a learned man, as can be judged from his work. While the language is good Spanish, it is very simple, almost the language of the uneducated" (19), but exactly what we would expect of an eighteenth-century New Mexican militiaman.

Works Cited

Anderson, Reed. "Early Secular Theater in New Mexico." *Pasó por Aquí: Critical Essays on the New Mexican Literary Tradition, 1542-1988*. Ed. Erlinda Gonzales-Berry. Albuquerque: U of New Mexico P, 1987.

Campa, Arthur L. "*Los Comanches*: A New Mexican Folk Drama" *University of New Mexico Bulletin*, Language Series 7.1 (1942): 5-43.

_____. "Spanish Religious Folktheatre in the Spanish Southwest (First Cycle)." *University of New Mexico Bulletin*, Language Series 5.1 (1934): 5-71.

Carroll, H. Bailey and J. Villasana Haggard trans. *Three New Mexico Chronicles*. New York: Arno, 1967.

Espinosa, Aurelio M. "*Los Comanches*: A Spanish Heroic Play of the Year Seventeen Hundred and Eighty." *University of New Mexico Bulletin* Language Series 1.1 (1907): 5-46.

Espinosa, Gilberto. *Heroes, Hexes and Haunted Halls*. Albuquerque: Calvin Horn, 1972.

_____, trans. "Los Comanches." *New Mexico Quarterly* (May 1931): 133-46.

Gillmor, Frances. "The Dance Dramas of Mexican Villages." *University of Arizona Bulletin* Humanities Bulletin 5 9.2: 5-28.

Noyes, Stanley. *Los Comanches: The Horse People, 1751-1845*. Albuquerque: U of New Mexico P, 1993.

Pino, Pedro B. *Exposición sucinta y sencilla de la provincia del Nuevo Mexico*. Trans. and Rpt. in Carroll.

Simmons, Marc. *New Mexico: A Bicentennial History*. New York: Norton, 1977.

Thomas, Alfred Barnaby. *The Plains Indians and New Mexico, 1751-1778: A Collection of Documents Illustrative of the Eastern Frontier of New Mexico*. Albuquerque: U of New Mexico P, 1940.

Luisa Capetillo: An Anarcho-Feminist *Pionera* in the Mainland Puerto Rican Narrative/ Political Tradition

Lisa Sánchez González

> love
> > knows
> > > no
> > > > compromise

—Tato Laviera

Introduction

In his 1985 *ADE Bulletin* essay, "Puerto Rican Literature in the United States: Stages and Perspectives," Juan Flores opens with a seemingly simple question: "Can anyone name the great Puerto Rican novel?" Assuming a silent response from his readers, he answers: Manuel Zeno Gandía's *La Charca* (1894).[1]

Flores asks this question as a rhetorical entry into a discussion of how publishing politics are linked with the realities of Puerto Rico's colonial condition. For Flores, the inattention to the Islands' "Great Books" is symptomatic of the violence of Puerto Rico's Americanization. He adds that this neglect seems outrageous given the intimacy and duration of the colony's relationship with the U.S. In his words; "After nearly a century of intense economic and political association, endless official pledges of cultural kinship and the wholesale importation of nearly half the Puerto Rican people to the United States, Puerto Rican literature still draws a blank among American readers and students of literature."

Flores' critique is important. It would certainly be naive to dismiss canon politics as a central issue in current struggles over representation in U.S. institutions, especially those involved in publishing and education. Read as a strategic intervention launched from within academic discourse—on the

ADE's turf, so to speak—Flores' piece begins to refocus attention away from traditional national literary canon formation, panning out to a fuller conceptualization of what Puerto Ricans must realistically confront as a quasi-"American" (or "AmeRícan")[2] identity in the twentieth century. As such, the implication of reading *La Charca* as a relevant text in evaluating the often violent convergences between U.S. and Puerto Rican social history, beginning with the latter half of the nineteenth century, problematizes an arena of literary, cultural and intellectual history that has been virtually ignored. More particularly, as Flores suggests, the Puerto Rican predicament of nearly one hundred years of U.S. colonialism is perhaps one of the most relevant—and least interrogated—issues for contemporary cultural analysis.

Yet, any gesture toward grounding the discussion of *mainland* Puerto Rican literature in social history opens up a number of crucial questions. Among them, how far a text like *La Charca*, a novel that represents the symptomatic elitism of Puerto Rico's nineteenth century ruling classes, will help us explore what Flores terms the "seamy, repressed side of the 'American century.'"[3] Like many "Great Books" in other national literatures, *La Charca* does little to recuperate the literary and cultural histories of the overwhelming majority of Puerto Rico's people, including those who have made the wage-labor pilgrimage to the continental United States. In fact, as socio-economic descendants (collectively speaking) of the peasants in *La Charca*, migrants to the States represent part of that "putrid pond" of pathos, poverty, ignorance and, most importantly, hopelessness metaphorically reflected in Zeno Gandía's title.

Granting the imperative to recuperate the lost and hidden narrative history of the Puerto Rican diaspora, insular "Greats" such as Zeno Gandía may not prove to be as relevant as Flores suggests. One of the defining elements of fin-de-siècle stateside Puerto Rican cultural and intellectual histories is the rupture they create in the seamless 19th century hegemonic narratives of both the United States *and* Puerto Rico. Consider that while Island intellectuals, such as Eugenio María de Hostos and Antonio Pedreira, were agonizing over the existential crisis of "being" in texts such as *La peregrinación de Bayoán* [Bayoán's Pilgrimage] and *Insularismo* [Insularism], Puerto Rican workers were *coming into being* for the first time as an organized class constituency. While Pedreira was writing in his academic magazines, Hostos was languishing in Paris, and Zeno Gandía was urging McKinley to invade Puerto Rico, thousands of Puerto Rican workers participated in the social movement of the 1890's, which coalesced under the anarcho-syndicalist agenda of the *Federación Libre de Trabajadores* [Free Workers Federation (FLT)] in 1899.

Thus, while *La Charca* is useful in understanding 19th century Puerto Rican literature, mainland Puerto Rican narrative history does not begin with

Zeno Gandía's peers, but with the humble exiles and activist nomads created by the social movement of the 1890s; among them, Bernardo Vega, Jesús Colón, Arturo Schomburg and Luisa Capetillo. All of these figures left behind significant bodies of work. And while Vega's *Memorias* [Memoirs] and Colón's *A Puerto Rican in New York* have been appropriated as the *pionero* generation's "Great Books," Schomburg and Capetillo have been virtually ignored.[4]

I suspect that this elision may be related to how both Schomburg and Capetillo struggled *within* the Puerto Rican and Cuban organizations of their time.[5] More specifically, Schomburg refused the tendency to put aside questions of racism within the community, and Capetillo insisted on the eradication of sexism as an integral part of revolutionary praxis. Consequently, their work attests to the inner contradictions that would mitigate our heroic/masculinist reconstruction of mainland Puerto Rican social and literary history; including their work would thus compromise the fragile epistemological foundation of our own literary canon.[6]

The work of all the early writers in the Puerto Rican diaspora must likewise be read in the context of a larger social and political milieu where the very act of writing for working class women and men of color was, in and of itself, a highly subversive practice. Describing this political and narrative ambient in Puerto Rico at the turn of the century, Julio Ramos remarks that:

> writing [*escritura*]—in the broadest sense of the word, which in addition to literature includes the administration itself of laws and state discourses—was the mechanism of social control and subordination [...] writing—more than a simple marker of certain subjects' prestige—was a technology [...] that provided the possibility of the administration of public life and, in the field of "symbolic" and cultural production, decided the legitimacy of all representational and hegemonic discourses.[7]

Ramos adds that the "entry" of Capetillo and other voices into the "technology" of Puerto Rican *escritura* was difficult and often dangerous. These writers, forcing themselves into the cultural symbolic arena—one of the "most jealously protected realms," where "power produced the fictions of its law"—often suffered as a result. In Ramos' terms, "in response to the loss of power in this zone," the agents of hegemonic authority "responded with violence, frequently and literally breaking heads and incarcerating those who produced alternative discourses."[8] Although Ramos focuses on Puerto Rico in this passage, his ideas are equally applicable to the U.S. context.

In a much longer version of this essay I discuss Schomburg, Capetillo and the historical juncture of fin-de-siècle Puerto Rico/New York in a more complete approximation of the *pionero* generation stateside.[8] In this essay, I will focus on Capetillo, and her particular understanding of mainland Puerto Rican political/narrative struggle as an anarcho-feminist.

Luisa Capetillo

Luisa Capetillo Perón was born in 1879 in Arecibo.[9] Her mother, Margarita Perón—a French national, probably from another Caribbean colony—migrated to Puerto Rico as a young woman. Perón worked for one of Arecibo's wealthier families, first as a governess and later as a washerwoman. Capetillo's father, Luis Capetillo, was a Spanish immigrant worker who also settled in Arecibo. According to Capetillo's biographer, Margarita frequented a neighborhood café called "*La Misisipí*" and was the only female participant in the *tertulias* [discussions] that were held there. She had a reputation for her liberal views and congenial temperament, characteristics that Luisa eulogized in the dedication to her penultimate text.

Capetillo's parents were autodidacts whose education was stimulated within the progressive circles of Puerto Rico's fledgling workers' movement. Luisa was their only child, and although education was scarcely available at that time to women—and even less readily available to working class children—Luisa's parents gave her a rather extensive education, primarily at home.[10]

Luis and Margarita were determined to nurture Luisa's intellectual growth, and while it seems insular Puerto Rican literature was not part of this project, they had a library that included texts of the literary vanguard in Russia, France, England and the U.S. Luisa read the work of Tolstoy, Hugo, Zola, Turgenev, Madeleine Vernet, Kropotkin and Mill, among others. She learned French from her mother, while her father taught her the basics of reading, writing and mathematics in Spanish.

Beyond this rather rough sketch, we know very little about Capetillo's childhood and adolescence. By 1897, when Capetillo was turning 18 years old, her father had apparently abandoned the family, and she had become involved in an amorous relationship with the son of her mother's employers. During their three year relationship Luisa gave birth to two children, and soon afterwards the couple separated (Valle Ferrer 54).

To support herself and her children, Capetillo became a garment worker in 1905, five years after the birth of her second child. As early as 1904 she was writing articles in Arecibo (Ramos 65). In 1906 she began her post as a *lectora* [reader] in one of Arecibo's tobacco workshops. These kinds of "lectures" were not an uncommon practice in Puerto Rico, particularly among tabaqueras/os; for a minimal fee, designated "readers" would provide workers with the latest news and fiction in circulation—usually materials related to socialist politics—by reading out loud and facilitating discussions while the rest of the employees were occupied with the day's labor.[11] Finally, according to her biographer, Capetillo formally joined the FLT's Arecibo organization in 1907 (Valle Ferrer 131).

For Puerto Rican women at the turn of the century, both on the Islands and in the states, the practice of reading aloud in workshops provided an invaluable educational opportunity. Few critics have discussed the ways women, who were also a significant part of the tobacco industry's work force (not to mention the workers' movement overall), took advantage of this type of education. And although Capetillo's early and extremely liberal studies at home certainly set her apart from most working class women of her time, her coming to consciousness as a political activist, and her subsequent literary contributions, began with her lectureship. Her contributions may therefore provide an important inroad to beginning our understanding of the specifically feminine concerns of her epoch.

My primary interest here is to analyze Capetillo's last surviving collection, *Influencias de las ideas modernas* [The Influences of Modern Ideas], published in 1916, which includes most of her fiction and experimental prose. This text also contains her final thoughts on feminism, anarchism and other related topics, and was written primarily during her stays in the U.S., beginning around 1912.[12] But in order to make sense of her work at that juncture, I will begin with her literary career in Puerto Rico.

All of Capetillo's earlier texts reflect her formative involvement as an anarchist organizer and agitator. These texts (published between 1907 and 1911) pivot around three major issues: an outline of daily practice for women; the course of current politics, primarily the socialist agenda in Puerto Rico, and; the negotiation of what she conceived of as a global, workers' social movement, grounded in the specific concerns of Puerto Rican women. In developing these ideas, Capetillo critiques the Catholic church and, more importantly, what she argues is the dogma that evolved out of Christian philosophy. She also offers numerous, critical examples of the corruption of the elite classes, works through the complexities of working class oppression and resistance, all the while critically engaging the organizational, institutional and political discourses of her time.

Capetillo's explication of a liberatory daily practice for women must be traced within an elaborate web of observations and occasional summary remarks about the plight of Puerto Rican women in general. As a writer, Capetillo is perpetually sliding between the everyday scenes of life, which she sketches at length, and her reading of their significance in relation to her paradigm of liberatory action and behavior. This movement between everyday practices in the immediate context, and the abstract projection of possible alternative systems of thought and action, constitutes what I have termed the *p'acá y p'allá* dialectic, and defines Capetillo's work as a writer/activist.[13] We have no record of how she engaged her audience in her public speeches, but we can assume that the performative moment would have added another dimension to this dialectical motion.

This strategy is clearly elaborated in her first collection, *Ensayos libertarios* [Libertarian Essays]. For Capetillo, people are good by nature, but this benevolence is mutilated by the sedimentation of lies and the coercion imposed by the ruling classes; long before Althusser would garner credit for calling our attention to "Ideological" and "Repressive State Apparatuses" in the 1970s, Capetillo, in solid anarchist form, was already moving beyond the Marxist-Leninist interpretation of power relations.[14] Education, in Capetillo's analysis, provides an antidote to this manipulation of power, by helping to peel away the many layers of hegemonically induced ideology that enforces complaisance with an oppressive social order. For Capetillo, the basis of this education should be philosophically grounded in liberatory Christianity—her own rendition of the alternative "third space"—which she uses to exhort even privileged women to change their ways:

> The point is not to give away worn out clothes, while keeping closets full of extravagant outfits, as if some people were more entitled to using new and luxurious clothes. You will tell me, "let them work for it if they want nice clothes." But they are continually working, and yet continue to be poorly dressed, barefoot and hungry. And do you think that the exploiters' wives and children work? Where are the daily practices, in deeds not formulas? And what right do they have to call themselves Christians, if they are vain, lazy, selfish, indifferent and arrogant? They are vain, because they do nothing privately; everything they do is heralded with announcements and self-flattery—for these reasons they do charity work or some poorly executed "good deed" for their fellow humanity.
>
> They are lazy, because they have another human being around to attend to their caprices, and don't do a thing for themselves.[15]

Puerto Rico's first working class feminist is also (not uncoincidentally) the first to insist on class and cultural specificity. Capetillo was exceptionally intolerant of those women who enjoyed relative luxury while others suffered for lack of the most basic necessities. I think it is fair to assume that her childhood experiences, growing up as the daughter of a domestic servant of one of Arecibo's wealthiest families, fueled the indignation of her first published text. Another passage from *Ensayos libertarios* clearly summarizes this outrage against the privileged classes:

> Selfish and indifferent, because after attending to their necessities and vices, they don't believe that others have the right to do the same, and they try to lower the measly salaries of their servants, and then horde all the money they can, feeling

indifferent to the fact that their brothers and sisters, their servants, are barefoot and sleep on the bare ground, and they call themselves Christians. (7)

Again, Capetillo's style weaves between the broader concept and the specific manifestations of these issues in daily life. Moving back and forth, *p'acá y p'allá*, between the concept of ruling class privilege and working class deprivations, while sketching how this relationship works itself out in the most basic material ways, Capetillo composes a dynamic pastiche of ideas and images that together catch the contours of social stratification without ever losing sight of everyday reality. Her clauses, which challenge the limits of standard syntax, are laced together with a vehemence that makes each phrase flow seamlessly from the next.[16] In ordinary terms, Capetillo speaks from the heart, and her conviction helps the listener follow the meandering lines of her argument. This style reflects the active basis of speech that was Capetillo's primary mode of language at the time, where proper grammar and coordinated clauses are not as important as making sense of a complicated cluster of issues for a listening audience.

Ensayos libertarios, published in 1907, marks Capetillo's entry into the public scene of politics and includes work she wrote between 1904 and the date of publication. Her next text, *La humanidad en el futuro* [Humanity in the Future], published in 1910, is a hastily prepared monograph exploring an ideal society. Her third work, *Mi opinión, sobre las libertades, derechos y deberes de la mujer como compañera, madre y ser independiente* [My Opinion, Concerning Women's Liberties, Rights and Duties as Partners, Mothers and Independent Beings], published in 1911, is a rambling and varied exploration of the roles of women.

Mi opinión is introduced in the preface as a humble effort to illustrate how, in Capetillo's words, "*¡Querer es poder!*" [Desire is power!] (vii). The prologue concludes with the premise that "the present social system, with all of its errors, is sustained by ignorance and the enslavement of women" (x). Capetillo continues this theme with the compelling argument in the opening essay, "*La mujer en el hogar, en la familia, en el gobierno*" [Women in the Home, in the Family and in Government], that marriage is the most culpable social construct in the perpetuation of women's bondage, offering a detailed analysis of how women must reconceptualize love in ways that make desire a productive force rather than a commodity exchanged between men for men, via women, and codified by the institution of marriage. The subsequent pieces include a translation of Madeleine Vernet's essay "Free Love," with a fascinating if controversial claim that sexual satisfaction is essential for women's health; that depriving a woman of her pleasure is a deformation of her physical, mental, spiritual, and moral well being (43). Other pieces in the collection contest the common misrepresentations of women and call for women themselves to take control of the situation and demand their "natural" rights in everyday life as well as the symbolic order. Building from the basic premise that the oppression of women is at the root of all oppressions, Capetillo finds sexual liberation the first step in the realization of a genuine social revolution.[17]

For Capetillo, the Anarcho-syndicalist agenda seemed the best avenue for social change, and we see in her first texts a tremendous faith in the ideals of Puerto Rico's anarchist movement and the FLT in particular. Yet her work suggests that she was under constant attack for her feminist perspective. Already in *Mi opinión*, Capetillo is condemning political leaders, and speaking as if she assumes her audience will be skeptical, even dismissive of her ideas. She confronts the challenge in the preface:

> I publish these opinions unpretentiously, not to gain glory or applause, and without regard for the criticisms of experienced writers. The only motive I have for putting this text in print is speaking the truth, which others—under better circumstances and with more talent—do not do. Why? because of the risk of taking a stand, because they won't support the concepts of an idea they consider utopian. (v)

She argues that these so-called "utopian" ideals are, in her opinion, realistic goals. She also condemns the politicos of her time as a self-interested and unenlightened bunch. In her words: "Such men are an obstruction to great plans and good work. And yet they call themselves patriots and the fathers of our nation. What conception do they have of the nation? A conceited conception, that begins and ends in them. All of them are like this" (vi).

From around 1910 on, Capetillo perpetually argued that Puerto Rico's so-called "patriots" were a fraud, and she never ceased to condemn the self-interested and misinformed maneuvers of the Islands' political elite as well as the socialist leadership. We do not have a clear idea of how her polemics were received, or who precisely posed as her antagonists. Perhaps comments such as the above would have targeted men like Manuel Zeno Gandía, who was elected legislative representative of Arecibo, Luisa's hometown, shortly after he helped negotiate the U.S. invasion. Or perhaps she was speaking of Santiago Iglesias and his retinue, the exclusively male leadership of the FLT. Bernardo Vega writes of a heated debate in the New York community, spurred by a polemic in which Luisa Capetillo participated, in particular her argument that "*La tiranía, como la libertad, no tiene patria, como tampoco la tienen los explotadores ni los trabajadores*" [Tyranny, like liberty, has no homeland, nor do the exploiters nor the workers].[18] Perhaps then she was under attack in New York, or even all these circles simultaneously, for her contentious critique of nationalism.

What we do know is that many of those within Puerto Rico's propertied and professional classes were actively supporting U.S. rule. We also know that the anarchist leadership had made a series of concessions after the U.S. invasion, particularly with the various national parties that were preparing themselves for the autonomy promised but never granted by the U.S. They had also negotiated formal ties with the American Federation of Labor (AFL) under the leadership of Samuel Gompers.[19] All of these gestures toward becoming part of the insular institutional apparatus and the most centrist U.S. labor union obviously compromised the anarchist spirit that had made the FLT so popular in the first place. The significance of these maneuvers was not lost on the organization's membership,[20] and ignited a major debate among the Puerto Rican workers in New York city as well.[21]

Like the other figures of our *pionero* generation, Capetillo never lost hope in the freedom of Puerto Rico's working classes, despite the disintegration and confusion that erupted in the aftermath of the Spanish American War. She continued her work with the FLT, however, amid a serious crisis in the anarchist movement.

Under pressure, the FLT leadership justified its bids to form official ties with the insular parties and the AFL as a necessary step given what they assumed was Puerto Rico's imminent independence. But by 1908, two local elections had been held on the Islands affirming the populace's desire for self-determination, and neither was recognized by the U.S. Congress as a legitimate "democratic" vote. Painfully aware that everyone had been duped by the empty promises of the U.S. government, the FLT decided to redefine its agenda. Trying to reconcile its original anarchist program of action with its syndicalist agenda, the FLT targeted two internal priorities: 1) propagating union organization and; 2) promoting working class solidarity by the development of an alternative proletarian culture (García and Quintero Rivera 59). The second aspect of the platform reaffirmed the early anarchist program which, as mentioned above, fully rejected party politics and institutional reform, and opted instead for educating and supporting workers in their own, self-determined projects, particularly cooperatives and mutual aid efforts. To amplify this aspect of the struggle, the FLT launched its *"Cruzada del ideal"* [Crusade of the Ideal], delegating worker "crusaders" to agitate and educate other workers on the concepts of a new, socialist world order where, in the words of a writer well-circulated among Puerto Rican anarchists, "each individual is a producer of both manual and intellectual work."[22] In what seemed a perfect project for her at the time, Luisa Capetillo joined the ranks of the Crusaders in 1909.

The milieu of the *Cruzada* around 1910 should have been an invigorating experience for Capetillo, whose education and idealism matched the program's timbre. The authors, texts and ideas in circulation that were read, discussed and evaluated by Puerto Rican workers, in their workshops and the programs sponsored by the Crusaders and the FLT, came from all over the world. These voices offered a wide array of analyses that applied to the unique situation of Puerto Rico's sudden shift to a colony of the rising U.S. empire. Anarchist newspapers and pamphlets arrived from places like Brazil, Panamá, Argentina and of course Spain, while some of the most popular polemics and novels were translations from Russian and French, such as the work of Tolstoy, Kropotkin, Bakunin, Chernyshevsky, Zola, Diderot and Balzac, with which Luisa was already familiar. But despite this seemingly perfect match, Capetillo, again, was disillusioned, critical and, like so many of her contemporaries, decided to leave the Islands in the hopes of making a better go of it in the United States.

This moment—this bitterness, solitude and exile—is what makes Capetillo such an important figure for reconceptualizing fin-de-siècle Puerto Rico and the first generation of writers and activists in the colonial diaspora. Her engagement with modernity, anarchism, organizational politics, feminism and the rhetoric of trade-unionism was crucially mitigated by her very personal recognition of their discursive limits; not as discourses in and of themselves, but rather as concepts that, in the problematic translation into practice, were bogged down by the contradictions inherent in her attempt to shape a viable fulcrum of praxis.

Using the standard Euro-American categories of literary taxonomy, Capetillo's final work, *Influencias de las ideas modernas*, can only be described as a postmodern piece, ironically produced during what is considered the Latin and Euro-American eras of high-modernism.[23] But although her experimental pieces challenge the limits of both traditional literary genres and the metaphysical conventions they imply—two of the common characteristics of postmodern literary expression—the postmodern label does not really fit either the context or content of Capetillo's work.[24] Fredric Jameson's reading of postmodern pastiche, for example, as "blank parody, a statue without eyeballs," converts pastiche into a "neutral practice" of parody, a "blank irony" that is "devoid of laughter and of any conviction" (Jameson 17). But the pastiche effect of Capetillo's text is not an experiment in emptying aesthetic form of life and humor, nor is her tone plagued with the exasperated despair or cynical pleasure of finding the parts not fitting the whole. Rather, her writing is inspired by, and saturated with, a political and philosophical conviction that serves as its textual and extra-textual logic. Furthermore, though we might read Capetillo's work as a particular type of *bricolage* or pastiche, the fragmentation and disjuncture of her texts may also be simply due to the fact that a working class woman of her times may not have had the luxury of revising and editing, of composing longer, more integrated narratives, or the resources (including editorial support) for publishing more extensive and polished volumes of prose.

And while the aestheticizing and nihilistic tendencies associated with postmodernism simply do not enable us to make meaning of *Influencias*, Jameson's invocation of the transition into "late capitalism" after WWII as a historical backdrop for postmodernism seems equally irrelevant. Puerto Rico has been a colonial satellite of Euro-American capital for nearly five hundred years, thus capitalism has always arrived "late" and as a virtual afterthought, creating a unique socio-economic context for Puerto Rican cultural expression.

Ultimately, the emplotment of Capetillo and other Puerto Rican authors into the analytical frames of Euro-American literary history points out both the limits of Euro-centric theories and the need to create new approaches to the Puerto Rican narrative tradition. Writing is indeed a type of technology, and how this technology is used will differ according to the circumstances under which it is available; this usage will depend on the user and her needs, and in a perpetual colonial context the applications of a given technology may stray farther and farther away from the metropolitan manufacturer's operating instructions.

Capetillo's experimentation with prose was an appropriation of the written word in an effort to elaborate her vision of the personal trajectories of her life and work as a political activist in ways that were self-conscious representations of the collective predicament of working-class feminist subjectivity within the early stages of transnational capitalism, most particularly the experience of U.S. imperialist designs in the hemisphere. Written language thus provided her with a particular set of tools that she could manipulate to craft a new lexicon of images, ideas and social identities. And although Capetillo recognized the formidable challenge of constructing a landscape uninterrupted by geo-political borders, she never gave up hope in making this vision a possibility; in fact, hope and love are the defining elements of her thought as she perpetually reaffirmed the imperative of social revolution in the fullest (and necessarily creative) sense.

Influencias de las ideas modernas, which includes plays, letters, journal entries, short stories, and a number of genre-defying fictional and quasi-fictional pieces, was composed primarily in New York City and Ybor City, Florida, during 1912-1916, although the title play and the prologue were composed in Puerto Rico in 1907. Three years after beginning her work in the *Cruzada*, on the magazine *Unión obrera* [Workers' Union] and founding a

feminist magazine, Capetillo traveled to the continental U.S. in 1912 to continue her work within the *colonias* of the Puerto Rican diaspora.

Like Lola Rodríguez de Tió, who travelled to New York City in 1903 despairing over the situation in Puerto Rico, Capetillo arrived in New York despondent but hopeful of gathering new strength and support in the Puerto Rican communities stateside (Vega 119-20). But again, it seems Capetillo was confronted with a whole new matrix of compromising conditions. And as the situation became more hostile, Capetillo's anarcho-feminism became more adamant.

As all her work insists, the status quo, in Capetillo's opinion, is an intolerably backwards affair. The appearance of things almost always masks an ugly truth, and relations of power distill the fuel that keep them in place. A decade before Gramsci would write his prison notebooks, Capetillo is already writing of the inversion of reality via the master discourses that continually reproduce them. In *Influencias*, she applies this analysis of power to the issue of political opportunism; crucially, the budding socialist organizations of her time were not immune to the critique.

Moreover, Capetillo's reading of power relations is vehemently positivist which, in the best of the humanist tradition, often appears as the most natural evocation of common sense. Words and concepts have essential meanings, according to Capetillo, and human usage of language—not language itself—is imprecise. We see this taken to near Platonic proportions in *Influencias*. For example, according to Capetillo, a corrupt politician is an oxymoron, for politicians should be naturally disinclined to corruption (54-55). Likewise, a woman who goes beyond the traditional occupations by becoming a legislator, doctor or lawyer, is still a "woman," despite her assumption of "masculine" roles, just as a man who learns to cook and clean is still a "man" (84-85). The established codes of licit and illicit behavior, for Capetillo, are also suspect: in her reading, the only differences between an entrepreneur and a petty thief are the scenes of their crimes and the intensity of the injustices they perpetrate, the capitalist being the exponentially more vile of the two (54). In the same vein, the term "civilization" is convoluted in its popular usage: the adjective "civilized" in Luisa's opinion actually refers to the ways westerners use fashion to mask their inattention to hygiene, while the so-called "barbarian races" do not need hats, breath mints and fancy overclothes, for their hair is habitually clean, they consume healthy food and they needn't hide dirty underclothes beneath expensive suits (96). Finally, what passes as "humanitarianism" in North America is actually not so humane: Capetillo calls our attention to the fact that while there were organizations to protect the rights of animals, no one seemed to have an interest in the welfare of the most vulnerable constituencies of human society, such as children, the elderly and the sick (60).

This method of essentializing concepts, grounded in poetic renditions of "Nature" as the originary and benevolent referent, is a common devise in nineteenth century Euro-American romantic realism and certain strains of modernism.[25] But the crucial difference in Capetillo, which she perhaps shares with certain Latin American and Iberian streams, is the constant imperative of literally returning to some semblance of the "natural" order by explicitly invoking revolutionary practice. And it is here precisely, as she approximates an anarcho-feminist ethical imperative in the practice of everyday life, that her writing undoes the binary logic that her essentialist method implies, because she derives her theory from the scene of practice, despite her positivist impulses. She cannot help but to de-essentialize and de-romanticize social constructs, because her feminist and anarchist epistemes require that she dwell on the very seams of the binary split; and dwelling on these overlapping edges, the contradictions become apparent, even glaring. In Capetillo's daily life, every choice—from what she ate to what she wore—was loaded with political significance. Like her suits, the trappings Capetillo borrows from the Occidental tradition don't quite "fit": the politically gendered valence of Capetillo's cross-dressing strategy—wearing clothes "cut" for men over a woman's body—might also be a useful metaphor for describing her (in)appropriate appropriation of patriarchal structures of thought and modes of writing. What may seem "awkward" at first glance may in fact suggest a specifically feminine *escritura*, a highly complex articulation of gendered ambivalence that can only be approximated by putting under question the very concept of male/female polarities and, with it, the binary logic endemic to the empirical tradition.

This cross-dressing effect is most clearly marked in her discussion of feminist practice. Capetillo desperately wants to base her ideas about gender in biological fact, or the most natural of the natural sciences, but her analyses ultimately overflow these constructs of nature. For example, in *Mi opinión*, as discussed above, Capetillo includes the Vernet piece, arguing that females who are not sexually satisfied run the risk of biological atrophy (41). But in *Influencias* we see Capetillo taking a skeptical stance on such biological determinism. In a fascinating section titled, "*Cartas interesantes de un Acrata de Panamá*" [Interesting Letters from a Panamanian Anarchist], Capetillo includes a series of letters written from her Panamanian admirer that omits her side of the correspondence. The anarchist's letters are reprinted in chronological order, and it is clear that Capetillo's side of the correspondence was contestatory, but since her letters are absent the reader is forced to figure out what Luisa's responses may have entailed. In general, his responses demonstrate Luisa's critique of his positions, particularly his cynicism and his varied but problematic takes on feminism. One of these letters states that women should be always gently treated, because tension causes her chest muscles to contract, damaging her ability to lactate properly (149). Judging by his next letter, Capetillo had written him to say how bitter she had become, because no one seemed to understand what she really meant to say; presumably, as his thoughts on lactating would suggest, her Panamanian comrade was not much of an exception (149-50).

Capetillo's own positions on feminism likewise begin to unfix themselves from their essentialist underpinnings. Sexuality in *Influencias* is no longer represented as male/female; love is now characterized by terms that are not gender specific, such as the union of souls and bodies (60). Likewise, the almost constant conflation of womanhood with motherhood in her earlier work begins to unravel: Capetillo argues at one point that to be "complete," a woman must have children, but then retracts this claim by stating that all women are "mothers," regardless of whether they literally bear children (65, 86).

Overall, *Influencias* tests the limits of romantic and modernist discourses of nature, finding them inadequate to the task of revolutionary feminist theory, fiction and practice. When Capetillo returns to the issue of feminism, she does so by rejecting any and all formulas for behavior, dress, sexual practice and love. Midway through the text, she writes an odd piece on the *"qué dirán"* syndrome,[26] exploring what others say about Elena, a woman they see getting into a car with a man named Andrés. Elena and Andrés are mutually attracted to each other, and rather rationally decide to spend an afternoon together exploring the option of carnal and metaphysical desire. A pair of *"curiosos"* [busybodies] is watching the action, and discuss the implications of Elena's behavior. One of these voices keeps complaining that a woman should "belong" to one man only, while men have the right—indeed the natural instinct—to pursue as many women as possible. The other busybody critiques this double standard, and they engage in a long (and amusing) stichomythia. In the end, the *machista* [male chauvinist] refuses to concede, so he is dismissed by his friend: "You are the representation of tyranny against women. See you later, liberator" (93). Meanwhile Elena and Andrés drive off and make love in the open air, forging a lasting relationship free of coercion and matrimony, creating a happy ending to the story of Elena, who did what she pleased with her own body (94).

This freedom of form and movement, both in ideational content and writing style, ultimately comes together as fiction; indeed, the implicit textual logic of Capetillo's final work depends on fiction as the best method for coming to grips with the ineluctable modality of revolutionary praxis.

The stories that Capetillo published in *Influencias* deal with the need to sublimate desire because of the existing social norms, and each story offers a way out of this type of repression and displacement. Her first story, entitled "The Cashier," revises the usual 19th century romantic realism of authors such as Dickens, Charlotte Brontë and Zola, by appropriating the trope of the orphaned youth (105-13). This character, Ricardo, receives the disinterested help of a kind benefactor who, pitying his plight, arranges and pays for his education. But unlike Jane Eyre, for example, who uses her mysteriously granted fortune to establish a bourgeois paradise, Ricardo is disgusted with his middle class lifestyle and, successfully robbing a huge sum of money from his employers, runs off with the cash—and his beloved—to St. Petersburg. In another piece, a play aptly titled "The Corruption of the Rich," a young noble-woman is engaged to marry a rich suitor against her emotional inclinations (167-96). On the eve of her marriage, she decides to elope with her true love, and in a very crafty way, sneaks off with her dowry and the extravagant collection of wedding presents her family has on display. And in yet another play, "A Marriage without Love, the Consequences of Adultery," the heroine Esmeralda, like Elena in the piece mentioned above, meets a handsome youth named Eduardo on the street while out shopping (171-78). Esmeralda's husband, Ricardo, is a boring businessman who treats his wife as a commodity. Rather than tolerate her loveless marriage, Esmeralda runs off with her lover. The consequence of adultery here is happiness; in Esmeralda's terms, she needed "to feel that natural and spontaneous feeling that makes you feel delirious, that makes you commit the grandest insanities" (173). Unlike the hapless Anna Karinina in Tolstoy, as well as many other adulterous tragic heroines in 19th and even 20th century literature, Capetillo's adulteress lives happily ever after.

In all of these stories, the uncontainable desires of women and men are allowed to break free from socially enforced constraints and the contradictions of capital accumulation. In the pursuit of love and the fulfillment of sexual desire, Capetillo's characters literally "run off" the scene of their oppression, and the stories close with the blurring trail of their escape.

Unfortunately, Capetillo's literary career comes to an end after this first attempt at fiction. Just six years after *Influencias* was published in 1916, Luisa died of tuberculosis. Unlike her characters, whose self-imposed exiles fulfill their lives, Capetillo's sojourn to the U.S. brought more trials, alienation and disillusionment. She never ceased to struggle within the anarchist and socialist organizations of her time, but the bitter end to her own story is a telling contrast to her literary tableaux. She was buried in Río Piedras' municipal cemetery, after a humble service attended by a small group of friends from her family and the FLT, just a few miles away from the *Ateneo Puertorriqueño*, where eight years later the cadaver of Manuel Zeno Gandía would lie in state, amid the glory of honor guards and an extravagant public funeral.[27]

Conclusion

In the interest of recovering Puerto Rican literature in the continental United States, the emplotment of great men, great books and great acronyms into the narratives of national culture and literature will not suffice. That is, if we want to conceive this project as a recuperation of texts that make meaning of the lives and experiences within the Puerto Rican diaspora, we need to reconceptualize literary studies and move beyond the basic assumptions that characterize traditional theory on canon formation. Returning to Flores' article, I would reassess his claim that mainland Puerto Rican narrative constitutes a "literature of straddling, […] operative within two national literatures and marginal in both" (*Stages and Perspectives* 66). This would imply a sort of stasis—one foot glued *p'acá*, the other *p'allá*, like a Caribbean Atlas—when in fact these texts, and this community is constantly moving, *p'acá y p'allá*, in a dialectical rhythm that underscores a species of cultural production that defies the rigid fixation of canon politics.

Of course, we need to recuperate our cultural and intellectual histories. But how we do this must be carefully evaluated. Among the texts produced by Puerto Rican diaspora writers and activists from the turn of the century, we will not find "Great Books," because our *pioneras/os* were actively struggling against what a national culture and literature would imply: the rigid taxonomical project of bourgeois cultural nationalism. If we emplot the *pioneras/os* in their historical context, we find a transnationalist milieu that believed they were fostering an impending social revolution; the very least of their concerns was producing the Great American Novel. Moreover, the first generation of stateside Boricuas was aggressively and creatively engaged in shredding the social, ideological and literary constructs endemic to the Occidental tradition, including those that were so dearly prized by Puerto Rico's insular dominant culture.

In the anarchist spirit of Luisa Capetillo, whose work has never fit into any traditional frames of analysis, I will close with the audacious assertion that until we effectively redefine the terms "great," "American" and "novel," canon politicking will be a game of deceptions. But once we do, Luisa Capetillo's *Influencias de las ideas modernas* will be a strong candidate for a genuinely American literary history.

Notes

[1]First published in the *ADE Bulletin* (Association of Departments of English), 91 (Winter 1988) pp. 39-44. Page references here will refer to the reprint in *Recovering the U.S. Hispanic Literary Heritage*, pp. 53-68. The literal translation for "*la charca*" is "the putrid pond."

[2]"American" here refers to the common usage of the term to signify U.S. cultural and national identity; in quotes since the term is equally applicable to the entire continent, or the Americas as a whole. "AmeRícan" is Tato Laviera's poetic affirmation of mainland Puerto Rican subjectivity. Cf. Laviera. pp. 94-95.

[3]In another article, Dr. Flores explains that, although published in 1894, *La Charca* is temporally situated in the 1850s and 60s, and thus implies a "critique of emerging capitalism" as it developed during that era. Consequently, Flores reads Zeno Gandía's novel as a romanticized realist rendition of pre-capitalist social relations, pitting the noble peasantry and the *hacendados* together—or, in hindsight, what they represented as a decaying social order for Zeno Gandía in the early 1890's—against the rising bourgeoisie (represented in the text as *el negocio*—or the business sector) that came to dominate in the late nineteenth century. Most of this argument relies on critical reinterpretations of two of the novel's main characters. Here Silvina, an abused young peasant woman, becomes the moral center of the novel, while Juan del Salto, the wealthy Hispanic patriarch, is read as an "ironic" character, whose narrative position is riven with complex ambiguities.

Although the essay is a brilliant re-reading of *La charca*, I find the class antagonism frame (between the dying *hacendado* elite and the incipient bourgeoisie) forecloses an analysis of the *gendered* social relations that are inextricably meshed in the historical and textual relations of power between class (and implicitly racialized) constituencies in nineteenth century Puerto Rican society. Flores acknowledges the novel's "class and sexual bias, buttressed...by overtones of racial determinism," but mitigates their effect in the novel by effectively deconstructing the patriarchal voice. This maneuver posits the patriarchal apex of the socio-economic pyramid as an ambiguous figure, whose contradictions compromise his moral authority. Certainly, this approach makes a lot of sense from a contemporary perspective, but I wonder how far the novel deconstructs that voice, or rather, how far Flores' reading teases out the ambiguities that, in Zeno Gandía's historical context, may have seemed unambiguous. Likewise, the novel's relevance to mainland cultural and literary history demands further discussion. Cf. Juan Flores, "Refiguring *La Charca*" in *Divided Borders: Essays on Puerto Rican Identity,* pp. 71-91. First published as "Introduction" to *La Charca*, trans. Kal Wagenheim (Maplewood, NJ: Waterfront Press, 1984), pp. 13-32.

[4]The most notable exceptions to this rule are: *Arthur Alfonso Schomburg: A Puerto Rican Quest for his Black Heritage* and *Amor y anarquía: Los escritos de Luisa Capetillo.*

[5]Though both are fleetingly mentioned in Bernardo Vega's text: *Memorias de Bernardo Vega,* pp. 120, 111-112, 88-89, & 134-135.

[6]Cf. Eugene Mohr's odd attempt to read Vega's *Memorias* as a heroic epic. Eugene Mohr, *The Nuyorican Experience: Literature of the Puerto Rican Minority*, chapter 1, "Proto-Nuyoricans," pp. 3-23.

[7]Ramos, Introduction, p. 14. This and all subsequent references will be my translation.

[8]Lisa Sánchez González, "*P'acá y P'allá*: Narrative and Political Struggle in the Puerto Rican Diaspora," chapter II.

[9]The only biography on Capetillo is Norma Valle Ferrer's *Luisa Capetillo: Historia de una mujer proscrita*. Most of the biographical information cited here comes from this work, along with Julio Ramos' chronology; Ramos, pp. 65-66.

[10]Valle Ferrer's introductory chapter provides an excellent overview of female education at the turn of the century. Also see Margarita Ostolazo Bey, *Política sexual en Puerto Rico* and *La Mujer en Puerto Rico: Ensayos de investigación,* ed. Yamila Azize Vargas.

[11]For an excellent, detailed discussion of the practice of *lectores* (readers) in workshops, see Ramos, Introduction, pp. 11-58.

[12]Capetillo published three earlier books: *Ensayos libertarios* (1904-1907); *La humanidad en el futuro* (1910); and *Mi opinión, sobre las libertades, derechos y deberes de la mujer como compañera, madre y ser independiente* (1911). None of these texts has been reissued since its original publication date.

[13]"*P'acá y p'allá*" literally signifies "*right here and over there*," but as phrase means a number of things, including "everywhere," denoting a universalizing inclusiveness, and "all over the place" in the chaotic sense. The *p'acá y p'allá* dialectic is my shorthand for a culturally and historically specific mode of expression that moves between the 'here and now' ('*p'acá*'), and a projection towards an abstract terrain 'over there' ('*p'allá*'), simultaneously negotiating both spaces as inextricable dimensions of material and ideational struggle (be they represented as somehow containable or out of control). This dialectic always implies motion and commotion, and a type of textual/contextual antiphony irreducible to structural frames of analysis or any reductive notion of determination. It also implies a certain dialectical rhythm between text and context that is far more involved than the concept of "syncopation" in Occidental musical traditions. Cf. Sánchez González, chapters I and V.

[14]Cf. Althusser, pp. 127-186.

[15]*Ensayos libertarios*, p. 6. This and all subsequent references to Capetillo's texts will be my translation.

[16]Of course, Spanish syntax is far more tolerant of this type of writing than English, especially current academic standards in English composition. The English translation here cannot avoid exaggerating Capetillo's oral technique.

[17]Capetillo's analysis here foreshadows some of the most compelling themes in Chicana/Latina theory in the 1980's and 90's, especially the (still) controversial Chicana lesbian writers, such as Gloria Anzaldúa, Emma Pérez and Cherríe Moraga, whose work centers on sexuality as the most important issue for contemporary cultural critique.

[18]Vega, pp. 134-35. Vega mentions Capetillo as an important historical figure but, beyond her curiosity as a woman with a big appetite, he offers little information on her work in New York City.

[19]For a full discussion, see L. García and Quintero Rivera, pp. 33-41.

[20]Igualdad Iglesias de Pagán claims that the FLT leadership and its membership had been critical of the Autonomist movement as early as 1897. Cf. Iglesias de Pagán, p. 38.

[21]By the time Luisa arrived, Puerto Rican anarchist organizations had been an integral part of the New York political scene for decades. Bernardo Vega recalls that the anarchist organization, *La Resistencia*, was one of the few surviving operations after the confusion and disintegration of the various clubs and organizations in New York after 1898 (Vega, pp. 107-109). Likewise a major scandal of that period was provoked by a speech given by Santiago Iglesias at a conference in Rochester, which Arturo Schomburg and others attacked for its racist overtones (Vega, pp. 111-12).

[22]Peter Kropotkin, *Fields Factories and Workshops*, pp. 22-23.

[23]Iris Zavala offers a compelling reading of "modernism" in Latin America at the turn of the century, which analyzes the emergence of new discursive strategies not unlike what I am discussing as Capetillo's unique take on the master narratives of her time. Cf. Zavala, pp. 28-49.

[24]Following Lyotard, "postmodern" signifies here a basic "incredulity toward metanarratives." Lyotard diagnoses postmodernism as a symptom of "the condition of knowledge in the most highly developed societies" (i.e. nation states entering a postindustrial phase after World War II), where the status of scientific discourse has been altered by the increasing commodification of knowledge, which requires that information be "translated" into readily consumable portions. Here "knowledge ceases to be an end in itself," and becomes something bought and sold rather than something we learn or know and, as a result, knowledge no longer needs to legitimate

itself with the old unifying assumptions about truth and the inviolability of empiricism. Instead, the "mercantilization" of information in late capitalism transforms the unifying principle of knowledge into nothing more than a process of exchange. Consequently, the "grand narratives" that previously legitimated Occidental discourses of knowledge (and therefore rationalized existing relations of power) break down like obsolete (and therefore abandoned) machines.

These ideas perhaps make sense within the "postindustrial" societies to which Lyotard refers, but cannot account historically for metadiscursive shifts in communities that have existed *outside* the postindustrial loop or on the periphery of those societies as (neo)colonial satellites. For if we read this metadiscursive incredulity and the obsolescence of Occidental discourses of knowledge as the defining elements of postmodernity (a gross oversimplication, but nevertheless its qualified "definition"), then much of the world has been "postmodern" for centuries. In literature, a number of texts produced prior to WWII would in fact qualify as postmodern works, since counter-hegemonic story-tellers and story writers in the Americas have been "incredulous" for centuries, compromising the Euro-American metanarratives all the while. Furthermore, the transformation of knowledge in "the most highly developed societies" has a distinct matrix of meanings in places where culturally specific understandings of what constitutes "knowledge" have different and equally complex histories that, among other things, include resistance to (and contradictory strands of complicity with) certain Euro-American philosophical traditions imposed as a result of annexation, colonization and other modes of imperialist domination.

This is why the emplotment of new voices and cultural traditions into the discussion of literary theory tests the limits of Euro-American "knowledge" and ultimately explodes the constructs endemic to this cultural and intellectual tradition. And I find it hardly a coincidence that postmodern theories attempt to explain away the demise of the "grand narratives" as a systemic shift in late capitalism (a system increasingly devoid of any and all human agency according to the major Marxist theorists) without attending to the historical resistance to this metadiscursive tradition outside the Euro-American mainstream.

In simpler terms, it is one thing for the emperor to realize the truth about his new clothes, but another thing entirely when his subjects point it out to him. I find many of the seminal postmodern texts cynical, nihilistic and hyper-aestheticized in elitist ways, which makes sense if we read these texts as the dying gasp of an outmoded cultural elite whose services as apologists for imperialism are no longer needed. Hence cynical and nihilistic posturing become perhaps the only way for the naked emperor to recuperate any semblance of dignity, while exhausting the recognizable limits of aesthetic form ensures that everyone's clothes will seem absurd. Cf. Lyotard, 1984.

[25]Consider, for example, the representation of nature in the novels of Emily Brontë or Emile Zola, and the canvases of artists such as Vincent Van Gogh.

[26]*¿Qué dirán?* literally means "What will people say?"

[27]Cf. "*Apuntes biográficos*," in the 1992 edition of *La charca*, which tellingly begins with the quote: "*El amo de la tierra es el amo de la patria*" [He who owns the land, owns the fatherland] (pp. v-xi). The reissue is part of the Instituto de Cultura Puertorriqueña's current popular library series.

Works Cited

Althusser, Louis. *Lenin and Philosophy and Other Essays*. Trans. Ben Brewster. New York: Monthly Review, 1971.

Azize Vargas, Yamila, ed. *La mujer en Puerto Rico: Ensayos de investigación*. Río Piedras, PR: Ediciones Huracán, 1987.

Capetillo Perón, Luisa. *Ensayos libertarios*. Arecibo, PR: Imprenta Unión Obrera, 1904-1907.

_____. *La humanidad en el futuro.* San Juan, PR: Tipografía Real Hermanos, 1910.

_____. *Influencias de las ideas modernas.* San Juan, PR: Tipografía Negrón Flores, 1916.

_____. *Mi opinión, sobre las libertades, derechos y deberes de la mujer como compañera, madre y ser independiente.* San Juan, PR: Biblioteca Roja/The Times Publishing Co., 1911.

Flores, Juan. "Puerto Rican Literature in the United States: Stages and Perspectives." In *Recovering the U.S. Hispanic Literary Heritage.* Eds. Ramón Gutiérrez and Genaro Padilla. Houston, TX: Arte Público, 1993, 53-68.

_____. *Divided Borders: Essays on Puerto Rican Identity.* Houston, TX: Arte Público, 1993.

García, Gervasio L. and A.G. Quintero Rivera. *Desafío y solidaridad: Breve historia del movimiento obrero puertorriqueño.* Río Piedras, PR: Ediciones Huracán/CEREP, 1982.

Iglesias de Pagán, Igualdad. *El Obrerismo en Puerto Rico: Época de Santiago Iglesias (1896-1905).* Palencia de Castilla, España: Ediciones Juan Ponce de León, 1973.

Jameson, Fredric. *Postmodernism, or the Cultural Logic of Late Capitalism.* Durham, NC: Duke University Press, 1992.

Kropotkin, Peter. *Fields, Factories and Workshops.* 1912; rpt. Brunswick, NJ and London: Transaction, 1993.

Laviera, Tato. *AmeRícan.* Houston, TX: Arte Público, 1985.

Lyotard, Jean François. *The Postmodern Condition: A Report on Knowledge.* Trans. Geoff Bennington and Brian Massumi. Minneapolis, MN: University of Minnesota Press, 1984.

Mohr, Eugene. *The Nuyorican Experience: Literature of the Puerto Rican Minority.* Westport, CT: Greenwood Press, 1982.

Ostolazo Bey, Margarita. *Política sexual en Puerto Rico.* Río Piedras, PR: Ediciones Huracán, 1989.

Piñero de Rivera, Flor, ed. *Arthur Alfonso Schomburg: A Puerto Rican Quest for his Black Heritage.* San Juan, PR: Centro de Estudios Avanzados de Puerto Rico y el Caribe, 1989.

Ramos, Julio, ed. *Amor y anarquía: Los escritos de Luisa Capetillo.* Río Piedras, PR: Ediciones Huracán, 1992.

Sánchez González, Lisa. "*P'acá y p'allá*: Narrative and Political Struggle in the Puerto Rican Diaspora." Diss. UCLA, 1995.

Valle Ferrer, Norma. *Luisa Capetillo: Historia de una mujer proscrita.* San Juan, PR: Editorial Cultural, 1990.

Vega, Bernardo. *Memorias de Bernardo Vega.* Ed. César Andreu Iglesias. Río Piedras, PR: Ediciones Huracán, 1988.

Zavala, Iris. *Colonialism and Culture: Hispanic Modernisms and the Social Imaginary.* Bloomington and Indianapolis, IN: Indiana University Press, 1992.

Zeno Gandía, Manuel. *La charca.* 1894; rpt. San Juan, PR: Instituto de Cultura Puertorriqueña, 1992.

The Recovery of the First History of Alta California: Antonio María Osio's *La historia de Alta California*

Rose Marie Beebe and *Robert M. Senkewicz*

The transformation of Alta California was as sudden as it was unexpected. From a population of less than 15,000 *gente de razón* [literally, people with the capacity to reason, meaning people born into Christianity; that is, any non-Indian people] in the mid-1840s, it contained over 100,000 inhabitants in 1850 and almost a quarter of a million two years later. Swarming over the landscape, hostile to the system of land ownership and use that had developed over the previous half century, the newcomers, imbued with their longstanding belief in Anglo-Saxon superiority, went where they willed and took what they wanted.

The *Californios* [any Mexican raised, or later, born and raised in California] adopted various strategies to meet this invasion. Some participated in the institutions set up by the conquerors, sitting in the 1849 Constitutional Convention and in the early state legislatures. Others prepared to defend themselves through North American courts and land commissions. Others withdrew from public life and public view, in the hope that they would be left alone. Others left and returned to Mexico.

This paper tells the story of another strategy, one man's attempt to preserve a world through the creation of history and autobiography. On April 4, 1851, in the city of Santa Clara, Antonio María Osio, who had been a bureaucratic functionary and officeholder in Mexican California for two decades, presented Father José María Suárez del Real with a densely written one hundred and ten page manuscript. In a cover letter, Osio told Suárez del Real that what the priest had asked him to do, "write the history of California," was beyond his ability. But he had decided, Osio said, to write a letter, a "*relación*" of events since 1815 and especially of "what I have known and seen since 1825."

Osio was well-situated to do this. A native of Baja California, he had married Dolores Argüello, the sister of Luis Argüello, the first Mexican governor of Alta California. He worked in the Customs Service in San Francisco and Monterey in the late 1820s. As a member of the *Diputación* [elected assembly that met at Monterey during the Mexican period in California] in the early 1830s, he was active in the successful movement to overthrow Governor Manuel Victoria. As a member of the Los Angeles *Ayuntamiento* [municipal government composed of a local magistrate and various members of a town council] and as *síndico* [public attorney], he participated in the movement against Governor Mariano Chico. He was a leader in the southern California resistance to Governor Juan Bautista Alvarado in 1837. In the late 1830s, he became both Collector of Customs at Monterey and a member of the *Tribunal Superior* [superior court], and he served in both positions until the 1840s. Politically and socially, Osio was a very well-connected man in Mexican California.[1] Yet his manuscript has never been published, or even widely studied. In this paper we would first like to demonstrate why the manuscript was consigned to historiographical oblivion. Secondly, we would like to highlight some of the reasons why we think it is an important and unique document in the history of Mexican California.

By early 1852, both Osio and Suárez del Real had left Alta California and returned to Mexico. Osio spent the rest of his life in his birthplace of San José del Cabo in Baja California, where he served as *alcalde* [local magistrate] in the 1860s and as a judge in the 1870s. The manuscript's existence remained almost completely unknown in California for a quarter century. Suárez del Real, who died in the 1850s, never returned to Alta California. Osio did return for brief visits at least twice, in 1864 and in 1875.[2]

By the time of that second visit, Hubert Howe Bancroft's staff, especially Enrique Cerrutti and Thomas Savage, were involved in collecting from the old *Californios* the reminiscences, dictations, and documents which would serve as the backbone of the Spanish and Mexican sections of Bancroft's seven-volume *History of California*. Osio had apparently heard about this, for he brought the manuscript with him to San Francisco. On April 18, 1875 Cerrutti wrote to Bancroft:

> A few days ago Mr. Osio, a resident of California in 1826, arrived in San Francisco, dragging along with him a manuscript history of the early times in California. I believe he originally intended to give it to your library, but certain persons whose acquaintance he happened to make induced him to reconsider his resolution, and made him believe that there was money in it. Actuated by that belief, he has given the manuscript to Mr. Hopkins, keeper of the Archives in San Francisco, with a prayer for enough subscribers to pay for printing it. I believe, with judicious diplomacy and a little coin, you could get some person to purchase the manuscript for your library. (Bancroft, *Literary Industries* 647)

Osio eventually returned to San José del Cabo, where he died in 1878. However, before he departed he left the manuscript at Santa Clara with Soledad Ortega, the widow of Luis Argüello. Upon her death, the manuscript passed into the possession of J.R. Arques, the executor of the Argüello estate. He gave it to one of Osio's daughters, Beatrice Osio de Williamson, who was living in San Francisco. During the late 1870s, three copies were made of it. One was made for John Doyle, who was collecting as many old documents as he could as part of his work for the Catholic Church in California on the Pious Fund case.[3] The second was made for James A. Forbes, who was a translator in the San Francisco Archives. Third, in 1878 a copy of the Doyle copy was made for Bancroft (Bancroft, *Literary Industries* 647-48).[4]

These events had two consequences. First, the fact that Osio did not freely make the manuscript available to Bancroft's staff soured them on him. Cerrutti's comments quoted above give a flavor of the negative way in which the emerging Anglo history establishment was beginning to deride Osio and his manuscript: Osio was "dragging along with him" the manuscript and was animated solely by the desire to make money. Actually, Cerrutti's letter points to something quite different. Osio was motivated by a desire to have the entire manuscript published on its own and rendered accessible to a wide readership. Osio was in fact something of a genuine amateur historian. He had at least browsed through the government archives in Monterey and when he was a member of the *Diputación* in the 1830s he was anxious to create and preserve an accurate historical record.[5] He may well have sensed that offering the manuscript to Bancroft would have been in effect to cede control of the historical record to the very people who had taken over his country and who tended to be scornful of Mexico's past rule in Alta California.

Such a fear would not have been unfounded. One need only contrast the paternalistic and heavy-handed manner in which the Mexican reminiscences are sometimes treated in Bancroft's *California* volumes with the reverential and awe-filled fashion in which the same author's *Popular Tribunals* handles the reminiscences of the San Francisco vigilantes of 1851 and 1856 to appreciate how pervasive was the denigration of Mexicans in the former works.[6]

Osio's experience made him very hostile to those who ruled the land where he had spent so many years. The experience was bitter. In 1839, he had been granted Angel Island in San Francisco Bay and in 1842 he received another grant of land near Point Reyes on the Pacific Coast north of San Francisco. He developed Angel Island quite effectively during the 1840s: by 1846 he had over 500 head of cattle grazing there and he was regularly selling beef to San Francisco. And, as the 1840s progressed, he spent more and more time at Point Reyes where he intended finally to settle so that he and his second wife could raise their young family in the country. In 1846 he had to abandon

Point Reyes because of the Bear Flag Revolt, and in the same year the U.S. Navy occupied Angel Island and slaughtered his entire herd of cattle. Soon North American squatters began to take possession of his land at Point Reyes.

Osio was associated with a group of Mexicans who had never made their peace with the American takeover of Alta California. Another of the group, Soledad Ortega, once told Mariano G. Vallejo, "They [the North Americans] rule over us in the same manner that the owner of a large farm rules his slaves. Our sweet Castilian tongue has given place to the unpronounceable English jargon—bless the Almighty I have not learned it" (Mollins and Thickens 109). Osio's manuscript was written in that same vein. It could be quite sharp on the subject of the North Americans. For instance, in relating Thomas A. Catesby Jones' premature capture of Monterey in 1842, Osio described the raising of the flag of the United States over the presidio in these words:

> The true *Californios*, people who loved their country and were proud of their nationality, were forced to witness a painful ceremony for the very first time. The national flag of the three guarantees was lowered from its native flagpole so that it could be replaced by the stars and stripes. This flag was alleged to be the symbol of liberty, but this actually was a lie. It belonged to an oppressor who displayed arrogance against the weak.[7]

In a similar fashion, Osio described the efforts undertaken by some *Californios* to resist the North American invasion in 1846 as follows:

> The North American flag waved in all the populated areas of Alta California, but the Mexican tricolor still flew in a few places as it wandered about its own country, passing through the deserted fields, unable to find shelter from the bad weather. It seemed as if the flag were revealing its despair; its brilliant colors had been faded by the strong rays of the sun, it had been torn by bullets and thorny branches, and worst of all, it had been orphaned with no distant hope of being helped. Nevertheless, the flag proudly waved in the wind, sensing the courageous heartbeats of the brave men who supported it. If they could not obtain an honorable surrender, they vowed to fight to the bitter end and die defending the flag. Let it be known for all time that even though they were unable to do more for their native land and for the country of their birth, these men should serve as an example for other places invaded by forces from the United States.

Osio's 1851 manuscript reflected the raw passions and the closely experienced bitterness of watching one's own country taken over by foreigners. In the document he described himself as "one who has experienced the sufferings of the *Californio* landowners, which the political change has caused." He was not, as were so many of the *Californios* who later gave their reminiscences to Savage or Cerrutti, ambivalent about the North American conquest.[8] He was emphatically and completely hostile to it. This attitude undoubtedly contributed to a negative assessment of his manuscript in what had been Alta California.

A second consequence of the way the manuscript came to be made available in the late 1870s was that Bancroft ended up with an unreliable version, for he had to content himself with a copy of John Doyle's copy. The Doyle copy, dated 1876 and now housed at the Huntington Library, is not one hundred percent accurate. The title was changed from "*La historia de Alta California*" ["The History of Alta California"] to "*Crónica de los acontecimientos ocurridos en California desde 1815-1846*" ["Chronicle of Events That Occurred in California from 1815 to 1846"], and the scribe, Gulielmo B. Chase, appears to have been editing the manuscript as he went along. He consistently made significant stylistic and grammatical changes in an apparent attempt to clarify or improve Osio's manuscript. Words, clauses, and complete sentences are missing.[9]

The Bancroft copy differs significantly in content and format from both the original and from the Doyle copy. As in the case of the Doyle copy, the Bancroft scribe may have been mechanically copying the pages before him. It is evident, though, that he was not a meticulous proofreader for, in addition to the omissions already noted in the Doyle copy, the Bancroft scribe compounded the inaccuracies and corrupted the manuscript even more by omitting additional material, from entire paragraphs to numerous pages. For example, twenty one consecutive pages of the original manuscript, which deal with the complex political controversies of 1836 and 1837 in which Osio was an active participant, are missing. At some point during his work on this section, the scribe, realizing that the material he was copying was not making any sense, observed in a parenthetical note at the bottom of the page: "*En todo este capítulo se nota alguna vaguedad y no parece sino que, o el autor por precipitación u otra circunstancia no describe claramente los hechos, o el copista del original dejó algo en el tintero.*" ["In this entire chapter one notices a certain vagueness and it seems that either because the author was in a hurry or some other circumstance, he does not describe the events clearly, or the scribe who copied the original left something in the inkwell."] (290-21).[10]

The corruptions of the Bancroft copy were taken to be inherent weaknesses of the manuscript itself. Bancroft himself called attention to some of these weaknesses and attributed them to Osio, rather than to the fact that he was using a corrupt copy of a copy.[11] In sum, the carelessness of the Bancroft scribe resulted in a confusing, unintelligible, and incoherent copy, and this is doubtless another reason why researchers have not consulted the Osio manuscript more frequently.

However, Bancroft did more than just criticize the Osio manuscript; he subsumed it into his own work. Had Osio been alive when *California* was published, he surely would have been outraged to learn that Bancroft had appropriated his manuscript into the corpus of dictations and reminiscences which *he* had collected. At the beginning of the first volume of the series Bancroft wrote:

> The memory of men yet living when I began my researches, as aided by that of their fathers, covers in a sense the whole history of California since its settlement. I have therefore taken dictations of personal reminiscences from 160 old residents. Half of them were native, or of Spanish blood; the other half foreign pioneers who came to the country before 1848. Of the former class, twenty-four were men who occupied prominent public positions, equally divided between the north and the south. (1: 55)

At the bottom of that page, in a footnote, right between "Ord" (actually Angustias de la Guerra y Noriega, the daughter of José de la Guerra y Noriega, longtime Commander of the Santa Bárbara Presidio) and "Palomares" we read "Osio" (1: 55).[12] In other words, Bancroft presented himself as the one who had called Osio's manuscript into being in the 1870s! In the pages of *California*, Bancroft and his staff stripped Osio of his own authorship.

The fate of the manuscript after Savage reported in 1883 that it was in the possession of Osio's daughter Beatrice is not entirely clear. Beatrice Osio de Williamson continued to live in the San Francisco Bay area for some time after her father's death.[13] We do know that the manuscript eventually came into the possession of Vallejo Gantner, son of John Gantner of the firm of Gantner and Mattern in San Francisco. It had probably come to his attention through some historic preservation efforts of the Native Sons and Daughters of the Golden West.[14] In the 1950s, he gave it to two of Herbert Eugene Bolton's research assistants, Margaret Mollins and Virginia Thickens, who planned to translate and edit it. When Herbert Eugene Bolton became ill and died, they had to return to teaching and were not able to complete the project. Later they arranged for the manuscript to be deposited at Santa Clara, its original home.[15]

Osio's manuscript is a significant document in the history of Mexican California for a number of reasons. First, it is the earliest narrative account of the period 1821-1846 that we have. The most utilized primary sources for the history of Mexican California have been documents concerning governmental and ecclesiastical affairs. Most of these sources have an ad-hoc quality about them. They were written to compile a required annual report, to deal with a current problem, or to answer a specific question. These sources have the closeness and the texture of day-to-day life, and that often gives them much of their value. However, historians know that to understand a culture and a people, one needs to know not only what they did in the lived ordinariness of their lives, but also how they viewed what they were doing. Explicitly self-reflective work—fiction, autobiography, memoirs—can be of great assistance as we seek to understand the past. Imagine, for instance, how incomplete our understanding of the Pilgrims would be if we did not have William Bradford's *Of Plimouth Plantation* or Mary Rowlandson's *Narrative of Captivity*, of colonial and revolutionary America if we did not have *The Autobiography of Benjamin Franklin*, or of the Jewish immigrant experience if we did not have Abraham Cahan's *The Rise of David Levinsky*. Analysis of these works, of course, is far from simple. However, they often provide a unique entry into a culture. Osio's manuscript does the same.

This leads to the second reason for its importance. The manuscript is clearly based on two types of sources: what Osio directly participated in and what he was told by others. The sources are then personal and oral. The oral nature of the sources is clearly revealed, for instance, in the way Osio treats non-Spanish names—he spells them out phonetically in the manuscript.[16] He had never seen these names in any sort of document; he had only heard them in the oral tradition of his people. The manuscript, therefore, brings together a number of stories that were undoubtedly current in Alta California in the 1830s and 1840s. Some of them, at least, bear the marks of having been worked on and refined either by Osio or by the tradition.[17]

Third, Osio's presentation of these stories is about as close as we are ever going to get to the oral culture as it existed before the North American invasion. The Osio manuscript differs markedly from other reminiscences by his contemporaries, notably the multi-volume works of Mariano Guadalupe Vallejo and Juan Bautista Alvarado, which were composed in the 1870s, more than a quarter century after the conquest and in some cases more than fifty years after the events they describe. With the passage of time a person's recollections do not always remain unchanged, memories tend to fade or become confused, and facts may be exaggerated or forgotten. People continually revise the memories of their lives to harmonize with the events that have happened or are happening at the present time (Couser, *Altered Egos* 17).

The Osio manuscript, on the other hand, was written a mere five years after the North American conquest of Alta California. The accounts of various events often tend to be more sober, less exaggerated, and less given to the grandiloquent pathos which one can find in some of the other reminiscences. In general, Osio's more matter-of-fact accounts are probably closer to the way these events were remembered to have been experienced by the *Californios*.[18]

Fourth, Osio offers a definite interpretation of the period he covers. We can gain the best perspective on his interpretive scheme by considering (a) his authorship; (b) the literary form of the manuscript, and (c) the emergence of Osio the man in the course of the work.

His Authorship

Osio clearly regarded his role as more than simply being the person who would collect and preserve a bundle of stories. He was deeply aware of what today we would term his authorship: he was the one who decided which stories to include and how to group them. This may well be the reason he decided to begin his account in 1815, even though he did not arrive in Alta California until 1825. For then there could be no doubt that he was the one responsible for the order which existed in the manuscript. He uses the pre-1825 section of his work, in fact, to introduce all the themes he wants to cover in the body of the work.[19]

The manuscript begins with a description of the sadness and sense of loss felt by the inhabitants of Alta California when their governor died and it ends with Osio stating that he himself has experienced the sufferings of the *Californio* landowners which the recent political change has caused. These themes of sadness and loss frame the entire manuscript. The work is Osio's lament on his and Alta California's lost possibilities and on the disorder and chaos that affected both of them after the North American invasion. Osio's history of California is not simply a record of scattered recollections but rather a carefully crafted response to the changes that were occurring around him.[20] Osio is attempting to come to terms with what it meant to be a *Californio* in 1851. The result is a historical manuscript that can also be read as a personal and collective autobiography.

Osio differs from the other *Californio* authors in that he maintained complete authorial control over his narrative and it is his voice that resonates throughout. Osio, alone, decided on the material that would be included and on the manner in which it would be presented and the manuscript was written in his own hand. The other *Californio* authors were not able to maintain this degree of control over their work because the material for their narratives was obtained through oral interviews conducted by Bancroft's staff.[21] The topics and the order in which they were to be discussed were partially controlled by the interviewers who would take notes as the person spoke. Later, the information would be transcribed. During the transcription process it was not uncommon for the material to be edited or "filtered" through the scribe's pen.[22] Informants' responses and opinions were often influenced by the manner in which the interviewer would ask the questions, which could be considered a form of manipulation. Osio, on the other hand, did not answer a set of pre-determined questions nor did he allow anyone but himself to edit the manuscript.[23] The form of the work was his and his alone.

The Literary Form of the Manuscript

Evidence of Osio's familiarity with many different literary traditions appears throughout the manuscript and Osio drew on a number of them.[24] For example, he could employ classical mythology. In one highly symbolic episode, Chico (whom Osio calls "Argos the observer") catches his mistress ("the beautiful Napea") flirting with a handsome young American ("Narcissus") she has met aboard ship.[25] Osio's obvious knowledge of and appreciation for a wide variety of literary genres may have influenced the stylistic framework he chose for his manuscript. Characteristics of three literary genres—epistle, memoir, and autobiography—appear in his work. The manuscript begins with the letter to Father Suárez del Real and ends with closing lines addressed to the same man. In this manner, the letter, which on the surface simply appears to be Osio's reply to the priest's request that he write a history of California, becomes the exterior framework for the work as a whole.

The conversational or dialogic tone of the narrative is characteristic of epistolary literature; the author writes the way that he speaks. Underlying the epistolary discourse is the important relationship between the reader and the author which will dictate the manner in which the information in the manuscript is conveyed.[26] The reader, Suárez del Real, plays a generative role in the creation of the work, for, the common memories, experiences, and trust shared by the two men give Osio the freedom to be honest, objective, and sincere as he composes. If one were to read the letter, or for that matter the entire manuscript, aloud, it would be easy to imagine Osio engaged in a long evening of conversation as he reminisced with his friend.[27] The dialogic motif is maintained throughout the entire manuscript. There are numerous instances where Osio adopts an explicitly conversational relationship with the reader as he says "Take note," "Look," "Notice," or "Imagine."[28]

Osio concludes the introductory letter by suggesting that Suárez del Real obtain letters from other friends who can provide him with information that Osio does not include. Although Osio appears to have taken his role as author very seriously, he never claims to be the supreme authority on California history. In fact, he openly submits his work to the scrutiny of others when he suggests that Suárez del Real ask for assistance from another friend who has the proper training and attributes of a good writer and who can help him compile a comprehensive history of California.[29] The closing lines of the introductory letter parallel the closing lines of the manuscript in which Osio states,

> As one who has experienced the sufferings of the *Californio* landowners, which the political change has caused, I would ask that you please allow me to conclude

the present letter here. Another friend of yours, with a very small pen, might continue the story. Please accept this brief work which your dear, devoted servant dedicates to you as a token of our friendship.

Here, as in the introductory letter, the ritual of closing allows Osio to reiterate the mood of the entire work, the tone of sadness and loss. He also implies that his work is incomplete and that it will take on a larger significance when different perspectives and interpretations are added to it. Epistolary texts are never closed. Rather, they are merely a selection from a larger body of information or just one side of an exchange (Altman 144-5, 162). The epistolary text is not merely a historical object or an antique curiosity but rather a living thing that can be framed and re-framed as part of an ongoing process of textual creation, transmission, and interpretation. A work such as Osio's becomes the sum of its readings and contains not only numerous readers but all the years of its existence (Blasing xxiv).

The Emergence of Osio the Man

While Osio is the narrator of the manuscript, his own personal presence does not stand out. Osio does not assume the role of narrator-protagonist and never overshadows or dominates the work. He chooses, instead, to slowly and subtly appear on the social and political scene, presenting different sides of himself in different contexts. He thus engages in an exercise of self-creation in which the reader is a witness and an indirect participant. This technique of subtle, progressive self-disclosure allows Osio, as narrator-observer, to position himself both inside and outside of his "history."

Osio refers to himself by name only twice in the manuscript, and then he calls himself "some fellow named Osio." As he becomes more involved in the political and social arenas, he appears in the text more frequently. However, he always describes himself in cryptic, indirect, or self-deprecating ways. He refers to himself as "the lowly Customs employee" or disguises himself as the "friend of Sepúlveda," "Gutiérrez' friend," or "the clumsy, foolish narrator." The restraint he employed in "creating" his public persona and in positioning himself in the manuscript in relation to other people indicates that he did not view himself as a person who operated and developed in isolation, but rather as someone who had been shaped by a collective experience.

Those two aspects of Osio—being described in a deprecatory fashion and being formed by a collective experience—also define the life of the other main character in the manuscript. That character is nothing else than Alta California itself. "Alta California" are the fifth and sixth words Osio placed in his manuscript, and it is never very far from the center of attention. Throughout the work, Osio often, indeed repetitively, adopts the point of view of the *Cali-*

fornio elite and criticizes Mexico for neglecting its welfare.[30] For instance, he breaks off an account of an artillery battle between the defenders of Monterey and one of Bouchard's ships to state, "*No hijo del país* [native son] was recognized by the Mexican government during its different periods." Or again: "The Mexican government declared itself California's stepfather and denied it protection as if it were a bastard child." Or yet again: "The government [of Mexico] never considered the advantages to be gained by stimulating development in different parts of this territory, which was so ready for it." The modest way in which Osio speaks of himself is matched in the manuscript by the minimal fashion in which the central government treats its faraway territory.

Osio emerges fully only at the end of the manuscript, as he writes about his own part in the history of the Bear Flag Revolt and the North American invasion. In this section he consistently refers to himself as a "*Californio.*" But in his mind this identity is inextricably intertwined with another identity. As he describes the help given to Stockton in San Diego by "some corrupt *Californios* and some Mexican traitors," he fumes, "Because I am a *Californio* who loves his country and a Mexican on all four sides and in my heart, as a point of honor, I should keep quiet about the following event or let it go unnoticed or be forgotten, but this would not be in keeping with the purpose of my narrative." This is the only time in the narrative section of the work that he refers to himself in the first person and refers explicitly to a design in the manuscript. For Osio, to be a *Californio* was always to be Mexican. And more: the "purpose" of this whole manuscript is to make that point against those who in 1851 were thinking that they could successfully negotiate the transition to North American rule. The quarrels with Mexico, really quarrels within an extended family, had blinded too many people, Osio thought, to their own identity.[31]

At the end of his work Osio describes the negotiations between Andrés Pico and John C. Frémont after the battle of San Pascual. He writes that even though the *Californios* might well become "*buenos ciudadanos de los estados de Washington*" [good citizens of the states of Washington]," they would always be "*en su propio país…extranjeros de México*" [in their own country…foreigners from Mexico]. Less than a year after he wrote those words, on February 2, 1852, Osio filed a claim before the United States Land Commission in San Francisco for Angel Island. Testimony on his behalf was offered by former Governor Juan Bautista Alvarado, former San Francisco Harbor Master William A. Richardson, and Jean Jacques Vioget, who had made the first survey of San Francisco and who testified to the Commission "I have never heard the title of Osio to the said Angel Island questioned or disputed" (Papers of the Land Commission). The Land Commission found in Osio's favor, and in 1855 the District Court in San Francisco upheld that judgment. However, in December 1859 the United States Supreme Court, straining for technicalities, threw out the claim in the case United States v. Antonio María Osio.[32] We would like to think that when Osio heard of that decision, he reached for his manuscript, re-read it, and realized that he had written more truly than he had known.

Notes

[1]No biography of Osio exists. The most convenient compilation of events in his life can be found in Hubert Howe Bancroft, *History of California* (4: 761-62). Bancroft states, "But for the record of offices held by him, there is a remarkable lack of information about the man." The information about Osio's life that we offer in this paper generally comes from the manuscript itself and from various other manuscript collections in The Bancroft Library and the Archivo General de la Nación in Mexico City.

[2]Maynard Geiger, O.F.M., *Franciscan Missionaries in Hispanic California, 1769-1848* (249-51), gives biographical information on Suárez del Real. Osio's 1864 trip is inferred from a letter from Edward Vischer to Osio at Santa Clara, September 30, 1864.

[3]The Pious Fund was an endowment established by Spain in 1697 to support the missions in Baja California. It was later used for the Alta California missions as well. In 1842 Antonio López de Santa Anna sequestered the principal and intermittently paid the interest until California became part of the United States. The Catholic bishop of California, Joseph Alemany, then claimed control of the fund. He successfully pressured the United States government to have the matter submitted to international arbitration.

Doyle served as Alemany's attorney in the case. He was also the first president of the California Historical Society. See Francis J. Weber, "The Pious Fund of the Californias" and "John Thomas Doyle, Pious Fund Historiographer."

[4]At the head of the copy of the manuscript made by Savage for Bancroft, which is now in The Bancroft Library, is this note from Thomas Savage:

San Francisco (Calif.)
January 8, 1883

I have this day examined a copy of the history of California, whereof the annexed is another copy; or rather, the former is, to the best of my knowledge and belief in the handwriting and bears the signature at the end of its author, Antonio María Osio, occupying about 162 pp. of paper of about fool's cap length. Sewed onto the first page is what purports to be the rough copy of a letter without a signature, from said Osio to Fray José Ma. Suárez del Real, dated at Santa Clara April 4, 1851, from which I conclude that Real had asked Osio for facts to enable him to write a history of California, and for the earlier parts of the history of the Californias, and the administrations of the various governors to Arrillaga inclusive, he refers to the works of Piccolo and others.

The original alluded to is in the possession of Mrs. Williamson, a Mexican lady who I understand is a daughter of the late Ant. M. Osio and lives now at 326 Polk St in this city, her husband being in Mexico.

Thos. Savage

The original of the manuscript is now in the archives at Santa Clara University. The Doyle copy is at The Huntington Library, and the Forbes copy is at The Beinecke Library.

[5]In the Archivo General de la Nación in Mexico City [General Archives of the Nation (AGN)], there are, for instance, a collection of copies of the minutes of the 1832 *Diputación*. At the conclusion of a number of the copies is the phrase *"Es copia, San Diego, 15 de mayo de 1832. Juan B. Alvarado."* ["This is a copy, May 15, 1832. Juan B. Alvarado"]. On the top left hand side of the first page of the same proceedings we find written in Osio's hand, *"Como de oficio para los años de 1832 y 1833, Osio."* ["Officially for the years 1832 and 1833, Osio"]. This indicates that at a later date Osio was asked by someone—or perhaps took it upon himself—to verify the accuracy of the copies. On the top of another document dealing with trade, again in Osio's hand is written *"Havilitado provicionalmente por la comisaría provisional de la alta California para el año de 1832, Osio."* ["Provisional quartermaster for the provisional commissariat of Alta California for the year 1832"]. This indicates the same type of verification on Osio's part (AGN, Gobernación, Legajo 120, Caja 191, Expedientes 2-4).

[6]In fact, the Mexican dictations and reminiscences in Bancroft's *History of California* were used in procrustean ways that made them serve the conquerors' notions of the superiority of what they termed Anglo-Saxon progress and development over what they were certain were Mexican indolence and laziness. On the denigration of Mexicans in Bancroft, see the comments of Genaro Padilla in *My History, Not Yours: The Formation of Mexican American Autobiography*, 254-55. On Osio's manuscript and the Mexican reminiscences in general, Bancroft states in *California*, "It [Osio's manuscript] is a work of considerable merit, valuable as a supplement to those of Vallejo, Alvarado, and Bandini, as presenting certain events form a different point of view; but like all writings of this class, it is of very uneven quality as a record of facts. None of them, nor all combined, would be a safe guide in the absence of the original records; but with those records they have a decided value" (4: 762). This statement, and others like it, might seem unobjectionable, until it is contrasted with statements like the one in *Literary Industries* about Andrés Pico: "There were several of the brothers Pico, all, for native Californians, remarkably knowing. Whether they caught their shrewdness from the Yankees I know not" (490). In *Popular Tribunals* (which was dedicated to "William T. Coleman, Chief of the Greatest Popular Tribunal the World has ever Witnessed")—Coleman gave Bancroft a dictation—the vigilante reminiscences are fairly consistently treated as the gospel truth, and the givers of the dictations congratulated for throwing one or other type of brilliant light on a difficult point. Vigilante Chauncey Dempster's reminiscence, for instance, is characterized as "able and eloquent...prepared for me with great care, in which the heart-beats of the movements seem to pulsate under his pen" (2: 73; see also 1: viii, 191). In *California*, on the other hand, the Mexican narratives are subject to a seemingly endless series of critiques in extensive footnotes (and it should be noted that both the critiques and the footnotes are absent from *Popular Tribunals*). Thus the reader is informed, for instance, that Osio's account of one scene is "amusingly absurd" (3: 208). Bancroft simply takes a figure of speech which Osio used ("But, in the end, providence proved the best commander at preventing bloodshed") interprets it literally, and then patronizingly denigrates it. The vigilante reminiscences were also at times inconsistent with each other, but Bancroft did not feel compelled to point this out to his readers. See Robert M. Senkewicz, *Vigilantes in Gold Rush San Francisco*, 193-94.

[7]All quotations from this point on, when not otherwise noted, are from our critical, annotated translation of the Osio manuscript.

[8]On this point, see especially Genaro Padilla, *My History, Not Yours*, 77-152.

[9]The Doyle copy did include a portion of text material which is missing from the original manuscript. In the original manuscript (page 101A), Osio indicated with a # symbol, as he had done in a previous section, that the rest of the paragraph on that page was written on a separate sheet. This particular sheet must have been lost or inadvertently discarded after 1876, because it

is not with the original. Fortunately, Chase had access to that extra sheet and included the information in his copy.

[10]Other examples of the corruption of the Bancroft copy are *Capítulo XII* [Chapter XII], where six pages of the original are missing, and *Capítulo XIII*, where the last six and a half lines are misplaced on the previous page.

[11]For instance, in *California*, Bancroft describes the maneuvers against Alvarado in 1837, noting that some of "the succeeding particulars are not expressed intelligibly by Osio" (3: 496).

[12]In his biographical sketch of Osio, Bancroft insists that Osio wrote his manuscript "in his later years," despite Savage's clear statement to the contrary. See Bancroft, *California* 4: 762.

[13]According to the 1900 census, she lived in enumeration district 357 on Maple St. in Oakland.

[14]John Gantner had married Adela Frisbie, who was the granddaughter of Salvador Vallejo, brother of Mariano Guadalupe Vallejo. Both John and Adela were quite active in the Native Sons and Daughters of the Golden West, who were interested in the preservation of historical documents. We speculate that the manuscript became known to John Gantner or Adela Frisbie through their connection with the Native Sons or Daughters. Since the manuscript mentions both Mariano and Salvador Vallejo, it stands to reason that John Gantner or Adela Frisbie would have been interested in it. See John O. Gantner, "Gantner and Mattern," a brief appendix to a longer manuscript, John Oscar Gantner, *Notes on the Life of My Father*. The information on Gantner's involvement in the Native Sons comes from the obituary of John Gantner, which is appended to the end of the "Gantner and Mattern" essay.

[15]This information comes to us through correspondence with Margaret Mollins and Virginia Thickens.

[16]"Bouchard," for instance, becomes "Buchard," and "Riley" becomes "Rayle." When he is discussing the Bear Flag movement, Osio has occasion to mention one of its leaders, William Ide. He assumed that "Ide" contained a silent Spanish "h" and was spelled "hide." So he joked that Ide could have been called *Señor Cuero* [Mr. Hide] since *cuera* means "hide" in Spanish and American merchants were dominating the hide and tallow trade. In addition, because of their leather jackets, Spanish and Mexican soldiers were called "*soldados de cuera*," and so Osio is also probably being sarcastic about the military escapades of the Bear Flaggers.

[17]In some places in the manuscript we can see Osio reacting to parts of the oral tradition. In describing the 1832 Battle of Cahuenga in which Governor Victoria's detachment forced a rebel group to flee, Osio becomes very critical of the rebel commanders José Antonio Carrillo and Pablo de la Portilla. He wrote, "It should be noted that even though they have bragged tremendously since the insurrection, they had twice as much left in reserve as their opponents. They never had the decency of saying later why they had not somehow aided Ávila and Talamantes, the only two men out of more than 200 in the force who joined the battle and distinguished themselves courageously."

[18]For instance, in his discussion of the Bouchard raid, Alvarado has a long story about how Bouchard, disguised as an English captain on a scientific expedition had visited Monterey in 1817 to scout Monterey's defenses (Alvarado, *History of California* 1:108-09). Speaking of the same episode, Vallejo says that Bouchard was frightened away from attempting to land at San Francisco when Commander Luis Argüello posted all of his soldiers in plain view of the privateer and fired a cannon at him (Vallejo, *Historical and Personal Memoirs* 1: 136). Neither account reflected what actually occurred, and are doubtless the results of the passage of time and perhaps of the designs of Alvarado and Vallejo as they were talking to the Bancroft staff almost sixty years after the events they had witnessed. Osio, whose oral sources included Luis Argüello, has neither story in his account of the Bouchard affair.

[19]The introductory section of the manuscript contains three large episodes: the attempts by Luis Argüello to develop San Francisco, the Bouchard raid, and the 1824 Chumash uprising. Osio chooses these three episodes to allow him to introduce three themes which will dominate his work: (1) the *Californios* did try to develop the resources of Alta California; (2) Spain, and later Mexico, never gave Alta California the support it needed if development were to succeed; and (3) the mission system never was so effective in converting and/or Hispanicizing the indigenous peoples as its proponents claimed. In fact, the very first incident that Osio recounts in his work sets a tone. Osio describes the scene when the head of the missions, Father Vicente Francisco de Sarría, finished his first meeting with Governor Pablo Solá: "When the Superior returned to the room in which he had left the other Fathers, he found them with some officers. One of the Fathers gestured with his head, as if to ask him if he had succeeded. The Superior understood, and in response placed his right arm all the way up his large left sleeve to indicate that he already had him in his pocket." This vivid picture of clerical manipulation and power is gradually undone in the course of the manuscript. In fact, the very last scene in the manuscript describes the Fathers' inability to find gold in California.

[20]At one point in the manuscript, when he is discussing "the veil of schemes which was drawn to hide the uprising by foreigners in 1840, an uprising which finally took place in 1846," Osio remarks, "That is why, today, those people with their *considerandos* [the word with which each item in a judgement begins…"whereas"] need to be reminded of a familiar story about two people who inherited vast expanses of adjoining lands." The reference to "*considerandos*" is a reference to the 1851 California legislature, which was meeting in San José, immediately adjacent to the city of Santa Clara, while Osio was composing the manuscript. Some *Californios* sat in this body and Osio may well have been specifically referring to them.

[21]Although, as Rosaura Sánchez says, Vallejo and Alvarado maintained authorial control over their memoirs by dictating the conditions of the sessions, they did not have the degree of control that Osio had over his manuscript. In his case there was no one else involved. There was no interviewer and no list of questions. See Rosaura Sánchez, "Nineteenth Century Californio Narratives: The Hubert Howe Bancroft Collection," 283.

[22]Sánchez states, "The manuscripts were always re-copied and carved up by topics, periods, etc., to create files of notations, excerpts and documents for the various writers hired to write Bancroft's California history" (286).

[23]There is evidence in the manuscript that Osio acted as his own editor, for at times he crossed out words and placed the corrections in the space above.

[24]Some of the authors and texts which served as sources for Osio include *The Bible*, Sir Walter Scott, the epic poem *Amadís de Gaula, Lazarillo de Tormes*, Cervantes' *Don Quixote*, Lope de Vega's epic poem *La gatomaquia*, Samaniego's *Fábulas*, and Lesage's picaresque novel *La historia de Gil Blas de Santillana*.

[25]In another episode, Osio recreates a meeting between Mariano Chico and Abel Stearns and uses a biblical reference as metaphor. Referring to the Gospel of Mark (chapter 15, verse 16), Chico is cast in the role of Pontius Pilate, administering bad justice.

[26]Janet Gurkin Altman writes: "The *I* or epistolary discourse always situates himself vis-à-vis another; his locus, his address, is always relative to that of his addressee. To write a letter is to map one's coordinates—temporal, spatial, emotional, intellectual—in order to tell someone else where one is located at a particular time and how far one has traveled since the last writing. Reference points on that map are particular to the shared world of writer and addressee" (87, 119).

[27]Osio recounts at least one episode at which he and Suárez del Real were both present: a wedding of an indigenous *alcalde* performed by the priest, which Governor José Figueroa also attended.

[28]Mutlu Konuk Blasing observes, "The *I* and the *YOU* whom the *I* addresses are both on stage; consequently, the work should not be seen as an object, because one cannot simply speak for oneself. Whom else one is speaking for depends upon which stage one is speaking from, what the props are, and who one's audience is" (xxvi). We might also note that Osio's clear division of the narrative into two parts, events before and after 1825, indicate that he was aware of the distinction between a *crónica* [chronicle] and a *memoria* [memoir]. In the *memoria*, the author explicitly states that he will only narrate what he has seen and experienced, however, he will highlight the narration with appropriate commentary. The *crónica*, on the other hand, may include material of which the author has no personal experience and no attempt is made to distinguish between the two. The inclusive nature of Osio's own personal experiences as well as those of his family and friends expands the structural dimensions of the text. Now the reader sees that the exterior epistolary framework is supported by a sub-structure, the *memoria*, which can be classified as both a personal and a collective autobiography.

[29]Osio suggests that Suárez del Real consult the work on Junípero Serra by Francisco María Piccolo, and, at another point in the manuscript, suggests that the author of the full history of California would have to take into account another published source, the work of Governor Figueroa on the abortive Híjar-Padrés colonizing effort: "*Señor* Figueroa, who was now free of the immediate problem, decided to print the official communications which had been exchanged between the *Jefe* [leader] of the territory, the *Diputación*, and the principal director of colonization. For the satisfaction of the public, this was done in the form of a printed manifesto. When the manifesto was finished he did not have time to have it printed since he became seriously ill and died in September 1835. However, his secretary, *Don* [title of respect] Agustín Zamorano, attended to it. After he had compiled various notebooks, he distributed them among the friends of the deceased general. In the notebook one is given an extensive view of everything that happened during *Señor* Figueroa's tenure in government. Therefore, it would be advantageous for the person who is entrusted to write the history of Alta California to make use of the notebook."

[30]See David J. Weber, *The Mexican Frontier, 1821-1846: The American Southwest Under Mexico*, 240-41.

[31]A major theme of the section of the manuscript which deals with the North American invasion is the loss of "*nacionalidad*" [nationality]. For instance, in describing the North American capture of Monterey, Osio writes, "At eleven o'clock the inhabitants of Monterey experienced the sorrow of seeing the stars and stripes wave for the second time from the flagpoles that had been erected for the tricolor flag of the three guarantees. However, this time it seemed worse as they began to think about the loss of their nationality and of everything they had worked so hard to create. For experience has always shown that conquerors never have been able to maintain a brotherhood with those they have conquered." And, in the same vein, Osio describes the resistance to the invasion: "Many people around Monterey and San Francisco were willing to defend with one last effort the nationality which they held so dear. In several skirmishes with the American troops, they fought like true Mexican soldiers and courageous victors."

[32]Osio sold his claim to Angel Island in 1853 (United States v. Osio, 23 Howard 273).

Works Cited

Altman, Janet Gurkin. *Epistolarity: Approaches to a Form*. Columbus: Ohio State UP, 1982.

Alvarado, Juan Bautista. "Historia de California." 15 vols. 1876, ms. The Bancroft Library, University of California, Berkeley.

Bancroft, Hubert Howe. *History of California*. 7 vols. San Francisco: The History Company 1884-1890.

Bancroft, Hubert Howe. *Literary Industries*. San Francisco: The History Company, 1890.

_____. *Popular Tribunals*. San Francisco: The History Company, 1887.

Blasing, Mutlu Konuk. *The Art of Life: Studies in American Autobiographical Literature*. Austin: U of Texas P, 1977.

Couser, G. Thomas. *Altered Egos: Authority in American Autobiography*. New York: Oxford UP, 1989.

Gantner, John O. "Notes on the Life of My Father." Ms. The Bancroft Library, University of California, Berkeley.

Geiger, Maynard, O.F.M., *Franciscan Missionaries in Hispanic California*, 1769-1848. San Marino: The Huntington Library, 1969.

Mollins, Margaret and Virginia E. Thickens, eds. *Ramblings in California: The Adventures of Henry Cerrutti*. Berkeley: Friends of the Bancroft Library, 1954.

Osio, Antonio María. "Antonio María Osio Papers, 1823-1853." The Bancroft Library, University of California, Berkeley.

_____. "Minutes of the 1832 meetings of the *Diputación Territorial* of Alta California." Archivo General de la Nación, Mexico City, Gobernación, Legajo 129, Expedientes 15 and 18.

Padilla, Genaro. *My History, Not Yours: The Formation of Mexican American Autobiography*. Madison: The U of Wisconsin P, 1993.

Sánchez, Rosaura. "Nineteenth Century Californio Narratives: The Hubert Howe Bancroft Collection." *Recovering the U.S. Hispanic Literary Heritage*. Eds. Ramón Gutiérrez and Genaro Padilla. Houston: Arte Público, 1993, 279-92.

Senkewicz, Robert M. *Vigilantes in Gold Rush San Francisco*. Stanford: Stanford UP, 1985.

United States Commission for Ascertaining and Settling Private Land Claims in California. Ms. The Bancroft Library, University of California, Berkeley..

Vallejo, Mariano Guadalupe. "Historical and Personal Memoirs Relating to California." 5 vols. Trans. Earl R. Hewitt. The Bancroft Library, University of California, Berkeley.

Vischer, Edward. "Edward Vischer Papers, 1853-1878." The Bancroft Library, University of California, Berkeley.

Weber, David J. *The Mexican Frontier, 1821-1846: The American Southwest Under Mexico.* Albuquerque: The U of New Mexico P, 1982.

Weber, Francis J. "John Thomas Doyle, Pious Fund Historiographer." *Southern California Quarterly* 49: 3 (1967): 297-303.

_____. "The Pious Fund of the Californias." *Hispanic American Historical Review* 43: 1 (1963): 78-94.

Adina de Zavala's Alamo: History and Legendry as Critical (Counter-Alamo) Discourse

Richard R. Flores

Adina De Zavala was born in 1861 not too far from Houston, Texas on her family's homestead of De Zavala Point near San Jacinto. Her grandfather, Lorenzo de Zavala, was the primary author of the Mexican constitution of 1824 and, after serving as the Mexican ambassador to France, settled in this part of what was then Mexico. When Antonio López de Santa Anna annulled the Mexican Constitution in 1835, Lorenzo de Zavala, acting on his liberal principles, sided with the Texan forces and served as the first Vice-President of the Republic of Texas until his untimely death from pneumonia in 1836.

Adina De Zavala, born in 1861, was educated at Ursuline Academy in Galveston and received her Master of Instruction degree from Texas Normal Institute in Huntsville. She founded the De Zavala Daughters, renamed the De Zavala Chapter and admitted into the Daughters of the Republic of Texas (DRT) in 1893, and later the Texas Historical Landmark Association. She served as a Vice-President of the Folk Lore Association of Texas and was a charter member and fellow of the Texas State Historical Society.

By the time of her death on March 1, 1955, Adina De Zavala was known as a woman committed to the preservation and restoration of Texas historical monuments as well as to the cultures and peoples who shaped the history of Texas. For all her accomplishments, De Zavala is perhaps least known, however, for initiating and substantially contributing to the preservation and restoration of the Alamo in the 1880s, an effort that requires some introduction.

The Alamo's Past

The mission of San Antonio de Valero was founded in 1718 under the direction of Fray Antonio de Olivares as part of the Franciscan missions in Texas. The mission complex consisted of a church, friary or *convento*, granary, workshops, storerooms, and housing for the native Indians. Today, what is known as the Alamo is only the mission church which was completed in 1744. In the 1750s the roof of the church collapsed due to poor construction materials and workmanship, and still in shambles, Mission San Antonio de Valero was secularized along with all other Texas missions in 1793.

The mission fell into disuse and disrepair until 1802 when it was occupied by a Spanish cavalry unit, the Segunda Compaña Volante de San Carlos de Parras del Álamo, from which the name "Alamo" comes from. This occupation marked the last time the Alamo was used as a church, since it was again abandoned in 1810 and remained so until it was occupied as a fort by the Mexican army from 1821 to 1835.

By the time of the "Battle of the Alamo" in 1836, the mission complex covered two to three acres and the roofless chapel was 75 feet long and 62 feet wide with stone walls 22 feet high and 4 feet thick. Attached to the northwest end of the church was the *convento* or long barracks which was 186 feet long and 18 feet wide and high. The rooms on the upper floor were used as a hospital while those on the first were soldiers' quarters (Ables 376).

In 1841 the Republic of Texas granted the mission church and the other local missions to the Roman Catholic church. And in 1848 the Alamo mission was leased to the United States, housing the U. S. Quartermaster's Depot. The U. S. government renovated the church in 1849, adding a top center gable and new upper windows. After the Civil War, the Alamo was again used by the Quartermaster's Depot as a grain reception facility.

The *convento* or long barracks of the mission was sold to Honore Grenet in 1877 who added wooden porticos to the structure above the stone walls. Upon Grenet's death, an advertisement for the sale of the Alamo in 1882 read:

FOR LEASE OR FOR SALE,
to the purchaser of its valuable and constantly kept-up stock of Goods, together with the lease of the ALAMO, and the goodwill of the business, so long and so profitably enjoyed by its deservedly popular founder. (Gould 16b)

A buyer for the Grenet business was found in the Hugo-Schmeltzer Company in 1886. In 1883, Grenet's lease to the mission church was purchased by the state of Texas, placing that portion of the Alamo in the hands of the City of San Antonio. From the activities of Grenet and the Hugo-Schmeltzer Co., it is clear that the primary function of the Alamo through the 1880s was commercial, being described as a "modernized and…mammoth business house," and only secondarily evoking interest as an historical site (Gould, inside page).[1]

An important organization in the effort to preserve the Alamo was the Daughters of the Republic of Texas (DRT), a group De Zavala was affiliated

with during the early years of the twentieth century. The DRT and De Zavala were themselves part of a growing nineteenth-century effort on the part of women to influence, preserve, and define aspects of American history and culture. While little has been written on this subject from the perspective of Texas women, Douglas and McCarthy have documented how women writers and philanthropists, mostly from places outside Texas, have been instrumental in shaping this crucial period in American history. Michael Kammen has included a brief discussion of Driscoll and De Zavala in his sweeping survey of American cultural history; and Ables's work has been invaluable in tracing the relationship between these two women

The DRT was established in 1891, dedicated to the preservation of historic sites and the memory of men and women responsible for the independence of Texas. Organized around local chapters, Adina De Zavala led the effort to establish the De Zavala Chapter, named after her acclaimed grandfather Lorenzo de Zavala.[2] By the time the De Zavala Chapter was admitted into the DRT in 1893, Adina De Zavala was already actively working to preserve the Alamo, having received a promise from Gustav Schmeltzer of the Hugo-Schmeltzer Co. "not to sell or offer the property [of the Alamo] to anyone else without…giving the Chapter [of the DRT] the opportunity to acquire it" (Quoted in Ables 378). Soon recognized for her vitality and vision, De Zavala became a member of the executive committee of the DRT in 1902.

De Zavala's initial agreement with Schmeltzer stated that the De Zavala Chapter of the DRT would have first option on purchasing the building that housed the Hugo-Schmeltzer Co., giving the DRT time to raise the sum of $75,000 which was the agreed upon price. However, early in 1903, De Zavala received word that a commercial interest group from the Eastern U. S. was interested in the Hugo-Schmeltzer property. Devising a strategy on how to raise the money, De Zavala heard of a "prominent, rich and very ambitious young woman who may be of some help" (Ables 381). This was Clara Driscoll, who initially collaborated with De Zavala and later openly feuded with her over the final historical portrait the Alamo would present.

Elsewhere (1995) I contrast De Zavala's efforts to restore the Alamo with that of Clara Driscoll, the woman credited by the DRT for restoring and preserving the physical site of the Alamo. In my attempt to understand how the private visions of De Zavala and Driscoll were transformed into the making of the Alamo as a site of public culture, I discuss the initial efforts of De Zavala, her collaboration with Driscoll, and their eventual public dispute over the historical portrait of the Alamo painted by the DRT. Juxtaposing Driscoll's romantic and sentimental historical and fictional texts with the equally romantic but utopian writings of De Zavala, I interpret these women's narratives as janus-faced texts that shed light on the contradictory perceptions of history and society they held. The discord between these two, I conclude, signals a critical moment: the transition to modernity. That is, the historical and political tensions between Driscoll and De Zavala are not exclusively matters of personal opinion but stances emblematic of racial and class distinctions associated with industrialization in Texas.

The emergence of the Alamo as one of the most important sites of public culture coincides with other preservation efforts across the country (cf. Kammen). These projects are not random occurrences but events whose traces point to the looming task of redefining American culture and society at a time of increased immigration and expanding capitalist economies. During this time, the search for collective icons that could fix particular images and identities yielded places of public culture, a process that converted the private visions of cultural elites into public markers of a new social order.

Only recently have the custodians of the Alamo recognized De Zavala's efforts at preserving the Alamo with a plaque in her honor. However, in a pamphlet published by the DRT entitled, "Women of the Alamo" De Zavala's name is absent. As I began exploring the life and work of De Zavala I could not, at least initially, imagine how this articulate, energetic, and intellectually astute woman of Mexican origin could be so passionate about restoring the Alamo. How could she not know of the legacy she was reproducing, a legacy established in the Republic period, and continued in her life time, when Texas-Mexicans were murdered or sent fearing for their lives across the Rio Grande in the name of the Alamo.

Let me state that after reading a good portion of her work and reviewing at least some of her personal papers, I continue to be surprised by De Zavala and this paper is less a definitive statement on her work and more an introduction to her critical, yet embedded, discourse of Texas history in general and the Alamo in particular.

I want to return to De Zavala's stories and discuss not only her Utopian collection of legends but her equally significant, and in fact, equally necessary, historical writing as a way of highlighting her critical, although only partially formulated, discourse of Texas history and the Alamo.

The Alamo Chronology

In 1917, several years after her chapter was voted out of the Daughters of the Republic of Texas, Adina De Zavala privately published *History and Legends of the Alamo and Other Missions in and around San Antonio*. This book begins with an extensive, and strikingly comprehensive, historical survey of the Alamo. De Zavala reconstructs the history of Mission San Antonio de Valero or the Alamo beginning with its founding as a Spanish mission. She includes Spanish documents portraying the allotment of mission lands as well as excerpts from church records from this period. She details how the Secularization Laws of 1793 led to the abandonment of the missions and their use by Spanish and Mexican cavalry as a frontier outpost.

De Zavala portrays the Battle of the Alamo, the events that precipitated it, and its final outcome using diary accounts of Fannin's soldiers, letters of Sam Houston, William Travis, and others. With maps and plats outlining the mission walls and structures, and archival documents, De Zavala weaves a richly-textured historical chronology. She concludes her historical chapter with an account of post-battle events and documents the Alamo's physical decline, its use, first by the U.S. Army, and second, as a supply store and whiskey house. She concludes this section of her narrative with details of her own effort to purchase and restore the property of Mission San Antonio de Valero.

Emplotting Legends

Immediately following this section De Zavala abruptly switches genres and provides a series of legends on the Alamo and other San Antonio missions. But unlike the numerous stories that speak of Bowie, Travis or Crockett, these tales have nothing to do with the Alamo "heroes," but portray a different understanding of turn-of-the-century Texas.

The first legend she recounts tells of ghosts with flaming torches that appear to anyone who attempts to tamper with the walls and physical structure of the Alamo. Following this is a legend about the statue of St. Anthony, the patron of the Mission San Antonio de Valero. Accordingly, all statues were removed from the mission after the Franciscans departed, except for that of St. Anthony which could not be dislodged. The legend claims that "Saint Anthony held his statue there, because he wished his church to be repaired and placed again at the service of the people he loved, whose mission and town had been given his name, and whom he was still anxious to serve!" (57). The statue was present during the battle in 1836, and years later when St. Joseph's Church was built only a few blocks away "all ideas of the use of the Alamo church for religious purposes was [sic] abandoned, and the statue of St. Anthony gave no more trouble, and was easily moved" (57).

It is the next series of legends that interest me, since they form a trilogy of narratives with a related motif. These legends come under the heading, "The Folk of the Underground Passages," with each legend depicting the presence of mysterious characters who come from the "enchanted city" to which underground passages of the Alamo are connected.

The first tale, "The Padre's Gift," concerns a man who appears to unsuspecting people, bringing them a special gift. According to this legend, the padre is one of the "good people who have power…to pass from the enchanted city of Tejas by way of the underground passages of the Alamo" (59). After providing some brief contextual material, the author, identifying herself as the narrator of the legend, recalls her own encounter with an old man dressed in a religious habit while riding outside the city as a young girl. Upon greeting her, the old man presented her with a thick book written in Spanish. The one condition of receiving the gift was that no one else was to touch it until she presented it to someone else under the same conditions of privacy. Agreeing, the narrator states, "I have always regretted that I did not ask the old man's name—but I thought, then, only of the precious old treasures and my wonderful good fortune in receiving them" (60).

The second legend concerns the mysterious woman in blue who emerges from the underground passages of the Alamo to seek out a Native Texan woman, "pure and good, well-bred, intelligent, spiritual and patriotic" (61), upon whom she will bestow a gift. "What is her gift? The gift of seeing to the heart of things! She sees…all that may vitally affect, for good or ill, the people of her city and State whom she ardently loves with a strange devotion" (61). This woman, the legend continues, is ready to help "the rich, the poor, the artist, the artisan, the writer, the children—the whole people of her beloved Texas land" (62).

The third legend describes the events of Ursula, a young girl, missing after playing with friends around the Alamo. Ursula's parents are facing difficult financial problems due to the father's ill health and when she fails to come home after playing, a search is organized by people from town. Fearing Ursula has been taken by Indians, the search party is relieved when they find her in a heavy sleep amidst the ruins of the Alamo. Upon her safe arrival home she recounts how, while playing hide 'n seek, she helped a woman who had stumbled and fallen. After aiding the woman she continued to hide from her friends when she fell into a deep sleep, awakening only after being found by the search party. The woman she helped had given her a small wrapped package and told her to stow it in her pocket. "The mother, realizing her daughter had met the 'good woman' of the underground" examines the package where she found "several very old Spanish gold coins, two diamonds and three pearls…and her first thought was that now, Joseph [her husband], could go to consult and secure the eminent specialists" who could cure his ailing health (65).

These stories are linked by their motif of gift-giving. In anthropological literature, discussion of gift-giving appears in relation to systems of exchange and, in many cases, heuristically paired with the Western discourse on commodity-exchange (Mauss; Sahlins; Strathern; Flores 1994). Gift- and com-modity-exchange are categories that attempt to capture qualitative distinctions between particular sets of social relations and the way such relations are signi-fied through the giving of objects. For De Zavala, however, in place of operat-ing as a form of exchange, the motif of gift-giving serves as an articulation of hope, or more specifically, the nostalgic hope for social restoration. Gift-giv-ing in these legends serves to restore elements of a world displaced by the rad-ical changes instituted by the social and economic reordering of South Texas.

In the first legend, the gift presented is a thick book written in Spanish from a man who comes from the enchanted city of "Tejas." In light of the Anglo-American's "repudiation of the Spanish past" for their own "self-iden-tity" (Weber 430), the use of the referent "Tejas" is instructive. It is derived from a Caddo word adapted by the Spanish as a name for the area, and was later kept by the Mexican government as the name of the province. Its pres-ence indexes a world of Spanish and Mexican influence, further indicated by the gift of the book, a prototypical literary and cultural document written in the Spanish language. The woman in the legend, whom the author claims is herself, makes an intriguing comment upon receiving the book. "I am sure it is wonderful, but it appears well nigh undecipherable [sic] with age, and besides, you see, I do not know the Spanish language well." Upon hearing this the *padre* responds, "No, use what you can, and pass it on" (60). The woman's comment contradicts the historical figure of De Zavala who, born into a Mexican family, was well-accustomed to communicating with her Mex-ican relatives in Spanish.[3] This legend, therefore, is not autobiographical but a sentimental narrative in which history gives way to hope. By encountering the man from the "enchanted" and "underground city"—motifs that speak to the unseen reaches of the unconscious where cultural symbols resonate with embedded sentiments of Desire (cf. Obeyesekere)—the young woman in the legend receives a gift that calls attention to and seeks to restore a social and cultural world of Spanish and Mexican making now lost.

In the "Mysterious Woman in Blue," the recipient of the gift is always a "native Texan woman…eyes of gray…not black" who is intelligent and good-hearted (61). The description of gray eyes is not a common feature: *Mexicanas* are usually described by their dark, often black or brown, eyes while Anglo-American women are seen as having blue or light eyes. Gray eyes are an amalgam, neither black, brown, nor blue but a combination of all of them. The woman who receives the gift, I suggest, is identified as neither Mexican nor American, but one who can claim that "All the children are her children—all the people are to her friends, and brothers and sisters!" (61).

The issue of social restoration is more clearly found in her gift of seeing. The woman in possession of the gift sees "to the heart of things" with the "clear-eyed vision of Joan of Arc," fighting for "justice" for the "whole people of her beloved Texas land" (61-62). Seeing to the heart of things is to see beyond the personal and sentimental, beyond the isolated events of everyday life. The woman's gift of sight serves to restore a sense of justice and unity only because such aspects have been lost. The same forces that displace the social and collective in favor of the personal and sentimental are those that merit a rethinking and critique. This will be taken up in the next section.

The third legend is that of the lost girl who, after helping an old woman, opens a gift of gold coins, diamonds, and pearls. This gift signifies another form of restoration by enabling the father to visit a medical specialist to cure his health. It is consistent with this reading that the gifts offered are forms of wealth and not, strictly speaking, money. That is, the coins and jewels are actually pre-capitalist forms of wealth and exchange and not, as Weber claims, the money-form—the most reified of all forms of exchange (Weber 331).

The gift of wealth serves to restore the father's health, and along with it, the economic and social health of the family since their economic troubles stem from the father's inability to work. Here, as in the previous two legends, the gift bestowed is not meant for personal use, even when given to an individual, but for the good of the "whole people of Texas," as in the gift of seeing in the legend of the mysterious woman in blue; or to be "passed on" as in the case of the Spanish book from the first legend.

On Legends and History

How are we to make sense of De Zavala's two different narratives about the Alamo? What is the relationship between De Zavala's historical text and her collected legends? Here, I turn to Paul Ricoeur's discussion of historical narrativity which I find instructive on these points.

Ricoeur states that every narrative "combines two dimensions in various proportions, one chronological and the other nonchronological." By chronological Ricoeur refers to the "episodic" aspects of narratives which "characterize the story made out of events"; by nonchronological, he means how plots configure "wholes out of scattered events" (178-79). While Ricoeur refers to the dialectical relationship between chronology and nonchronology in the same text, it is quite clear that he understands texts to be weighted in one direction or another. My concern in this paper is first, to see how De Zavala's narratives are weighted in different directions; and second, to demonstrate how the meaning of these two texts can be more fully appreciated through Ricoeur's dialectical relationship: that is, De Zavala's historical narrative is only historical when paired with her collected legends, and these legends make interpretive sense when paired with the historical texts.

Finally, as Ricoeur states, an historical event is more than a single occurrence and contributes "to the development of a plot" (171). As such, an historical text is one that not only provides a chronology but situates this chronology within a processual frame.

Equipped with these briefly stated notions of Ricoeur, I now return to De Zavala's writings. I understand her chapter on the history of the Alamo as a chronological narrative that tells an "episodic" story. But this chapter, replete with "data" and "facts" is only a partial history and must be read alongside her nonchronological legendry since it is there that we find the "plot" to this story. De Zavala's collected legends allow us to understand the "historical" significance of the Alamo, not as a place with a chronology but as an event whose meaning is situated within the larger process of Texas social life.

In order to accomplish this I turn to the works of Ann Douglas and Fredric Jameson. Building on various literary and critical traditions, including the structuralism of Levi-Strauss, Jameson demonstrates how narratives operate as "symbolic resolution(s) of real political and social contradictions" (80). Placing Jameson's critical perspective alongside Douglas's keen reading of the role of nineteenth-century women in literary and cultural practice makes De Zavala's critical discourse apparent. Following Douglas, the "problem" a poetics of restoration, as I refer to the organization of De Zavala's legends, seeks to resolve is the impact of "laissez-faire industrial expansion" and its "inevitable rationalization of the economic order" (Douglas 12). It is critical to remember that De Zavala's legends were coterminous with capitalist expansion and modernization in South Texas, the effect of which was the dismantling of *mexicano* traditional society and its subsequent reorganization by capitalist entrepreneurs into a more efficient and pragmatic economic form. Developments in both the railroad and large scale commercial agriculture were two activities that eroded the traditional, family-based, cattle ranching society of South Texas and reshaped it to the needs and logic of a market economy (Montejano; De Leon and Stewart).

That De Zavala's poetics of restoration are a response to the social and economic displacement experienced by *mexicanos* at the turn of the century is fairly clear. These Utopian legends seek to fix the problem of socioeconomic displacement by pointing to various forms of restoration and recalling the "enchanted city of Tejas" where social and racial cleavage are unknown.

De Zavala's position regarding the Alamo is not quite so evident. She worked diligently and energetically to restore it as shrine of Texas liberty—a bastion, in many cases, of anti-Mexican sentiment. And yet, in spite of all her colonial interests—that is, her concern for "things" and "places" of the past with seemingly no concern for their social effect—there remains a critique, a critical discourse, embedded, perhaps even repressed, in her narratives. For we find that the processual frame De Zavala constructs, the plot in which she embeds the Alamo, is the modernizing social displacement of Mexicans. According to this plot, the fictive restoration of Mexicanos is necessary since their real condition is one of degradation brought forth by the cultural, economic, and social reorganization of Texas as an industrialized state. Read as a singular text, the historical chronology De Zavala provides of the Alamo configures a past for a place, but as a narrative whose plot has itself been displaced, embedded in these collected legends, we find an historical text that prescribes a social place for a people. It is not surprising, following the deep, resistive role that *mexicano* expressive culture has played, to find De Zavala's critical practice portrayed in such a way (Flores 1992, 1994; Limón 1983a, 1983b, 1994; Paredes). This reading of De Zavala's narratives serves to counter the monological discourse of the DRT and the growing sentiment surrounding the Alamo in the early 1900s. Her legends that call for a return to "Tejas," precisely *because* of their Utopian impulse, express an allegorical unity whose necessity emplots a very different kind of Alamo in a rather unheroic historical narrative. With a fuller discussion of De Zavala's historical and folkloric work in process I want, at this point, to allow her embedded critical discourse to remind us that keeping Mexicans in line has been the central plot of the Alamo all along.

Notes

[1]There was, according to Gould, a growing trade in Mexican curiosities and souvenirs of the Alamo, although these items were only loosely tied, if at all, to the physical place of the Alamo.

[2]Adina De Zavala, for reasons unknown to me, later officially changed the "de" in her name so as to write it in upper-case letters.

[3]For example, I have seen letters she received from her uncle, Lorenzo de Zavala, Jr., written entirely in Spanish.

Works Cited

Ables, L. Robert. "The Second Battle for the Alamo." *The Southwestern Historical Quarterly* 3 (1967): 372-413.

De León, Arnoldo and Kenneth L. Stewart. "A Tale of Three Cities: A Comparative Analysis of the Socio-Economic of Mexican-Americans in Los Angeles, Tucson, and San Antonio." *Journal of the West* 24.2 (1985): 64-74.

De Zavala, Adina. *History and Legends of the Alamo and Other Missions In and Around San Antonio*. San Antonio: Privately published by the author, 1917; 2nd edition, edited by Richard R. Flores, Houston: Arte Público Press, 1996.

Douglas, Ann. *The Feminization of American Culture*. New York: Doubleday, 1977.

Flores, R. "The *Corrido* and the Emergence of Texas-Mexican Social Identity." *Journal of American Folklore* 105 (1992): 166-182.

_____. "'Los Pastores' and the Gifting of Performance." *American Ethnologist* 21.2 (1994): 270-85.

_____. "Private Visions, Public Culture: The Making of the Alamo." *Cultural Anthropology* 10.1 (1995): 100-16.

Gould, Stephen. *The Alamo City Guide*. New York: MacGowan & Slipper, 1882.

Jameson, Fredric. *The Political Unconscious*. Ithaca: Cornell UP, 1981.

Kammen, Michael. *Mystic Chords of Memory: The Transformation of Tradition in American Culture*. New York: Vintage Books/Random House, 1991.

Limón, José E. "Folklore, Social Conflict and the United States-Mexico Border." *Handbook of American Folklore*. Ed. R. Dorson. Bloomington: Indiana UP, 1983. 216-26.

_____. "Western Marxism and Folklore: A Critical Introduction." *Journal of American Folklore* 96 (1983): 34-52.

_____. *Dancing with the Devil: Society and Cultural Poetics in Mexican-American South Texas*. Madison: U of Wisconsin P, 1994.

Mauss, Marcel. *The Gift: The Form and Reason of Exchange in Archaic Societies*. 1925. Tran. W. D. Halls. New York: Norton, 1990.

McCarthy, Kathleen D. *Women's Culture: American Philanthropy and Art*. Chicago: U of Chicago P, 1991.

Montejano, David. *Anglos and Mexicans in the Making of Texas, 1836-1986*. Austin: U of Texas P, 1987.

Paredes, Américo. *With His Pistol in His Hand: A Border Ballad and its Hero*. Austin: U of Texas P, 1958.

Ricoeur, Paul. "Narrative Time." *Critical Inquiry* 7.1 (1980): 169-90.

Sahlins, Marshall. *Stone Age Economics*. Chicago: Aldine, 1972.

Strathern, Marilyn. *The Gender of the Gift*. Berkeley: U of California P, 1988.

Weber, David J. *The Spanish Frontier in North America*. New Haven: Yale UP, 1992.

Weber, Max. *From Max Weber: Essays in Sociology*. New York: Oxford UP, 1946.

PART IV
Writing the Revolution

Práxedis G. Guerrero: Revolutionary Writer or Writer as Revolutionary*

Ward S. Albro

Peter Kropotkin, the aristocratic Russian anarchist whose ideas probably had the greatest influence on the Mexican anarchist movement led by Ricardo Flores Magón, believed strongly that it was "by means of the printed word that the cause of revolution could best be served" (Joll 150). Flores Magón certainly shared those sentiments. For more than two decades he directed his greatest efforts at either writing or obtaining a means of publishing and distributing his writings. While his refusal to re-enter revolutionary Mexico from his self-imposed exile in the United States was seen by some as, at worst, cowardice, or at the very least as dooming his cause to failure, Flores Magón remained true to his belief that his role as a revolutionary anarchist was to write, and he could best perform that function north of the border (Albro *Always a Rebel*; Cockcroft; Hernández Padilla).

An avid reader of Kropotkin as well as a leader in the Flores Magón, or *magonista* movement, Práxedis G. Guerrero seemed in agreement with both mentors when he wrote, in an article entitled "*Working*," a description of the task of the revolutionary:

> And so, gloomy and pensive, the revolutionary meditates; he leans over any old piece of paper and he writes strong phrases that hurt, that shake, that vibrate like the bugles of storm; he wanders and he ignites with the flames of his words, the extinguished consciences, he sows rebellion and discontent; he forges the weapons of freedom with iron from the chains that he destroys; restlessly, he goes

*Acknowledgments: This study is drawn from research for a larger work entitled *To Die on Your Feet: The Life, Times, and Writings of Práxedis G. Guerrero* (Fort Worth: Texas Christian University Press, 1996). A grant from the Recovering the U. S. Hispanic Literary Heritage Project at the University of Houston enabled me to complete this study of Guerrero. In translating the writings of Guerrero I acknowledge the able assistance of Arturo Ramos of Cuernavaca, Morelos, México, and María de Jesús Ayala Schueneman and Lydia Nevárez-Méndez of Kingsville, Texas.

> through the crowds taking to them the ideas and the hopes; he works, he works.
> (Bartra 195-196; Cortés 118-121; Guerrero 70-73)

This article was published in *Regeneración*, the Flores Magón newspaper in Los Angeles, in October 1910, although it may have been composed earlier. In a letter in August 1910 to longtime friend Manuel Sarabia, Guerrero expressed a dramatically different view, writing:

> I believe that you will agree with me that the word is an excellent medium whose efficacy is well known, but it should not become the "chronic weapon for demolishing tyranny." The revolutionary phrase, when not accompanied by deeds, or followed by them, acquires the insensitive soporific monotony of Christian prayers. (Cortés 51)

Less than five months after this letter Guerrero died attempting to initiate revolution in the Mexican state of Chihuahua. His determination to be a revolutionary actor cut short an increasingly significant career as a revolutionary writer. This central contradiction in Guerrero's short life—to be a writer encouraging revolution or to be a revolutionary actor who also wrote—was a conflict he could never resolve.

Práxedis G. Guerrero was born in 1882, the sixth of eight children of the owners of an *hacienda* in the state of Guanajuato, about 45 kilometers from the city of León. Educated through secondary school in León, Guerrero capably entered all the family enterprises, both on the *hacienda* and traveling over the Republic. Service in the Second Military Reserve, organized by General Bernardo Reyes, Minister of War in the government of Porfirio Díaz, provided more travel opportunities. An avid reader and a curious traveler, Guerrero became increasingly disturbed the more he saw and learned of life in Porfirian Mexico. A nation said to consist of "900 large landowners and 9,000,000 landless *peones*," a nation where the foreign entrepreneur could do no wrong, a nation undergoing "modernization" at a heavy cost to much of its own population were all factors driving Guerrero to a momentous decision—to leave his native land (Martínez Núñez 27-36).

Entering the United States in September 1904 he joined many of his countrymen in supplying much of the labor for the American Southwest. Working as a laborer in Colorado and California and then in the mines in Arizona (and later in the mines and railroad yards in Texas), Guerrero, who had renounced all help from home, supported himself the rest of his life. His experiences in 1905 and 1906 also helped forge a revolutionary, as he began to organize workers in Morenci, Arizona, and he affiliated with the *Partido Liberal Mexicano* (*PLM*) of Ricardo Flores Magón, then headquartered in St. Louis, Missouri. He also began his career as a writer in this era as he became convinced that Porfirio Díaz must be overthrown, and that his writings might hasten that event (Martínez Núñez 37-41).

The *PLM* was the primary opposition to the *Porfiriato* from its origin around the turn of the century until the movement launched by Francisco I. Madero supplanted it in late 1910. Although begun in Mexico, most of the leaders, fleeing suppression and fearing for their lives, came to the United States in 1904. First from Texas and then from Missouri, Flores Magón organized the *PLM* and published the newspaper, *Regeneración*, which he had first published in Mexico City and which would be synonymous with his cause. In July 1906 the *PLM* published its manifesto and program, the first thoroughgoing indictment of the Díaz system, plan for a new nationalistic and socially reformed Mexico, and call for revolution. The Liberals envisioned coordinated uprisings led by affiliated clubs in Mexico with groups of adherents from the United States crossing the border to support, and even lead, the movement (Albro, *Always a Rebel*; Cockcroft).

From the beginning the Flores Magón movement was thoroughly infiltrated by agents hired by the Mexican government, working with cooperative local, state, and national government agencies in the United States. Unsuccessful attempts at revolt were attempted in 1906 and 1908, but constant harassment, legal and extralegal, kept the leadership on the run or in custody. The main charges in the United States related to neutrality law violations. Ultimately, almost all the principal leaders of the movement ended up incarcerated, facing in many cases long, drawn out legal battles (Raat). It was precisely this situation which opened the door for the emergence of Práxedis Guerrero as a leader of the *PLM*. His talents enabled him to be the major figure in the movement from 1907 to 1910, while Flores Magón was in custody. He also became the leading *PLM* publicist in this period, and his writings in some respects sustained the cause.

Guerrero first joined the movement while working in a copper mine in Morenci, Arizona. Apparently, he had befriended Manuel Sarabia, a *PLM* Junta member in Arizona at the time, and formed a group of workers, *Obreros Libres* [Free Workers], to propagate *PLM* ideas (Cortés 52-53; Martínez Núñez 78). These activities came shortly after the occurrence of the celebrated strike and riot at the American owned copper mine at Cananea, Sonora, blamed by some on *PLM* agitation (Raat 65-91). In the Fall 1906 came the first attempts by the *PLM* to initiate revolution in Mexico. There is no evidence that Guerrero participated, either directly or indirectly, in any of these events. The aborted revolt was to have a great effect on Guerrero, however, as the arrests that followed these events opened the way for his assumption of leadership.

Junta vice president Juan Sarabia was arrested in Ciudad Juárez, México, and imprisoned in that country. Junta secretary Antonio Villarreal was arrested in El Paso, Texas, although he escaped to rejoin Ricardo Flores Magón, who had fled to California. Guerrero had moved to Douglas, Arizona, on the border, sharing a home with Manuel Sarabia. When Flores Magón launched a new periodical, *Revolución*, in Los Angeles in June 1907 Guerrero became one of the contributors. Shortly thereafter Manuel Sarabia was kidnapped in Douglas and taken to Mexico with the collusion of Douglas officials and representatives of the Mexican government (Albro, *Secuestro*; Raat 46-48,53, 118, 142-146, 185). Guerrero contributed to the outpouring of outrage that got Sarabia released. His article *"Justice,"* appearing first in loose-leaf form in Douglas and later in *Revolución*, was one of his first efforts to attract attention from *magonistas* throughout the Southwest.

Blaming Díaz for manipulating the kidnapping, Guerrero called on Mexicans to "clean the Porfirian stain from their country," concluding with: "Let's erase the word tyranny from the fatherland and replace it with another on which rests the only peace acceptable for man: JUSTICE!" (Cortés 57-60). Later, in a letter to a brother, Manuel Sarabia described the author of this work as "a fighter who knows no fear... Ah! If only we had more Guerreros!" (*Archivo* L-E-927). When Flores Magón, Villarreal, and Junta member Librado Rivera were arrested in Los Angeles in August 1907, Guerrero almost immediately assumed a larger role, sending out circular letters calling for financial support for the defense of the leaders (*Archivo* L-E-928). The next month in *Revolución*, Guerrero warmed to the task of "writing" the revolution in a piece entitled *"Make Way!"*:

> Out of the cluster of clouds that the hurricane whirls around to darken the skies, comes the flaming sword wielded by an invisible arm, and with dazzling zig-zags writes on the page roaring with black smoke, the words MAKE WAY! And as the shadow becomes darker, the sword glows even brighter.
>
> Out of the squall of hatred that besieges us; out of the black bosom of the tempests that the tyranny unleashes over our foreheads, comes the invulnerable sword of the Idea and writes with the lightning of the word, in the very heart of darkness, pages of honor to the inextinguishable cry: MAKE WAY! (Bartra 187-188; Cortés 61-62; Guerrero 83-84)

After further arrests in Los Angeles, Guerrero and Sarabia, in October 1907, arrived in California to take over direction of *Revolución*. Feeling the urgency of the situation with most of the *PLM* leaders under arrest, Guerrero wrote: "We cannot stop for a moment...we cannot sleep... If we cannot reach liberty walking, we must jump..." He concluded this call to labor by writing:

> Double the labor, we will rest later when the body of the old buffoon of Tuxtepec [Díaz], on the end of a rope, serves as the lead weight for the architect of the future to raise the walls of the houses of the people. (Cortés 63-64)

In the same issue appeared another piece by Guerrero entitled "*Listen,*" demonstrating a style that would come to identify him for many readers:

> Do you hear it? It is the wind rustling the branches in the mysterious forest. The gust of wind of the future, which wakens the quiet and sleepy underbrush; it is the first sigh of the virgin grove receiving on its bowed head the kiss of the impetuous Aeolus.

After a few more references to Greek mythology, and building the dramatic effects, he continued:

> It is the breath of the Revolution.
> Do you feel it? It is the quaking of granite cracking to pieces, beaten by the iron fists of Pluto: it is the heart of the world beating beneath its enormous chest; it is the fiery spirit of a giant who breaks from his prison to hurl curses of flame into space.
> It is the trembling announcing the birth of a crater of a volcano.
> Do you feel it? It is the vibrations made by the hammers of the gods…
> It is the force of the Revolution advancing. (Cortés 65; Guerrero 24)

In December 1907, Guerrero again pointed out the importance of the writer in bringing on the revolution when he wrote:

> Our silence can be obtained only with death, but even so, the rebel pen we grasp will implacably continue cutting the mantle of Caesar to show the sword the way to his rotten heart; the immortal spirit of the revolution, identified with the sword, will find a hundred hands prepared to replace us in the fight… We are standing, we will kneel before no power. We face the enemy; we will not turn our backs before any danger. (Cortés 66-67; Guerrero 51-52)

In California, Guerrero met Flores Magón for the first time, visiting him briefly in the Los Angeles County Jail. Flores Magón, Villarreal, and Rivera were fighting extradition to the Arizona Territory, where United States officials, in consultation with Mexican authorities, wanted to try them on neutrality law charges. Altogether, Flores Magón and his compatriots would be locked up about three years, not gaining release from Arizona prisons until August 1910. For the moment, however, Flores Magón saw his movement in good hands, writing to Sarabia in December 1907: "*Revolución* is beautiful. I congratulate everyone and especially Práxedis. What a brilliant pen!" (Martínez Núñez 116). His joy was short-lived as Sarabia was arrested in January 1908 and the newspaper suppressed in February.

Subsequently, Flores Magón wrote Guerrero several times about the possibility of acquiring other newspapers, letters that indicate that personal contacts must have been infrequent. The *PLM* leader told Guerrero that he would "need all the help you can lend us in the editing of the newspaper… The newspaper is indispensable not only for our defense…but to encourage those who are growing cold since they know nothing of the fight." Later, he wrote:

> The newspaper is needed. This is understood by our own enemies, and so well, that they make every effort to leave the cause without a press. We have come to the United States, and are in the same condition as in Mexico, without the freedom to write. (Martínez Núñez 120-121)

Toward the end of April 1908 Guerrero, working with Modesto Díaz, published a few more issues of *Revolución* before the paper was suppressed for the final time by the end of May (Martínez Núñez 122).

In the meantime Guerrero's father died and, due to his growing notoriety and increasing commitments to the *magonista* cause, he was unable to go to his family in Guanajuato. He left Los Angeles in late May, accompanied by childhood friend Francisco Manrique, to go to El Paso to direct the second attempt at armed revolution. In essence, this was to be Guerrero's revolt. He selected the date. He sent representatives into Mexico to alert the Liberal groups there while he traveled the borderlands from California to South Texas to rally supporters. Again, the border at El Paso-Ciudad Juárez was to be the key area, just as in 1906. When Guerrero indicated he would cross the border there to direct activities in Chihuahua, the Flores Magóns were alarmed. Younger brother Enrique wrote Guerrero urging he remember that "Ricardo always recommends and even begs of us, that we do not expose ourselves and risk falling into the hands of our enemies" (Martínez Núñez 127-130). Práxedis was being asked to choose whether to be a writer or to be a revolutionary.

The movement was as always totally infiltrated. Proposed revolts in Mexico never got started. Guerrero and Enrique Flores Magón escaped capture when the main conspirators in El Paso were arrested, their stores of arms and ammunitions confiscated. Revolts in 1908 occurred in Viesca, Coahuila, near Torreón, and in an attack on Las Vacas [now Ciudad Acuña], across the border from Del Rio, Texas. With the failure of these efforts, the final assault of the 1908 uprising was an attack on the small town of Palomas, Chihuahua, led by Guerrero himself. Leading only ten men to attack this Mexican customs station about 100 kilometers west of Ciudad Juárez was rather quixotic, perhaps reflecting frustrations with the complete lack of success in the efforts to bring on revolution (*Archivo* L-E-918 to 954; US Department of Justice

90755-277). On the other hand, it also illustrated Guerrero's determination to be a leader in the field.

"Eleven and not one more," he wrote, "to attempt, with an audacious move, to save the revolution which seemed to be shipwrecked in the surf of treachery and cowardice" (Bartra 218-220; Cortés 164-167; Guerrero 42-46). The attack, coming in the early morning hours of July 1, 1908, was rebuffed, the attackers suffering only one casualty—Guerrero's dear friend Manrique. Guerrero later wrote accounts of the three 1908 revolutionary episodes in the borderlands—Viesca, Las Vacas, and Palomas. The last account began:

> This chapter in the history of freedom should be called *Francisco Manrique*; it should carry the name of that youth, almost a child, who died by the bullets of the tyranny on July 1, 1908, in the frontier village of Palomas. (Bartra 218; Cortés 164; Guerrero 42)

As in 1906, the Mexican government publicly dismissed the 1908 raids as the work of bandits, but as yet had not realized that Guerrero had become the main leader of the movement (*Archivo* L-E-935).

Additional arrests in 1908 further decimated the *PLM* ranks. Guerrero was increasingly carrying the movement on his own strong back after he left Palomas and crossed the border back into New Mexico. Over the next two and one-half years he would criss-cross the borderlands from California to Texas. He made a trip deep into Mexico, visiting his family one last time. He went into the midwestern United States for the first and only time. Working, writing, publishing, organizing, plotting, encouraging, and staying one jump ahead of the many agents of two nations, who finally recognized his importance but who could not catch him. Guerrero was the only significant *magonista* leader who was never arrested.

From New Mexico, Guerrero returned for a time to Douglas, Arizona, and then went to El Paso to try to plan the next attempt at revolt. In February 1909, Flores Magón and his fellow prisoners were finally taken to Arizona to stand trial. Still hoping to get something going that year the Junta leaders asked Guerrero to go to Mexico to assure supporters in the central and southern areas of the Republic that success was in sight. Guerrero was able to visit his family one last time before going on for quick stops in Mexico City, Puebla, and Oaxaca. Back in the United States, Guerrero went on a mission into the Midwest to try to explain *PLM* programs to important American socialists. With the many legal battles both financial and popular support from American radical groups grew more important. Surprisingly, Guerrero's travels to Mexico and the Midwest were not detected by the numerous agents pursuing him (Martínez Núñez 51-55, 176).

With the conviction of the Junta leaders in Arizona 1909, Guerrero realized the burden of leadership would continue to be on him. He moved his base
of operations to Texas, dividing his time between El Paso and San Antonio.
Leadership seemed to rest easily on Guerrero but his increasingly strong commitment to anarchism caused him some intellectual problems. As he told
Jesús María Rangel, one of the leaders of the attack on Las Vacas: "I believe
that a popular revolution should be spontaneous, without leaders." He added,
"…I am not a mere political enemy of General Díaz. I am an anarchist; I don't
fight because I hate government, but for the love of a free humanity…"
(Martínez Núñez 176-177). Meanwhile, Guerrero had been issuing manifestos
and proclamations and writing letters, often filled with instructions on buying
arms or other revolutionary activities (US Department of Justice 90755-176).
He was the leader.

Since the suppression of *Revolución* in May 1908 Guerrero had not had a
regular outlet for his writings. This obviously bothered him as much as it had
Flores Magón. Finally, in August 1909, he made a modest step toward rectify-
ing this shortcoming by publishing a paper entitled *Punto Rojo* [Red Point] in
El Paso. Printed on a small press in the home of William Lowe, an El Paso
socialist sympathizer, *Punto Rojo* was at first a small, four-page digest size
paper. In a letter to a supporter Guerrero said he "selected El Paso for geographical considerations, as being the most central point, where we could
extend both north and south as well as east and west" (*Archivo* L-E-951). In
Punto Rojo, from the beginning, he proclaimed: "I am not merchandise, I am
an idea; and ideas are not bought, they are defended" (*Archivo* L-E-951).
Gradually the paper grew to standard size, with the quality also improving.

Inasmuch as Guerrero was a wanted man, under indictment for neutrality
law violations, and also had to continue to work to support himself, it is amaz-
ing that he kept *Punto Rojo* going for nine months. Given the circumstances
some of his writings were hurried and definitely not memorable. While the
paper was published in El Paso, Guerrero was often in other parts of Texas,
sometimes on the run to escape some of his more determined pursuers. On
one occasion he avoided capture only by leaping out a third story window in a
Houston boarding house (*Archivo* L-E-952; US Department of Justice 90755-
175). Later, writing his sister about this event, he reassured her:

> Don't worry about me. I am like an eagle that burnt its feathers crossing over the
> flames of a volcano. I feel them growing again, and I see from my retreat the
> space that will soon be mine… (Martínez Núñez 183).

Much of the writing in *Punto Rojo* denounced the passivity that Guerrero
found along the border. "Passivity never! Rebellion, now and forever," he
urged (Cortés 76-77). Comparing begging for bread to begging for liberty, he

wrote, "Beggar of liberty… Beggar of bread…do not beg anymore, demand it. Stop waiting, take it!" (Cortés 78). Taking a different approach, Guerrero hoped an appeal to women might inspire some action as he wrote, "Whom do you love? Whom do you love? To whom do you give that tenderness that only an honorable and free man knows how to value, to deserve and conserve, to increase and defend?" (Cortés 79-80). Often his writings were specifically directed toward the Mexican population in the United States, as in the following protest to the proposed El Paso meeting of Díaz with United States President William Howard Taft:

> In Mexico there is an excuse for those who pretend to coexist with the Tyrant; that excuse is terror. But you do not have this excuse, you cannot have it, and if you accept any part given you in this degrading farce, there will be no valid subterfuge; not even the water of one hundred biblical floods will remove the stain you will have thrown on yourselves.
>
> Defend dignity or wait for me to burn your face with the word that will distinguish you in the future: Wretches! (Cortés 81-82)

On the upcoming hundred year anniversary of Mexico's movement for independence, he asked: "Will the sun of the Centenary burn the backs of a flock of sheep or will it kiss the proud forehead of a people?" (Cortés 85-86).

Shortly before *Punto Rojo* was suppressed by El Paso authorities, in May 1910, Guerrero wrote his sister some comments about his writing style:

> Unfortunately, in this fight one must use terms of argument similar to those that oppose us; philosophy does not penetrate a rock, you have to use a crowbar and a hammer. When writing pages destined to energize the people, I often become violent and use a language that intimately I reject; but the sublimely cold language of philosophical truth is not the most fit language to awaken the enthusiasm that every revolution needs in order to achieve victory. (Martínez Núñez 56)

Even though he was now being described by United States Secretary of State Philander Knox as "a notorious revolutionist who is still at large along the border," Guerrero continued to avoid capture (US Department of Justice 90755-175). From his narrow escape in Houston he went to Bridgeport, in north Texas, to work in the coal mines. From there he made his way back to San Antonio. A ten thousand dollar reward was offered for his capture. Writing his sister about the attempts by both the United States and Mexico to capture him and to stifle the movement in view of what he saw as the inevitable revolution, he wrote: "Sad blindness. There are things that you cannot kill and you cannot imprison…" (Martínez Núñez 189).

He was still in San Antonio when Flores Magón and his colleagues were released from prison in early August 1910. With signs of revolt from Texas growing daily, and with many other exiles now in San Antonio, it seemed strange that Flores Magón returned to Los Angeles to direct *PLM* activities and to publish again *Regeneración*. Guerrero was torn between rejoining the junta leaders in California or returning to Mexico to foment revolt. Writing Manuel Sarabia, now in England, he made clear his ultimate determination to be an active participant:

> The fight becomes more intense every day. For my part, I will soon abandon this land; I will go to Mexico and will experience the same luck as Lugo [José Lugo was executed for his role in the Viesca revolt in 1908] or I will fulfill my purpose. Nobody sends me and I go against the opinion of some comrades, who without doubt wish to see me die of boredom in this hypocrite country. (Cortés 52-53)

For the moment, however, Guerrero did go to California, arriving near the end of August and becoming one of the most active contributors to *Regeneración* when it resumed in September. Ethel Duffy Turner, who helped edit an English page in the newspaper, remembered this period as an exciting epoch. Ricardo and Enrique Flores Magón, Antonio Villarreal, Librado Rivera, Anselmo Figueroa, along with friends, wives, and children were all together writing, talking, and expecting the imminent downfall of Díaz (Turner, Interview; Turner, *Ricardo Flores Magón* 206-207).

Guerrero's writings in *Regeneración* throughout the Fall 1910, some of which had been published elsewhere earlier, were varied and extensive. He wrote several general pieces on the nature on revolution and, without specifically stating his adherence to anarchism, how the elimination of government would benefit society. He also published several of his dramatic, more poetic works, meant to inspire support for revolutionary change. His accounts of the revolutionary actions of 1908 were also published. Beginning with the second issue, *Regeneración* each week featured Guerrero's *puntos rojos*—short commentaries, aphorisms, call to arms, and the like (Bartra; Cortés; Guerrero). In his last writings, Guerrero also evidenced increasing concern for the treatment of Mexicans and Mexican Americans in the United States.

In this last regard he argued that the exploitation and discrimination against Mexicans in the United States was directly related to conditions in Mexico. Mexicans north of the border accepted the insults of a racist society because the economic opportunities in the United States at least allowed them to feed their families. Yet, the misery and hunger they left in Mexico would overcome them in the United States if they did not cease being "passive and indifferent workers." Caught between "two hungers," which he described as the "universal companions of the impotent," Mexican workers could escape their dilemma through support for revolution in both countries (Cortés 92-94; Guerrero 90-91).

Ricardo Flores Magón, frustrated by his imprisonment, had earlier lashed out at citizens of the United States for not lending more support:

> The *norteamericanos* are incapable of feeling enthusiasm or indignation. This is truly a country of pigs. Look at the socialists: they cowardly break up in their campaign for free speech. Look at the resplendent American Federation of Labor with its million and a half members which cannot prevent the declaration of judicial "injunctions"... If the *norteamericanos* do not agitate against their own domestic miseries can we hope they will concern themselves with ours? (Abad de Santillán 47-55).

Guerrero resisted outbursts such of this until he learned of a lynch mob action in Rock Springs, Texas in November 1910, shortly before he left the United States for the final time. The victim, Antonio Rodríguez, was a ranch worker accused of killing a white woman (De León 50). Guerrero described the event in an article entitled "*Whites, Whites*":

> A man was burned alive.
>
> Where?
>
> In the model nation, in the land of freedom, in the home of the brave, in the piece of land that still has not come out of the shadow projected by the hanging of John Brown: in the United States, in a town in Texas, called Rock Springs.
>
> When?
>
> Today, in the tenth year of the century. In the age of airplanes and dirigible airships, of the wireless telegraph, of the wonderful rotary press, of the congresses of peace, of the humanitarian and animal societies.
>
> Who?
>
> A crowd of white *men*, to quote the name they prefer; white, white, white *men*.
>
> The people who burned this man alive were not a horde of cannibals, they were not blacks from Equatorial Africa, they were not savages from Malaysia, they were not Spanish Inquisitors, they were not red-skinned Apaches, nor Abyssinians, they were not Scythian barbarians, not trogolytes, nor illiterate and naked inhabitants of the jungles. They were the descendants of Washington, of Lincoln, of Franklin; it was a well dressed crowd, educated, proud of their virtues, civilized; they were the citizens and white *men* of the United States.
>
> Progess, civilization, culture, humanitarianism. A lie turned into an ember with the bones of Antonio Rodríguez. Dead fantasies of asphyxia, in the fetid smoke of the stake in Rock Springs.
>
> There are schools in every town and every settlement of Texas; those schools were attended, when they were children, by the *men* of the lynch mob, their intellect was shaped in those schools; they graduated from them, to push smouldering brands into the flesh of a live man, only to say a few days after the transgression that they had done the right thing, that they had acted with justice.
>
> Schools that educate men to launch them beyond the point where the beasts are. (Bartra 251-252; Cortés 144-145; Guerrero 95-96)

Guerrero touched on all manner of subjects in his work on *Regeneración* in the Fall 1910. Meanwhile, the likelihood of revolt in Mexico grew daily. Francisco I. Madero had come to San Antonio and issued his call for revolution to begin on November 20. Guerrero had earlier scoffed at Madero's claim to represent agrarian workers in Mexico and now he feared the *PLM* might be swept up in the *maderista* movement (*Regeneración*, June 3, 1911). By the end of November 1910 supporters of the Liberals were fighting in Sonora, Chihuahua, Tlaxcala, Morelos, Durango, Oaxaca, Tabsco, and Veracruz. If Madero entered Mexico and the *magonista* leaders did not, such groups might easily go over to the *maderista* cause. Guerrero might intellectually agree with Flores Magón on the role of the revolutionary as writer, but in September he had also published the following: "Without me, all the aspirations and ideals would roll around in the minds of men like dry leaves whirled about by the north wind. Progress and Liberty are not possible without me. I am Action" (Cortés 103; Guerrero 28).

So, against the wishes of Flores Magón, Guerrero left Los Angeles at the end of November 1910. Before leaving he gave his books, his most valued possessions, to the son of Librado Rivera. Then he went to the home of John Kenneth and Ethel Duffy Turner, who had become close friends, leaving most of his personal effects there. "If I do not return, Ethel, send them to her [his sister in Guanajuato], and I know I will not return." Accompanied by Lázaro Gutiérrez de Lara he went on to El Paso, Texas, to prepare to enter Mexico (Martínez Núñez 223; Turner, *Ricardo Flores Magón*, 207).

Calling on a number of veterans of his 1908 efforts at revolt, Guerrero gathered enough troops to cross into Mexico shortly before Christmas. His main target was Casa Grandes, with the expectation that additional recruits in Mexico would enable him to advance on toward Chihuahua City. After sending Gutiérrez de Lara and Prisciliano Silva to operate in other parts of Chihuahua, Guerrero boldly led his force of thirty-two toward Casas Grandes. Realizing he could not take that strongly fortified position, he turned northwest toward Janos, hoping to obtain both supplies and recruits. He attacked and took that town the night of December 29, but in the early morning of December 30 troops from Casas Grandes arrived and in heavy fighting Guerrero was killed. The death of their leader inspired his troops who, though outmanned, drove the federal troops from town. Later, the rebels were forced out, leaving the body of Guerrero behind (Almada 179; Martínez Núñez 221-239).

When word from Chihuahua reached the *Regeneración* offices in California, the sense of loss was immense. John Kenneth Turner wrote:

> The price of despotism in a given country is the blood of her best and bravest sons. Of the thousands of good and brave men whom Porfirio Díaz has killed in

order to perpetuate his personal rule over Mexico, I cannot believe that any was better or braver than Práxedis Guerrero. (*Regeneración*, Jan. 14, 1911)

Ricardo Flores Magón, for all the involvement of Guerrero in his movement, had actually only spent a short three months—September to November 1910—in close contact with him. Yet it is obvious that he understood how important Guerrero was to the cause. He wrote:

> …on the glorious day of Janos Práxedis G. Guerrero, the young fighter for liberty gave up his life…
>
> Práxedis was the soul of the movement for freedom. Unhesitatingly it can be said that Práxedis was one of the purest, worthiest, most intelligent, self-denying and bravest men that ever espoused the cause of the disinherited, and the vacancy caused by his departure can never be filled. Where can a man be found so free from personal ambitions of any kind, all brain and heart, brave and active as he was?
>
> …Without exaggeration it may be said that it is not Mexico that has lost one of her best sons, but that it was all humanity, for Práxedis was a fighter for the freedom of all…
>
> And yet I cannot grasp the loss and give credence to the terrible reality. At any moment a hope hidden deep within my heart tells me that a comforting telegram will come saying that Práxedis is still among the living. The brutal truth cannot destroy in the deepest recesses of my heart a last remnant of hope like a flickering light ready to go out. And my tortured mind still hopes to meet him in his favorite haunts, in the office where we used to dream with him the dream of the dawn of social emancipation, and my restless eye seeks the martyr bent over his table of toil, writing, writing, writing. (Cortés 12; Guerrero 16-17)

Ricardo Flores Magón could and did, write, write, write, all the rest of his life. His writings continue to be subject matter for scholars in several countries. His contributions to the coming of the Mexican Revolution, to Mexican political and intellectual history, to anarchist theory and thought, and to numerous other topics continue to be evaluated, interpreted, and reinterpreted. Práxedis G. Guerrero may well have been the equal of Flores Magón in matters of the pen, but he could not separate the word from the deed—a conviction that cost his life.

Works Cited

Abad de Santillán, Diego. *Ricardo Flores Magón, el apóstol de la revolución social mexicana.* México, DF: Grupo Cultural "Ricardo Flores Magón," 1925.

Albro, Ward S. *Always a Rebel: Ricardo Flores Magón and the Mexican Revolution.* Fort Worth: Texas Christian UP, 1992.

_____. "El secuestro de Manuel Sarabia." Historia Mexicana 18 (1969): 400-407.

Almada, Francisco R. *La Revolución en el Estado de Chihuahua.* México, DF: Instituto Nacional de Estudios Históricos de la Revolución Mexicana, 1964.

Archivo *"Genaro Estrada" de Secretaría de Relaciones Exteriores*, L-E-918 to L-E-954. México, DF: Secretaría de Relaciones Exteriores.

Bartra, Armando, ed. *Regeneración, 1900-1918: La corriente más radical de la revolución mexicana de 1910 a través de su período de combate.* México, DF: Ediciones Era, 1977.

Cockcroft, James. *Intellectual Precursors of the Mexican Revolution, 1900-1913.* Austin: U of Texas P, 1968.

Cortés, Omar, ed. *Práxedis G. Guerrero: Artículos de Combate.* México, DF: Ediciones Antorcha, 1984.

De León, Arnoldo. *Mexican Americans in Texas: A Brief History.* Arlington Heights, IL: Harlan Davidson, 1993.

Guerrero, Práxedis G. *Práxedis G. Guerrero: Artículos literarios y de combate; Pensamientos; Crónicas revolucionarias, etc.* México, DF: Grupo Cultural "Ricardo Flores Magón," 1924.

Hernández Padilla, Salvador. *El Magonismo: Historia de una pasión libertaria, 1900-1922.* México, DF: Ediciones Era, 1984.

Joll, James. *The Anarchists.* New York: Grosset and Dunlap, 1966.

Martínez Núñez, Eugenio. *La vida heróica de Práxedis G. Guerrero.* México, DF: Instituto Nacional de Estudios Históricos de la Revolución Mexicana, 1960.

Raat, W. Dirk. *Revoltosos: Mexico's Rebels in the United States, 1903-1923.* College Station: Texas A&M UP, 1981.

Regeneración (Los Angeles) 14 Jan. 1911.

Turner, Ethel Duffy. Personal interview. June 1965.

―――――. *Ricardo Flores Magón y el Partido Liberal Mexicano.* Morelia, Michoacán: Editorial "Erandi" del Gobierno del Estado, 1960.

US Department of Justice, Record Group 74, File 90755. Washington, DC: National Archives.

Before the Revolution: Catarino Garza as Activist/Historian*

Elliott Young

Principio pues por inspirarle sueño al lector, dándole ligeros apuntes de mi emigración a este Estado, al decir sueño no carezco de razón, porque no se encontrará en todo el concurso de los escritos, una sola frase galana ni imágenes delicadas, ni erudiciones ni mucho menos pinturas literarias porque mi pluma no sabe pintar, pero si reproducir, fotografiar y estampar verdades cuya luz reseña las pruebas.

—Catarino Garza, "La lógica de los hechos"

Todos los discursos de los miembros del aparato gubernamental no hacen sino cantar las bondades del régimen institucional que permite continuar con la 'Revolución Mexicana', por la vía pacífica. El mismo nombre del partido oficial 'Revolucionario Institucional', nos da una muestra de la importancia de este objeto discursivo ('institucionalidad') para conformar prácticas que evitan un cambio revolucionario.

—Rafael Sebastián Guillén, AKA Subcomandante Marcos, "Filosofía y educación," Thesis, UNAM, late 1970s

The new mestiza copes developing a tolerance for contradictions, a tolerance for ambiguity. She learns to be an Indian in Mexican culture, to be Mexican from an Anglo point of view. She learns to juggle cultures. She has a plural personality, she operates in a pluralistic mode—nothing is thrust out, the good the bad and the ugly, nothing rejected, nothing abandoned. Not only

*Acknowledgment: An earlier version of this paper was presented at the Latin American Studies Association, XVIII International Conference, March 1994.

213

> does she sustain contradictions, she turns the ambiva-
> lence into something else.
>
> —Gloria Anzaldúa, *Borderlands/ La Frontera*

Broad economic and political structures set limitations on human activity, yet it is people that make history move. In focusing on identity formation I hope to illuminate the process by which human agents make sense out of their lives and thereby lay the foundation for individual and collective action. Although this paper does not detail the process of capitalist development in the South Texas and Northern Mexico border region, it is within this framework that Catarino Garza launched his 1891 revolution. Rather than highlight the actual events of the revolution, a worthy endeavor in itself, I will address the process before the revolution in which Garza constructed himself as a Texas Mexican border hero and justified resistance to Anglos and Porfirista Mexicans (see Young, 1996).

Identity, whether class, national, racial, or gender, can be used as a tool for social control or as a means of resistance. Discourses that enforce social hierarchies naturalize the socio-economic subordination of subaltern classes at the same time as they impede resistance to that subordination. The ability of hegemonic classes to define and categorize people allows them to rule without relying exclusively or even primarily on the police and military to keep order; the coercive forces are always on hand, however, to be called upon when the ideological mechanisms of control fail. Yet, no matter how dominant the ruling class, counter-hegemonic practices and ideas are always present and competing with the "natural order." The ability of subaltern groups to rename, define, and classify themselves can be a powerful counter-hegemonic tool, a strategy of resistance that prepares the ideological ground for structural change (see Gramsci, 1988).

In his autobiography, Garza challenged the definitions of Texas Mexicans espoused by Anglos in Texas and by the Díaz regime in Mexico, and thereby set the stage for his revolution two years later. Nonetheless, Garza's reconstruction of Texas Mexican identity, though resistant to some forms of social control, reinforced others. For instance, the Anglo/Mexican racial hierarchy was questioned but the white/black hierarchy was not, and while male dominance took on a racial inflection it was not radically challenged. In analyzing Garza's construction of his racial, national and masculine identity I will illustrate the complex intersections of these categories and show how they were marshaled as a means of struggle and of social control.

Catarino Garza: From Journalist to Revolutionary

After arriving in Corpus Christi, Texas, at the beginning of 1888, Catarino Garza, began writing the story of the last twelve years of his life. His autobiography was meant to be more than just a personal account; it was also intended to be read as a history of Mexicans in Texas. In addition to its value in reconstructing the life of Garza, an important yet understudied figure, his autobiography provides a rare account of the complex racial and political issues confronting Mexicans in Texas in the late nineteenth century. While Garza's experience cannot represent the diversity of experiences had by Texas Mexicans, the broader structural issues that he identified in his autobiography touched the entire Texas Mexican population. Thus, Garza's autobiography is both a personal story of his life and a collective history of Mexicans in Texas.

Garza is best known for the insurgency that he led against Mexico's President Porfirio Díaz in 1891. Yet even this major political and military event has escaped the attention of most historians. It would be mistaken, however, to seek the meaning of Garza's revolution, or any revolution for that matter, by only analyzing the actual event, i.e.. the armed actions. The outbreak of violence in any revolution is like the tip of an iceberg. Most of an iceberg lays beneath the water, and thus one must dive beneath the surface of the water in order to get a sense of its size and shape. Similarly, to see the foundations of a revolution one must dive beneath the surface of society. I am not proposing a materialist analysis, where one focuses on the base, usually conceived of as an economic structure, and then assumes that the cultural superstructure merely reflects the material base. Rather, I am suggesting that the foundation for a revolution, or any other extraordinary activity, is history itself, both material and cultural. The histories that all individuals make for themselves, often not in written form, integrates personal experience with a broader understanding of how society functions. These informal auto-histories serve as a guide to present action by making a coherent or at least logical narrative out of past experiences. These new meanings, or what the Marxist cultural critic Raymond Williams calls an "emergent culture," form the wellspring from which the revolution draws its strength (Williams 40-42).

Revolutionary declarations and manifestoes come only after the protagonists have written, metaphorically or literally, their own histories. Revolutionary consciousness is thus only the end result of a long mental process of making sense of everyday experiences and of giving those experiences new meaning. Most people process their experiences mentally, orally, or through some other non-written medium, and therefore it usually remains unrecorded. For Garza, however, we are fortunate to have his autobiography which provides us with a tangible record of how he made sense of his life, of how he conceived of his own history. This essay therefore examines Garza's construction of himself as a revolutionary before the revolution. When he began writing in 1888, he probably had no idea that in a couple of years he would lead an armed insurrection against Mexico's Porfirio Díaz. In retrospect, however, one can see how the chronology of events and conclusions reached in his autobiography helped him to arrive at the decision to take up arms. Writing his autobiography played an important role in ideologically preparing him for leading a revolution. Although the specific events leading up to his declaration of revolution and the actions of the revolution should not be ignored, this essay will focus on the arguments made in his autobiography that prepared the ground for the actual battles.

Garza's autobiography began with a description of his arrival in Brownsville, Texas, in 1877 and covers the twelve subsequent years he spent living and working in different towns along the U.S.-Mexico border. He took a particularly active part in defending the Mexican community as a founder and officer of several mutual aid societies and as the editor for their newspapers. These activities, often involving vociferous attacks on Anglo racism and Mexican corruption, helped him to gain the support of many Texas Mexicans, but they also provoked the enmity of those whom he denounced. By the time he returned to Texas after a couple of years in St. Louis, Missouri, he had become quite well known to a larger public due to a series of highly publicized incidents. In response to the acerbic commentary in his newspaper, *El Comercio Mexicano*, xenophobic Anglos and Díaz supporting Mexicans used legal pressure and extra-legal coercion to silence Garza. In December 1887, fearing for his life, Garza left Eagle Pass and went to Corpus Christi where he began to write his autobiography. While in Corpus Christi, Garza continued to organize Texas Mexicans and to publicize their cause in *El Comercio Mexicano*. His autobiography ends in 1888 with a description of a visit to Palito Blanco, a small Texas Mexican rural community where he had been invited to speak for a Cinco de Mayo celebration.

By using consular reports, newspaper clippings, and U.S. army records it was possible to reconstruct a broad outline of the next seven years of his life (see AREM and NA). In September 1888, several hundred armed supporters of Garza briefly took control of Rio Grande City after Victor Sebree, an Anglo customs inspector, shot and nearly killed Garza. One day later, Garza's supporters disbanded and returned to their homes when they had been assured that Sebree would be brought to justice. In February 1891, Díaz agents assassinated Dr. Ignacio Martínez, an opponent of Díaz and a friend of Garza's. Given his brush with death in 1888 in Rio Grande City and the killing of his friend Dr. Martínez in the streets of Laredo in 1891, Garza worried that he would be killed next. On September 16, 1891, unable to continue his non-vio-

lent journalistic opposition, Garza declared a revolution against the Mexican government. Although it is impossible to place an exact number on Garza's supporters or those who directly took part in the raids into Mexico, the evidence suggests that he had widespread support among the Mexican population of Texas and that there were at least several hundred active insurgents. The United States and Mexican governments responded to the revolution by sending thousands of troops to the border region. The U.S. authorities, however, unable to enlist the cooperation of the local population, were largely unsuccessful in their efforts to squash the rebellion. After a year and a half of insurgency and war on the border, U.S. authorities convinced some prominent Mexican ranchers to cooperate with the government's counter-revolutionary operations. They argued persuasively that if Garza's revolution were allowed to continue, the instability would be bad for business along the border. With the help of the collaborating ranchers, the U.S. army became successful in arresting Garza's supporters. After scores of his followers were arrested in Spring of 1893, Garza understood that his revolution was unraveling. Rather than wait to be captured, he took a boat from New Orleans to Nassau and eventually entered Costa Rica under a false name.

Garza's reputation preceded him, thus undermining his effort to remain incognito. Shortly after his true identity had come to light, the President of Costa Rica invited him to dinner and he was ultimately recruited to be part of the movement for Central American Unity. The Colombian liberals, who were fighting to gain power in Colombia, asked Garza, who had a reputation as a skilled tactician, to lead a military attack on Panama. In April 1895, Garza led a small band of armed men into Bocas del Toro, Panama, as part of a coordinated campaign against the Colombian government. Garza's band was discovered and he along with most of the other fighters were killed. Six months later Garza was spotted in Cuba fighting with the Cuban independence movement against Spanish rule. Garza's legend continued for years after his death, kept alive by occasional sightings along the Texas Mexico border.

Garza's trajectory from journalist to revolutionary occurred in a relatively short period of time. Although "La lógica" ends in 1888, before Garza took up arms, the narrative helps to explain why Garza became increasingly radicalized during his stay in the U.S.. Perpetual racial harassment from Anglos and political attacks from his enemies in the Mexican government prompted Garza to write "La lógica" when he did. Ultimately, his words were not enough and so he chose armed revolution. His eloquent words, however, provided the intellectual foundation for his revolution. The act of writing "La lógica" was part of the process by which Garza became a revolutionary, every bit as important as his decision to, as Garza later commented, "abandon[ar] la pluma para empuñar la espada" [put down the pen to pick up the sword] ("La era de Tuxtepec," 268; all translations are mine). Perhaps it was his ability to pick up his pen in 1888 to write history that allowed him to pick up his gun in 1891 to make history.

The Logic of Events

In the dedication and preface of his autobiography Garza explained that "La lógica" should not be read as art or literature, but as history or the narration of actual events. I am basing my hopes, wrote Garza, "no en las aptitudes de mi pluma, sino en la seguridad de que cumplo fielmente como mexicano en extranjero suelo al narrar las circunstancias de nuestros nacionales en este país" (61) [not in the aptitude of my pen, but in the security that I faithfully fulfill my duty as a Mexican on foreign soil of narrating the circumstances of our nationals in this country]. His autobiography entitled "La lógica de los hechos: O sean observaciones sobre las circunstancias de los mexicanos en Texas, desde el año de 1877 hasta 1889" [The Logic of Events: Observations on the Circumstances of Mexicans in Texas, from 1877 until 1889] thus served as part of his ongoing defense of Mexicans in Texas. Garza began writing a history of the last 12 years of his life because he was afraid that he would be killed, either by agents of Porfirio Díaz or by hostile Anglos. His autobiography would thus allow his voice and his explanation of events to be heard even after his death. More immediately, he hoped that it would publicize the difficult plight of Mexicans in Texas and "suscitar el celo entre los representantes de [su] país" (61) [arouse the zeal of the representatives of [his] country]. Although his 431 page handwritten autobiography stops abruptly in 1888, leaving unfinished chapters and blank pages where he intended to include photographs, it provides invaluable insight into the way Garza conceived of the world and of himself.

Although he wrote a personal narrative as well as a collective one, he denied the individuality of his writing by identifying himself as an "hijo del pueblo" [son of the people] whose mission was to "educar las masas" (65) [educate the masses]. He even denied his own literary and artistic skills in the first chapter, claiming that he merely reproduced a story made by "el pueblo." Garza proclaimed to the reader that "no se encontrará en todo el concurso de los escritos, una sola frase galana ni imágenes delicadas, ni erudiciones ni mucho menos pinturas literarias porque mi pluma no sabe pintar, pero sí reproducir, fotografiar y estampar verdades" (69) [you will not find in all of these writings, one elegant phrase, nor delicate images, nor erudite phrases, much less literary portrayals, because my pen does not know how to portray, but it does reproduce, photograph and print the truth].

Garza's subjectivity can be seen, however, in his choice of which events to include in his narrative. Deciding to use the autobiographical form also had consequences, such as making his individual story dominate the collective one and allowing him space to discuss aspects of his personal life. Garza also attempted to efface his own artistry thereby positioning his story as a collective rather than an individual one. While Garza implicated himself throughout the narrative, and rarely used the impersonal third-person, he wanted his text to speak for a shared experience of Texas Mexicans. However, Garza did more than just "reproducir y fotografiar" a story made by "el pueblo." Throughout the text he commented on the events that he described and drew broad conclusions about the nature of racial relations and gender roles.

In spite of his protestations to the contrary, "La lógica" must be analyzed as both a personal expression and as a collective history. Thus, the conclusions he drew about race and gender tell us as much about Garza as they do about the society he characterized. The analysis of "La lógica" demonstrates the artificiality of making a rigid distinction between personal experiences and broader structures. Rather than attempting to draw strict lines between these two aspects of the autobiography, a futile and unproductive task, I will show how they relate to each other. This investigation will thus explore the relationship between Garza's personal experience and the broader conclusions he drew about life for Mexicans in Texas in the late nineteenth century.

Constructing a Complex Racial and National Identity

The first chapter of "La lógica," entitled "Pluma en desorden" [Pen in Disorder], addressed racial and national identity and described the complexity of dealing with this issue in the border region. Garza's first negative experience with Anglos happened the very moment, or perhaps even before he stepped onto Texas soil. As he crossed the border from Matamoros into Brownsville, a U.S. customs official stopped him and without any cause emptied all of his belongings onto the floor. After disturbing Garza's clothes, the customs guard simply said "all right." Garza described this episode ironically and noted the impolite speech of the customs official by consciously mistranslating the English "all right" for the Spanish "dispense usted la molestia," a formal way of saying excuse me for having bothered you. In the next clause Garza made it clear to his readers that everything was not "all right," "visto el desorden en que dejó mi ropa" [given the disorder in which he left my clothes] (ibid.). Throughout "La lógica" Garza made the point that he, and Mexicans in general, had better manners than the coarse and rude "americanos" (read Anglos) with whom he had contact. His insistence on the respectability, dignity, and decency of Mexicans must be understood within a context where Anglo's claimed superiority on these same grounds. Thus, culture and custom became the ideological battleground upon which Garza strove to prove the equality, if not superiority of Mexicans over Anglo Americans.

Although national identity clearly had racial overtones, the national differences manifested themselves most apparently in cultural variation. While Garza defended all Mexicans, he also condemned those Mexican Americans who had betrayed their Mexican culture. In his description of Brownsville, he criticized the Mexican American customs as "tan sencillas, que a semejanza de las salvajes, se manejan unos con otros" (70) [so simple, that they treat each other like savages]. What most bothered Garza, however, was the servile role played by Mexican American political leaders and the way in which Mexicans were used as voters in elections. Both of Brownsville's political clubs, the popular México-texano (azul) and the democrático México-texano (colorado), were, Garza complained, "presididos por mexicanos de origen y gobernados por distintos círculos americanos, quienes…lo han convertido en instrumento servil (70) [presided over by people of Mexican origin and governed by distinct groups of Americans, who…have made [them] into servile instruments]. Garza pointed to the practice of bringing Mexicans over to Texas a few days before an election to make them into U.S. citizens and have them vote as evidence of the "degradado" [degraded] state of these people. Aside from having to lie by saying that they had been in the U.S. for one year, they also had to swear to defend the U.S. against any enemy, even Mexico. But perhaps most upsetting to Garza was that these Mexican voters would show up drunk at the voting booth after a night of revelry, all paid for by the "especuladores de la política" [political speculators]. In reference to this scenario Garza remarked, "qué vergüenza da decir que México ha sido la patria de seres tan degradados" (71-72) [what a shame to have to say that Mexico has been the country of these degraded beings]. He continued that "México está mal juzgado por los emigrantes a este País" [Mexico is badly judged because of the immigrants to this country]. Though Garza himself judged these Mexicans harshly, he always sought to find the deeper societal causes for these people's degradation.

While holding Mexicans to a high standard, expecting them to be more respectable and polite than their Anglo counterparts, he also recognized the challenges they faced in Texas. He had himself been the recipient of rude and violent treatment by Anglos simply because he was Mexican and was well aware of the process by which Anglos appropriated, legally and illegally, the private land of Mexicans in South Texas. He thus applauded the "gran número de mexicanos que han podido conjugar su nacionalismo y que por sus intereses y su familia residen en el Estado sufriendo injustamente las deprivaciones de centenares de texanos ambiciosos, que por medios ilegales y con el apoyo

de funcionarios públicos de mala fe se echan sobre sus propriedades" (72) [great number of Mexicans who have been able to maintain their nationalism and who reside in this state for their interests and that of their family, suffering the unjust depredations of hundreds of ambitious Texans, who by illegal means and with the help of corrupt public officials throw them off of their land]. Thus while Garza condemned aspects of the Mexican American society of which he was a part, he understood that they all suffered under the weight of Anglo oppression.

Not long after his arrival in Brownsville, Garza became embroiled in a public debate over a racist insult made by an Anglo lawyer. Ties to Matamoros, on the Mexican side of the river, had been cut by authorities in Brownsville after Matamoros refused to stop traffic from Veracruz, the site of an outbreak of yellow fever. The workers of Brownsville called a meeting to ask for free passage between the cities. At the meeting an American lawyer, Rossell, argued that the quarantine should not be lifted because of the danger that yellow fever from Matamoros would spread to Brownsville. Rossell callously asserted that "si el pueblo obrero se perjudica o se muere de hambre nada nos importa, lo que debemos ver es que no nos invada la fiebre amarilla, porque bien puede morir alguien americano, y como 'un blanco vale más que un mexicano'; asi es que yo protesto contra la idea de levantar la cuarentena" (75-76) [it does not matter to us if it hurts the working people or if they die of hunger, what we should see to is that yellow fever does not invade us, because some American could die, and as 'a white is worth more than a Mexican;' this is why I protest against the idea of lifting the quarantine].

Seeing no sign of protest about this remark, Garza wrote his own response and had it printed in a Spanish language newspaper. Garza argued that men like Rossell "no merecen penetrar en la sociedad justa; porque desde luego atropellan a la cortesía, a la delicadeza y al respeto a sí mismo" [do not deserve to be admitted into civilized society; because it is only a matter of time before they ride roughshod over courtesy, delicacy, and their own self-respect]. He went on, saying that "ese abogado blanco que miente villanamente al asegurar que un americano vale más que diez mexicanos, pues en las casas de los Señores Blowmberg and Raphael está un mexicano (sin ser negro) que puede probarle en el terreno que quiera que vale tanto como él o cualquiera otro de sus correligionarios" (77) [this white lawyer who villainously lies in asserting that one American is worth more than ten Mexicans, should know that in the house of Blowmberg and Raphael there is one Mexican (without being black) who can prove in whichever terrain that he is worth as much as him or any other of his cohorts]. Garza, who worked at Blowmberg and Raphael's trading company, thus challenged "ese abogado blanco" [this white lawyer] to a fight to defend the dignity and honor of Mexicans.

Although Garza quite ably defended Mexicans with his words he was always ready and willing to physically fight for their rights. Another important aspect of Garza's response to Rossell was the insertion in parentheses of the statement "sin ser negro" [without being black]. Garza placed Mexicans on the same level as whites, but he considered blacks a different matter. At one point Garza even claimed that "no valía más un blanco americano que diez mexicanos" [one white American was not worth more than ten Mexicans] but again he felt compelled to include the parenthetical exclusion "(sin ser negro)" [without being black] to qualify the Mexicans to whom he referred (76).

The response to Rossell was Garza's first piece of published writing and it began his career as a journalist. Garza began to receive more harassment as he wrote more openly against corruption in the Mexican American community and against racism in the Anglo community. In 1879 Garza joined with Leon A. Obregón and Antonio P. Treviño in forming the Sociedad Juárez and establishing the society's newspaper *El Bien Público* [The Public Well-being]. Right from the start they were attacked for publishing this newspaper. Obregón even suffered an assassination attempt at the hands of the newspaper's enemies. His life was only barely saved because a bundle of newspapers he carried in his bag prevented the assassin's knife from puncturing his chest. Such threats did not intimidate Garza who continued to write provocative articles. One such article, entitled "derecho de la ciudadanía" (78) [The Right of Citizenship], chastised as "renegados" [renegades] those Mexicans who sold their votes for money. According to Garza, publishing articles such as these in their newspaper awoke "en unos el entusiasmo, en otras la curiosidad y en la mayor parte el odio" (84) [enthusiasm in some, curiosity in others, and hate in most].

While some of the animosity generated by Garza's writings came from within the Mexican community, he also had to suffer the insults of obnoxious Anglos. One such incident occurred at the Opera House in Brownsville where Garza was the target of a group of Anglos who were throwing orange peels. After Garza confronted them, one admitted to having thrown the peels. Garza grabbed his arm and led him outside. As he saw the Anglo reaching for his revolver, Garza pulled out his own pistol and pressed it against the Anglo's breast. Garza claimed that "cuando éste vió que el cañon de mi pistola estaba en contacto con su pecho, hizo lo que la mayor parte de los texanos hacen, gritó de la manera más cobarde" (84) [when this one saw the barrel of my gun in contact with his breast, he did what most Texans do, he screamed in a cowardly manner]. Garza attributed the orange peel harassment to the work that he was doing to "liberar socialmente la raza mexicana" (85) [socially liberate the Mexican raza].

From his first contact with the Brownsville customs agent all the way through his twelve years in the U.S., Garza continually defended himself and Mexicans in general from Anglo insults and offenses. Garza made a special point of providing a detailed description of these incidents of racial conflict. For example, the St. Louis *Globe Democrat* complained about a convention of Mexican journalists being invited to St Louis, arguing that "haya aceptado a esa chusma de escritores mexicanos sin precaver si puedan traer piojos" [this mob of Mexican writers had been accepted without checking if they carried lice] (115). Garza, who had invited the journalists and hosted them, noted proudly how they protested this article by refusing to accept a dinner being given in their honor by the *Globe Democrat*.

In another incident in Corpus Christi in 1888, one of several physical confrontations with Anglos, Garza beat up a rowdy Anglo "cowboy" in a bar room brawl. He was in a bar drinking with a friend when for no apparent reason an Anglo insulted him and threw a glass which barley missed his head and smashed against the wall. Garza punched the Anglo in the face, but spared his life "porque jamás he querido manchar mi mano con sangre de desgraciados" (199) [because I have never wanted to stain my hand with the blood of low-lifes]. These incidents show the full range of Garza's responses to racial harassment. In some cases he publicized the issue in newspapers, in another case he boycotted the offending party, and in many other cases he used physical violence to make his point. All of the incidents he described end with him being victorious over Anglos whom he characterized as "cowardly" and "disgraceful." One may wonder whether he chose these incidents, as opposed to others where Anglos won the day, to encourage more Mexicans to stand up against Anglo insults. Did he merely reproduce the events as they happened or did he mold them into a triumphant narrative to foster greater resistance to an increasingly powerful and aggressive Anglo presence?

After being treated badly by the Anglo customs guard on his way into Brownsville, Garza found himself working with Spaniards who also had a low opinion of Mexicans. One Spaniard even remarked that "si los españoles no hubieran conquistado a México, aún sería fecha que anduviéramos con pabico y chimal huyendo por los campos" (70) [if the Spaniards had not conquered Mexico we would still be running through the countryside with a flag and shield]. Although Garza found this comment particularly insulting, he did not accept this challenge and ended up becoming a friend of this Spaniard. Later in his narrative Garza commented on the effect of colonialism on the Mexican people. He asserted that "en México nuestra tradición es de servidumbre y errores, nacida del poder colonial que se basó o quiso basarse en la incomunicación con el extranjero, en la legitimidad de la esclavitud, etc. más no estamos obligados a seguir cargando el yugo de aquellas tradiciones, porque es

precisamente convenir [con] tales errores, tales vicios morales producen en
alta escala al malestar social; así como el internarse estos errores en las clases
imbéciles engendran falsas opiniones rancias, así pues el pueblo americano
nos ha dado calificativos impropios e insultantes" (87) [our tradition in Mexico is one of servitude and mistakes, born in the colonial power that based
itself or wanted to base itself on the lack of communication with the foreigner,
in the legitimacy of slavery, etc., we are no longer obligated to carry the yoke
of these traditions, because it is precisely agreeing with these mistakes and
with these moral vices that produces a high level of social illness; also as the
imbecilic classes internalize these errors they engender the age-old fallacies,
and thus the American people have called us inappropriate and insulting
names]. Garza thus blamed the colonial powers for Mexico's legacy of servitude, but he also argued that some Mexicans had internalized these mistakes
and had thus become "imbéciles" [imbeciles]. He rejected colonialism, not
because he disagreed with the notions of progress that went along with imperial expansion, but because he felt Mexicans had not assumed their role as proponents of progress.

Garza's admiration for the imperial conquerors comes through forcefully
in his description of his second encounter with Spaniards. He was feeling isolated as he walked aimlessly in the streets of St. Louis, a city to which he had
just arrived and in which he had no friends. His spirits lifted upon hearing two
men conversing in his native language. He had not heard Spanish for several
days and so he approached these two men, one of whom turned out to be a
Spaniard and the other of Moroccan descent. Garza quickly became friends
with these Spaniards who invited him to a celebration of Mexican Independence day. Whereas he had previously commented on the negative effects of
the Spanish conquest, he made a toast at the celebration to his new Spanish
friends and in honor of the "madre de mi patria" [mother of my country].
Garza began his toast by assuring the Spaniards that although speakers
throughout Mexico would be praising their independence leaders, nobody in
Mexico would be offering "insultos a la gran nación civilizada, intrépida y
valerosa conquistadora, a la madre de mi Patria, 'España.' No señores, nuestras dos naciones, ligadas de antemano por los vínculos sagrados de afecto y
simpatía, fundadas en su comunidad de origen y lengua están llamadas a ser
una misma…España es México y México, España. No idénticas instituciones,
pero sí iguales costumbres" (95) [insults to the great civilized nation, the
intrepid and valiant conquerors, the mother country, Spain. No Señores, our
two nations connected beforehand by the ties of affect and sympathy, founded
in your community and language of origin are called to be one…. Spain is
Mexico and Mexico Spain. Not identical institutions, but equal customs]. The
ambivalence that Garza felt towards Spain and the legacy of the conquest

stemmed not so much from the fact that it had happened, but from Mexico's inability to emulate its imperial "madre." Although he would publicly defend Mexico's dignity and honor against anyone who tried to denigrate it or its people, Garza also believed Mexicans were less progressive and modern than their Anglo American counterparts.

Garza's admiration of Anglo culture may have been the product of his internalizing the dominant racial ideology which held lighter skin superior to darker skin. Though he railed against racial discrimination directed towards Mexicans, Garza expressed a similar discrimination towards African Americans and African Spaniards. When he met the two Spaniards in St Louis, he described one as a young Moroccan "de corteses maneras a pesar de ser moro" (94) [with courteous manners even though being a Moro]. From this off-handed comment and others like it one can surmise that Garza believed that darker people could be expected to be less civilized than their lighter counterparts. His surprise at finding a darker complexioned person, such as the Moroccan, to be so friendly and courteous sheds light on some of Garza's own racial prejudices.

Garza's attitude about Anglo Americans was as complex and ambivalent as his attitude toward Spaniards. In spite of negative experiences with Anglos who treated him badly simply because he was Mexican, Garza admired and became close friends with several Anglos. Garza even referred to one Anglo woman in Laredo, Laura Jones, as "un ángel en mi defensa" [a guardian angel]. Laura Jones sat at his side as he presided over Laredo's mutual aid society Union Mexicana. Her presence, according to Garza, compelled the members "por respeto al bello sexo [que] se moderaban un tanto los escándolos" (89) [for respect of the fair sex to moderate a bit the scandals]. Garza also referred positively to Anglos in a glowing description of a Mexican Independence Celebration in Eagle Pass. Though he recognized that the "armonía" [harmony] of that evening where Mexicans and Americans danced together was only a temporary respite from the tempestuous race relations, it expressed his desire for Mexicans and Anglos to live together peacefully. He ended the description of the celebration with a passage praising the "americano," Santiago Riddle, as "[uno] de los más populares en la frontera del estado de Coahuila y de los más queridos por el pueblo obrero" [one] of the most popular on the border of the state of Coahuila and one of the most loved by the working people]. Though Riddle's first name, Santiago, leaves some question as to his ethnicity, Garza usually used the marker "americano" to refer exclusively to Anglos. The mixture of an hispanicized first name and anglicized last name might indicate inter-racial marriage, something quite common along the border, but nevertheless Garza viewed Riddle as an "americano." Garza dedicated five pages (which remained blank) to a description and portrait of

Riddle, his "fiel y verdadero amigo" (173) [faithful and true friend]. While having some "americano" friends did not erase the reality of conflict and racial hatred between Anglos and Mexicans, Garza may have included these accounts in "La lógica" to demonstrate his hope that "las dos razas" would live together in harmony and even as friends.

Garza's battle lines were never clearly drawn and he often found himself with enemies on both flanks. When a Mexican citizen living in Eagle Pass was illegally handed over to Mexico and then executed, Garza condemned both the U.S. and Mexican authorities, thus earning him disdain from both. This incident exemplifies the difficulty that Garza had in trying to negotiate the racial politics of the border. The basic facts of the story that became an international incident are as follows: Maverick County Sheriff Oglesby arrested Francisco Erresures, a twenty year old Mexican citizen living in Eagle Pass. After being handcuffed, Oglesby secretly brought Erresures to Coahuila, Mexico, and handed him over to Francisco Mondragón, the County Judge for the Rio Grande district. The next day Erresures was killed while in the custody of Mondragón.

As this incident heated tensions along the border, Garza was abandoned by his newspaper colleague and became the target of attacks by both Anglos and Mexicans. In his newspaper, *El Comercio Mexicano*, Garza criticized both the U.S. and Mexican governments' handling of this incident. English language newspapers also quoted Garza's statement that Mondragón was "un criminal" and that both Sheriff Oglesby and Mondragón should have been sent to prison (146). While imprisoned on libel charges, Adolfo Duclós Salinas, who co-edited and published *El Comercio Mexicano*, tried to fire Garza from his position as editor; Garza later concluded that Duclós Salinas had betrayed him as a way of currying favor with Mondragón. Meanwhile, Garza had also inspired the wrath of the *Galveston News* and the Veteran Volunteers of Texas, who were mobilizing to fight Mexico in response to this incident. A *Galveston News* article argued that they were not sorry the two countries were on the verge of war because the U.S. could take Mexico in 15 days, "lo que sí sentimos es que nuestro pueblo tenga que regar su sangre con la de los mexicanos, suya bajeza no merece tal distinción" (149) [what we are sorry about is that we will have to mix our blood with that of Mexicans whose lowliness does not deserve such an honor]. Garza responded with a stinging article attacking the "estúpidos editores" [stupid editors] of the *Galveston News* and "los Veteranos borrachos voluntarios" [drunk Volunteer Veterans] and reminding them how thirty young cadets held off the attack of more than 300 "yanquees comedores de bellotas" (149-50) [dirt-eating Yankees] in the Mexican American War. Garza responded to the racist remark about the lowliness of Mexican blood with his own interpretation of racial purity: "los condiseramos los mexicanos con más pureza de sangre que los americanos, supuesto que en nuestro país, sólo hay una mezcla, la de español e indio y entre ellos la generalidad son de aventureros irlandeses, mendigos polacos, rusos, prusianos, y más que todo, africanos asquerosos" (150) [we Mexicans consider ourselves to have purer blood than the Americans, given that in our country there is only a mixture of Spanish and Indian, and they are generally descendants of Irish adventurers, Polish beggars, Russians, Prussians, and more than anything else filthy Africans]. Rather than rejecting the racism inherent in the argument made by the *Galveston News*, Garza accepted the logic and turned it around to criticize the Americans. Mexicans were superior to Americans, reasoned Garza, because they had less racial mixing and purer blood.

The day that Garza's article appeared, eight armed Americans forced Duclós Salinas to sign a retraction. When they showed up at Garza's office, he refused to sign the retraction, proclaiming that "jamás acostumbro contrariar mis principios o convicciones [I am not accustomed to contradicting my principles or convictions]. The Americans threatened that if he did not leave the county within twenty-four hours they would not be responsible for his life. Garza replied that "yo resido en un país libre y soy tan hombre como ustedes para responder en cualquier terreno por mis acciones" (151) [I live in a free country and I am as much a man as you to be responsible for my actions anywhere]. The American Consul, Eduardo Linn, intervened on Garza's behalf, allowing him to carry a pistol and promising to settle the conflict with the Volunteer Veterans of Texas. The situation was ultimately resolved peacefully. Garza remarked that in the end the Veterans, who had threatened him, became his "mejores amigos y protectores" (153) [best friends and protectors] in his conflict with the Governor of Coahuila, José María Garza Galán.

Aside from showing the dangers of being a journalist in Garza's position, the Erresures incident illustrates the tangled and changeable position in which he often found himself. He had to defend Mexico in the face of Anglo offenses, yet he also had to attack Mexico's government for its offenses against its own people. In this case he antagonized all sides by criticizing everyone. The racial divide, though clearly significant, was not the only factor determining Garza's alliances on the border. The changeable political context in Mexico and Texas made for very deep divisions within the Mexican community, thus rendering friends of enemies and enemies of friends. As Garza's narrative indicated, alliances along the border, like the Rio Grande border itself, changed over time as circumstances changed. Analyses that focus exclusively on racial or on political differences will therefore not grasp the shifting and multi-dimensional terrain upon which alliances cohered and disintegrated.

Garza fiercely criticized the Mexican government, but he did so in the name of Mexican nationalism, being careful to reiterate his own patriotic sentiments. He defined his anti-government, pro-nationalist stance in response to an article in the *Eagle Pass Times* written by an Anglo lawyer. The lawyer accused Garza of defending the country that was responsible for murdering Erresures, namely Mexico, while at the same time condemning the U.S., the country which gave Garza safe haven from Mexico. Garza answered these charges in *El Comercio Mexicano*: "Defender las instituciones de un país no es marchar de acuerdo con su gobierno. Nostotros defendemos a México pero no así a sus actuales gobernantes. Atacamos a los filibusteros americanos y no a los hombres dignos y honrados" (158) [To defend the institutions of a country is not to go along with its government. We defend Mexico but not its current administration. We attack the American filibusters and not the dignified and honorable men]. Garza's situation was difficult. To defend Mexicans in Texas, he had to criticize Americans, and to defend Mexicans in Mexico, he had to criticize Mexico. In Texas he was accused of being anti-American and in Mexico he faced the charge of being anti-Mexican. Garza found support for his cause among Texas Mexicans on the border, the people that lived in the interstices between the two nations and understood the complexity that he described.

Garza's struggle to define himself against the Díaz regime but for the Mexican people can be seen in the way he handled a conflict with the Mexican Consul in Eagle Pass, José María Calvo. Garza came into direct conflict with Calvo at a meeting of a mutual aid society when Calvo opposed his offer to draft the by-laws for this society. Garza accused the Consul of never representing Mexicans in the courts and of wanting "convertir aquel círculo de obreros, en un instrumento servil" (162) [to turn that circle of workers into a servile instrument]. In spite of the opposition of Calvo, the society approved Garza's idea to publicly celebrate Mexican Independence. Although both Calvo and Garza were chosen as the keynote speakers for the celebration, Calvo never spoke because he claimed illness at the last moment. In his speech in front of an audience of more than 400, Garza condemned the Consul, criticized the Mexican government, and raised the banner of patriotism: "Si el Cónsul en estos momentos de convulsiones políticas internacionales, le da vergüenza y miedo decir que es mexicano, a mi por el contrario, me da honra y valor decir que soy hijo de Anáhuac, de esta patria de Hidalgo, Morelos, Abasolo, Allende, Matamoros y otros de igual temple, que es la más envidiada por los filibusteros ambiciosos y miserables.... Se me dirá que ataco a los gobernantes; pero señores, estos no son la patria, ni son las leyes, ni son el pueblo; sino unos verdaderos sirvientes. Defiendo a la república Mexicana y no a los tiranos que la gobiernan" (167-68) [Though the Consul is afraid and ashamed to say that he is Mexican in these times of international political conflict, I am honored to say that I am the son of Anáhuac, from the country of Hidalgo, Morelos, Abasalo, Allende, Matamoros, and others of equal stature who are hated by the ambitious and miserable filibusters.... They tell me that I attack those who govern; but *señores*, they are not the country, nor the laws, nor the people; but are truly only servants. I defend the Mexican republic and not the tyrants who govern it]. In addition to making the distinction between the country and the "tiranos" who govern it, Garza ran through a brief history of Mexico, marking 1877, the year Díaz came to power, as a moment when "el sol se opacó y la opresión reinó" (172) [the sun darkened and oppression reigned]. In this speech, Garza reached back into Mexico's past, both to the pre-Columbian era, Anáhuac, and to the Independence period, Hidalgo and Morelos, as inspiration for a new government in Mexico. Although he had previously been critical of officials of the Díaz government, this was the most vehement public attack on the Díaz regime up to this point and it came the closest to advocating overthrowing the Mexican government.

Through these descriptions of encounters with people of different ethnicities, Anglos, Spaniards, and Texas Mexicans, Garza began to define his own ethnic and national identity. Although he clearly proclaimed himself to be a Mexican patriot, the exact meaning of this label was clarified through his descriptions of complex relationships between and among ethnic groups. His Mexicanness was inflected with a particular political stance vis-à-vis progress, modernity, and the Díaz regime. Garza used the language of nationality negatively to attack the Mexican Consul and those Mexicans who sold their votes to US. politicians. He also invoked his national heritage positively to legitimize his present political struggle. Garza's exploration of national and racial identity in "La lógica" helped him to define and justify his political opposition to Díaz. Being a Mexican patriot was, however, only part of a complex political persona. Another equally significant aspect of Garza's political identity was his masculinity. In this next section I will examine Garza's construction of masculinity and how his view of gender roles intersected with his national identity.

The Border Hero: Garza's Construction of Masculinity

Garza's definition of masculinity comes across forcefully in "La lógica." His notion of masculinity, like his national identity, formed an essential part of his persona as an oppositionist leader. By analyzing his interactions with women one may discern, not only his perspective on gender, but also his beliefs about Mexican nationalism and racial relations between Anglos and Mexicans. Much of Garza's cultural and racial nationalism can be discerned from reading his political manifestoes and speeches to mutualistas. His pessimistic view about the possibility for harmonious relations between Anglos and Mexicans, however, emerged in his discussions about women in a way that it does not in the rest of his narrative. In "La lógica" Garza devoted a considerable amount of attention to his interactions with the "bello sexo." After almost all of these descriptions, Garza concluded with some comment about the virility and heroism of Mexican men as compared with Anglo men. Although these comparisons never directly appear in his public speeches and newspaper articles, they indicate that Garza's political vision came, not only from ideas of liberty and freedom, but also from racialized and gendered conceptions of the differences between Mexicans and Anglos. His descriptions act to portray him as the paradigmatic male border hero who single-handedly defends Mexicans against Anglo oppression (see Paredes and Limón). Casting himself as a benign patriarchal figure who had the responsibility to rescue *señoritas* in distress did not by itself lead him to take up arms against Díaz. Nevertheless, Garza's construction of masculinity in "La Lógica" was an important part of his larger persona as a political opposition leader.

Garza's concept of masculinity as expressed in "La lógica" was in many ways not unique to Garza or to border males. Nineteenth century notions of gender in Mexico and the U.S. saw men and women as fundamentally different, each with his or her own "separate sphere." Men were expected to function in the public realm and civic society, while women were largely relegated to the private sphere, the home. The separate sphere ideology contended that men and women had different strengths and weaknesses and that the public/private division allowed each to make use of their special "gifts." Men's intellectual capabilities and lack of emotionality prepared them for government service and work outside of the home. Whereas women's "morality" and "purity" made them particularly well suited to be guardians of "civic virtue." Men were supposed to provide for and protect their families, while women were in charge of nurturing their children and husbands (see Kerber 7-11). Garza's masculine persona fits well with these nineteenth century notions of gender roles. However, his use of this nineteenth century concept of masculinity to construct himself in the border hero tradition is more specific to Texas Mexican border society. The point is not to judge Garza by late twentieth century standards of "correct" gender ideology or behavior toward women, but rather to examine the ways in which Garza's notions of masculinity worked together with his national and racial identities to form his persona as a border hero and a revolutionary leader.

In "La lógica," Garza made a point of re-counting several instances of his chivalrous and gentlemanly behavior. In each case, he offered to help a woman by giving her money and taking care of her problems. One such instance occurred in April 1886, while on a walk through Lafayette park in St.

Louis., Missouri, Garza approached what he described as a "preciosa" [precious] young woman with beautiful blond hair and a black dress. This young telegraph operator, Maine, introduced herself to Garza whom she recognized as she had just delivered flowers to him a few days earlier in Milwaukee. Maine explained that she had come to St. Louis to visit her sick mother who had died four days earlier. She had no surviving relatives except for her brother in Philadelphia. Upon hearing of her sorrows, Garza offered to pay for her to go visit her brother. She refused the money, but they became close friends (133).

The recounting of this incident allowed Garza to portray himself as a gentleman and at the same time to criticize Anglo American society. For instance, he argued that "entre estos primos son costumbres abolidas ayudar a un huérfano o proteger a las viudas" (134) [among these cousins helping orphans and protecting widows are abolished customs]. This critique of Anglo males for not assuming their male responsibility to protect women and children says as much about Garza's view of women as it does about his view of Anglo American society. Garza's explicit connection between widows and orphans equates a woman without a husband to children without parents. In this way, Garza cast women as children, and husbands as their guardians. Maine ended up marrying another man, but Garza commented proudly that she named her children Kate (Catarino) and Erasmo after him. He thus served as a symbolic father to Maine's children, further reinforcing his image of himself as the paternal protector. Garza expressed this familial paternalism by placing himself in the position of her brother when he stated that he loved her "como a una hermana" (135) [like a sister].

Along with the notion of paternal protection, Garza's concept of heroism helped him to distinguish Anglo Americans from Mexicans. One day while walking along a street in St. Louis, Garza observed two young women who were injured as they tried to enter a buggy being pulled by a wild horse. The six foot tall, agile Garza grabbed hold of the horse and brought it under his control. One of the women injured by the horse asked Garza for his business card because she was so impressed by his gallantry; a few days later he received an invitation to her house. When Garza arrived at Miss Blanche's house, he discovered she was a very wealthy Anglo woman. Garza explained to Miss Blanche that "exponer la vida por una señorita o por un amigo, nada valía para un mexicano" (136) [to risk ones life for a young woman or for a friend is nothing for a Mexican]. In reference to the same incident, Garza concluded that "para ser un héroe entre los americanos se necesita muy poco, y para serlo entre nosotros los mexicanos, necesitamos morirnos defendiendo a la Patria" (136) [to be a hero among the Americans one needs very little, but to be one among us Mexicans, we need to die defending the Fatherland].

These two statements show how gender and nationality intersected. The first one expresses the chivalrous concept of men risking their life for young women and the second invokes the notion of the heroic male who dies "defendiendo a la Patria." However, both statements specifically equate Mexicans with chivalry and heroism. Therefore, in the guise of a compliment, he delivered a critique of American nationalism and Anglo males. His portrayal of Mexican males as virile heroes willing to die defending the nation contrasts with Anglo males, who are presumably emasculated, weak, and unwilling to defend their nation.

In "La lógica," Garza uses eight descriptions of bar-room brawls and gun fights to portray Anglo men as weak and cowardly. These descriptions also serve to glorify violence and cultivate his image as a man of superior strength. One such incident occurred in a hotel lobby in St. Louis when he overheard an Anglo lawyer saying that "los mexicanos eran lo mismo que los perros, que por un hueso se peleaban" (137) [Mexicans were just like dogs, they would fight over a bone]. Without missing a beat, Garza announced that he was a Mexican, called the lawyer a "miserable difamador" [miserable defamer], and whacked him with his umbrella. The lawyer ran away screaming for help. After an article appeared in a local newspaper accusing Garza of hitting the lawyer without cause, Garza went to see the reporter and in plain view of everyone gave him a good whipping too. In glorifying this almost reflexive resort to violence, Garza exemplified his own strength and virility. In contrast, he always described his enemies as weak men who either ran away or screamed "de la manera más cobarde" (84) [in the most cowardly manner].

Garza's contradictory attitude toward Anglo women, respecting them as women while disrespecting them as Anglos, led him to praise their beauty on the one hand and dismiss them as unworthy on the other. A short while after the incident of beating the Anglo lawyer had occurred, the lawyer's sister approached him and apologized for her brother's behavior. They later became lovers. In his retelling of this story Garza boasted that she had given him several presents, including a portrait and a ring. He then flippantly commented that he did not even remember whether he gave these presents to another woman. While this male form of boasting, whereby he inflated his own value by showing disdain and disrespect for this woman, can be seen as somewhat universal behavior for Western men, Garza gave this boast a nationalist twist. He concluded that because "Los americanos aman por conveniencia, así como son fáciles para amar, son fáciles para olvidar y abandonar" (139) [Americans love for convenience, as they are easy to love, they are easy to forget and to abandon]. Thus he suggested that Mexican women were more deserving of deeper and more committed love than were Anglo women. His comments not only demonstrated his insensitivity to this woman, but also served as a critique of all Anglo women. Garza's descriptions of Anglo women often seem contradictory because at the same time as he felt a need to protect and praise what was feminine about them, he felt compelled to criticize and put down what was Anglo about them.

By showing the undying gratitude of the women whom he helped, Garza displayed his chivalry. Whether it was Garza's explicit intent or not, "La lógica" portrayed Garza as a paternal protector. On May 6, 1886, while at the train station in St. Louis, waiting for his train to Eagle Pass, Texas, Garza noticed an "hermosísima" [very beautiful] Mexican woman with a child in her arms. After introducing himself, he learned that she was on her way to New Mexico to visit her ill husband but had missed her train as she did not understand the announcements that were being made in English. Garza wrote, "desde aquel momento me hice cargo de la expresada señora y su niña" [from that moment on I took charge of this woman and her child]. Garza helped the woman with her train arrangements and paid for her passage to Fort Worth, Texas. A few months later he received a letter from this woman saying that her husband had died and that she needed assistance getting to Paso del Norte, present day El Paso. Garza commented that "como ella era viuda y yo soy hijo de 'viuda,' creí mi deber atenderla" (139) [as she was a widow and I am a son of a 'widow,' I thought it my duty to help her]. Not only did he send her money from Eagle Pass, but he went so far as to surprise her by meeting her as she disembarked from the train in Paso de Norte. Garza described the scene at the railway station in some detail. The little girl noticed Garza first and called out, "Mamá, el Señor Garza." Then the mother exclaimed, "usted es el angel de mi guarda. ¡Qué hubiese sido de mí, si en este país no me hubiera encontrado con usted!" (139-40) [you are my guardian angel. What would I have done if I had not met you in this country!]. This and other similar episodes in "La lógica" portray Garza as an indispensable "guardian angel" of women.

Why does Garza choose to include these stories about his relations with women and what do they mean? Garza recognized that these stories did not fit with the rest of his political narrative and felt it necessary to explain why he included them. In chapter seven, Garza apologetically introduced this section entitled 'de todo un poco" [a little bit of everything] by stating that he thought it "necesario distraer un tanto cuanto mi pluma para narrar accontecimientos que al paracer son de poca importancia [necessary to distract my pen a bit to narrate events that seem to have little importance]. Yet, he continued, "en mi carrera de historiador, los recuerdo, y no puedo menos que mezclarlos con otros de más interés" (133) [in my career as an historian, I remember them, and cannot do otherwise than include them with others of more interest]. These stories, far from being random digressions, complemented his narration of "more interesting" events by linking ideals of male responsibility, paternalism, and heroism to a nationalist, cultural, and racial struggle. One must remember that Garza's view of proper gender relations was neither unique to him nor to Mexicans. However, Garza deployed these popular conceptions of gender roles to express the more contentious claim of Mexican cultural superiority. Women, especially Anglo women, became the objects of a territorial battle between Anglo and Mexican males. Penetrating and occupying Anglo women's bodies and then discarding them had the dual purpose of asserting male control over women and Mexican control over Anglo "property."

Garza's concepts of male responsibility, paternalism, and heroism not only informed his behavior toward women, but was itself part of his political persona as a revolutionary leader. The feeling of responsibility toward women complemented his belief that he had a special responsibility to defend and protect the Texas Mexican community and overthrow the Díaz regime. Also, as shown above, Garza's patriarchal beliefs had a racial and national inflection. Therefore, Garza's patriarchal concepts of masculinity and femininity should not be viewed as insignificant "distractions" despite Garza's desire for readers to see them in that manner. Rather, his gender ideology should be seen as part of his complex world-view that led him to his pursue the dual goals of overthrowing Díaz and defending Mexicans from Anglo oppression.

Constructing Identities

On September 15, 1891, Catarino Garza issued his revolutionary "Proclama" on the banks of the Río Bravo, near Mier, Mexico. "Conciudadanos: Levantaos en masa para derrocar en unos cuantos días á los tiranos que con el nombre de Gobierno Federal y de los Estados nos oprimen; y salvemos á nuestra querida Patria que está proxima á desaparecer, víctima de la esclavitud, del robo, del asesinato y de la miseria.... ¡Abajo los tiranos! ¡Viva el pueblo mexicano! Vuestro compañero de sacrificios y de peligros. C. E. Garza" [Fellow Citizens: Rise up en masse to overthrow in a few days the tyrants who using the Federal and State governments' name oppress us; and save our dear country that is almost disappearing, victim of slavery, of robbery, of assassinations, and of misery.... Down with the tyrants! Long live the Mexican people! Your comrade of sacrifices and danger. C. E. Garza] (CPD). Though his revolution never succeeded in overthrowing the Díaz regime, he evaded capture by both the U.S. and Mexican armies for a year and a half. Ultimately he fled to Costa Rica where he continued to develop his concept of himself as a revolutionary, but this time as a pan-Latin American revolutionary leader. The language and purpose of "La lógica" stands in stark contrast to Garza's "Proclama," yet one can see how the latter implicitly rest-ed on the former. "La lógica" thus prepared the ideological ground for the revolution by helping Garza to define himself as a leader and by making sense of the "circunstancias" [circumstances] facing Mexicans in Texas.

Garza's formulation of his own racial, national, and gender identity thus served as a means of struggle against the oppression of Mexicans in Texas by Anglos and in Mexico by Porfiristas. While the ability to define himself and the larger community to which he belonged may have helped him to cope with everyday physical and psychological stresses, in the end it would not by itself be enough to resolve the problems he confronted. He would need to as he said, "abandon[ar] la pluma para empuñar la espada" [put down the pen to pick up the sword]. Though his phrase seems to establish a dichotomy between the "pluma," his journalistic and intellectual pursuits, and his "espada," his armed revolutionary activities, the two elements are inter-dependent.

Garza's own history teaches us that people's understanding of who they are and how they fit into the larger society is crucial in determining their actions. Historians should thus focus not only on what people do, but on the long process of identity formation whereby people articulate a view of themselves as individuals and as members of society. Most people do not lead revolutions or major political movements and have therefore been left out of history by historians who focus on extraordinary individuals or broad structural transformations. A shift in attention away from the larger political events to the everyday mechanisms of social control and struggle may help historians grasp the depth and richness of this arena and bring new actors onto the historical stage. By resurrecting from obscurity those people who have been most silenced by the ruling classes we may begin to change history as well as write about it.

Works Cited

Archivo Histórico de la Secretaría de Relaciones Exteriores de México (AREM). Top., 18-27-112, 9-1-45, and Legajo 834.

Garza, Catarino. *La era de Tuxtepec en México: O sea Rusia en América* (Costa Rica, 1894). In Celso Garza Guajardo, comp., *En busca de Catarino Garza*. Monterrey: Universidad Autónoma de Nuevo León, 1989. Original pamphlet can be found at Tulane University.

_____. "La lógica de los hechos: O sean observaciones sobre las circunstancias de los mexicanos en Texas, desde el año 1877 hasta 1889." In Celso Garza Guajardo, comp., *En busca de Catarino Garza*. Monterrey: Universidad Autónoma de Nuevo León, 1989. The manuscript of this work, that remained incomplete and unpublished, can be found in the Benson Latin American Collection at the University of Texas, Austin. It was donated to the University of Texas in 1927 by Garza's daughter, Amelia Pérez of Alice, Texas.

_____. "Proclama," Matamoros, México , Sept. 1891, in Colección de Porfirio Díaz (CPD), Universidad Iberoamericana, México D.F., doc. 11418.

Gramsci, Antonio. *An Antonio Gramsci Reader*. Ed. David Forgacs. New York: Shocken Books, 1988.

Kerber, Linda K. *Women of the Republic: Intellect and Ideology in Revolutionary America.* New York: W.W. Norton, 1986.

Limón, José E. *Mexican Ballads, Chicano Poems: History and Influence in Mexican-American Social Poetry.* Berkeley: U of California P, 1992.

National Archives (NA). General Records of the Department of State, RG 59. "Despatches from United States Consular Officials in Nuevo Laredo, Mexico, 1871-1906," microcopy no. 280, roll 2; and National Archives, Records of U.S. Army, RG 393, "Garza Revolution Papers."

Paredes, Américo. *With His Pistol in His Hand: A Border Ballad and Its Hero.* Austin: U of Texas P, 1990.

Williams, Raymond. "Base and Superstructure in Marxist Cultural Theory." *Problems in Materialism and Culture.* London: Verso, 1981.

Young, Elliott. "Remembering Catarino Garza's 1891 Revolution: An Aborted Border Insurrection," *Mexican Studies/Estudios Mexicanos* 12 (2), Summer 1996.

PART V

Recovering the Creation of Community

Spanish-Language Journalism in the Southwest: History and Discursive Practice

Gabriel Meléndez

> Necesario se hace que la Prensa, ese espléndido altar que la civilización moderna ha erguido a las instituciones populares,—comprendiendo su alto ministerio y la importancia que ella representa en las mismas— abandone la frivolidad con que desde tanto ha venido enervándose, para ocuparse seria y conscienzudamente del desarrollo intelectual de las masas populares hispano-americanas que habitan todavía una porción del Oeste y el Sudeste de esta gran república del Norte.
>
> —José Escobar, Denver, Colorado, 1896.[1]

> [It becomes necessary for the Press, that splendid altar that modern civilization has erected to popular institutions,—taking note of its high ministry, and the importance it represents in those institutions—to abandon the frivolity which for so long has weaken it, in favor of employing itself in the intellectual development of the masses of Hispanos that still inhabit a portion of the West and Southwest of this great republic of the North.]

A Culture of Print Among *Nuevomexicanos* [New Mexicans]

Nuevomexicanos [New Mexicans] became Mexican Americans by political default in 1848. But even prior to becoming a conquered people they long held a desire to know the liberating benefits that would accrue to them with the establishment of the press in their particular corner of the world. Before the conquering armies of the United States visited them, poverty, isolation and lack of educational opportunities slowed Nuevomexicano social, cultural and historical development.

The acquisition of the press by Padre Martínez and others in New Mexico in 1834 pushed what had been essentially an oral and a colonial manuscript culture toward the development of a complex system of communication resulting from the ability to produce multiple imprints of written material. The hallmark of a "culture of print" is precisely that it involves many other individuals besides the author in the production of printed materials. The exchange of ideas by way of their inscription in print is not solely the domain of technology, but of the intellectual grist and entrepreneurial skills that drive and sustain such activity. Print discourse as it emerges from the journalistic activity of New Mexico's Spanish-speaking people is framed by its intellectual and cultural purpose, that is, by the use of print technology in service to cultural maintenance and educational advancement. Crucial to this project is the coming together of the producers of print (authors, editors, reporters, printers) and a community of readers. A culture of print is thus activated through the consonance of thought, the complicity of action, and the orchestration of initiatives that Robert Darnton terms the "communications circuit" of print discourse (30). What is important here is the way and manner by which the viewpoint of the group finds its way into public discourse, not in spite of, but precisely because of this complexity and concordance of activity.

Popular and literary journalism in New Mexico grew out of two momentous and seemingly antithetical developments in the nineteenth century. On the one hand, the territorial expansion of the United States into the Southwest resulted in the subordination of Nuevomexicanos and other Mexican-origin groups in their homeland: the Southwest. Nuevomexicanos became the object of an intense Anglo-American cultural hegemony which threatened the survival of their communities and would eventually impede their right to self-actualization. Military occupation preceded the economic conquest of the region and the push to open new markets in the Southwest. Shortly thereafter, New Mexico entered the industrial age and, for the first time in their long history, Nuevomexicanos had access to manufactured goods and the scientific and technological advances that characterized economic life in the United States. Among the items that could be acquired were typographical mechanical presses which, heretofore, had been extremely scarce in Mexico's northern provinces.

Spanish-language newspaper publication lasted well over half a century. From 1880 to 1935 more than 190 newspapers were established in over thirty communities in Colorado, New Mexico, Arizona and Texas. In volume alone, the establishment of Spanish-language newspapers under the guidance of native-born Mexicano editors and proprietors in the 1890s constitutes irrefutable evidence that a culture of print shaped and influenced their communities. The shift from orality to print represented by newspaper publication induced the emergence of other agents of cultural expression. Cultural voicing widened beyond orality to include written composition. A development that is not without its consequences, as Ong notes, "This gives thought different contours from those of orally sustained thought" (96). Likewise, authority to voice the experience of the group extended itself to include those who were educated and trained as *periodiqueros* [newspaper journalists].

In cultures where orality predominates or in regions which Walter Ong describes as "preserving massive residual orality" (69), a description that is easily applicable to widespread maintenance of traditional verbal forms in the Southwest, the viewpoint of the group often resides with its bards, its orators, its *ancianos* [elders]. In them one finds those agents of culture authorized by tradition to speak in the name of the group. Prior to the introduction of the press, Nuevomexicanos relied heavily on these cultural guardians to transmit and validate their society's cultural epistemology. Known variously to the community as *bardos, trovadores, oradores,* [bards, troubadours, orators] and the like, ʻhey expressed a distilled knowledge of the past through speech forms grounded in a tradition of oral poetics, oratory and rhetoric. This backdrop of residual orality echoes in the work of Nuevomexicano journalists who relied heavily on the modes of thought and expression of their *antepasados* [ancestors].

The emergence of a print culture in Mexican-origin communities in the Southwest remains an expression of resistance and opposition to Anglo-American political, social and cultural hegemony in the Southwest after 1848. As such, it is subject to the vicissitudes of a policy of maceration of the "cultural other" by the dominant group. Contained and never totally free, this culture of print, like the group it represents, is held in check, often coerced into angered discursive posturing and defensive response.

The Press in the Wake of American Conquest

In the decade following the signing of the Treaty of Guadalupe Hidalgo the number of presses in New Mexico slowly increased. Anglo-American editors and publishers entered the region in greater numbers and began to establish newspapers at Santa Fe, Taos, Las Vegas and Albuquerque. During the same period Nuevomexicano periodical activity abated dramatically, a reaction due to the political and cultural estrangement produced by martial law and, in no small measure, owing to the loss of the Martínez press, the one press in the region that was previously at the service of the Spanish-speaking population. However, Nuevomexicanos continued to influence the development of the press and print discourse in New Mexico in two key ways. First, Anglo-American editors and publishers quickly came to understand that the predominance of the Spanish language among the majority of the citizens of the territory meant that the "American press" would need to respond to this linguistic reality by publishing materials in Spanish. As a result most newspapers after 1848 were either partially or totally printed in the Spanish language. According to territorial historian Porter Stratton, "most territorial editors followed the bilingual practice" (12). Nuevomexicanos, as the majority readership of these newspapers, came to shape the scope and nature of early Anglo-American periodical activity. A second way in which Nuevomexicanos, influenced print discourse was as associate editors, translators and the printers in many of these newspaper endeavors. Arrangements of the sort between Nuevomexicanos and Anglo-Americans favored the latter group since Nuevomexicanos were engaged principally to provide language and translating skills to these newspapers, although presumably, Anglo publishers allowed Nuevomexicanos to contribute items of interest to the Spanish-speaking public. The relatively small number of autonomous Nuevomexicano presses during this period is explained by the continued lack of educational opportunities available to Nuevomexicanos and to the difficulty most aspiring journalists would necessarily have encountered in attempting to raise the capital to buy presses of their own.

The Flowering of Spanish-language Journalism in New Mexico

From 1848 to 1879 Nuevomexicanos established only a handful of Spanish-language newspapers over which they exerted complete editorial autonomy and authority. However, important work in printing and publication among Nuevomexicanos continued in those years. Nuevomexicanos were just beginning to position themselves to enter the professions. Local historian Benjamín Read reported that Urbano Chacón had set up a newspaper called *El Explorador* [The Explorer] in Trinidad, Colorado in the late 1860s and in the first years of the next decade was publishing *El Espejo* [The Mirror] in Taos, New Mexico. Chacón's newspapers clearly inspired others to follow suit, and, as an editor, Chacón was in a position to guide the work of younger Nuevomexicanos in journalism. Enrique H. Salazar, for example, one of the founders of *La Voz del Pueblo* [The Voice of the People] in Santa Fe, credited Urbano Chacón with giving him his start in journalism by providing him an apprenticeship at *El Espejo*.

By the late 1870s Nuevomexicano journalists hearkened back to early concerns over the lack of educational advancement in the region, a situation exacerbated by increasing discontent and disillusionment with New Mexico's status as a territory. Adhering to the conviction that "literacy and education are the avenue to social and economic advancement" (Salvino 140), Nuevomexicanos encouraged the use of the press as the vehicle to liberate the mind and spirit. At Las Vegas, several Nuevomexicanos began issuing *El*

Anunciador de Nuevo Méjico [The New Mexico Announcer]. This weekly began publication on October 12, 1871, and continued to be published until January of 1879. Although only one issue of the paper survives into the present and very little is known otherwise about the publication or its publishers, *El Anunciador* appears at the outset of a sustained period of journalism for Nuevomexicanos. The disposition of Nuevomexicanos to increase their influence in the pubic sphere accounts for the high expectations that accompanied the appearance of new publications in these years. *El Anunciador*, for example, contains the prospectus for *La Estrella de Mora* [The Star of Mora], a paper which, in the words of its editor, would speak "for the society in which we live, especially for the *nativos* [natives] of this territory..." The prospectus of *La Estrella de Mora* sounds a familiar note intoned with the same urgency that guided Padre Martínez and others earlier in the century to consider the press as an instrument to educate the native populace. Severino Trujillo, the author of the prospectus, declares:

> Desde tiempo he estado observando atentamente y examinando con escrupulosidad las circunstancias que rodean nuestro país, el cual á no dudarlo, está muy atrás de las demás naciones en lo que respecta á la cultura del entendimiento, el desarrollo de los poderes mentales del hombre. De aquí esa aciaga miseria que cual contagiosa gangrena ha ido cundiendo por casi todas las clases de la sociedad. ("Prospectus..." 12 Jan. 1878)

> [For sometime now, I have carefully observed and examined the circumstances that encircle our homeland, which, without doubt, lags far behind other nations, in regards to a culture of knowledge and the development of the mental abilities of mankind. From whence stems the ominous destitution that has spread like a contagious gangrene that has infected every social class.]

Trujillo's mission, "the development of the mental abilities of mankind," evinces his generation's belief in the power of literacy, equating such work to a moral cause. Trujillo continues:

> Pues si tales son los hechos que nuestro país yace en miseria, y que esta miseria se origina y mana directamente y principalmente de la falta de instrucción en la masa del pueblo quién no ve en este caso la necesidad que todos tenemos de un medio de instrucción pública, el cual iluminando nuestras ideas y operando eficazmente el desarrollo de nuestro espíritu nos conduzca, en fin, digámoslo así, como por la mano á mayor grado de prosperidad, y nos ponga al nivel de todos los pueblos cultos que existen sobre la superficie de la tierra. (12 Jan. 1878)

> [Such is the case, that our homeland lies in misery. This misery originates and emanates directly from the lack of instruction of the masses of the people who are not aware of the need that we all have for some manner of public instruction which will, by enlightening our ideas and operating effectively on the development of our spirit, will lead us by the hand—shall we say— to a higher degree of

prosperity, [one] that will place us at the same level as the rest of the civilized nations on the surface of the Earth.]

The Trujillo text is telling: first, in the manner of its appearance as a prospectus revealing an intensification of journalistic activity among Nuevomexicanos in the late '70s, and second, for what can be inferred from its content regarding the factors that mitigated against such discursive agency. The deployment of printing technologies among Nuevomexicanos follows other situations in which as Davidson argues "the implementation of new print technology is not necessarily a first cause but can be seen as a response to preexisting political processes and social needs (real or perceived)" (18). The social maladies in the New Mexican case were poverty, isolation, social enclavement and Anglo antagonism to Mexicano culture, factors Trujillo gingerly refers to as "the circumstances that encircle our homeland."

Nuevomexicanos continued to inhabit a viable regional community which, social historian Sarah Deutsch suggests, "played host to the incoming Anglos" (7). This explains, in part, the fact that Nuevomexicano discursive agency, via new newspaper enterprises, continued to grow and expand in subsequent decades. Even as Nuevomexicanos "found themselves *partially incorporated* into an increasingly powerful national international capitalist economy controlled by an alien culture," (7) this paradigm continued to be marked by "evidence of initiative, enterprise and autonomy" (7) on the part of the region's *nativos*.

Not surprisingly the greatest outpouring of Nuevomexicano periodical activity occurred in the decades following the arrival of the railroad in 1879. As book historian, Ronald J. Zboray has pointed out, rail development and dispersal of print technology were wedded technologies at mid-century:

> Because the West and South lagged far behind the North in economic development, the rails, and, indeed, the roads and waterways, served as avenues through which ideas, responses and approaches of the more mature capitalism of the North penetrated into the interior of the country to compete with regional cultures. (478)

In the thirty years since the American conquest, Nuevomexicanos had managed to install a culture of print that operated with a high degree of efficacy. By Porter Stratton's count, thirty-five new Spanish-language papers were founded in the decade of the 1890s alone (36). The ability of the Mexicano press to communicate with the greater part of the citizenry in the Southwest obligated English-language publications to assume the role of serving a linguistic minority.

Print culture encouraged a sense of cultural ascendancy among the Spanish-speaking people that began to reveal itself in terms used to self-identify group membership. Throughout the Territorial period the term *mexicano* [Mexican] in both the public and private spheres of discourse was prevalent among the Spanish-speaking population of New Mexico. It is clear, however, that los periodiqueros consciously moved to create a space in the context of their publications for the use of the terms *nuevomexicano, neo-mexicano* and, to a lesser degree, *novo-mexicano*. The wide spread use of the Latin prefixes *neo-* and *novo-* among these literates was a deliberate and conscious attempt to draw attention to a shared sense of promise which they had come to believe would allow them to break the bonds of social stultification. Sensing the magnitude of that promise, Camilo Padilla, editor of *El Mosquito*, advised the youth of his generation to break with servility. Writing on *Cinco de Mayo* [the Fifth of May] 1892, Padilla cites for his readers the case of Mexican youth organizing against the Díaz regime as an example for self-actualization: "Let us celebrate the valor and intrepidity of the youth in the neighboring Republic of Mexico. And by this, filled with enthusiasm and patriotism we admonish, 'Why cannot, New Mexican youth, do likewise?'" Provoking Nuevomexicanos to action, Padilla continues, "What is not possible for New (Neo) Mexican youth?—these young people who were not born to be dictated to by some or another corrupt politician—unite and organize yourselves, and by this make yourself known and respected" ("A la juventud…" [To the Youth…], 5 May 1892).

The trend announced by *El Anunciador* toward the establishment of Neo-Mexicano-controlled newspapers throughout the territory continued unabated through the decade of the 1890s and through the years leading to statehood in 1912. By 1900 Nuevomexicano newspapers had been founded in every important settlement along the Rio Grande corridor. Soon, this line of newspapers reached beyond the territorial borders of New Mexico to include El Paso, west Texas, the Clifton-Morenci mining districts of Arizona, and Spanish-speaking settlements of southern Colorado. In New Mexico, four cities in particular—Las Cruces, Albuquerque, Santa Fe and Las Vegas—became the hubs of a journalistic network extending into other areas of the Southwest.

Neo-Mexicanos at Las Cruces had managed to support several Spanish-language periodicals during the decade of the 1880s. The most important and long-running of these was *El Tiempo* [Time] which had been established in 1882 and continued to be published under that title until 1911. Further North, at Albuquerque, *La Bandera Americana* [The American Flag] began publication in 1895 as did *El Nuevo Mundo* [The New World] two years later in 1897. Santa Fe, by now long-acknowledged as the birthplace of journalism in New Mexico, had seen the establishment of *El Boletín Popular* [The Popular Bulletin] under the able direction of José Segura in 1885; *El Nuevo Mexicano*, the Spanish-language edition of the *Santa Fe New Mexican*, began publication in 1890. Also established in Santa Fe in 1888 was *La Voz del Pueblo*, a paper that was later moved by its founder and editor, Enrique H. Salazar, to Las Vegas, N. M. The Mexicano community of Las Vegas had been served by *La Revista Católica* [The Catholic Review] since 1875. This paper, under the direction of Italian Jesuits, could boast of publication on the first cylinder-model mechanical press in the area. Its impact on the predominantly Catholic, Spanish-speaking Mexicano community in the Las Vegas vicinity was immediate. Nuevomexicanos themselves, influenced by the work of the Jesuits, pursued with unbridled vigor other journalistic endeavors in Las Vegas in the 1890s. *La Voz del Pueblo* resumed publication after its relocation in the summer of 1890 and two other newspapers followed. *El Sol de Mayo* [The May Sun] was founded by Manuel C. de Baca in 1891 and *El Independiente* [The Independent] by Enrique H. Salazar in 1894. All totaled over ninety Spanish-language newspapers were published in New Mexico alone during the period marked by the coming of the railroad in 1879 to statehood in 1912.

New Mexico's periodiqueros also began to organize themselves into a press association as early as 1890.[2] *La Prensa Asociada Hispano-Americana*, [The Spanish-American Press Association] brought together editors from every important Spanish-language newspaper in New Mexico and west Texas for its first organizational meeting held in Las Vegas, New Mexico, in late 1891. In the ensuing months of 1892 the association met regularly at Las Vegas, Santa Fe, Las Cruces and El Paso, Texas. In March, 1892, La Prensa Asociada met in Albuquerque to install its officers and draft a preamble and resolutions that would guide the work of the organization. Victor L. Ochoa of *El Hispano-Americano* [The Spanish-American] of Las Vegas was installed as La Prensa Asociada's president and Camilo Padilla of *El Mosquito* of Mora became the organization's first vice-president. La Prensa Asociada continued to draw other members to its ranks. José Segura of Santa Fe's *El Boletín Popular* reported that several of the most prominent Spanish-language journalists were in attendance at a meeting of *La Prensa Asociada* held in Santa Fe in early December, 1893. Present at the meeting were Camilo Padilla of El *Mosquito* (Mora, New Mexico), José Escobar of *El Progreso* [Progress] (Trinidad, Colorado), Teófilo Ocaña Caballero of *La Lucha* [The Struggle] (El Paso, Texas), Marcial Valdez of *El Tiempo* (Las Cruces), Pedro G. de la Lama of *La Opinión Pública* [The Public Opinion] (Albuquerque), and Marcelino Lerma of *La Flor del Valle* [The Flower of the Valley] (Las Cruces). Other important Spanish-language publications from across the territory were represented at the meeting as well. The organization progressed rapidly with *La Voz del Pueblo* of Las Vegas suggesting that the benefits of the collaboration represented by La Prensa Asociada would soon spread to the neighboring states of the Southwest and to Mexico, "Ya no en materia de duda, que en corto tiempo

se inaugurará uno de los movimientos que pueden beneficiar á la raza latina, más que ningún otro, esto es, la asociación de la prensa española en Nuevo México, Arizona, Texas y parte de México." ("La Prensa…" 5 Mar. 1892) [No longer a matter of doubt, but that in a very short time will begin a movement that can benefit the Latin race more than any other, this is the association of the Spanish press in New Mexico, Arizona, Texas and part of Mexico.]

The synergism of purpose of La Prensa Asociada, when viewed against the backdrop of poverty, isolation and the scarcity of technology that had been so prevalent in the years prior to the arrival of the railroad, seemed to confirm the growing sense of confidence and enthusiasm among Neo-Mexicanos who began to see themselves as agents of change in the progress of their community. Editors and writers were also defined by the process in which they engaged. Partaking of *el don de la palabra impresa* [the gift of the printed word] molded them into an identifiable cultural force. As an organic intelligentsia, periodiqueros channeled the ethnopoetics of the region into print discourse for the first time.

Publication created a public venue that allowed for the expression of thoughts, ideas, attitudes, and concerns rooted in the experience of Nuevomexicanos. This activity went well beyond the prosaic, matter-of-fact business of reporting the news of the day. Newspaper publication stimulated debate and gave voice to the overriding concerns of the period. It also provided an outlet for creative and artistic work among New Mexico's Spanish-speaking populace. Newspapers functioned as a forum for elucidating the cultural debate Nuevomexicanos found themselves embroiled in with their Anglo-American counterparts. At the same time such development inspired a generation to take up journalism as a profession. Drawing strength from intellectual activity and civic concern, Neo-Mexicano print culture posited language as a principal tool in the struggle for cultural survival. Thus, the use and maintenance of the Spanish language in particular was promoted in a public forum. Moreover, the Spanish language was displayed in a variety of forms; its literary and artistic potential was promoted by publishing the writings of local and regional authors, alongside the work of writers and thinkers of the broader Spanish-speaking world.[3] This work in journalism establishes the contours of a Nuevomexicano cultural resurgence, one that bespeaks a concrescence of elements including the material means to support such activity. The full extent of the work of La Prensa Asociada attains greatest acuity in the work of individual editors, and is best represented in the impact wrought by the enterprises they established along the Río Grande.

Neo-Mexicano Discursive Agency: Camilo Padilla, Pioneer Publisher

Camilo Padilla's contributions to the development of Neo-Mexicano journalism and culture are important for two reasons in particular. First, Padilla's work spans his entire public life. His lifelong dedication to promoting the educational and cultural progress of his community lead to increased professionalism and the improving quality of Neo-Mexicanos in journalism. Second, Padilla's career points the way to greater specialization and increased sophistication among New Mexico's periodiqueros. Camilo Padilla, born in 1865, was in fact responsible for producing the first and only specialized publication to feature poetry, art, essays, and other creative expression by Neo-Mexicanos. A graduate of El Colegio de San Miguel [St. Michael's College] in Santa Fe, Padilla spent over ten years working as a compositor for the *New Mexican*, a paper published in Santa Fe by W. H. Manderfield.

Camilo Padilla was among the best read and most seasoned travelers of his generation. In 1890, Padilla traveled to Washington serving as the private secretary to Antonio Joseph, New Mexico's territorial delegate to the United States Congress. In the early years of the decade Camilo interspersed visits to Washington as Joseph's secretary with time spent time working on newspapers in Mora County when Congress was not in session. From 1898 to 1901 Padilla resided continually in the nation's capital. During periods of time spent in New Mexico, Padilla began to lay the foundation for his own work in journalism. From July to September, 1890, he edited *La Gaceta de Mora* [The Mora Gazette]. In December, 1891, he began publication of his own paper to which he gave the feisty name, *El Mosquito*; and, shortly thereafter, Padilla became a founding member of La Prensa Asociada.

For reasons that are not yet clear, Camilo Padilla moved to El Paso, Texas in 1907, where he began the publication of *Revista Ilustrada* [The Illustrated Review]. Information regarding the issuance of his magazine is sketchy and incomplete and is obscured by the fact that no extant issues of *Sancho Panza*, the title under which the magazine was published for some time, have ever made their way to libraries or archival repositories. Furthermore, the publishing history of *Revista Ilustrada* is marred by its issuance at different locations and in different cities. Padilla reverted to using the earlier name *Revista Ilustrada* and continued to publish under that title in Santa Fe through the first decade of the 20th century. Sometime in the 1920s, Padilla once again returned to El Paso and began to issue *Revista Ilustrada*. Padilla remained in El Paso until the summer of 1925. Shortly thereafter, he moved the magazine to Santa Fe for the last time where he published *Revista Ilustrada* until shortly before his death in 1933.

Among Padilla's first submissions to Spanish-language newspapers is a letter to the editor of *La Voz del Pueblo* in Las Vegas in May 1889. Padilla's submission appeared with the title "Crónica nacional" [National Chronicle]. The communiqué was meant to provide *La Voz* and its readership with news and information from Washington, D.C. During the early part of the decade, Padilla contributed many such items to Santa Fe's most important Spanish-language newspaper, *El Boletín Popular.* His association with *El Boletín* was no doubt encouraged by the fact that José Segura, the editor and proprietor of the paper, was Camilo's first cousin. Through communiqués sent back to *El Boletín*, Padilla came to be seen as the paper's official correspondent in Washington. His items were frequently signed "Gus," and appeared with the note "De la capital nacional: Correspondencia particular de El Boletín" [From the nation's capital: Special correspondence to El Boletín]. He submitted other items to the paper as well, including editorial opinions, travel narratives, and cultural observations.

In April 1894, Padilla submitted a short essay he entitled "Nuestra única salvación" [Our Only Hope] to *El Boletín*. Padilla spoke to the issue of disharmony and discord that had begun to manifest itself among Nuevomexicanos, observing that this disunity had become most pronounced in the territory from 1874 to 1894. This twenty-year period encompassed the arrival of the railroad in New Mexico and a subsequent and unprecedented immigration of Anglo-Americans to the Territory. In his essay, Padilla alludes to the political and cultural fissures that had come to disfigure the contours of self-reliance and cohesiveness which he asserts characterized Nuevomexicano society of earlier times. Padilla noted that an atmosphere of discord and dissonance pervaded Nuevomexicano communities, a condition that was exacerbated by the menace of an alien culture and its attendant moves to dominate the region:

> El tiempo transcurrido entre estas dos fechas—1874 y 1894—significa mucho para nosotros. Ahí encontramos la llave de nuestra situación. Sólo veinte años median de una a otra fecha, mas ¡cuánto cambio y materias ofrece ese período do al observador! Durante ese lapso se ha operado en nuestras conciencias una marcada tendencia al apartamiento, un movimiento de desunión que de día en día aumenta en progresión verdaderamente aterradora. En nada existe verdadera comunión de ideas; los grandes principios que daban unidad á nuestras acciones y que establecían entre los hombres de una misma raza una especie de confraternidad ó se han desmoronado ó amenazan ruina.
>
> Consecuencia fatal de esta disgregación es la envidia, la ambición y la mala voluntad que nos tenemos, que han venido á suplantar y á empequeñecer no sólo los grandes principios de confraternidad que heredamos de nuestros padres sino hasta nuestra fé. La intriga y la mentira—esos mónstros (sic) que acompañan la política del día—han venido á suceder á la sinceridad y la verdad. El sentimiento particular ha tomado el lugar del sentimiento colectivo; el último hoy no existe, ó

si existe, avergonzado de ver tanta perfidia, se oculta en el pecho de uno que otro de nosotros.... (12 Apr. 1894)

> [The time that has transpired between these two dates—1874 and 1894—means much for us. Here we find the key to our situation. Only twenty years separate one date from the other, however, how much change and evidence is offered to the observer by this period of time. During this interval of time a marked tendency to separatism has moved our conscience, a movement towards disunity that increases day to day with terrifying progression. Nowhere can be seen a communion of ideas; the great principles that brought unity to our actions and that established among men of the same race a kind of brotherhood have crumbled away or are threatened by ruin.
>
> The fateful result of this dissolution is envy, ambition, and the ill will we have for each other; [these things] have come to supplant and shrink the great principle of brotherhood that we inherited from our forefathers, even in matters of our very faith. Intrigue and falsehood —those monsters that keep company with the politics of the day—have come to overtake sincerity and truth. Individual concern has replaced the collective sentiment; the latter does not exist today, or if it exists, it is shamed by such treachery as lays hidden in the heart of one or another of us. . . .]

Padilla's submissions to *El Boletín Popular* in the 1890s are characterized by clear, concise, and polished language. In them one finds the work of a keen observer and chronicler of people, places, and events. Sharing in detail the experience of his travels with his readership back in New Mexico, Padilla was aware of the importance of providing such accounts to other Nuevomexicanos who had not had the opportunity to travel. Life for the great majority of Padilla's fellow Nuevomexicanos centered on subsistence farming and ranching, and few citizens of the Territory had either the occasion or opportunity to consider the roots of the cultural, economic, political, and religious disparity that existed between their community and Anglo-American émigrés to New Mexico. Added to this, encounters with Anglo-American immigrants were strained by cultural differences and mutual distrust. Nuevomexicanos were left to imagine and speculate on the background and way of life of these newcomers.

In his communiqués from Washington, Padilla attempted to register a sense of awe and excitement with his own discovery of eastern American cities, in this way gaining insight into the workings of the country that only a few decades prior had so profoundly affected and forever changed the fate of his homeland and the way of life of his fellow Nuevomexicanos. Padilla's views of Washington, D.C., and other cities represented incursions into a social world that was foreign and alien to most Nuevomexicanos in the nineteenth century. Nuevomexicanos had little information and few means to appreciate the enormity of the socio-economic disparity that existed between New Mexico and the rest of the United States. This lack of understanding was exacerbated by the air of haughtiness and superiority that conditioned Anglo-American interactions with the native populations of the Territory. Padilla obviously sensed the importance of issuing his communiqués from Washington, where the experience of travel and fellowship with other New Mexicans living in Washington continually returned him to a deeper reverence for New Mexico as cultural homeland: "…when finding ourselves far away from our beloved homeland, we thought often about this land which today, like an old plow is on the auction block; when, in company of the young patriot, Maximiliano Luna, we contemplated the future of our peaceful and righteous people, and thought about the discord of our fellow citizens,—which has arrived here like a plague" ("Nuestro Patrio Suelo," [Our Homeland] *El Mosquito*, 10 Dec. 1892). In pieces such as "Camilo en Virginia" and "Historia Original Neo-Mexicana: ¡Pobre Emilio!" [Original New-Mexican Story: Wretched Emilio!], a short story published in *La Gaceta de Mora* under the pseudonym "Zulu," Padilla began to delineate the social and cultural boundaries that conditioned interactions between Nuevomexicanos and the dominant Anglo-American social and political reality.

Padilla's "Historia Original Neo-Mexicana"

"Historia Original Neo-Mexicana: ¡Pobre Emilio!" (1890) is among the first pieces of prose fiction written by a native New Mexican with the intent of capturing the personal experience of Nuevomexicanos as they attempt to make sense of the ethnic and cultural differences that set them apart from the Anglo-American society. "Historia Original Neo-Mexicana" is the story of Emilio, a young man who, we are told, is a close friend of the narrator. Emilio, we discover, is about to embark on a journey that will take him *al oriente* [back East] to work in the nation's capital. Camilo Padilla's own travel and work in Washington obviously inform the details of Emilio's story.

Upon taking his leave of Emilio at the train station in Santa Fe, the author reflects on the possibility that this separation will forever change their lives. The narrator's intuition will prove to be prophetic. Two years later, the narrator makes a trip to Washington where he has the opportunity to visit his friend once again. The two rekindle their friendship and indulge in long conversations about, as might be expected, New Mexico:

> Obtuve un cuarto cerca de Emilio y todas las noches nos juntábamos ya para platicar, ya para tomar un paseo.
> ¡Qué ratos tan memorables aquéllos!
> Ya platicamos sobre Nuevo México y la raza neo-mexicana, ya sobre aquella hermosa ciudad y sus atractivos.

¡O pláticas benditas, que habeis, cual ingratos pájaros, emprendido el vuelo para no volver jamás. Mientras duraban aquellas pláticas, los hermosos ojos negros de mi amigo se hallaban bañados en lágrimas. Me recuerdo de un capítulo de su residencia en ese lugar, y del cual los voy á dar alguna idea al narrar lo siguiente: ("Historia Original…" 14 Aug. 1890)

[I obtained a room close to Emilio's and each night we would get together to talk or to take a walk.

Oh what memorable times were those!

Now, we would talk about New Mexico and the New Mexican race, now about the beautiful city and its attractions.

Blessed talks, which like uncaring birds have taken flight and will never return again! While those conversations lasted my friend's beautiful dark eyes were bathed in tears. I remember a chapter regarding his stay in that place, of which I shall give some idea in the following narration:]

But indeed, things had changed. Emilio relates how he has fallen madly in love with a young woman in the capital. He is willing to give up everything in order to have her love: "Sacrificaré religión, familia, honor, futuro—todo por ti.…" [I will sacrifice everything, religion, family, honor, the future, all for you.…] he declares upon asking her one evening to marry him. But she has already told him, "…tú eres católico; yo presbiteriana. Es imposible para mí cambiar de credo religioso, así como también lo es para ti." […you are Catholic, I am Presbyterian. It is impossible for me to change my religious beliefs, just as it is impossible for you to do so.]

Emilio, dejected and torn, is given to bouts of depression. He confesses his folly at believing he could cross the cultural divide into the Anglo world by seeking the hand of this Anglo maiden. Despondency invades his spirit and his conversations are filled with nostalgia for New Mexico, in particular, for the New Mexican woman. The narrator relates those moments of intimate disclosure when Emilio confesses all to him:

A menudo me decía: "O, no hay en este mundo mujeres tan tiernas apasionadas, sinceras, como las nuestras—las mexicanas. Lo que nuestras primitas son todo lo contrario—frías, metalizadas, especuladoras. ¡Mexicanas, mujeres nobles, Dios las bendiga mil veces!" Y cuando llegaba á esto afirmaba que realmente sentí lo que decía, consagrándolas una lágrima. (ibid.)

[Many times he would say to me: "Oh, in this world there aren't women as tender, passionate, sincere as our women—the Mexican women. Indeed our cousins here are quite the opposite—cold, hard, speculative. Mexican women, noble women. God bless you all a thousand times!" And when he would come to this, he would affirm that he truly felt what he had said by shedding a tear for them.]

Emilio, though no longer infatuated with the young woman, cannot rid himself of the humiliation at being spurned by the woman he loves. One day, having made the decision to kill himself, Emilio takes up a revolver and, at the very moment when he is about to end his life, a vision suddenly appears before him. The vision is of two shadows or shapes which represent his most cherished ideals. In one he sees a vision of the homeland, of New Mexico; in the other he sees the image of his own mother. Emilio's dream occasions a profound transformation and change in the young man at the very moment that he has thought to take his own life. Emilio confesses to his friend the following:

> Al momento puso el revolver sobre la mesa é hincado y llorando dijo: "Si no fuese por Vdes. ¡O mi patria y querida madre! yo me volaría la tapa de los sesos. Pero como ciendo [sic] que tal vez necesiteis mis humildes servicios, debo de ocultar debajo de una falsa sonrisa mis penas, y defenderos con mi voz, pluma y espada. Es contigo, ¡patria querida!, con la que me esposo, y no es sino por ti quien vivo. (ibid.)

> [At that moment he placed the revolver on the table and kneeling and crying he said, "If it were not for the both of you, my homeland and my beloved mother, I would blow off the top of my head! But it being the case that you may have need of my humble services, I am obliged to hide my pain beneath a false smile and defend you with my voice, my pen, and my sword. I am with you beloved homeland; to you I am betrothed, and it is only because of you that I live.]

Although Emilio's story is cast in the mold of a nineteenth century romantic narrative filled with melancholic undertones and overstated pathos, it nonetheless accords emotional valence to the profound identification of Nuevomexicanos with a homeland and a cultural inheritance distinct from and at times at variance with Anglo-American sensibilities. While Padilla's protagonists appear as emotional caricatures suspended in the contrived situation provided by the story of an unrequited love, the subtext of "Historia Original" has everything to do with the clash of cultural values between Nuevomexicanos and the Anglo-American social order. The story's overt symbolism centers on themes revered in Mexicano culture. It is no coincidence that questions of religion, honor, motherhood, homeland, the idealization of the feminine, and a culturally-prescribed abhorrence to suicide should figure so prominently in the psychological dilemma young Emilio confronts. From the vantage point of cross-cultural dissonance, the story, then, is less about personal sentimentality than it is about the exploration of contrasting world views and ideologies.

Padilla's Revista Ilustrada

Camilo Padilla published his "magazine" *Revista Ilustrada* for twenty-seven years. *Revista Ilustrada*, a contemporary of *El Palacio* [The Palace], the

New Mexico Historical Society's publication, was no doubt born out of the need Nuevomexicanos felt to have their language, art, and literature featured in an analogous publication. As was the case with the histories of the day, Nuevomexicanos increasingly were becoming aware of the manner in which Anglo-American publications were restrictive and elided the local culture. In the best of cases, the ethnocentrism of these publications was reflected in the consistent omission of Nuevomexicano-authored pieces. In the worst of cases, articles on Nuevomexicano life and society were filled with countless distortions authored by a multitude of uninitiated observers of Nuevomexicano cultural practices. Camilo Padilla was himself a member of the Anthropological Society and maintained an association with such leading figures in the cultural life of New Mexico as L. Bradford Prince, ex-governor and founding member of the New Mexico Historical Society. Padilla had made the acquaintance of the historian Colonel Ralph Twitchell, and, in later years, of Senator Bronson Cutting and Willard Johnson, the editor of *Laughing Horse Magazine*. *Revista Ilustrada* was launched at the exact time that Anglo-American specialized publications on art, history, archeology, and literature made their first appearance in New Mexico.[4] Camilo Padilla's resolve as a publisher was sharpened by this kind of development. It moved him to conceive of *Revista Ilustrada* as a specialized venue specifically tailored to Nuevomexicano needs. Padilla described his magazine in its early titles as "Publicación mensual de industria, comercio, literatura y arte" [A monthly publication of industry, business, literature and art]. Later, with the magazine's permanent relocation to Santa Fe, Padilla subtitled it "Magazine de hogar," [Home magazine] and described its purpose to be, "Crear interés por el idioma de nuestros padres" [To create interest in the language of our forebears].

With its inaugural issue published in El Paso, *Revista Ilustrada* opened up a heretofore unknown space for representing the creative work of the Nuevomexicano community in art and literature, and its format was, for most of its years, that of a literary magazine. The poems, short stories, and historical articles featured in each issue were enhanced with illustrative photographs, wood-block prints, and other graphics. The magazine's columns and features promoted leading figures from all walks of life in the Spanish-speaking community of the Southwest. Padilla's collaborations with editors in El Paso and in Mexico lent the magazine a dynamic and transnational outlook. Its inclusiveness reduced the tendency to view Nuevomexicano issues and concerns as unrelated or disconnected to realities in other areas of the Southwest, and made patent a cultural affinity to the El Paso border area, to Mexico, and to other parts of the Hispanic world.

Revista Ilustrada is, then, the first publication issued by a Neo-Mexicano to recognize the importance of contemporary work in the arts and literature.

Spanish-language newspapers of earlier days, arbitrarily divided as they were between news, announcements, editorial commentary, poems, and other writings, were subject to the immediate concerns of daily life. The poems, essays, or other writings supplied by local editors and writers were filled with an urgency that took precedence over more formal refinements of the texts. *Revista Ilustrada* presented texts that were removed from the immediate context of social, political, and cultural happenings; thus, it benefited and encouraged a process of distillation in the thought and writing of Nuevomexicanos as they achieved greater sophistication in literature by the early years of the twentieth century.

The magazine's mission was aided by the fact that by this time there were several established voices in the community who were speaking to the matter of the ascendancy of Neo-Mexicano culture and arts. *Revista Ilustrada* published the works of Benjamín M. Read, Eusebio Chacón, Aurelio M. Espinosa, Luz Elena Ortiz, and Isidoro Armijo, along with the commentaries of Camilo Padilla, who often offered his work in a column entitled, "A través de mis cristales" [From My Point of View] or under the pseudonyms "Dimas" or "Ignatus." In its format and presentation, *Revista Ilustrada* rivaled the work of its contemporaries in the local English-language press. Far from being parochial and provincial—a charge often directed at New Mexico's Spanish-language press—it displayed the works of Mexican and Latin American authors and opened its venue to include New Mexican women writers. It featured the arts in the form of wood-block prints, graphics, and photographs. Camilo Padilla also provided his readership with a list of books available for purchase from "La librería de la Revista" [The Revista Book Shop]. The list included a number of works of world literature (Hugo, Dumas, Verne, Cervantes, etc.), works from the national literature of Latin America (*María* by Jorge Isaacs, *El perriquillo sarniento*, by Fernández de Lizardí, etc.), and a number of works of a regional and local nature such as "La llorona" [The Weeping Woman], "Cuento: Pedro de Urdimalas" [The Story of Pedro de Urdimalas], and "Chucho el roto" [Chucho, the Bum]. Presumably, Padilla authored some of the latter works which he sold for fifteen to thirty cents a copy.

All in all, its typical sixteen-page issues were carefully edited and executed. At the time of Padilla's death the Santa Fe New Mexican noted of *Revista Ilustrada*, "It was well edited, attractively illustrated and was full of literary gems. It did much to stimulate interest in the Spanish language throughout the Southwest" ("Camilo Padilla...," 23 Nov. 1933).

Esteem was often voiced by Padilla's contemporaries, many of whom had worked with equal fervor in the cause of a Nuevomexicano cultural movement. That praise should come from Eusebio Chacón is especially telling. In

October, 1914, Chacón responded to Padilla's request for the submission of an article on the history of New Mexico to be included in *Revista Ilustrada*, taking the occasion to note that he was much honored by the solicitation. Chacón ended his note with praise for Padilla's long career in journalism and for the noble, albeit difficult, task Padilla had set for himself in attempting to bring literature and art to the masses of Nuevomexicanos. Chacón writes that he found the idea of having a submission published in *Revista* as fanciful a notion as Padilla's own dream to bring high quality literary journalism to the state:

> He leído esta carta varias veces; me hé dado pellizcos por desengañarme de no estar soñando... Ah, sí, soñando uno de esos sueños color de rosa de mi amigo Padilla, que con tanto heroísmo se dedica al periodismo elegante y culto en Nuevo México, como quien dice, sacrificando su vida en "arrojar margaritas"... a un pueblo que no aprecia como debería tales sacrificios. ("Cosas raras de la historia...," [Oddities of History...], 15 Oct. 1914)

> [I have read this letter several times; I have pinched myself to make sure that I am not dreaming... Oh yes, dreaming one of my friend Padilla's rose-colored dreams, my friend who so heroically dedicates himself to elegant and refined journalism in New Mexico, as one would say, sacrificing his life by "tossing marigolds"...to a citizenry who does not appreciate as it should such sacrifice.]

At Padilla's death in 1933, praise for his work as editor, educator, civic, and political figure continued to be voiced in many quarters of New Mexico. The *Santa Fe New Mexican* observed:

> In his passing, New Mexico loses a pioneer educator, a trenchant publicist, pioneer printer, editor and publisher; a distinguished orator in two languages; famous interpreter, political leader of outstanding ability, keen student of public affairs, a life-long worker of the Spanish-speaking people of the southwest, and an enthusiast in the cause of preserving the Spanish traditions, customs, art, music, language and culture. ("Camilo Padilla...," 23 Nov. 1933)

Camilo Padilla had spent a lifetime attempting to ameliorate the neglect in education and the arts that typified life for most Nuevomexicanos. But in a few short years after his death, his name and the record of his achievements dropped from public memory.

Conclusion

Several factors hampered the success of Spanish-language publication in the post-statehood period. Anglo-Americans reached numerical parity just as New Mexico entered the Union. The Spanish-language press began to show the effects of the hegemonic constriction of Nuevomexicano language and culture by Anglo-dominated social institutions. The privileging of English, which had been mandated as the language of instruction in the public schools by the Public Education Law of 1890, had given rise to a language shift that threatened to reverse whatever gains Spanish-language journalism had made to retain Spanish at the center of public life in New Mexico. The history of Spanish-language publication and of the periodiquero cultural movement was likewise excised from the public record as more and more public institutions began to reflect the installation of Anglo-American cultural and political hegemony. With the death of Camilo Padilla, the most dynamic period in the periodiquero movement drew to a close, and, once again, Nuevomexicano cultural practices, to the degree that they would survive into the future, would do so by the sheer force of will vested in the residual orality of an earlier epoch.

Notes

[1]"Deberes que la prensa tiene para el pueblo" [The Responsibilities of the Press to the People], *Las Dos Repúblicas* [The Two Republics], Denver, Colorado, 15 Feb. 1896. Variations in punctuation, accentuation and orthography routinely appear in texts taken from Spanish-language newspapers and other nineteenth sources in New Mexico. Most often these discrepancies are the result of the informality of the medium and the haste with which these materials were prepared for publication. In some cases, grammatical forms reflect the orthographic conventions of the Spanish language of the period. In citing these materials, I have elected to quote these materials in their original form, noting only the most extreme instances where usage or grammatical form obstruct the meaning and intent of the writer. Translations to English of original documents and newspapers, except in cases where previous published translations exist, are my own.

[2]For a complete discussion of La Prensa Asociada and the activities of its members, see my essay "Contesting Social and Historical Erasure: Membership in *La Prensa Asociada Hispano-Americana,*" *Essays on Hispanic Expressive Culture in New Mexico*, Genaro Padilla & Victor Sorrel, editors (forthcoming, U of New Mexico P.)

[3]From the ranks of los periodiqueros came the first inklings of a native and indigenous intellectual tradition that coalesced the work of native poets, writers, historians, and publicists. Benjamín M. Read and Eusebio Chacón were two of the best known authors in the group that included poets, editors, and other literati. Read (1853-1927), a prominent Santa Fe attorney, authored *Guerra méxico-americana* [Mexican American War], (1910) and other works. *Guerra méxico-americana* was the first work of its kind which registered a Nuevomexicano perspective to events surrounding the U.S. War with Mexico. Eusebio Chacón (1870-1948) received a degree in law from Notre Dame University in 1888. While attending to a full and active practice as an attorney in Santa Fe, Las Vegas, and Trinidad, Colorado, Chacón also managed to author novellas, poetry, and essays which found their way into print in Spanish-language newspapers in Santa Fe, Las Vegas and Trinidad, Colorado.

[4]The title of Padilla's magazine may have been inspired by the work of publicist N. Pérez Bolet who had begun the publication of *La Revista Ilustrada de Nueva York* [The New York Illustrated Review] in 1895. See Veron A. Chamberlin, & Ivan A. Schulman. *La Revista Ilustrada de Nueva York: History, Anthology and Index of Literary Selections*. Colombia, Missouri: U of Missouri P, 1976.

Works Consulted

Primary Sources (Newspapers)

El Anunciador de Nuevo Méjico. Las Vegas, New Mexico; weekly; Spanish; October 12, 1871-January 12, 1878.

La Bandera Americana, Semanario Dedicado a los Intereses y Progreso del Pueblo Neo-Mexicano. Albuquerque, New Mexico; weekly; English and Spanish; May 6, 1895-c. December 3, 1938.

El Boletín Popular, Periódico Político, Literario y de Anuncios. Santa Fe, New Mexico; weekly; Spanish; English and Spanish; October 21, 1885-c. 1910.

El Combate. Mora, New Mexico; weekly; Spanish; 1902-1910; 1914-September 15, 1917.

La Crónica de Mora. Mora, New Mexico; weekly, English and Spanish; June 1889-January, 1890; 1894-1896.

El Eco de Norte. Mora, New Mexico; weekly, Spanish; August 31, 1908-1922.

El Eco del Valle. Las Cruces, New Mexico; weekly, Spanish; November 18, 1905-October 13, 1917.

La Estrella. Las Cruces, New Mexico; weekly; Spanish; February 6, 1910-December 26, 1931.

La Gaceta de Mora and Mora Gazetta. Mora, New Mexico; weekly, English and Spanish; March 27-November 22; 1890, English and Spanish, January, 1891; March 27-November 22, 1890; January, 1891.

El Hispano-Americano, Organo de la Orden de los Caballeros de Mutua Protección. Las Vegas, New Mexico; weekly; Spanish; April 7, 1892- November 1, 1920.

El Independiente, Dedicado a los mejores intereses del estado de Nuevo México y en particular del condado de San Miguel. Las Vegas, New Mexico; weekly; Spanish; 24, 1894-c. August 24, 1928.

El Mosquito. Mora, New Mexico; weekly, English and Spanish; November 1891- June 30, 1892.

El Nuevo Mexicano. Santa Fe, New Mexico; weekly; Spanish; August 2, 1890- April 30, 1958.

El Progreso. Trinidad, Colorado; weekly, Spanish, 1891-1944.

El Sol de Mayo, Periódico Independiente, de Noticias, Variedades y Anuncios. Las Vegas, New Mexico; weekly; English and Spanish; January 18, 1894- November 22, 1894.

La Revista Católica. Las Vegas, New Mexico and El Paso, Texas; weekly; Spanish; January 2, 1875-September 16, 1962.

La Revista Ilustrada. Santa Fe, New Mexico; weekly: English and Spanish; March, 1907-c. August, 1933.

El Tiempo. Las Cruces, New Mexico; weekly, Spanish, October 5, 1882- July 8, 1911.

La Voz del Pueblo, Semanario Dedicado a los Intereses y Progreso del Pueblo Hispano-Americano. Las Vegas, New Mexico; weekly; English and Spanish; June 14, 1890-February 10, 1927.

Secondary Sources

Chamberlin, Veron, A. & Ivan A. Schulman. *La Revista Ilustrada de Nueva York: History, Anthology, and Index of Literary Selections.* Colombia, Missouri: U of Missouri P, 1976.

Darnton, Robert. "What is the History of Books?" *Reading in America: Literature and Social History.* Ed. Cathy Davidson. Baltimore: John Hopkins UP, 1989. 27-52.

Davidson, Cathy. *Reading in America: Literature and Social History.* Baltimore: John Hopkins UP, 1989.

Deutsch, Sarah. *No Separate Refuge: Class, Culture, and Gender on an Anglo-Hispanic Frontier in the American Southwest, 1880-1940*. London: Oxford UP, 1987.

Grove, Pearce S., et. al., eds. *New Mexico Newspapers: A Comprehensive Guide to Bibliographical Entries and Locations*. Albuquerque: U of New Mexico P and Eastern New Mexico UP, 1975.

Ong, Walter. *Orality and Literacy: The Technologizing of the Word*. New York: Mathuen, 1988.

Padilla, Genaro. *My History, Not Yours: The Formation of Mexican American Autobiography*. Madison: U of Wisconsin P, 1993.

Patterson, C. S. *Representative New Mexicans*. Denver, CO: 1912.

Read, Benjamín M. *Historia Ilustrada de Nuevo México*. Santa Fe, NM: New Mexican, 1911.

Salvino, Dana Nelson. "The World in Black and White, Ideologies of Race and Literacy in Antebellum America," *Reading in America: Literature and Social History*. Ed. Cathy Davidson. Baltimore: John Hopkins UP, 1989: 140-56.

Sánchez, Pedro. *Memorias sobre la vida del presbítero don Antonio José Martínez*. Trans. Ray John de Aragón. Santa Fe: The Lightning Tree, 1978.

Stratton, Porter A. *The Territorial Press of New Mexico, 1834-1912*. Albuquerque: The U of New Mexico P, 1969.

Twitchell, Ralph, Emerson. *The Leading Facts of New Mexican History*. Cedar Rapids, IA: The Torch, 1917.

Zboray, Ronald, J. "The Railroad, the Community and the Book," *Southwest Review*, 71 (1986): 474-87.

Cultural Continuity in the Face of Change: Hispanic Printers in Texas

Laura Gutiérrez-Witt

Introduction

The printing medium has been the principal means for conveying ideas for the last five hundred years. Invented in Mainz, Germany, by Johann Gutenberg in 1439, moveable type made possible the editing and correcting of texts to be distributed in multiple copies. The economic exploitation of the press began in 1450, and the printing industry quickly spread across Europe. Although ecclesiastical and/or royal patronage was an important consideration for the early printers, retail sales to the expanding middle and professional class provided the printers some of the capital to expand their businesses.

Print historians such as Elizabeth Eisenstein and Lucien Febvre consider the invention of printing and its rapid dissemination across Europe a "communication revolution" (Eisenstein 21) and "a new means of communicating ideas" (Febvre 12). Eisenstein suggested that printing made possible the spread of old ideas in new combinations and the consequent creation of new systems of thought. The press hence served as an agent for change in established—though evolving—societies.

Printing in Mexico

Soon after the arrival of Hernando Cortés and his armies in Mexico, the press became an instrument to implant and spread European ideas. The license to import books to Mexico was granted by Emperor Charles V in 1525 to Jacob Cromberger, a German master printer who resided in Seville, and the monopoly to import books to Mexico was held by the Cromberger family until 1551. This lucrative business was based on the demand for European books by religious houses and libraries, by individual clergy, and by laymen who wished to add new texts to their private libraries (Leonard 95-97).[1]

In 1539, Cromberger contracted with a Lombard printer, Giovanni Paoli, who later was known as Juan Pablos, to establish a press in Mexico City. This endeavor was approved by the Crown at the behest of Archbishop Juan de Zumárraga, the *Doctrina breve muy compendiosa* [Short Complete Catechism], of 1544. The Mexican book production of the sixteenth century—which included confessionals, missals, vocabularies, grammars, dictionaries, sermons, funeral orations and devotional books—served the purpose of evangelizing the native populations and also provided materials for the first educational institutions in the country. By the end of the sixteenth century nine presses were functioning in Mexico and over 200 publications had appeared (García Icazbalceta).

The development of the printing industry in Mexico during the sixteenth to the eighteenth centuries is relevant to the topic of Hispanic printing in Texas because the practices and traditions of the Mexican printing endeavor provide many antecedents. The Cromberger-Pablos press printed not only the books mentioned above but also occasionally newssheets called *hojas volantes* [flying sheets], considered to be the precursors of the newspapers. As early as 1541 the Cromberger-Pablos press printed an *hoja volante* describing an earthquake in Guatemala, and the publication of *hojas volantes* continued in Mexico and indeed in the Americas throughout the seventeenth and into the early eighteenth century. The focus of the *hoja volante* was generally a single event, but at times several events were mentioned on one sheet (Garner 3-5).

During the eighteenth century the Mexican presses began to issue what can be considered serial publications which appeared at regular intervals in a more or less standardized format. The first serial publication was the *Gazeta de México y noticias de Nueva España* [Gazette of Mexico and News of New Spain] edited by Juan Ignacio Castorena y Ursúa, which began on January 1, 1722, issued more or less monthly. The *Diario literario de México* [Literary Daily of Mexico] was begun in 1768 by Father José Antonio Alzate y Ramírez to cover matters other than current political and news events. He wrote articles on science, the arts, natural history, and literature. Periodical publications other than newspapers were also produced by the Mexican presses: *almanaques, calendarios,* and *guías de forasteros* [almanacs, calendars, and guides for travelers].

It was only after 1790, however, that the press in Mexico and Latin America was used for political agitation. Since its arrival in 1539 the press served either church or government or both to promote their particular objectives. After 1790 the press began to act as a true agent for change (Pierce and Kent 231). In Mexico, the 1810 decree on freedom of the press issued by the Spanish Cortés was officially proclaimed only in October, 1812, but freedom of the press was a fragile right, and more often than not, the authorities monitored all printing closely. Political publishing was a precarious activity for the printers who risked arrest, imprisonment, and at times, execution for issuing books, broadsides, pamphlets or periodicals which served to incite rebellious acts against those in power.

Printing in Texas

The press reached Texas in the early nineteenth century. Two issues—possibly the same publication with a title change—of a newspaper, *La Gaceta de Texas* [Texas Gazette] and *El Mexicano* [The Mexican], appeared in June, 1813 (Gutiérrez; Wallace). Written and set in type in Nacogdoches, Texas, the two bilingual numbers were actually printed in Natchitoches, Louisiana, because the publishers, William Shaler and José Álvarez de Toledo y Dubois, quarreled with Bernardo Gutiérrez de Lara and were forced to leave Texas.

The first printer in Texas, however, is generally considered to be Samuel Bangs, a young printer from New England (Spell). Bangs was recruited by General Francisco Xavier de Mina for his expedition to Mexico of 1816. Mina, Father Servando de Mier, and a small number of European soldiers were hoping to join the Mexican insurgents fighting for independence from Spain. To this end, Mina recruited 200 men and raised $200,000 for ships and supplies in the United States. A press and a printer, Samuel Bangs, were part of the expedition (Spell 12). After a rather circuitous journey from Boston, the expedition landed in Gálvez Town, now Galveston, in late 1816. Bangs printed various proclamations in Galveston but none have survived (Spell 19).

In March, 1817, Mina landed in Mexico at Soto la Marina. Here Bangs began to earn his pay. Broadsides were printed and distributed at various villages, urging the inhabitants to join the insurgent armies against the Spaniards. Mina's engineering crew designed and built a small fort to serve as a base of operations while Mina marched to the interior of Mexico. The few men left to defend the fort were no match for the royalist army of General Joaquín Arredondo. The fort fell on June 15, 1817, and Bangs and his press were captured (Spell 30-31).

Bangs was imprisoned and worked on a chain gang in Monterrey for several months. But he was soon set to work printing for General Arredondo: cards, letterheads, forms, proclamations, directives, and pamphlets. In 1821, at age 23, Bangs was technically released from prison but retained as a government printer. General Arredondo fled Monterrey after the insurgents assumed power, and the governing official became Colonel Gaspar Antonio López who moved the seat of government to Saltillo. Bangs and the press followed.

In 1823 Bangs was able to return to Boston, but four years later he journeyed south again to become the government printer for the state of Tamaulipas in Ciudad Victoria. He expanded this enterprise by importing presses, type, and printing supplies for the region. The following year he took over the printing activities of the Mexican state of Coahuila and Texas in Saltillo. Bangs moved to Galveston in 1838 and started its first newspaper, the *Commercial Intelligencer*. He was associated in the following years with English-language printing enterprises in Galveston, Houston, Corpus Christi, Point Isabel, and Brownsville.[2] He died in 1854 at age 53 in Georgetown, Kentucky.

The event which changed the lives of Hispanic citizens in Texas was obviously the independence of the province from Mexico. As early as 1819, English-language publications were begun by the colonists coming into Texas from the United States, and at least 81 newspapers were published in Texas by 1846 (Wallace 1, 48). What publications did the Spanish-speaking population of Texas have access to before 1848? More research is needed to answer this question. Certainly after 1848, English-language newspapers began to add Spanish sections, and the milestone Ríos-Castillo bibliography listed thirty-eight Spanish-language newspapers in Texas for this period. But what about other printing—books, pamphlets, circulars, broadsides? At least one historian cited the fact that literacy was on the rise and the Spanish-language press contributed "to the development of a more overt Mexican public opinion" (Gómez-Quiñones 198). Gómez-Quiñones further commented that ships from Veracruz to Galveston "disseminated newspapers, books, and pamphlets, as well as people, from Mexico" (198). Where were the books sold and by whom? Another as yet unanswered question. The sources for answering these questions are often the publications themselves, some of which are extant but many titles are known only through secondary sources.

Spanish-Language Printing in Texas after 1900

The Texas Revolution and the Mexican American War caused deep and lasting changes among the Hispanic population of Texas during the nineteenth century. In the twentieth century the Mexican Revolution and its prelude was the backdrop for cataclysmic change. The Spanish-language press and the Hispanic printers in Texas were significant agents in these movements.

During the last three decades of the 1800s numerous critics of the Porfirio Díaz government—Paulino Martínez, General Ignacio Martínez, and Catarino Garza among them—emigrated to Texas to escape persecution, and began to publish highly articulate anti-Díaz newspapers. This steady stream of exiles, which soon became a flood, added not only greater numbers and diversity to the native Texas Mexican population, but they also stimulated cultural and intellectual endeavors, printing and publishing among them. For some emigrants, publishing was politically motivated, but for many others publishing and printing provided a livelihood and a means to keep and reinforce their cultural identity.

Many historians and literary critics have discovered and mined the numerous Spanish-language newspapers which were published in the Southwest and in Texas during the nineteenth and twentieth centuries (Leal; Gutiérrez). These publications were discovered very early by pioneer scholars, even before they found archival and other primary sources.

For the study of the history of Hispanic printing in Texas, the best sources are often the publications themselves, if they exist. As Leal has pointed out, many newspapers are known only by title (157). Hence, information about the publishers, editors, or printers of newspapers and other publications is sketchy and incomplete.

Four Hispanic Printers in Texas

This study encompasses the lives and careers of four printers in Texas, two in San Antonio and two in Laredo. The four men were representative of the many Hispanic printers active in Texas during the first half of this century. Three of the four emigrated to Texas from Mexico for economic and political reasons; the other was born in Texas. Two of the four learned the printing art in Mexico and two learned it after their arrival in Texas. Hence the study of each individual offers a different picture of the printer, his enterprise, and how his publications were disseminated to the reader community.

Ignacio E. Lozano

When one speaks of Hispanic printers in Texas, the name of Ignacio E. Lozano is certainly the best known, and for good reason. As a journalist, founder, and publisher of the widely distributed newspaper, *La Prensa* [The Press] of San Antonio, Lozano was eminently successful, and this success gave him high visibility as a leading figure in the Hispanic world of San Antonio and the southwestern U.S. But the newspaper was only one aspect of his activity as a publisher and printer. His printing establishment also produced many works of fiction and non-fiction. He founded a bookstore to distribute his own publications and those imported from Mexico and abroad. His life and work has been studied extensively. His newspaper, *La Prensa*, and its influence and significance in San Antonio was the subject of a conference in 1988 organized by Juan Bruce-Novoa and the Universidad Nacional Autónoma de México [National Autonomous University of Mexico] in San Antonio (Bruce-Novoa, Introduction 121-124). Luckily, some of the more relevant papers presented at the conference were published in 1989 (*The Americas*

Review). Scholars have relied on his newspapers and publications to tell the story of Ignacio E. Lozano. Oral interviews and personal correspondence with surviving participants have been other sources used by scholars (Medeiros). It is assumed that when the newspaper in San Antonio was sold and then ceased publication that its archives and business records were lost.

Ignacio E. Lozano set a standard for Hispanic printing and publishing in Texas in the twentieth century. Yet when he and his family arrived in San Antonio in 1908, Lozano had only limited experience in the printing industry (Ríos-McMillan 136). He had written poetry and essays for his local newspaper, *El Pueblo Libre* [Free People] of Mapimí, Durango. In San Antonio, he began to work for a Mexican publisher, Adolfo Duclós Salinas, who had resided in Texas since the 1880s. Lozano quickly learned the details involved in publishing periodicals and also the market for books and newspapers. When Duclós Salinas died, Lozano continued to publish his weekly, but was not financially able to sustain it. He went to work for another publisher, Francisco Chapa, of *El Imparcial* [The Impartial] where he soon had administrative responsibility for the newspaper.

In 1913, Lozano decided to invest his savings in a new weekly newspaper, *La Prensa*, for which he hired Leonides González, also a recent arrival from Mapimí, Durango, to be managing editor and business manager (Ríos-McMillan 137). The first issue appeared on February 13, 1913, and its success was instantaneous. The Mexican population, growing with new arrivals daily (García 28), was starved for news from Mexico and the Revolution. Ríos-McMillan has called *La Prensa* "the voice of 'el México de afuera' [Mexico abroad]" (137). *La Prensa* was indeed the voice of the exiles who remained hopeful of a timely solution to their country's political problems and of a return to the homeland. Bruce-Novoa, in fact, noted that "it flaunted itself as a newspaper of Mexico for Mexicans written by Mexicans" (Chicano Community 150). In addition to news from Mexico and abroad, the newspaper published poetry, literary essays, historical sketches and biographies, and commentaries by noted authors and intellectuals from Mexico and elsewhere. Not only for the exiles but also for the Texas Mexicans, the newspaper provided a "window on Mexico" (Bruce-Novoa, Chicano Community 151). The newspaper became a daily on October 10, 1914 (Ríos-McMillan 138), and continued as a Lozano enterprise until 1957.

It is important to note that the financial success of *La Prensa* probably made possible Lozano's other publishing and bookselling activities, namely the establishment of the Casa Editorial Lozano [Lozano Publishing Company] in 1917 and the Librería Lozano [Lozano Bookstore]. Income derived from the newspaper's broad subscription base, wide distribution (Bruce-Novoa, Chicano Community 150-151),[3] and extensive advertisements gave impetus to the editing and publishing of monographs and their dissemination. Subsequently, the foundation of another successful newspaper, *La Opinión* [The Opinion], in Los Angeles supported these other publications as well. The Lozano printing activities did not seem to include commercial printing as a means of livelihood; the newspapers provided that. As I will note later, the exclusion of commercial printing was not usually the case for the other printers included in this study.

The Lozano publishing house produced the well-known novels of the Revolution by José Asención Reyes, Teodoro Torres, Miguel Arce, and Alfredo González (Parle) as well as non-fiction. The bookstore stocked the Lozano publications in addition to imported works by contemporary authors such as Amado Nervo, Rubén Darío, Enrique González Martínez and romantic writers such as Manuel Acuña and Ignacio Altamirano (Parle 166-167). The stated objective of Ignacio E. Lozano for *La Prensa* was to maintain a strong Mexican cultural identity among his readers and to promote unity among the exile community and the Texas Mexican community. The activities of the publishing house and bookstore worked towards the same ends. Bruce-Novoa has suggested, however, that *La Prensa* also "molded" the Mexican community of San Antonio and indeed in Texas "into a *de facto* Chicano one in spite of itself" (Chicano Community 150).

Rómulo Munguía

The other printer from San Antonio included in this study is José Rómulo Munguía y Torres, whose experiences and indeed life contrasts rather dramatically with that of Lozano, yet there are also many similarities in objectives and philosophies between the two. Born in Guadalajara in 1885, Munguía did not emigrate to San Antonio until 1926 at the age of 41 (Munguía).

Munguía's forty years in Mexico involved printing and politics from a very early age, and the two activities were to consume him his entire life. Munguía's life was touched by politics at age eight when his father, a government official, was incarcerated for his political opposition to Porfirio Díaz, and indeed died in prison in 1893. The printing experience for Rómulo began vicariously when his two older sisters began to work as compositors in the printshop of the newspaper *El Sol* [The Sun] in Guadalajara soon after their father's death. At age twelve, the young Rómulo began his own printing career, working for Loreto, Ancira y Hermanos, a printing company in Guadalajara. With the death of his mother in 1900, Rómulo moved to Mexico City to live with his sister Elvira. He began an apprenticeship with Francisco Gutiérrez, a friend of the family who also printed the satiric political weekly, *El Hijo del Ahuizote* [Son of the Critic], for the Flores Magón brothers. Rómulo thus early learned the influence of the press and its use as a political tool.

In 1903 the police arrested more than eighty persons at the printshop, including employees as well as the Flores Magón brothers. Rómulo was pardoned due to his "tender age." He then went to work for Ignacio Cumplido, a well-known and established publisher and printer in Mexico City whose clients included the Mexican railway company. Rómulo's contacts with political and labor organizing had not been lost, however, and in 1907 he organized the first union of typographers, the "Sindicato Ignacio Cumplido." Government disapproval caused the group to disband almost immediately.

In 1908 Rómulo was working as composing room foreman for *El Diario* [The Daily], a major Mexico City newspaper which also printed political propaganda for Ramón Corral. Munguía privately supported Bernardo Reyes, Corral's opponent, so he kept the Reyes camp informed of the pro-Corral printing activities at the newspaper (Munguía 8). Munguía's first trip to the United States occurred in 1909 when he spent several weeks in New York City learning linotype operation at the Mergenthaler Linotype Company in preparation for its installation at the plant of *El Diario*.

For the next five years Munguía became involved in revolutionary activities, using his printing skills to advance the cause of workers and of the Carrancista faction. In 1911 he organized an association of workers, "La Cámara Nacional del Trabajo" [The National Chamber of Workers] in Mexico City and published a newsletter, *El Obrero* [The Worker]. The group disbanded after Madero's assassination in 1913, and Rómulo went to Puebla to join the Carrancistas. He helped to establish a Constitutionalist newspaper, *El Demócrata* [The Democrat]. He was also sent to Veracruz where he worked on several newspapers for the Constitutionalist cause, *El Pueblo* [The People] and *Dictamen* [Opinion] among others. He traveled south as an "information officer," writing and printing propaganda for mass distribution. It was in Mérida that Rómulo was captured and almost executed by the opposing armies (Munguía 19). Saved by the counterattacking Constitutionalist forces, he continued working as editor and writer and doing labor organizing as possible.

Munguía returned to Puebla in 1915 to operate an office of revolutionary propaganda for the military governor. He met his future wife at this time and married in 1916. In addition to his work as printer, Munguía also continued labor organizing. A union of yarn and textile workers and one for workers in graphic arts were established, as well as an office to oversee employer-employee relations, "La Junta de Vigilancia de Patrones y Trabajadores" [Oversight Committee of Employers and Employees]. As the social revolution unraveled over the next decade, however, Munguía grew more and more disenchanted and finally left Mexico in 1926.

Munguía's first employer in San Antonio was none other than Ignacio E. Lozano. The two had corresponded and Lozano was aware of Munguía's expertise and experience as a printer and linotype operator. Three months after he began work for Lozano, Munguía became *La Prensa's* mechanical superintendent (Munguía 45). His wife and four children joined him within the year.

Although Munguía left Mexico because of his disenchantment with its political situation, he continued to consider himself Mexican and indeed kept his Mexican citizenship until the day he died. Working at *La Prensa* could only serve to reinforce his *mexicanidad* [Mexican nationalism] and his desire to see the Mexican cultural identity preserved in San Antonio. His wife, Carolina, began broadcasting in early 1931 with La Estrella [The Star], an independent Spanish-language radio program on KONO Radio. Her half-hour segment included local talent, conversation, classical music, and advertisements for businesses seeking a wider Mexican clientele. When she retired to give birth to a child the following year, Rómulo took over the program and gave it an even more Mexican slant, playing Mexican music, commenting on Mexican customs and traditions, editorializing on the political situation in Mexico and on the socioeconomic condition of Mexicans in the United States.

Munguía found much of the Spanish-language publishing trade in San Antonio preempted by Lozano and his enterprises, who was of course his employer. Hence attempting to establish his own press was not economically feasible in the short term. Nonetheless, from 1927 to 1930, Rómulo enrolled in correspondence courses on advertising, undoubtedly in preparation for establishing his own business. His son Rafael can be said to have founded Munguía Printers when about 1930 he bought a small hand-press and a few fonts of type. On the back porch of his home, Rómulo began to print business cards!

Soon thereafter, Munguía bought printing equipment belonging to Severo González: an Italian-made cylinder press said to have been used by the Villistas [followers of General Francisco Villa] to print edicts and currency. This time the garage became the printshop of La Imprenta Estrella [Star Printers]. A family enterprise, La Imprenta Estrella employed the oldest son Rafael as the linotype operator, the younger son Rubén served as general manager and compositor, another son Guillermo was the pressman, Rómulo Junior and Enrique were press feeders, and a daughter Elvira answered the telephone and did odd jobs! Needless to say, the enterprise flourished.

The company formally became Munguía Printers in 1936, and the printshop became a training ground for master craftsmen, and for a number of neighborhood teenagers who served as apprentices. The business was primarily a commercial printshop in contrast to a publishing concern like Lozano's, although a few pamphlets survive which bear the imprint of Ediciones Munguía [Munguía Editions]. Commercially, the Munguía enterprise did fill a void that the printshop could provide both English and Spanish copy. Its clientele included many businesses, particularly grocery stores who needed broadsides, announcements, circulars to advertise their specials. Some of its earliest clients were the Chinese grocers for whom La Imprenta Estrella had printed materials when no other shop would. By 1941 the printshop had twenty full-time employees who worked for at least minimum or better wage with overtime pay (Munguía 48). The war years brought a downsizing of the plant due to the departure of many employees who joined the military forces—as did three of the Munguía sons. Advertising was limited and so were supplies.

After the war, Munguía Printers regrouped and provided a place for returning war veterans to acquire new skills. The Munguía children branched out into other careers with the exception of Rubén who returned to printing. Recalling his roots in labor organizing, in 1953 Rómulo Munguía converted Munguía Printers into the first all-union printshop in San Antonio.

Despite the fact that Munguía's enterprise was almost solely a commercial printshop, he published a number of local interest periodicals and probably numerous pamphlets. One of his more successful—though not moneymaking—publications was a Spanish-language parish newsletter that Munguía published for Father Carmen Tranchese, *La Voz de la Parroquia* [The Voice of the Parish]. The newsletter proved so popular and effective in communicating with Spanish-speaking parishioners that the Archbishop preempted the publication for the diocese (Castañeda 229), changing printers in the process!

Munguía very soon after his arrival in San Antonio involved himself in activities to advance the cause of Mexico and Mexicans, as we have seen with the radio show. He also joined or helped to establish organizations such as the Cámara Mexicana de Comercio [Mexican Chamber of Commerce] and the Agrupación de Ciudadanos en el Extranjero [Association of Citizens Abroad], and worked with the Mexican consulate not only on holiday celebration projects but also with visits in the southwestern district to observe social and economic conditions of Mexican citizens. He was particularly active in promoting correspondence courses given by professors from the Universidad Nacional Autónoma de México in San Antonio in a effort to maintain cultural and intellectual contacts between Mexicans in San Antonio and Mexico. Rómulo Munguía died in 1975, but Munguía Printers continues to function as a successful business.

There is much research left to be done concerning the influence of Munguía the printer. His personal papers at the Benson Collection, nineteen boxes, hold the record of his personal involvement in the cultural life of San Antonio. His strong political and social beliefs, his highly refined technical skills, and a rigorous work ethic were fully dedicated to preserving some semblance of cultural continuity in a fast-changing society. The Munguía Papers include personal correspondence, his own writings, organizational records, personal financial records, photographs, press releases, copies of some of his publications, and taped oral interviews.

Eduardo Idar, Sr.

San Antonio was a major destination for the economic and political exiles leaving Mexico during the first decades of the twentieth century, but in earlier years the communities along the Rio Grande River also provided shelter and livelihood for emigrating Mexican citizens. Given the proximity of the mother country, the native Texas Mexican population of these communities maintained close familial and cultural ties with Mexico. This same population moved up, down, and across the river with ease, depending on economic and political circumstances. Similarly, printers and publishers moved where they were able to earn a living from their trade. One can almost be sure that each small community on the Texas side of the border had at least one Spanish-language newspaper. These newspapers often traded stories with other newspapers in the region, in addition to exchanging copies of their own editions (*La Crónica* 1 January 1910: 1).[4]

The city of Laredo had several such newspapers, some which began in the 1880s and possibly earlier.[5] One such publication which may have begun sometime in the 1890s was the weekly, *La Crónica* [The Chronicle] (Límon 87). The January 8, 1910, issue of *La Crónica* included an editorial thanking its contributors and subscribers for its success during its first year of life (1). Its masthead, however, cited the present series as "segunda época" [second series].

La Crónica was published and edited by Nicasio Idar, a native of Point Isabel, Texas, born in 1853. Nicasio Idar moved to Roma about 1870 from Corpus Christi where he was raised and educated and then to Laredo in 1880. He learned English during a cattle drive which he worked from Corpus Christi to Kansas City when he was fifteen years old (E. Idar 28 March 1991). His earliest experiences as a printer or journalist are yet to be determined, but it may be that he learned the trade after his second move to Laredo. Married in 1881 to Jovita Vivero, a Methodist minister's daughter, Nicasio worked for the Mexican railroad system as a conductor and later a yardmaster during the period 1881 to 1894. Apparently his wife and family lived with him in Mexico at intervals, although his middle son, Federico, was the only one born in Mexico, in Monterrey, 1893. In fact, his family believe that Nicasio organized a railroad workers' union in Acámbaro, Mexico.

There is evidence that Nicasio was already editing the newspaper *La Crónica* in 1899 (Limón fn 12), and was publishing in Laredo as early as 1895 when he was threatened with a libel suit (E. Idar 7 March 1991). During the second epoch of the newspaper, 1909?-1914, Nicasio wrote editorials, but two sons, Clemente and Eduardo, and a daughter, Jovita, produced many of the articles and prepared the copy.

The newspaper reflected the freethinker, anticlerical views of its owner. While attacking and counterattacking the stance of *La Revista Católica* [The Catholic Review] of Las Vegas, New Mexico, *La Crónica* also included a wide variety of articles dealing with current events, news from Mexico, local and regional news, biographical and historic essays, poetry, literary essays, commentary, and, of course, lots of advertisements. More importantly, however, *La Crónica* gave voice to the serious social and economic disparities suffered by Mexicans in Texas and the U.S.

In February, 1910, the Idar establishment expanded, becoming the Nueva Imprenta de Idar e Hijos [New Press of Idar and Sons]. An announcement in *La Crónica* solicited printing projects, offering free translations of publications on mechanical, commercial or legal subjects (*La Crónica* 26 February 1910: 2). The newspaper provided a vehicle for the dissemination of the particular philosophies of its owner, but the commercial printing enterprise gave the family additional income for its sustenance. The newspaper and printshop evolved as only one of Idar's activities, however. Early during his residency in Laredo, Idar served as assistant city marshall and was later elected as Justice of the Peace for Precinct 2. He also owned a cigar factory which advertised in *La Crónica*. Nicasio Idar was active as well in many community endeavors: the Washington Birthday Celebration program committee, memberships in *mutualista* [mutual aid] societies and in Masonic groups, and the Club Internacional [International Club] of the Mexican Consulate, serving with other Laredo printers and publishers on its publicity committee, to prepare a celebration for the centennial anniversary of Mexican independence (*La Crónica* 30 April 1910: 1).

The expansion of the Idar printing business continued during 1910 and 1911. Correspondents and agents were commissioned in at least eighteen cities in Texas, New Mexico, and Mexico (*La Crónica* 11 June 1910: 2), and Nicasio Idar purchased a large building to house his family, his justice of the peace office, the cigar factory, the printing plant, and the newspaper editorial offices (*La Crónica* 2 July 1910: 2). Clemente and Jovita (the latter under a pseudonym) signed more and more pieces on the injustices suffered by Mexicans in the U.S. (C. Idar 1).[6] At this time Eduardo began to travel as a roving reporter and agent for *La Crónica* to the lower Rio Grande valley. His reports from Brownsville on the revolution in Mexico began in early 1911 and replaced the earlier anti-Catholic Church articles, probably due to space considerations but also because news of the revolution was what the public wanted.

The March 15, 1911, issue announced the organization by Clemente Idar of the Primer Congreso Mexicanista de Texas [First Mexicanist Congress of Texas] (Límon), and beginning on September 28, 1911, the newspaper published reports of the congress held from September 14 to 22, 1911. In 1912 the Tipografía de N. Idar [Printshop of N. Idar] published the proceedings and selected speeches in a small pamphlet (*Primer Congreso*). *La Crónica* and a sister publication of the Idar group, *La Revista de Laredo* [The Laredo Review] continued to be published at least until 1914, when the patriarch of the family, Don Nicasio, died at age 61. According to interviews with Ed Idar, Jr., most members of the family—the widow and nine children survived—with the exception of Eduardo, Sr., moved to San Antonio within the next few years (E. Idar 7 March 1991).

Eduardo Idar, Sr., remained in Laredo and probably continued a reduced printing operation after 1914. In 1916, the Compañía Publicista Idar [Idar Publicity Company] began to publish a daily newspaper titled *Evolución* [Evolution]. It is uncertain how many of the Idar siblings were involved in this enterprise. Clemente and Federico soon went their separate ways, Clemente following the labor cause in the United States and Federico working in the political arena in Mexico. It is likely, then, that Eduardo and Jovita probably worked together on *Evolución*.

Earlier, another newspaper was published in Laredo with the same name. On April 2, 1910, *La Crónica* in fact announced the founding of a newspaper in Laredo titled *Evolución* and published by José Peña Barrera and José María Mora as "un semanario defensor de las doctrinas del librepensamiento" [a weekly in defense of freethinking doctrines]. It is unknown how long this newspaper was published or if the Idars assumed its ownership or editorship in 1916. The newspaper started by the Compañía Publicista Idar in 1916 with the same title had a new numbering sequence and appeared daily. Its agenda was news, and few, if any, free-thinker articles appeared in its pages. The format of the newspaper conformed more to that of a big-city newspaper than to the older *La Crónica*, and its printing style was more attractive. The newspaper included many articles on international and Mexican news as well as editorials, classified advertisements, local news including social events, poetry and literary pieces. The Idar group also branched out into bookselling, advertising in the newspaper the availability of books on history, science, literature, novels, religion, pedagogy, medicine, and languages, and listing in an advertisement in *Evolución* of March 1, 1917 (2), nineteen titles from Spanish, Mexican, French, and American authors, the latter two in translation, available at the Compañía Publicista Idar (2).

On March 11, 1917, *Evolución* (2) announced the organization of a Sociedad Mutualista de Tipógrafos Laredenses [Mutual Aid Society of Laredo Printers] with twenty-one members. Hence, the printing industry in Laredo seemed to support numerous establishments and enough members willing to collaborate on mutually beneficial projects. The Idar company continued the commercial printing operation in addition to publishing a newspaper and selling books. In fact, the newspaper regularly included advertisements of the printing services available at the printshop. By the end of 1918 the company was advertised as an "imprenta, librería, papelería" [printery, bookstore, stationery shop], and later offered binding services and sheet music for sale. It is likely that the Idar group also trained apprentice printers who later developed their own newspapers or printshops. One example was Pedro G. Chapa who later edited and owned the *Jim Hogg County Enterprise*, a bilingual newspaper in Hebbronville (Chapa).

Evolución was published until 1920, and Eduardo concentrated on commercial printing thereafter, according to his son, Ed, Jr. (E. Idar 28 March 1991). Increased competition and the onset of the depression were unfavorable for printing activities, and the Idar printshop was closed about 1928. Eduardo Idar continued to work as a printer for a time, possibly in Falfurrias, before returning to Laredo. In 1932 he helped to found a new political party opposing the ruling Laredo Independent Club, but the new party lost the election. He worked as a deputy county tax assessor-collector for several years thereafter, always dreaming of setting up his own printing establishment again. Ed, Jr., mentions how difficult it was for him to tell his father in 1946 when he returned from World War II that the was going to use his savings and the G.I. Bill to return to college rather than go into the printing business with his father. Eduardo, Sr., died in 1954.

The Idar legacy of publishing and printing spanned at least two generations. There are some parallels in the directions that the Idar enterprise took with the work of Lozano in San Antonio, but the distribution of the Idar newspapers and publications did not reach that of the Lozano productions. Lozano did no commercial printing, an area which was probably profitable for the Idar group. Although there is only scant evidence of publication of books, monographs, or pamphlets by Nicasio or Eduardo, their newspapers and community activities reinforced the cultural and linguistic identity they sought to pass on to their children. And it was really in his remarkable children that the social conscience of Nicasio Idar lived on.

José García Roel

The Mexican Revolution touched large and small communities on both sides of the border. In 1913 José García Roel of Ciudad Guerrero, Tamaulipas, saw his house burned and his prized possession, a printing press, melt in the flames. He then became one of many Mexican citizens to cross the river into Texas escaping with his life and his family and little else.

Born in Monterrey in 1882, José García Roel graduated from normal school and held several teaching positions in the states of Nuevo León and Tamaulipas before becoming principal of the municipal school in Ciudad Guerrero sometime after 1904. In Guerrero he became a self-taught printer, acquiring a small press and some type to set up a printshop. About 1910 he was publishing a small newspaper titled *El Pueblo*, but he was also writing prose and poetry. The newspaper, *La Crónica* of Laredo, dated April 2, 1910, congratulated him for a well-written article, "Fanaticismo" [Fanaticism] (2). A later issue of *La Crónica* (July 2, 1910) listed a play, "Sangre Azteca" [Aztec Blood], by José G. Roel, as part of a program by school children to be held June 2, 1910, in Hebbronville. Later the same year, Everardo Torres of Zapata dedicated a poem printed in the November 12, 1910, issue of *La Crónica* to Professor José García Roel. García Roel was therefore in fairly close communication with *La Crónica* and probably other newspapers of the region. He very likely exchanged his newspaper and local news with others, and possibly also circulated other publications which he issued from his press. How much of his own work did he publish and how did he circulate copies to interested readers? There is as yet no evidence to answer these questions.

His son, Virgilio G. Roel, recalled that Professor García Roel was a public speaker who was often asked to give patriotic speeches or eulogies at various types of public events in Laredo (Roel). It may be that in Ciudad Guerrero and in surrounding communities on both sides of the border, Professor García Roel was already known as a public speaker before his arrival in Laredo in 1914. He undoubtedly was writing articles and possibly some poetry for his newspapers in Ciudad Guerrero.

In Laredo Professor García turned to teaching, to public speaking, and to writing poetry and plays on commission. He purchased a printing press as soon as he was financially able to do so, and began to publish a series of weeklies, titled *El Combate* [The Fight], *El Fronterizo* [Borderlander], and *El Chile* [The Pepper] (Roel). Copies of these newspapers may not have survived. *El Combate* and *El Chile* apparently were noted for their political criticism and calls for reform—which at times resulted in fines for Professor García Roel for insulting public officials. *El Fronterizo* was a more news-oriented weekly which included local, regional, and Mexican news as well as advertisements. The approximate dates of publication for the latter newspaper, Virgilio Roel recalled, were from about 1928/9 to the early 40s. It is certain that the newspaper was in operation in 1934, because that year Professor García Roel published his novel *El hombre que mató a su alma* [The Man Who

Murdered His Soul] at the "Talleres de *El Fronterizo*" [Workshop of the Borderlander]. It is likely that he published other books as well, but they have not yet been found. He did produce ephemeral materials such as "calaveras" [skeletons, i.e., Day of the Dead satiric verses], announcements, circulars, broadsides, and similar items.

The printing business was precarious, however, and Professor García Roel also worked for the *Laredo Times*, an established, well-financed daily newspaper, as editor of the Spanish section. His obituary in the *Laredo Times* issue of January 21, 1949 (1), mentioned that he held this position at various times, probably between 1926 when the Spanish section began and the early 40s. How much influence did he have in deciding what to publish in this section of that newspaper? That remains to be determined. The obituary noted that he was a brilliant speaker, often called upon to deliver addresses at patriotic and civic functions, and he was "engaged in the printing business in its various branches." He was the author of various pamphlets, several novels, and many essays and poems.

Conclusion

What did these four printers—Ignacio E. Lozano, Rómulo Munguía, Eduardo Idar, Jr., and José García Roel—have in common? They were well-read, though often self-educated individuals with strong social consciences. The self-identity of each was secure, and each was proud of his *mexicanidad*. Their enterprises often involved the entire families: the Lozano, Munguía, Idar, and even the Roel children contributed to the success of their respective businesses. More importantly, the printers were actively promoting linguistic and cultural continuity through their work. The environment in which each lived and worked was in flux—Lozano, Munguía, and Roel were displaced by events outside their control. They brought the world they left with them and recreated it, but they could not fully control their new worlds either. But they could mold, as Bruce-Novoa has noted, this new world and give it some semblance of home. In the process, this new environment and its inhabitants, both immigrants and natives, were reborn, not once but again and again. The cyclical nature of these cultural rebirths suggested by several scholars is supported by what little is thus far known about Hispanic printing in Texas.

Documentation of the four printers included in this study is incomplete and what is available varies considerably from individual to individual. The existence of documentation depends in each case on the body of work which has survived, on their individual social status and personal influence, on their activities in non-publishing areas which would lend them prominence and notice, on the distribution and influence of their publications, and on the availability of personal records. The study of these four individuals, however, provides an opportunity to contrast motivations, lifestyles, printing environments, and influences under which each worked. There are ties among the four, some quite direct, others not so clear, but one can suppose that they knew some of each other's work. García Roel may have been somewhat removed from the center of the Lozano orbit, but as a well-read and educated person, he probably read *La Prensa* along with many other Spanish-language publications. The lack of extant issues for *La Crónica* for 1913 and 1914 obviates the possibility of citing mention of *La Prensa* in *La Crónica*, but the Laredo newspaper in 1910 and 1911 mentioned many other Spanish-language newspapers, and it is not unreasonable to suppose that *La Prensa* was probably noted as well when it appeared.

In fact, repeated citations in the extant issues of *La Crónica* point to the existence of a network of newspapermen and printers who seemed to be in close communication with each other across the south Texas region during the early decades of this century. They apparently published each other's stories, sometimes without citing the source. The editors were not in agreement on all issues, and rebuttals and responses to accusations of favoring one position over another were not unusual. The printers banded together for mutual benefit when opportunities existed for collaboration; the Laredo mutual society for typographers announced by *Evolución* and cited above is an example. The printers apprenticed with other printers until they set up their shops, i.e., Lozano and Munguía. During difficult financial times, printers/publishers such as Eduardo Idar or García Roel could find employment with other publishers or printers. Undoubtedly, research in other extant newspapers will reveal additional evidence of what was probably a close-knit network of professional journalists, writers, editors, publishers, and printers.

The printer is often a forgotten cog in the network of cultural production and cultural continuity. Every newspaper, monograph, pamphlet, or piece of newsprint which is known to have been published was produced by a printer, whose life and background is generally unknown and unstudied. Sometimes the printer was also the editor, journalist, writer, and publisher, but not always. Nonetheless, the location of documentation on printers and their printshops is valuable for the study of cultural continuity since the end products, the publications themselves, would not exist without the technological expertise of the printers. Finding the printers can often lead to the discovery of previously unknown authors and works.

Notes

[1] For a more complete discussion of the Cromberger enterprise, see Clive Griffin's study, *The Crombergers of Seville: The History of a Printing and Merchant Dynasty* (Oxford: Clarendon, 1988).

[2] In Spell's biography of Samuel Bangs, see "Appendix II: Extant Specimens of Samuel Bangs' Printing, A Tentative Listing," 167-199, for a list of Bangs' publications in Mexico and Texas.

[3] Bruce-Novoa noted that "half of its production ended up in Mexico, but that still meant that the newspaper was of interest to some twenty to thirty thousand readers on this side of the border."

[4] This issue of *La Crónica* mentioned exchange with newspapers in Laredo, Zapata/Uribeño, Alice, and Brownsville. A later issue (12 February 1910) cited newspapers in San Diego and Del Rio, all small Texas communities along the Rio Grande River.

[5] See the newspaper listing for Laredo and other Texas cities in the Ríos and Castillo compilations.

[6] This study does not attempt to follow the career and writings of Jovita Idar who was a publisher and author in her own right. See *The Rebel* by Leonor Villegas de Magnón (Houston: Arte Público P, 1994) which cites the work of Jovita Idar. Its editor, Clara Lomas, has researched the life and writings of Jovita Idar, and her introduction and appendixes for *The Rebel* provide additional information on Jovita Idar.

Works Cited

The Americas Review 17.3-4 (1989).

Bruce-Novoa, Juan D. "*La Prensa* and the Chicano Community." *The Americas Review* 17.3-4 (1989): 150-56.

Bruce-Novoa, Juan D. "*La Prensa*: Introduction." *The Americas Review* 17.3-4 (1989): 121-24.

Castañeda, Carlos E. *Our Catholic Heritage in Texas. Vol. 7: The Church in Texas since Independence, 1836-1950. Supplement, 1936-1950.* Austin: Von Boeckmann-Jones, 1936-58.

Chapa, Pedro G. Obituary. *Austin American-Statesman*, 2 October 1994: B4.

La Crónica (Laredo, Texas). 2nd, 1 January 1910-28 December 1911, 18 April 1914.

Eisenstein, Elizabeth. *The Printing Revolution in Early Modern Europe*. Cambridge: Cambridge UP, 1983.

Evolución (Laredo, Texas). 1 March 1917-29 February 1920.

Febvre, Lucien, and Henri-Jean Martin. *The Coming of the Book: The Impact of Printing, 1450-1800.* London: NLB, 1976.

García, Richard A. "Class, Consciousness, and Ideology—The Mexican Community of San Antonio, Texas: 1930-1940." *Aztlán* 9 (1978): 23-69.

García Icazbalceta, Joaquín. *Bibliografía mexicana del siglo XVI*. México: Fondo de Cultura Económica, 1954.

Garner, Jane. "Flying Sheets, Early Newspapers Important to Scholarly Inquiry." *General Libraries Newsletter* [University of Texas at Austin] Fall 1987: 3-5.

Gómez-Quiñones, Juan. *Roots of Chicano Politics, 1600-1940.* Albuquerque: U of New Mexico P, 1994.

Gutiérrez, Félix. "Spanish Language Media in America: Background, Resources, History." *Journalism History* 4.2 (1977): 34-41, 65-68.

Idar, Clemente. "¿Ya se olvidaron los Tratados de Guadalupe?" *La Crónica* 2. 104 (December 31, 1910): 1.

Idar, Ed, Jr. Taped interviews. By Margo Gutiérrez, Austin, Texas. 7 and 28 March 1991.

Laredo Times 21 January 1949.

Leal, Luis. "The Spanish-Language Press: Function and Use." *The Americas Review* 17.3-4 (1989): 157-62.

Leonard, Irving A. *Books of the Brave*. Cambridge: Harvard UP, 1949.

Limón, José E. "El Primer Congreso Mexicanista de 1911: A Precursor to Contemporary Chicanismo." *Aztlán* 5.1-2 (1974): 85-117.

Medeiros, Francine. "*La Opinión*, A Mexican Exile Newspaper: A Content Analysis of Its First Years, 1926-1929." *Aztlán* 11.1 (1980): 65-87.

Munguía, Kathleen. "A Man in Two Countries: The Biography of Rómulo Munguía Torres, 1885-1975." Senior honors thesis, Yale U, 1975. Rómulo Munguía Collection, box 17, U of Texas, Austin.

Parle, Dennis J. "The Novels of the Mexican Revolution Published by the Casa Editorial Lozano." *The Americas Review* 17.3-4 (1989): 163-68.

Pierce, Robert N. and Kurt Kent. "Newspapers." *Handbook of Latin American Popular Culture*. Ed. Harold E. Hinds, Jr. and Charles M. Tatum. Westport: Greenwood, 1985.

Primer Congreso Mexicanista, verificado en Laredo, Texas…14 al 22 de Septiembre de 1911. Discursos y Conferencias Por la Raza y Para la Raza. [Laredo] Tipografía de N. Idar, 1912.

Ríos, Herminio and Guadalupe Castillo. "Toward a True Chicano Bibliography: Mexican American Newspapers, 1848-1942." *El Grito* 3 (1970): 17-24; "Toward a True Chicano Bibliography, Part II," *El Grito* 5 (1972): 40-47.

Ríos-McMillan, Nora. "A Biography of a Man and His Newspaper." *The Americas Review* 17.3-4 (1989): 136-49.

Roel, Virgilio G. Personal interview. Austin, Texas. 1 November 1994.

Spell, Lota Mae. *Pioneer Printer: Samuel Bangs in Mexico and Texas*. Austin: U of Texas P, 1963.

Wallace, John Melton. *Gaceta to Gazette. A Checklist of Texas Newspapers*. Austin: U of Texas, 1966.

The Tradition of Hispanic Theater and the WPA Federal Theatre Project in Tampa-Ybor City, Florida

Kenya C. Dworkin y Méndez

> The new theatre should fulfill only one condition: stage and auditorium should alike be open to the masses, contain a people and the actions of a people.
>
> —Romain Rolland[1]

Introduction: "We Live in Order Not to Die"[2]

In order to reconstruct the rich and meaningful past of Hispanic theater in Tampa-Ybor City, Florida, we must first understand how it was that in the 1890s Cubans, Afro-Cubans, Spaniards, and Sicilians were brought together in a sleepy southern town to forge what is known as the Tampa Latin community. This community's uniqueness lies in the extraordinary alliance that it created. Ybor City's already indisputable diversity was further enhanced by the presence of several hundred Cuban-Chinese, Spanish-speaking Rumanian Jews, German Jews, and African-Americans.[3] Born of socio-economic and political necessity, Ybor-City became an enclave that allowed literally tens of thousands of immigrants to escape political and economic oppression, racism, and national instabilities. As a result of the entrepreneurial, immigrant bourgeois class and the tremendous capacity of its concomitant working class, the one manufacturing industry that would single-handedly bring prosperity to Tampa flourished—the hand-rolled cigar industry.[4] The magnitude of this feat, which in itself is a wonder given the fact that it was accomplished by non-Anglos in the predominantly Anglo, agricultural south, is augmented when one considers that the people who were responsible for it were 'racially' segregated from most of the city that benefited from their success.

Accompanying this enormous economic and population growth, and in an effort to take 'personal' responsibility for the health and well-being of its residents, Cuban-style mutual aid societies were built by each of the ethnic groups represented among Ybor City's population—Spaniards (ethnic Asturians and Galicians), *Criollos* (Cuban-born Spaniards), Sicilians (and later, non-Sicilian Italians), white Cubans, and, eventually, Afro-Cubans.[5] These societies, among them *El Centro Español, El Centro Asturiano, El Círculo Cubano, La Unión Martí-Maceo*, and *L'Unione Italiana*, were voluntary associations that offered health services, hospitalization, burial insurance, worker's compensation, cultural events, instruction, and community gathering places to community residents. Furthermore, they were indispensably instrumental in the establishment and preservation of a strong theatrical tradition in Ybor City-Tampa.[6]

The Tradition of Hispanic Theater in Tampa-Ybor City[7]

Historically, Tampa-Ybor-City's Hispanic theater, which began in the 1890s upon the city's founding, was different from all other Spanish-language theater in the United States in that it was primarily supported and operated by ethnic mutual aid societies. Every mutual aid society had its own building that housed the organization's various functions, and in most cases the theaters in which the stage productions were produced, rehearsed, and performed (Mormino & Pozzetta 175-209). These societies were supported by the same working class that in the 1890s had donated one day's salary to the cause of independence in Cuba and selected and paid the *lectores* who daily would read to the workers in the cigar factories. Historian Louis Pérez, Jr., specialist in nineteenth- and twentieth-century Cuban history, cites in his "Reminiscences of a *Lector*" that "'[t]he *lectura* was itself a veritable system of education dealing with a variety of subjects, including politics, labor, literature, and international relations'" (445). This idea is reiterated by Tampa historian Gary Mormino. In his singular book about the immigrants of Ybor City, he underlines the importance of the *lector* to the cigar makers by stating that,

> [t]he custom of reading to workers from a raised platform, *la tribuna*, began in Cuba but [it] had often run afoul of Spanish colonial authorities. In Tampa, it became a cherished right, more so because the cigarmakers chose factory readers, paid their fees, and selected the items to be read. (102)[8]

The informally educated cigar makers considered themselves an elite working class as a result of the *lector* tradition, and each one of the mutual aid *centros* maintained a 'show committee' made up of members who contracted and managed the performances. Therefore, in Tampa-Ybor City, an unusually educated working class was involved in a cultural and economic enterprise traditionally claimed by a higher, more educated class of people.[9] Hispanic theater in other parts of the U.S., in cities such as Los Angeles, San Antonio, and New York, was primarily supported by professional, commercial endeavors. In his seminal text *A History of Hispanic Theatre in the United States: Origins to 1940*, Nicolás Kanellos comments that it is 'ironic' that the Federal Theatre Project (FTP) agreed to situate its only Hispanic theater project in Tampa-Ybor CIty, given the abundance and professional nature of "units in Los Angeles or New York…[that were] more in line with the stated purposes of the Works Project Administration (WPA)" (156). The answer to the question of why the government established a FTP in Tampa and not in other cities with Hispanic theatre, lies, at least in part, in the fact that two Tampans took the initiative in the enterprise by contacting the FTP forthwith.[10] This illustrates once again the perspicacity and entrepreneurial spirit of Ybor City patrons.

Returning to Kanellos's concern that the FTP, itself, might have been better put to use in other cities with established Hispanic theater activity, I must agree that the establishment of the Tampa FTP was unorthodox, given the primary stated purpose of the WPA. However, I also think it was providential. Had it not been for the Spanish unit in Tampa, one of the most unusual Hispanic communities in the United States might never have gotten the attention it deserved from the national government. This unwritten episode in Hispanic, and more specifically, American history, has much to offer in the way of lessons and strategies for a minority community's cultural and economic survival. The truth is that the tradition of Hispanic theater ranks with the cigar industry, immigration, and mutual aid societies in its importance within the range of significant reasons Tampa-Ybor City ought to be studied in the first place. Finally, what is truly tragic about the fact that the FTP decided to develop a Spanish-language unit in Tampa is that they didn't do it anywhere else. Given that at the national level the FTP supported French and German theater, albeit to a very limited degree, it certainly must be true that there were many more Hispanic actors out of work than there were French or German ones. A surprising situation? I think not. Just as there were proportionately more Latins on relief in Ybor City, a community whose population reflected a very limited number of immigrants from Western Europe, there were infinitely more people of Western European descent on the relief roles elsewhere, to the exclusion of many Hispanics in numerous cities. It is possible that Hispanics may not have seemed 'mainstream' enough to be deserving of relief over their more 'American' counterparts. What is indeed ironic is that sixty years later the U.S. government is thinking the same thing.

Federal Theatre Project: "Unemployed actors get just as hungry as anybody else."[11]

In addition to the strong precedent for community-organized theater, the significant yet short-lived establishment of a local, federally-funded, Spanish-language theater in 1936-1937 causes Tampa-Ybor City to stand out from all other U.S. Hispanic communities because it became home to the only project of its kind in the country. While the depression-era Federal Theatre Project funded a significant amount of foreign-language (particularly Yiddish) and African-American theater in cities such as New York, Chicago, etc., the only government-sponsored, Spanish-language theater unit was the one headquartered in Tampa-Ybor City, Florida. Despite the unique nature of the Tampa Latin community, its theater tradition, and its FTP Spanish unit, the paucity of research or even preserved materials relating to this project is disheartening. Alan Kreizenbeck, in his 1979 dissertation entitled *The Theatre Nobody Knows: Forgotton Productions of the Federal Theatre Project, 1935-1939*, suggests in his title and then later reiterates in his introduction that he will "discuss the FTP in terms of its less well-known productions...." (2). Indeed, he goes on to state that although

> several accounts of Federal Theatre Project have already been written...the focus is on how the organization worked rather than on what the organization did...There is also a tendency in these works to concentrate on productions in New York and California—understandable, as those two states employed the majority of the Project's personnel and spent the lion's share of Project funds. (2)

One would think that Kreizenbeck would uncover much-lacking and urgently-needed information about projects precisely like the Tampa-Ybor City FTP. Yet, he included one paragraph on the subject, in which he reports an erroneous number when totaling the productions that the Spanish unit produced in Tampa and provides no information on the project's background. Moreover, there is no mention of the cause of the Spanish unit's demise. The only mildly interesting observation that he made, one found in the FTP national director's book *Arena*, was that the Spanish unit's "potential audience comprised nearly half the population of [Tampa]—of the 105, 000 who lived in Tampa, 45, 000 of them were Latins" (276). Kreizenbeck, like Florida FTP director Dorothea Thomas Lynch before him, would attribute the Spanish unit's great success in part to the large Spanish-speaking population, the "ready-made audience." While the Tampa population statistic may seem important, Kreizenbeck's use of it says more about the enterprise and entrepreneurial spirit of the Tampa Latins, who out-developed their Anglo Tampan neighbors, than it does about any potential success its FTP might have had. His theory demonstrates a profound lack of understanding of the important relationship between a community's cultural tradition and the success or failure of a theatrical enterprise. This commitment to and even dependency on the salubrious effects of continued, uninterrupted avenues of ethnic cultural expression was certainly more responsible for the success of Hispanic theater in Tampa-Ybor City than the percentage of the Spanish-speaking population per se. Kreizenbeck's assumption does not take into account other factors that could determine a project's success or failure such as conservatism, unemployment, poverty, and cultural impoverishment.

If we used the same argument presented by Kreizenbeck apropos of the potential success of the Tampa project and applied it to other areas, such as predominantly English-speaking Dallas, Houston, and Fort Worth, Texas, all of which had FTPs, we would find that the theory of a direct relationship between population size and success was faulty. These Texas FTP units failed, not because there weren't enough English-speaking patrons, but as a result of cultural conservatism in the face of theatrical and literary innovation, an inattentive, unpromoting press, and poverty.[12] Rather than flourish, they suffered because of the devastating economic conditions the Texan population endured throughout the Depression and FTP era. The following anecdote provides poignant evidence of the last of the above-stated reasons for the failure of the Texas FTP—poverty. Upon asking a woman with three children who was sitting at the back of a hall during rehearsal whether she could attend the function if ten cents per person were charged, the FTP national director was told that they [the free productions] "were the only place we ever had to go...That'd be forty cents even if my husband and I parked the littlest one somewhere. We live a long time on forty cents" (Flanagan 94).

Notably, the Spanish unit of the FTP, housed at the magnificent *Centro Asturiano*, in Ybor City, ran theatrical shows concurrently with continued local zarzuela and *teatro bufo* (Cuban farce) productions at other mutual aid societies. The FTP Spanish unit did not perform particularly socially relevant material, with the exception of the Spanish-language version of *It Can't Happen Here* (*ICHH*). However, it is important to note that the other theater groups did maintain a healthy tradition of socially and politically relevant farce as well as zarzuela and musical revue—one that had existed long before the FTP and continued after its demise (Mormino & Pozzetta 157-9). It is important to note that the FTP planned the debut of *ICHH* so that it would open in multiple cities and in multiple languages across the nation. The play was being staged as a protest on the part of FTP administrators against the government's impending discontinuation of the Federal Theatre Project. Apropos of Sinclair Lewis's *It Can't Happen Here*, which was first rendered into Spanish as the ill-conceived, grammatically imperfect *Esto no lo pasará aquí*, the Tampa Spanish unit first received a devastatingly inaccurate translation that was totally unlearnable and unpresentable. Despite state director Lynch's misgivings and with just a few weeks to spare, the play was subsequently translated into the acceptable *Eso no puede ocurrir aquí* and hastily produced, the translations of the last acts arriving just days before the debut. In her conversation with the national director, Hallie Flanagan, Lynch responded to inquiries about why she seemed unwilling to stage *ICHH* using the Spanish unit by stating that she did not know "whether those players [could] do it or not" (Interview 52). Lynch goes on to explain in her 1977 interview with John O'Connor that the clash between Spanish and American theater traditions caused her to doubt the success of such a venture. Whereas the Spanish tradition produced actors who were accustomed to presenting multiple plays concurrently, using a prompter to coach them with their varied lines, the American tradition called for single, long-running productions in which actors were expected to learn all their lines without benefit of a prompter.

While it is clear that both traditions facilitated the survival of both theatrical styles, one can also appreciate why the state director worried that the Spanish unit might have had difficulty due to the late-coming translation, the lack of time, and the difference in the expectations for the actors involved. When enumerating the potential problems with such a production, Lynch went on to explain, "we had been fighting our way through this down in Miami, and they sent us a literal translation...Of course, everything is done by the *puntador*, the man in the box. They had to learn their lines, and they couldn't understand why they had to learn their lines" (Interview 52).

Nevertheless, Lynch obscured what seemed to be legitimate concerns by insinuating that the Spanish unit became so involved in the actual technical production of *Eso no puede ocurrir aquí* that it never had the chance or, perhaps, the wherewithal to understand the political significance of Lewis's play about the internal fascist takeover of an American town. She ascribed the same shortcomings to the Spanish-speaking audience, as well. Lynch, who throughout her interview takes on what becomes a familiar and increasingly patronizing tone, commented of the Spanish unit's endeavors to produce *ICHH* that

> they were so loyal, and the man who played the villain, the president, he said to me, 'Oh, (in accent) Miss Lynch, I never dreamt in all my years that I would be playing the president of the United States.' (Laughter) All the implications went out the window. But, oh, really, it was wonderful, what they did with that, and no time at all to do it.... It didn't attract the Spanish people. They didn't know what the heck it was all about, naturally. But, they did it, and they did a beautiful job with it, and it was eternally to their credit. (Interview 52-3)

First, in forcing the Spanish unit to perform *ICHH* in translation, thereby succeeding in making every effort to pull off a successful national debut, it would seem that the FTP bureaucracy put uninformed and, perhaps, unreasonable expectations far above the needs or traditions of the Tampa Latin unit's members. Put differently, Lynch was more concerned about the intellectual capacity of the Spanish unit and its audience than she was about the fact that they were both forced, in very short order, to either perform or appreciate an American play that remained totally devoid of familiar context for them, despite its translation. Second, Lynch's concern for the Tampa Latins' inability to fathom the meaning behind *ICHH* seems ill-founded, at best, when one considers the varied and sophisticated political experience of both the Cubans and the Spaniards involved in the Spanish unit, as well as that of the Tampa Latin community (Spaniards, Cubans, and Sicilians) at large. Moreover, and more specifically, fascism was hardly an unknown concept for a large part of the Ybor City populace in the wake of the Spanish Civil War, whose beginnings coincided precisely with the existence of the Tampa-Ybor City FTP. The same could be said about local Italians in the face of the continued aggression on the part of Mussolini's 'Black Shirts' in Ethiopia and in Italy.[13]

ICHH's implications for those who saw it were that, as Flanagan said in her FTP account *Arena,*

> hundreds of thousands of people all over America crowded in to see a play which says that when dictatorship threatens a country it does not necessarily come by way of military invasion, that it may arrive in the form of a sudden silencing of free voices. (129)

Ironically, the day after the national debut of the English, Yiddish and Spanish versions of *It Can't Happen Here*, in Los Angeles, Boston, San Francisco, Tampa, Birmingham, Bridgeport, Chicago, Cleveland, Denver, Detriot, Yonkers, Indianapolis, Omaha, Miami, Newark, Seattle, and Tacoma, Adolf Hitler invaded the demilitarized Rhineland, setting the European stage for a decade of fascist invasion, war and genocide.

The demise of the FTP's Spanish-unit:
The 'Mysterious' ERA Act of 1937

Cultural and language difference, racism, and misunderstandings about citizenship led to the Spanish-language FTP's severe limitation.[14] For example, the Tampa-Ybor City unit was actually four units combined, one Spanish, one Latin, and two American. The first two groups experienced considerable success due to the "ready-made" Spanish-speaking audience available in Ybor City proper. Furthermore, the Spanish unit tried to allay any linguistic or cul-

tural differences that might keep Anglo-Tampans away from their own productions by providing English-speaking audiences with programs containing
translated plot summaries of the infinitely more successful Spanish-language
plays, zarzuelas, and musical revues. Nonetheless, the Anglo Tampans stayed
away in great measure. In contrast, Dorothea Lynch, state director of the
Florida FTP, in a 1977 interview, illustrated exactly how supportive the
Tampa Latins were of their theater by saying of the Ybor City patrons that
their

> loyalty…was one of the things that was amazing to me, because most of our lead-
> ing ladies were over fifty. Some of them are living now and they must be close to
> my age. But once a leading lady, once you had your public, you had your public,
> and they came loyally—they just loved them…Paying a quarter to get in when
> they probably didn't have a quarter for anything else. (Interview 15)

Her final remark about the 'quarter' highlights the reality presented by
Flanagan in our earlier discussion of the potential theater patron in Texas who
in the mid-1930s found ten cents to be too much to pay for a ticket. In the
1920s and 1930s, members of Tampa-Ybor City's mutual aid societies paid
an average of two dollars a month for membership and were eligible for up to
two dollars a day in worker's compensation benefits (Mormino & Pozzetta
203). While this comparison serves to illustrate the dramatic difference
between Texan and Tampan economic conditions during the time of the FTP,
I do not mean to undermine the need of the Tampa-Ybor City workers for
government relief. The Depression, complicated by a series of labor strikes
and advancing technology, brought about the catastrophic decline of the hand-
rolled cigar industry in Tampa. In 1935, there were as many as three thousand
unemployed cigarworkers, with thousands already having left the city. The
number of Latin workers employed by cigar factories had declined by nearly
forty percent (Mormino & Pozzetta 290-91).

Unfortunately for the two Anglo groups, their success was precariously
contingent upon the willingness of Anglo Tampans to venture into the Latin
neighborhood (Ybor City) where the *Centro Asturiano* was located. This does
not mean, though, that the Spanish-language FTP was not successful when
compared to other FTP units, particularly in Florida. Sadly, Robert Mardis, in
his 1972 dissertation entitled *Federal Theatre in Florida*, deemed the project a
failure because there had been no establishment of a permanent professional
theatre, which was one of the WPA goals, and because the Spanish unit, like
all the other Florida units, had needed subsidy (201).[15] However, Kanellos is
quick to point out that

> this judgement reveals a lack of awareness that these actors were continuously
> involved in professional theatre on their own terms before the Federal Theatre

> Project was instituted in Tampa, and the documentary records show that they con-
> tinued to perform at area theatres and mutual aid societies afterwards. (159-60)

Attributing failure to the project by FTP standards, Mardis obviously chose to
ignore the strong precedent for community theatre that had already existed in
Tampa-Ybor City since the early twentieth century. Perhaps this is another
case of cultural misunderstanding, for had Mardis understood the unique
nature of the theatrical tradition in the Tampa Latin community, with its singular working class origins, he would not have overlooked the fact that a 'professional' theater had already existed and continued to thrive despite the FTP
efforts. He also wouldn't have judged the Tampa FTP effort by WPA standards alone since its circumstances were indeed extraordinary in both a positive and negative sense, as we shall soon discuss. Furthermore, and as regards
of a 'national' theater, which was another of the WPA's less clearly stated
goals, the productions of Tampa-Ybor City's mutual aid societies and other
independent houses deeply reflected a tradition of 'national' or ethnic, popular
theater. Of course, an acceptance on the part of mainstream American society
that Spanish-language theater, farce, and operetta might become a representative part of what would later be called 'American' theater implied a legitimation of a non-English language popular imagination and a tradition of social
engagement. Loren Kruger, in her book about the concept of a national theater, *The National Stage. Theatre and Cultural Legitimation in England,
France, and American*, says of the FTP that

> [i]n challenging the hegemony of connoisseurship and the social relations of
> patronage, [it] also undermined the authority of connoisseur taste. Instead of pro-
> ducing novel commodities to satisfy that taste, Flanagan argued [that] the FTP
> should offer performances that engage the 'vast new audience' with 'plays of
> authentic popular material' performed in ways 'interesting to a modern audience.'
> In other words, it should respect popular taste for vaudeville and stock comedy,
> even while working to create an audience for classical and experimental theatre.
> (135)[16]

If Kruger's analysis of what the FTP should have presented is accurate, then
the Tampa Spanish unit more than fulfilled the expectation that the theater
represent the people, indeed, 'contain' the people, to paraphrase Romain
Roland. In Tampa-Ybor City, the theater was literally born of the people; it
was the people—the working people.

The greatest blow dealt to the Spanish-language FTP in Tampa-Ybor City
was the passage of the ERA Act of 1937 that virtually removed 'foreigners'
(non-citizens) from government relief roles. The Tampa Spanish unit lost a
total of twenty-five people, most of them the most experienced in the group,
thereby causing the disbanding of the group. The younger, English-speaking

members that remained were shipped off to complement other existing, English-speaking theater troupes in various Florida cities. Many of the people in question had lived in the United States for a number of years and believed that they were, indeed, American citizens. However, they had not gone through the official process of naturalization, rendering themselves unqualified for federal assistance. It is difficult to understand why there is hardly any mention of this incident in Hallie Flanagan's book *Arena*, since one would expect it to be the most reliable source of inside information about the FTP. Yet, despite the fact that she devoted a forty-page chapter to the demise of the FTP, there is no discussion of the Tampa Spanish unit's fate. While she did provide some information about the Relief Act of 1935 and the Emergency Relief Appropriation Act of 1938, there is no specific mention of the ERA Act of 1937 nor did she elaborate on how government legislation dictated that non-citizens were not eligible for WPA relief.

In her first chapter, "Danger: Men Not Working," Flanagan included actual wording from the 1938 Act, which specifically outlawed the denial of work to any person "on account of race, creed, color, or any political activity, support of, or opposition to any candidate or any political party in any election," (36). Yet she gave no explanation of whether any other part of the Act, or any other congressional document stated the illegality of non-citizens receiving relief in the form of work. Upon learning of the impending demise of the FTP on a national scale, President Franklin Roosevelt, creator of the WPA and the New Deal, told the press that "[t]his single[d] out a special group of professional people for a denial of work in their profession. It is discrimination of the worst type...and we have as a result an entering wedge of legislation against a specific class in the community" (Flanagan 363). Certainly the same could be said about the fate of the Tampa Latins.

In the following excerpt from an exchange between Dorothea Lynch (DL) and her husband Larry Lynch (LL), which took place during John O'Connor's (JO) 1977 interview with the former Florida FTP director, the couple discusses the confusion surrounding the issue of citizenship and naturalization on the part of many members of the Spanish unit, and consequently, of older Tampa Latins:

> LL: Latins there, the older Latins entered this country for twenty years and had never become citizens. Nobody paid any particular attention to it in those days.
> DL: Oh, they did have to learn to speak English.
> LL: They considered themselves American citizens. They voted and everything else, and may have held office for all I know (laugh).
> DL: Well, I don't know about that, but they (laugh)...
> LL: They considered themselves Americans, American citizens. But they had never gone through the formality of becoming...
> DL: Just the first papers.

JO: What happened that they got checked up on? Was there a statewide campaign to...

DL: It was nationwide—that came from up above. That was a national WPA policy that they had to be citizens to benefit from being on WPA. I think in any instance.

LL: I'm not sure of this at all, but...

DL: Ours were just all plotted.

LL: I think some Texas congressman or something originally raised it, but once it was raised—the law was the law. (Interview 14-15)

It is unclear precisely what the state director was saying when she speculated that members of the Spanish unit 'were just all plotted.' Perhaps she meant marked or singled out but she did not elaborate. It is difficult to understand why both Flanagan, in her book, and Lynch, in her interview, failed to explain what the ERA Act of 1937 mandated or how it directly effected members of the Tampa Latin unit. Furthermore, Lynch both contradicts and betrays herself when she equates the naturalization process with having to learn "to speak English." Earlier in the interview, when she describes her initial meeting with the Tampa Latins who would help organize and manage the local FTP, she states very clearly that "some of the best players spoke very little English...My first interview was at a big, long table...and all of the Latin people that were going to be in charge were around it. I sat at the head and then an interpreter introduced them to me...." (Interview 5). If communication between Lynch and the Latins was hampered enough to require an interpreter, it would seem that the older Cubans and Spaniards had not 'had' to learn English, as Lynch suggested in her discussion of the citizenship issue, to survive in their entirely Spanish-speaking environment.

Furthermore, in her accolades for Manuel Aparicio, the group's director, she betrays the premium she placed on English as a vehicle through which immigrants might earn respect. Of Aparicio she said "[he], the head man, the director, [was] trained in the old tradition of the Spanish theatre. He was a great person, and he could speak English. So, that was all right" (Interview 5). In contrast, when talking about other members of the Spanish unit, she is patronizing and belittling. When describing her first meeting with the prompter, who is a key, indispensable figure in Spanish theater, she described him as "a little man [who] said, 'I am a puntadore [sic]!' Well, (laugh) I tried not to look too ignorant, but of course he was the one who sat in the little prompter's box. 'I am the prompter,' and believe me, he was the king pin! (Laughter)" (Interview 5). A little later, when referring to the women in the unit Lynch repeatedly used terms such as 'little dancers,' 'pretty little women,' and 'girls' while describing them as 'perfectly delightful' and 'very talented' (Interview 6). Kanellos, himself, in his own book on Hispanic theatre, suggests that the FTP's attitude [was] a model of condescension and that, ultimately, the Hispanic unit disbanded because of congressional xenophobia (156).

Upon termination of the Hispanic FTP in Tampa, Dorothea Lynch, the Florida FTP director files a report with the national FTP suggesting necessary changes that would be essential to any future, government-funded, Spanish-language theater project. Among them was a recommendation that the issue of citizenship be clarified, implying that those Hispanics who participated in the Tampa project had failed to understand

> one of the fundamental functions of the WPA…While the traditions of the theater involved should be preserved, they should be used in the interests of international good will, in this case the heightening of our "Good Neighbor Policy" with South America. Or they should be used to increase the understanding of the finest things in the "Old country" by young Americans who have not been able to travel. Members of the company should participate in an Americanizing process…This is partly a matter of adjusting character to the democratic idea. (Kanellos 160)

It is difficult to understand exactly why the FTP bureaucracy believed that providing a community such as Ybor City with a mechanism such as a subsidized local theater would 'Americanize' people or help them adjust 'to the democratic idea.' It is certainly clear by Lynch's statement that her idea of 'preserving' or respecting foreign theater traditions was to trivialize culturally-specific theater for the purposes of promoting a political ideology (the Good Neighbor Policy). Despite the fact that the Tampa-Ybor City FTP had, perhaps, an unwitting hand in preserving the tradition of Hispanic theater, Lynch would have us believe that it was never intended to do so. Therefore, in its efforts to establish a 'national' theater, the FTP would not seem to have been promoting multiculturalism for the long term. As Kanellos quite candidly observes, "the Spanish-language theater was seen [by the WPA] as possibly a passport into the melting pot but not as an end itself" (160).

Conclusion: The Ghost of the ERA of 1937— *'It can't happen here?'*

There is so little known at the moment about the Tampa-Ybor City FTP, that it is difficult to say whether the experience had any lasting repercussions. Furthermore, documentation of it was so poor that a project to reconstruct actual details about the players and performances will require a combination of archival research, oral interviews, sleuth-like snooping, and not a little luck. The paucity of information is compounded by the fact that there is, in general, little organized, documentary evidence of the local theater. Furthermore, there has been no attempt to reconstruct and then analyze exactly how the theater aided in the survival of the thoroughly unique Tampa Latin identity. A pertinent question is, what effect did the political and cultural subject matter of the Cuban *teatro bufo* or the *farsa* have on Ybor City residents? There are few playscripts or other production-related papers to be found, although there is a smattering of playbills, FTP-related correspondence, and the O'Connor interview in the Dorothea Lynch, Fernando Mesa, and Hedley Gordon Graham collections at George Mason University, the Library of Congress, and the National Archives. Curiously, National Archives' Record Group 69 even contains an unmarked folder containing numerous letters written by members of the Spanish unit to President Roosevelt, thanking him for the FTP and expressing their urgent desires for his success in the next election. Yet, there is not much known about the lives of these people. Upon reading the following letter by Jaime Fernández, it becomes clear that there is a great deal that can be learned about the circumstances surrounding the Tampa-Ybor City community, its theatre tradition and its FTP from the project's participants, themselves:

> Honorable President, Franklin D. Roosevelt
> Washington, D.C.
>
> Thanking God for designated you as president of this great nation at the moment that we, the workers were passing the worst crisis known to history…You and your Government came to our rescue and have helped us carry this crisis that soon will be over.
>
> Before my necessities made me turn to relief, I worked as Reader to the Cigar Makers; reading daily to 600 Cigar Makers the most important news of the day; but on Nov. 27, 1931, this work was taken away from us by the owners of the factories…To-day I am working as actor in the Federal Theatre Project #702T., and am satisfied as I can take the necessities of life to my wife and my son, and furthermore, I can help in the educational campaign, as the theatre is a place that you enjoy yourself and in the meantime you educate yourself. Hundreds of laborers go to our shows.
>
> Hoping to God that in the next elections, you will be our president again; and wishing that you can extend our project, I remain truly yours.
>
> Jaime Fernández
> 1411-11th Ave.[17]

There is no doubt that Fernández's history, along with many others, is contained in interviews yet to be held and boxes collecting dust in someone's attic.

One thing must remain clear. The importance of the theater tradition in Tampa-Ybor City is paramount. The Tampa Latin identity is unique among that of other U.S. Hispanic communities for its origins, its ethnic diversity, and its survival, despite a sharp economic downturn in the 1930s and 1940s. A study of the Tampa Latin community's linguistic and cultural survival, and particularly of the role theater had in providing strategies for education and resistance, will provide an innovative model for other ethnically, racially, and culturally juxtaposed minority communities in the U.S.. There are in its history, profound implications for Hispanic and minority studies in the United States. These can be seen in the fact that the Tampa Latin community has maintained its self-defined 'Latin' [Cuban, Spanish, and Italian] identity for over a century despite the tremendous influx of subsequent immigrants from their own and other countries, Spanish-speaking or not. It has rejected and remained unaffected by U.S. government efforts to create an all-inclusive label, 'Hispanic' or 'Latino' with which to categorize people from many different racial, sociocultural, and ethnolinguistic backgrounds.

One can still go to Ybor City and hear some Spanish spoken in its cafes. Indeed, one can still buy Cuban bread and *pastelitos de guayaba* in several local Tampa-Cuban bakeries. There is still piping hot *café con leche* to be had at the Tropicana or paella and *tablao* to be enjoyed at the Columbia restaurant. You might even be able to buy a thing or two at an Italian food emporium. *La Gaceta*, although slightly diminished, is still published in its trilingual format. The mutual aid societies, among them *L'Unione Italiana*, *La Nuova Sicilia*, *La Società Italia*, the Sons of Italy, *El Centro Español*, and *El Centro Asturiano* are still functioning at a more or less minimal level. If you walk into the *cantina* at the *Centro Asturiano* or *L'Unione Italiana* on a Saturday afternoon, you will be transported in time. There will be old men playing *briscola* or dominoes, and having a *cafecito*. What you can't do is go into the still sumptuous *Centro Asturiano* theater and witness local theater—or any theater at all. The voices from center stage have been silenced for a very long time—too long. The strategies for resistance and survival that could be learned precisely from things like community theater, of which the Ybor City example is crucial, will be lost if an effort is not made to document and analyze them. If we do not retain our past, learn its lessons and build upon them, there will be no future at all. In essence, recovery will mean survival.

Notes

[1]This is a translated excerpt from Romain Rolland's *Le Thèâtre du peuple* (1903), written in turn-of-the-century Paris. In this book Rolland discussed popular theater in the context of a national theater, the latter of which was generally associated with canonical works of critical drama. See Kruger 21-9.

[2]This quote is part of title for the first chapter of Mormino & Pozzetta's *The Immigrant World of Ybor City. The Immigrant World of Ybor City. Italians and Their Latin Neighbors in Tampa, 1885-1985.*

[3]For a vivid account of the ethnic diversity contained in Ybor City see José Yglesias *The Truth About Them*; Mormino & Pozzetta 43-62, 233-59.

[4]For a summary of the founding of Tampa see Durward Long, "The Making of Modern Tampa: A City of the New South, 1885-1911," 333-45; Mormino & Pozzetta 43-62.

[5]Ybor City's Afro-Cubans, who for decades had participated openly and actively in the *Círculo Cubano*, formed their own society, *La Unión Martí-Maceo*, after white Cubans succumbed to pressure to push them out from Anglo Tampans, who supported the Jim Crow laws. See Mormino & Pozzetta 185-88.

[6]For a description of the mutual aid societies see See Durward Long, "An Immigrant Cooperative Medicine Program in the South, 1887-1963," 417-34; Mormino & Pozzetta, 175-209.

[7]In using the toponymic 'Tampa-Ybor City' I am specifically referring to the Latin area known as Ybor City (and to an almost equal degree, West Tampa), to the exclusion of greater Tampa, which was predominantly White and Anglo-Saxon, with the exception of 'the Scrub,' an African-American ghetto. See Mormino & Pozzetta, 3-15.

[8]For a more detailed account of the origin and practice of the *lector* see Muñiz, "La Lectura en las Tabaquerías," *Revista*, 190-272; Muñiz, "La Lectura en las Tabaquerías," *Hoy*, 78; Ortiz, *Cuban Counterpoint: Tobacco and Sugar*, 89.

[9]See Nicolás Kanellos, *A History of Hispanic Theatre in the United States: Origins to 1940*, 146-7.

[10]Kanellos, in his chapter on Tampa, explains that "[a]ccording to *La Gaceta*..., it was Juvenile Court judge T. B. Castiglia and Joseph Chamoun (El Turco) who took the initiative to contact the Federal Theatre Project authorities about founding a unit in Tampa...and then set about recruiting the actors for the unit." See Kanellos 156.

[11]Harry Hopkins, Works Progress Administrator in 1934, is quoted by Hallie Flanagan, whom Hopkins would ask to become national director of the Federal Theatre Project. *Arena* , 9.

[12]For more information about the Texas Federal Theatre Project see *Arena*, 93-5.

[13]For a summary of the fascist movements in Europe see Garraty, John A. and Gay, Peter. (eds) *The Columbia History of the World*, 1044-58.

[14]For a description of the racist and intolerant Anglo attitudes towards Tampa Latins see Gary Mormino, "Tampa and the New Urban South: The Weight Strike of 1899," 337-56.

[15]For further discussion on the short-sightedness of Mardis's remarks see Kanellos, 159.

[16]For more detailed discussion on the topic of a 'peoples' theater see Kruger, 219n8, 220n9.

[17]This letter, along with about fifteen others, is contained in FTP Record Group 69, Box 63. An interesting historical note is that when Mr. Fernández explains that he and other Ybor City *lectores* were fired, he was referring to an attempt, on the part of factory owners, to break the cigar workers' unions. The owners knew very well the vital role the readers had in informing the workers about labor issues. In doing away with them, they expected to be able to keep workers in ignorance, cause them to disband, and consequently, avoid strikes. Cf. notes 7 and 13, Mormino & Pozzetta 97-141; . For general information see Cooper, *Once a Cigar Maker. Men, Women, and Work Culture in American Cigar Factories, 1900-1919*.

Works Consulted

Cooper, Patricia A. *Once a Cigar Worker. Men, Women, and Work Culture in American Cigar Factories, 1900-1919*. Urbana: U of Illinois P, 1987.

Flanagan, Hallie. *Arena*. New York: Duell, Sloan and Pearce, 1940.

Garraty, John A. and Peter Gay, eds. *The Columbia History of the World*. New York: Harper & Row, 1972.

Kanellos, Nicolás. *A History of Hispanic Theatre in the United States. Origins to 1940*. Austin: U of Texas P, 1990.

Kreizenbeck, Alan D. *The Theatre Nobody Knows: Forgotten Productions of the Federal Theatre Project, 1935-1939*. Diss. New York University, 1979.

Kruger, Loren. *The National Stage. Theatre and Cultural Legitimation in England, France, and America*. Chicago: U of Chicago P, 1992.

Long, Durwood. "The Making of Modern Tampa: A City of the New South, 1885-1911," *Florida Historical Quarterly* 49 (April 1971): 333-45.

_____. "An Immigrant Cooperative Medicine Program in the South, 1887-1963," *Journal of Southern History* (November 1965): 417-34.

Lynch, Dorothea Thomas. Personal interview. 14 March 1977. By John O'Connor. O'Connor, John. Dorothea Lynch Collection, Research Center for the Federal Theatre Project, George Mason University, Fairfax, VA. (Unpublished)

_____. *Report*. Np: [c. 1939?].

Mardis, Robert Francis. *Federal Theatre in Florida*. Diss. University of Florida, 1972.

Mormino, Gary R. and Pozzetta, George E. *The Immigrant World of Ybor City. Italians and Their Latin Neighbors in Tampa, 1885-1985*. Urbana: U of Illinois P, 1987.

Mormino, Gary R. "Tampa and the New Urban South: The Weight Strike of 1899," *Florida Historical Quarterly* 60 (January 1982): 337-56.

Muñiz, José Rivero. "La Lectura en las Tabaquerías," *Revista de la Biblioteca Nacional* 2 (October-December, 1951): 190-272.

_____. "La Lectura en las Tabaquerías," *Hoy* (May 1, 1948), 78.

Ortiz, Fernando. *Cuban Counterpoint: Tobacco and Sugar*. New York: A. A. Knopf, 1947.

Pérez, Louis A., Jr.. "Reminiscences of a *Lector*: Cuban Cigar Workers in Tampa," *Florida Historical Quarterly* 52 (April 1975): 443-49.

Yglesias, José. *The Truth About Them*. New York: World, 1971.

Contributors

Ward S. Albro is a professor of History and Director of International Programs at Texas A&I University-Kingsville.

Rose Marie Beebe is an assistant professor of Spanish in the Department of Modern Languages at the University of Santa Clara in California.

Sandra Dahlberg is an instructor at Highline Community College and a doctoral student in English at the University of Washington in Seattle.

Kenya C. Dworkin y Méndez is an assistant professor of Spanish and Latin American Literature and Cultural Studies at Carnegie Mellon University in Pittsburgh, Pennsylvania.

Richard Flores is an associate professor in the Department of Anthropology and Chicano Studies at the University of Wisconsin-Madison.

Margaret García Davidson is Assistant Professor of English at Southern Methodist University in Dallas. She is completing a doctoral study entitled "Borderlands and Issues of Cultural/Ethnic Identity in Early Mexican American Writers" at the University of California, Davis.

Anne E. Goldman teaches Jewish American Literature in the Women's Studies Department at the University of California in Santa Cruz.

Erlinda González-Berry is a professor in and chair of the Department of Modern and Classical Languages at the University of New Mexico in Albuquerque.

John M. González is a doctoral student in the Department of English at Stanford University in California.

Laura Gutiérrez-Witt is Head Librarian of the Benson Latin American Collection at the University of Texas in Austin.

Timothy R. Libretti is an assistant professor in the English Department at Northeastern Illinois University in Chicago.

Manuel M. Martín Rodríguez is an assistant professor in the Department of Spanish and Portuguese at Yale University in New Haven, Connecticut.

A. Gabriel Meléndez is an assistant professor in the Department of American Studies at the University of New Mexico in Albuquerque.

F. Arturo Rosales is an associate professor in the Department of History at Arizona State University in Tempe.

Lisa Sánchez González is an assistant professor in the Department of English at the University of Texas in Austin.

Robert J. Senkewicz, S. J., is an associate professor and chair of the Department of History at Santa Clara University in California.

Charles M. Tatum is a professor in the Department of Spanish and Portuguese and Dean of Humanities at the University of Arizona in Tucson.

Elliott Young is a doctoral candidate in the Department of History at the University of Texas in Austin.